双墙对话：哈德良长城与中国长城保护管理研讨会文集

Wall to Wall: the Hadrian's Wall and Great Wall of China Management Seminar Proceedings

中国文化遗产研究院 Chinese Academy of Cultural Heritage

英格兰遗产委员会 Historic England

编　著

文物出版社

图书在版编目（CIP）数据

双墙对话：哈德良长城与中国长城保护管理研讨会
文集：汉英对照 / 中国文化遗产研究院，英格兰遗产委
员会编著 . -- 北京：文物出版社，2019.10
　　ISBN 978-7-5010-6292-8

Ⅰ.①双… Ⅱ.①中… ②英… Ⅲ.①长城—文物保
护—中国—国际学术会议—文集—汉、英②城墙—文物保
护—英国—国际学术会议—文集—汉、英 Ⅳ.
① K878.34-53 ② K885.618.34-53

中国版本图书馆 CIP 数据核字 (2019) 第 206236 号

双墙对话：哈德良长城与中国长城保护管理研讨会文集

Wall to Wall: the Hadrian's Wall and Great Wall of China Management Seminar Proceedings

编　　著：中国文化遗产研究院
　　　　　Chinese Academy of Cultural Heritage
　　　　　英格兰遗产委员会
　　　　　Historic England
责任编辑：李　睿　宋　丹
封面设计：王文娴
责任印制：苏　林

出版发行：文物出版社
　　　　　Cultural Relics Press
地　　址：北京市东直门内北小街2号楼
　　　　　Building No.2, Dongzhimennei Beixiaojie, Dongcheng District, Beijing
网　　址：http://www.wenwu.com
邮　　箱：web@wenwu.com
邮政编码：100007
经　　销：新华书店
印　　刷：北京京都六环印刷厂
开　　本：889mm×1194mm　1/16
印　　张：23.5　插页：1
版　　次：2019年10月第1版
印　　次：2019年10月第1次印刷
书　　号：ISBN 978-7-5010-6292-8
定　　价：380.00元

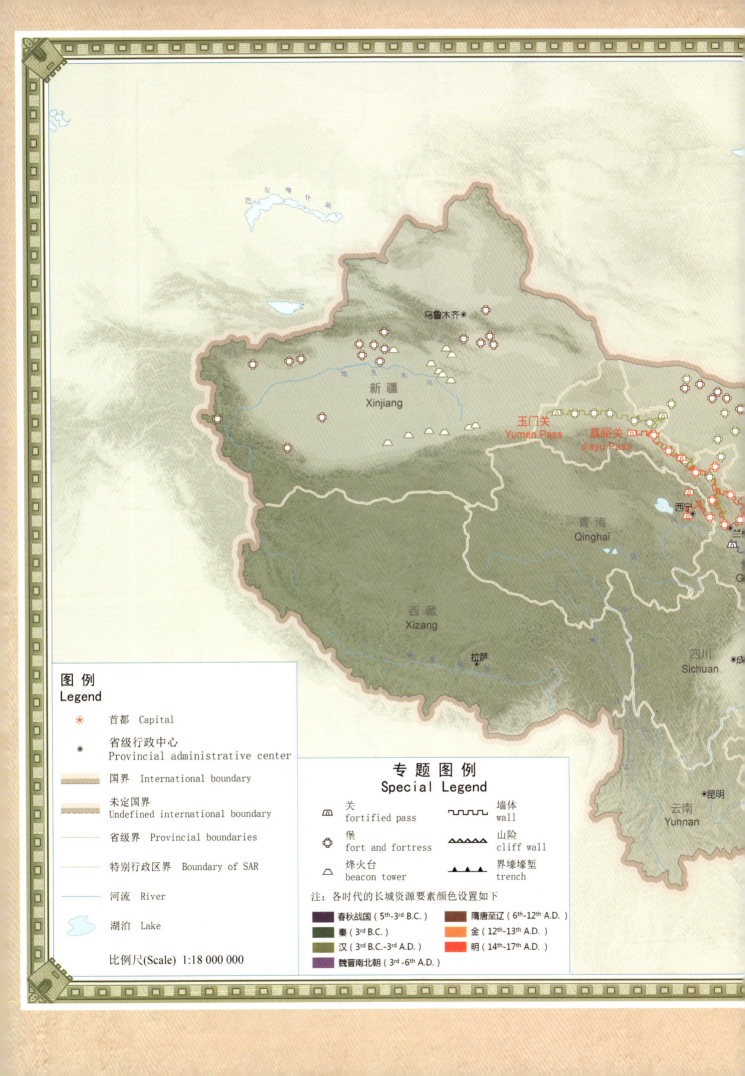

巴尔喀什湖

乌鲁木齐◎

新 疆
Xinjiang

塔 里 木 河

玉门关
Yumen Pass

嘉峪关
Jiayu Pass

西宁◉

青 海
Qinghai

黄 河

西 藏
Xizang

拉萨

四 川
Sichuan

成

G

昆明

云 南
Yunnan

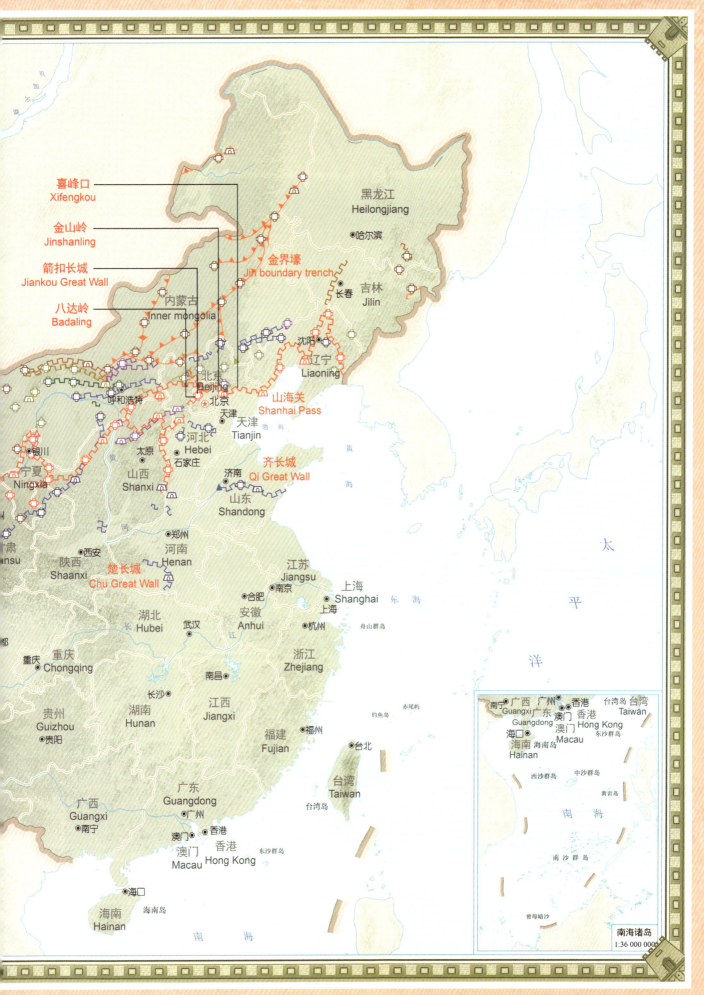

喜峰口
Xifengkou

金山岭
Jinshanling

箭扣长城
Jiankou Great Wall

八达岭
Badaling

黑龙江
Heilongjiang

哈尔滨

金界壕
Jin boundary trench

长春

吉林
Jilin

内蒙古
Inner mongolia

沈阳

辽宁
Liaoning

北京
Beijing

北京

山海关
Shanhai Pass

天津
Tianjin

呼和浩特

河北
Hebei

太原

石家庄

济南

齐长城
Qi Great Wall

银川

宁夏
Ningxia

山西
Shanxi

山东
Shandong

郑州

河南
Henan

西安

陕西
Shaanxi

楚长城
Chu Great Wall

甘肃
Gansu

江苏
Jiangsu

南京

上海
Shanghai

上海

合肥

安徽
Anhui

杭州

湖北
Hubei

武汉

舟山群岛

重庆
Chongqing

浙江
Zhejiang

南昌

长沙

湖南
Hunan

江西
Jiangxi

福建
Fujian

福州

台北

贵州
Guizhou

贵阳

钓鱼屿

赤尾屿

广东
Guangdong

广州

台湾
Taiwan

台湾岛

广西
Guangxi

南宁

澳门
Macau

香港
Hong Kong

东沙群岛

海口

海南
Hainan

海南岛

南 海

太

平

洋

东 海

黄

海

南宁 广西 广州 香港 台湾岛 台湾
Guangxi 广东 澳门 香港 Taiwan
Guangdong 澳门 Hong Kong 东沙群岛
Macau
海口
海南 海南岛
Hainan

西沙群岛 中沙群岛

黄岩岛

南 海

南沙群岛

曾母暗沙

南海诸岛
1:36 000 000

中国长城分布示意图（版权：国家文物局；制图：国信司南）

Map of the Great Wall of China (© NCHA; drawing: Geo-Compass)

主　　编　**Editors in Chief**

于　冰 Yu Bing
[英] 大卫·布劳夫 David Brough

协助编辑　Assistant editors

汉佛瑞·维尔法 Humphrey Welfare
卡罗尔·派拉 Carol Pyrah
刘方舟 Liu Fangzhou

特别致谢　Special acknowledgements

双墙对话：哈德良长城与中国长城保护管理研讨会由纽卡斯尔大学于 2018 年 3 月承办

Wall to Wall: the Hadrian's Wall and Great Wall of China Management Seminar was hosted by Newcastle University in March 2018

目录

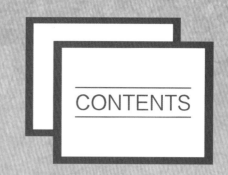

CONTENTS

Chapter One
National Management Systems

Chapter Two
Conservation Principles and Practices

Chapter Three

Survey, Research and Monitoring

Chapter Four

Tourist Management and Social Engagement

Chapter Five

Concluding Remarks   341

序

中国长城和哈德良长城有许多共同之处。它们在 1987 年同时被列入联合国教科文组织世界遗产名录，两者虽然规模上相去甚远，但都面临很多挑战和机遇。数个世纪以来，两座长城都深刻地影响了周边人民的生活，并在当代世界中持续扮演重要角色。它们引人注目，因此每年吸引着成千上万的游客参观游览。但是，两座长城地位重要，所处环境复杂多变，引人入胜，需要悉心管理。

2018 年中国文化遗产研究院和英格兰遗产委员会迈出第一步，开启了中英两国专家在这两处世界遗产地的管理和保护方面独一无二的合作。2018 年 3 月，由双方主办、纽卡斯尔大学承办的专家研讨会在英国纽卡斯尔市召开。两国的长城专家出席并分享了各自保护世界遗产地的经验，探讨如何吸引和满足游客需求，如何讲述各自遗产地故事以及如何鼓励当地人参与方面。

我们非常荣幸能够发表研讨会成果的文集，里面包含了中英两国突破性的学术研究，以及遗产保护与鼓励公众参与的方法。

中国文化遗产研究院与英格兰遗产委员会的崭新合作振奋人心，此文集更是合作结出的首个硕果。我们希望这一合作为双方在遗产环境保护、遗产管理和旅游业方面带来互惠共赢的绝佳机遇。

柴晓明　　　　　　　邓肯·威尔逊　（官佐勋章）

中国文化遗产研究院　院长　　　英格兰遗产委员会　首席行政长官

FOREWORD

The Great Wall of China and Hadrian's Wall have much in common. Inscribed as UNESCO World Heritage Sites in 1987, the two Walls are very different in scale but share many challenges and opportunities. Both of them have profoundly influenced the lives of the people around them for many centuries, and they continue to play a part in the modern world. They are instantly recognisable and, as a result, they are visited and enjoyed by huge numbers of people every year. However, each of the Walls is a centrepiece to a complex and intriguing ancient landscape which needs to be carefully managed.

In 2018 the Chinese Academy of Cultural Heritage and Historic England took the first steps in a unique collaboration between Chinese and UK experts in conservation and management of the two UNESCO World Heritage Sites. In March 2018 Historic England and CACH organized, and Newcastle University hosted an expert seminar that brought together specialists on the two Walls to share their experience in protecting and conserving World Heritage Sites, in attracting and catering for visitors, in telling the stories of each site, and in engaging local people.

We are honoured to be publishing in this volume the papers given at the seminar, from ground-breaking academic research to conservation, and public engagement approaches from both sides of the globe.

These are the first fruits of an exciting new collaboration between the Chinese Academy of Culture Heritage and Historic England. We hope that this partnership will bring about great opportunities for mutual benefit in the fields of conservation of the historic built environment, heritage management, and tourism.

CHAI XIAOMING   DUNCAN WILSON OBE
Director, Chinese Academy of Cultural Heritage   Chief Executive , Historic England

前　言

大卫·布劳夫

英国纽卡斯尔大学

　　本文集是中国文化遗产研究院和英格兰遗产委员会于 2018 年在英国纽卡斯尔大学合作举办研讨会的成果。此次研讨会是哈德良长城和中国长城首度开启广泛对话和合作的标志。之前的 2017 年 2 月，英国文化协会和北京大学考古文博学院组织中英文化遗产高级别对话，对话中首度提议举办哈德良长城与中国长城研讨会。中国文化遗产研究院和英格兰遗产委员会特别有资格在文化遗产保护和管理领域进行合作，也希望以此为平台带动中英其他伙伴参与合作，促进哈德良长城和中国长城两个标志性世界遗产的研究和公众认知。

　　此研讨会聚集来自"双墙"的顶尖学术研究人员和高阶管理人员。或许令人吃惊的是，虽然两处长城十分类似，面临相似的挑战，但这样的聚会却是史无前例。"双墙"的类似之处包括形式、历史功能，以及重要影响。相似的挑战包括：实现经济和社会利益最大化的同时如何保护遗迹本体；在遗产保护和开放利用及访客管理间取得平衡；深化对长城的考古学学术认知和价值学术认知；促进和扩大公众及社区参与长城保护，从而升华其价值内涵。

　　但是，即便拥有很多共同点，中英双方也承认各自对对方长城的本体、历史、管理体制和保护实践了解有限。因此，研讨会的首个目标即为向彼此介绍各自概况，从而为双方探讨未来合作内容领域和合作内容提供参考。确认未来可能的合作内容则为研讨会的第二个目标。

　　以此为目标，研讨会分为五场；前四场介绍"双墙"的考古及其管理；第五场则是全体讨论，讨论未来合作的潜在机会。

　　本论文集也遵循与研讨会相同的结构。第一章的文章基于研讨会中的发言，描述"双墙"的历史和遗存，以及各自适用的法律制度和行政管理体制。马修·西蒙兹介绍了在不断变化的历史背景中哈德良长城的原始设计和建设，以及随后三百年来其形式和材质的多样变化，同时也概述了后世对哈德良长城目的和功能解读的学术探索。段清波随后讨论中国长城的历史起源和影响，及其在中国文明和文化中的象征意义和功能的重要性。亨利·欧文·约翰描述英国遗产管理保护的国家立法和制度体系，并概述构成这些体系的关键原则和理念。汉佛瑞·维尔法介绍了哈德良长城战略管理和日常运营的管理结构。于冰则描述了中国长城在本体认知、宏观环境和管理体制上的复杂性，以及近年来长城整体保护方面的探索实践。本章最后，赛巴斯蒂安·索默从罗马帝国边疆的总体系统来看哈德良长

INTRODUCTION

DAVID BROUGH
Newcastle University

The Seminar of 2018 on which this publication is based was organised in partnership between the Chinese Academy of Cultural Heritage (CACH) and Historic England (HE) and was hosted by Newcastle University. It marked the first substantive expression of a wider emerging programme of collaboration between Hadrian's Wall and the Great Wall of China that was first proposed during the UK-China Cultural Heritage High Level Dialogue, organised by the British Council and the School of Archaeology and Museology, Peking University, in February 2017. CACH and HE are especially well qualified to collaborate in the conservation and management of cultural heritage, and it is intended that there will be further joint working between other partners in China and the UK in research and in raising public awareness about these iconic World Heritage Sites.

The Seminar brought together leading academic researchers and senior managers from the two 'Walls'. Acknowledging the many parallels between the two, and the similarities in the challenges each face, it was perhaps surprising that this was the first time such a gathering had been held. The parallels include the form and historic function, and the heritage significance of each site. The challenges include those of: conserving historic fabric while maximising the economic and social benefits; balancing visitor management and greater visitor access with conservation; developing greater academic understanding of the archaeology and its significance; and promoting and broadening public and community engagement with these historic structures, and strengthening the value placed upon them.

Despite all of this common ground, it was acknowledged that each country had a limited knowledge and understanding of the fabric, history, and management structures and practices of the other Wall. The first objective of the Seminar was therefore for each site to provide the other with an introductory overview. This mutual orientation provided the basis for informed consideration and discussion of the scope and substance of potential future collaborations, the identification of which formed the second objective of the Seminar.

Reflecting these objectives, the Seminar was divided into five sessions; the first four provided an introduction to the archaeology of the Walls and their management; the fifth session was devoted to a structured plenary discussion concerning potential opportunities for future collaboration.

This publication follows a similar structure. Chapter 1 consists of papers based on presentations describing the history and fabric of each site, and the regulatory and administrative frameworks through which they are managed. Both the original design and construction of Hadrian's Wall and

城的历史，介绍了包含更广范围的罗马帝国边疆系列跨国世界遗产地的申报背景，及其对管理的影响。

第二章探讨的主题是中英长城保护实践和保护理念。蕾贝卡·琼斯结合英国文化遗产保护原则和政策，重点阐述其在安东尼长城——哈德良长城的姊妹墙，同属罗马帝国边疆世界遗产地——如何贯彻实施，侧重说明遗产价值和遗产认定的重要性，以及"历史遗产循环"和"周边环境"的概念。麦克·考林斯呈现哈德良长城沿线的一系列保护实施案例，而贾海麟介绍中国金山岭长城平衡保护管理、资源利用和开放旅游的案例研究，两篇文章相得益彰。接下来的保护实践案例研究，一个是在北京和河北长城试点案例中利用非财政资金并探索创新方法，另一个是英国大切斯特要塞，分别由侯珂及麦克·考林斯呈现。此章节以张俊的文章作结，通过长城小站的案例来探索民间组织的角色。

第三章的主题是"双墙"考古研究相关的考古调查及与保护相关的监测。本章开头，托尼·威尔莫特回顾哈德良长城两个多世纪来考古调查和发掘技术的演变，并指出新兴技术的价值以及考古发掘持续不变的重要性。李一丕接着提供了对中国长城世界遗产地最古老区段之一——河南楚长城的考古调查、发掘及保护方法的真知灼见。罗伯·柯林斯通过哈德良长城研究框架的编制介绍如何确定未来研究的挑战及机会，并说明如何调动非学术资源来应对这些挑战和机会。在本章最后大卫·布劳夫 - 约翰·史考特和张依萌的文章讨论"双墙"监测的方法以及这些方法如何为管理决策提供信息。

第四章，也是论文集正文的最后一章，主要讨论访客管理及公众参与。麦克·考林斯和佩吉特·拉扎里以哈德良长城国家步道为例，讨论如何通过游客管理来保护长城考古遗址。接下来，张朝枝通过国际文件系统分析遗产保护领域呈现责任基层化趋势，对认识和推动遗产旅游利益相关者参与遗产保护和可持续利用非常重要。比尔·格里菲斯基于已出版的哈德良长城阐释规划框架，概述哈德良长城沿线实施的各种阐释主题和阐释方法。本章最后，马尧详述中国长城阐释中广泛运用的数字技术，及技术对增进公众认识、理解和参与长城保护的效果。

本论文集的最后，基于研讨会最终的全体讨论环节总结概述了哈德良长城与中国长城未来合作的想法和期望。不过，合作内容还会随着中国长城和哈德良长城之间的合作发展而深化。未来将会见证更多研讨会与交流，包括 2019 年 10 月将在河北金山岭举办的第二届"双墙对话"研讨会。

本文集用中英双语出版，涉及大量翻译工作。其中，中国作者的论文由作者自行提供英文翻译版本，大卫·布劳夫、卡罗尔·派拉和汉佛瑞·维尔法和于冰负责英文翻译的校对、编辑，并确保翻译的一致性。英国作者的论文由黄思源、张容榕、马艳鑫和徐逢时翻译为中文，于冰负责中文翻译的校对、编辑，并确保

the various alterations to its form and fabric over three centuries are placed in their changing historical context by Matt Symonds, who also outlines subsequent academic endeavours to explain its purposes and functions. Duan Qingbo then discusses the historical origins and impact of the Great Wall, and its symbolic and functional significance in the shaping of Chinese civilisation and culture. The national legislative and regulatory systems of heritage management and conservation in the UK is then set out by Henry Owen-John who summarises the key principles and concepts which underpin these systems. The operational and governance structure through which strategic and day to day management of Hadrian's Wall is conducted are explained by Humphrey Welfare, while Yu Bing describes the complexity of the management of the Great Wall in terms of its fabric, context and regulatory system, and the recent effort in its integrated conservation. To conclude this chapter, Sebastian Sommer places the history of Hadrian's Wall within that of the overall system of Roman imperial frontiers, and explains how its present day management fits within the context of the development of the wider Frontiers of the Roman Empire serial transnational World Heritage Site.

The theme of conservation practices and philosophies in China and the UK is then explored in Chapter 2. Rebecca Jones provides an overview of how UK conservation principles and policies are implemented through practice along the Antonine Wall, the sister site in the UK to Hadrian's Wall within the wider Frontiers of the Roman Empire World Heritage Site, and highlights the importance of significance and designation and the concepts of "the heritage cycle" and "setting". A range of examples of conservation practice from across Hadrian's Wall are presented by Mike Collins, which are complemented by Jia Hailin's case study of balancing conservation management and use and access at the Jinshanling section of the Great Wall. Further case studies of conservation using non-government funds and exploring innovative practice from pilot restoration projects in Beijing and Hebei, and from the fort of Great Chesters, are presented by Hou Ke and Mike Collins respectively, before the chapter concludes with Zhang Jun's exploration of the role of non-governmental organisations through the example of the work of the Great Wall Station.

The papers in Chapter 3 consider the topics of survey as it relates to archaeological research, and of monitoring as it relates to conservation within the two monuments. The chapter opens with Tony Wilmott's reflections on the evolution of survey and excavation techniques over more than two centuries of research on Hadrian's Wall, acknowledging both the value of emerging technologies and the continuing importance of excavation. Li Yipi then provides an insight into the survey, excavation and conservation methodologies at the Chu Great Wall in Henan, one of the oldest sections of the Great Wall of China World Heritage Site. Future research challenges and opportunities, as identified through the Hadrian's Wall Research Framework process, are summarised by Rob Collins who then illustrates how non-academic resources can be mobilised to help address them. Papers from David Brough and John Scott and from Zhang Yimeng complete this chapter with discussions of the methods used to monitor the two monuments and how these approaches can inform decision-making in management.

翻译的一致性。为便于读者理解和长远"双墙"对话合作，特别整理一份相关词汇互译表（附后）。实习生刘方舟在文集的编辑汇总、体例统一、文字图片校对、参考文献和图片说明翻译等方面做了大量工作。

　　中国文化遗产研究院资助本文集的排版编辑。中国文化遗产研究院和英格兰遗产委员会各自负责本文集在中国和英国的出版印刷。

The main body of the volume concludes with papers discussing visitor management and public engagement, which are presented in Chapter 4. Conservation of archaeological deposits through the management of visitor access is discussed by Mike Collins' and Paget Lazzari's case study of the Hadrian's Wall Path National Trail. This is followed by Zhang Chaozhi's more general analysis of a bottom-up system of responsibility for heritage conservation reflected by international documents, an understanding of these by everyone is important for the conservation and sustainable use of heritage. Bill Griffiths then provides an overview of the variety of interpretation themes and methods being implemented along Hadrian's Wall, based on the published Interpretation Framework. The chapter concludes with Ma Yao's detailed description of the extensive use of digital technologies in the interpretation of the Great Wall, and their effectiveness in raising public awareness, understanding and participation in the conservation of the Great Wall.

The papers in this volume illustrate that there continue to be many areas of academic debate concerning the definition, history and function of these two enormous and complex ancient frontier systems. Similarly, different opinions continue to be held on the relative merits of different approaches and practices in respect of all aspects of present day management of the monuments discussed in this volume.

The concluding section of this publication summarises current ideas and aspirations for future collaboration between Hadrian's Wall and the Great Wall of China. Although based on the discussions of the final plenary session of the Seminar, these ideas will continue to be developed as cooperation between the Great Wall of China and Hadrian's Wall evolves. This process will be taken forward through further seminars and exchanges, commencing with the Second Wall to Wall Seminar to be held at Jinshanling, Hebei, in November 2019.

As a bilingual publication, translation work involved is substantial. For the papers by Chinese authors, the authors themselves have been responsible for providing their English translations, and David Brough, Carol Pyrah, Humphrey Welfare, and Yu Bing have been responsible for the English proofreading, editing and ensuring consistency in translation. For the papers by UK authors, Huang Siyuan, Chang Jungjung, Ma Yanxin and Xu Fengshi have undertaken the translations into Chinese, and Yu Bing has been responsible for the Chinese proofreading, editing and consistency in translation. In order to facilitate reader understanding and long-term dialogue between the two Walls, a glossary of translation has been prepared and included in the publication. CACH intern Liu Fangzhou has made a lot of input into the aggregation of papers, format consistency, text and illustration formatting and reference translation.Liu Fangzhou has also assisted Yu Bing and David Brough in the compilation of the bilingual Glossary.

Design of the publication has been funded by CACH, and CACH has financed the printing of the publication.

GLOSSARY
术语表

于 冰 大卫·布劳夫 汉佛瑞·维尔法 刘方舟
YU BING, DAVID BROUGH, HUMPHREY WELFARE, LIU FANGZHOU

INTRODUCTION
介 绍

The tables below are divided into four sections.

以下表格分为四部分。

Section 1.1 includes English translations and explanations of some specific terminology related to the archaeology of the Great Wall.

1.1 部分包括与长城考古相关的一些特定术语的英文翻译和解释。

Section 1.2 includes English translations and explanations of key regulatory, administrative, conservation and heritage management organisations and terminology related to the management and conservation of the Great Wall of China.

1.2 部分包括与中国长城管理和保护相关的监管、行政、保护、遗产管理组织的关键术语的英文翻译和解释。

Section 2.1 includes Chinese translations and explanations of some specific terminology related to the archaeology of Hadrian's Wall together with some further terminology specific to its management and conservation.

2.1 部分包括与哈德良长城考古相关，以及一些特定于其管理和保护的术语的中文翻译和解释。

Section 2.2 includes Chinese translations and explanations of key regulatory, administrative, conservation and heritage management policies and organisations related to the management and conservation of Hadrian's Wall.

2.2 部分包括与哈德良长城管理和保护相关的监管、行政、保护、遗产管理政策以及相关组织的中文翻译和解释。

1. 中文术语的英文对照表
1. ENGLISH GLOSSARY OF CHINESE TERMINOLOGY

1.1 与长城相关的专用术语与词汇
Section 1.1 Great Wall specific terminology and vocabulary

Original Chinese (Hanzi and Pinyin) 中文原文（加拼音标注）	Meaning in Chinese 中文释义	(Recommended) English translation 英文翻译	Meaning / Description in English 英文释义
土墙 Tuqiang	构筑时外观以土筑为主的墙体。	Earth Wall	Refers to wall whose exterior at the time of construction was mainly built with earth.
石墙 Shiqiang	构筑时外观以石筑为主的墙体。	Stone Wall	Refers to wall whose exterior at the time of construction was mainly built with stone.
砖墙 Zhuanqiang	构筑时外观以砖筑为主的墙体	Brick Wall	Refers to wall whose exterior at the time of construction was mainly built with brick.
山险墙 Shanxianqiang	利用险要，经人为加工形成的险阻。	Cut Wall	Sections of the Wall created by cutting away sections of hills or mountains.
自然险 Ziranxian	指在地势险要之处，与墙体共同构成防御体系的山体、河流、沟壑等自然地物。	Natural Barriers	Natural features such as mountains, rivers, and gullies which, together with the Wall, constitute a defensive system.
壕堑 Haoqian	墙体和壕沟的组合防御体，汉代称壕堑。	Trench Wall	An integrated defensive system, consisting of wall and ditch. Named Haoqian in Han Dynasty.
马面 Mamian 其他名称 城垛 Chengduo 墙台 Qiangtai 墙垛 Qiangduo	依附于城墙外侧、与城墙同高的台子。	Horse Face	A terrace attached to the exterior and at the same height as the Wall.
马道 Madao	墙体内侧供人、马上下通行的道路。	Horse Path	A road on the inner side of the Wall for people and horses going to and from the Wall.
铺舍 Pushe 其他名称 楼橹 Loulu 铺房 Pufang	建于城墙或者敌台上，供守城士兵巡逻放哨时遮风避雨的建筑物，也是戍卒休息和储备军用物品的场所。	Sentry House	A building built on city walls or on defensive towers for the patrolling soldiers to find shelter from harsh weather, also used by garrison soldiers to rest and store materiel.
垛口 Duokou 其他名称 女口 Nvkou 雉堞 Zhidie 垛口墙 Duokouqiang	建于城墙或者敌台上，供守城士兵巡逻放哨时遮风避雨的建筑物，也是戍卒休息和储备军用物品的场所。	Battlement	The crenellated parapet on top of the Wall.

续表 Continued

Original Chinese (Hanzi and Pinyin) 中文原文（加拼音标注）	Meaning in Chinese 中文释义	(Recommended) English translation 英文翻译	Meaning / Description in English 英文释义
水门 Shuimen 其他名称 水窦 Shuidou 水关 Shuiguan		Watergate	A channel built into the Wall to allow streams to pass underneath and rainfall to be drained from the Wall.
城楼 Chenglou 其他名称 门楼 Menlou 战棚 Zhanpeng 楼子 Louzi 敌团 Dituan 堞楼 Dielou	建于长城墙体上用于瞭望和射击的建筑物。	Gate Tower	Buildings built above gates within walls for observation and defence.
障墙 Zhangqiang	为防止守城士兵暴露于敌人的视线和射程之内而构筑在墙体上横向防御的短墙。多建于墙体陡峭处。	Barrier Wall	A series of short walls constructed on the Wall perpendicular to the battlement to prevent the defending soldiers from being exposed to enemy vision and fire, usually only built on steep parts of the Wall.
坞墙 Wuqiang	敌台外侧的低矮围墙，上有箭孔用于防御。	Outskirt Wall	A low wall built surrounding some defence towers, with arrow slits to bolster the defence.
战台 Zhantai	升起的建于长城外侧的进攻平台，可从上攻击来敌，为金山岭长城较典型设施。	Battle Platform	A raised platform, typically on a branch wall exterior to the Great Wall, from which the advancing enemy could be attacked, a typical facility at Jinshanling section.
炮台 Paotai	建于长城墙体上设置火炮的平台。	Artillery Platform	Platforms built on top of the Wall as artillery emplacements.
烽火台 Fenghuotai 其他名称 烽燧 Fengsui 墩台 Duntai 烽堠 Fenghou 烟墩 Yandun 狼烟台 Langyantai 狼烟墩 Langyandun	指在长城沿线用于点燃烟火传递重要信息的高台，是长城防御体系的重要组成部分。	Beacon Tower	A high platform on the top of which a signal beacon could be placed, constituting an integral part of the Great Wall Defence System.
空心敌台 Kongxinditai	内部中空的敌台，更适于保护守城士兵。	Chambered Tower	A type of defence tower, with internal rooms offering greater protection to soldiers guarding the Great Wall.
敌台 Ditai 其他名称 敌楼 Dilou 墩台 Duntai	突出于城墙的防御型高台，可分为空心和实心两种。	Defence Tower	A tower built along the Great Wall itself to protect against attacks, which can be either chambered or solid.

续表 Continued

Original Chinese (Hanzi and Pinyin) 中文原文（加拼音标注）	Meaning in Chinese 中文释义	(Recommended) English translation 英文翻译	Meaning / Description in English 英文释义
关 Guan 其他名称 口 Kou	一般指筑有城、围的屯兵地，一般依托于墙体。	Fortified Pass	A fortification system guarding a mountain pass.
关隘 Guan'ai	处于险要位置的关城。	Strategic Pass	A fortified pass of particular strategic significance.
堡 Bu or Bao 其他名称 城障 Chengzhang 障城 Zhangcheng 镇城 Zhencheng 障塞 Zhangsai 城堡 Chengbao 寨 Zhai 戍堡 Shubao 边堡 Bianbao 军堡 Junbao 屯堡 Tunbao 民堡 Minbao	筑有城、围的屯兵、居住地，为长城防御体系的重要组成部分，与墙体不发生直接关联。	Fort Fortress	A large and strongly defended enclosure containing barracks or living quarters, constituting an integral part of the Great Wall Defence System but not attached to the Wall itself.
挡马墙 Dangmaqiang 其他名称 羊马垣 Yangmayuan 副墙 Fuqiang 小长城 Xiaochangcheng	构筑在长城墙体外，平行于长城墙体或护城壕的墙体，多用于抵挡骑兵。	Horse Wall	An external wall parallel to the Wall or trench wall, often used to prevent or impede cavalry attacks.
镇 zhen	明朝年间，北部边境沿长城防线设立九边，即区域性军事指挥区，每边设一军事指挥所，称为镇，有时"边""镇"通用。	Zhen	During the Ming Dynasty, there were nine Bians, or regional military frontier or boundary areas along the Great Wall, a Zhen was where the headquarters of each Bian was located. Sometimes Zhen is also used interchangeably with Bian, denoting a military region.
边 Bian	长城沿线的区域性边境军事指挥区。	Bian	A regional frontier or boundary military command area along the Great Wall.

1.2 与长城相关法规、行政管理、保护和管理机构相关的用语

Section 1.2 Chinese regulatory, administrative, conservation and heritage management organisations and terminology related to the Great Wall

Original Chinese (Hanzi and Pinyin) 中文原文（加拼音标注）	Meaning in Chinese 中文释义	(Recommended) English translation 英文翻译	Meaning / Description in English 英文释义
中国文物保护基金会 Zhongguo wenwu baohu jijinhui	成立于1990年，由国家文物局主管的具有独立法人地位的全国公募性公益基金组织于2017年成为注册慈善组织。	China Foundation for Cultural Heritage Conservation	A national charitable foundation founded in 1990, with independent legal status under the supervision of the National Cultural Heritage Administration (NCHA), and accredited as a registered charity in 2017.
中国文化遗产研究院 Zhongguo wenhua yichan yanjiuyuan	国家文物局直属的唯一国家级文化遗产保护科学技术研究机构。	Chinese Academy of Cultural Heritage	The sole national academic body providing technical and policy advice on the management and conservation of cultural relics which reports to NCHA.
文物 Wenwu	中国基本概念和法律术语，涵盖所有可移动和不可移动物质文化遗产，因其历史、艺术、科学价值而受到保护。	Cultural relic(s)	A basic legal term and fundamental concept in China. It is used to cover all movable and immovable material objects of cultural heritage that should be protected for their historic, artistic and scientific values.
中华人民共和国文物保护法 Zhonghua renmin gongheguo wenwu baohu fa	最早颁布于1982年，并于2002年修订。总共八章，包括总则、不可移动文物、考古发掘、馆藏文物、民间收藏文物、文物出境进境、法律责任、附则。	Cultural Relics Protection Law of the People's Republic of China (CRPL)	First promulgated in 1982 and revised in 2002. There are 8 chapters including: general provisions, immovable cultural relics, archaeological excavations, cultural relics in museums, private collections of cultural relics, import and export of cultural relics, legal responsibilities, supplementary provisions.
文物部门 Wenwu bumen	省、市、县级政府部门及其下属机构，主要负责本辖区内所有文物的保存、维护和管理。	Cultural Relics Departments	The departments at Provincial, Municipal and County-level governments, together with their subordinate agencies, with principal responsibility for administration and management of protection and conservation of all cultural relics within their jurisdiction.
"四有"工作 "Siyou" gongzuo	《文物保护法》要求文物保护单位应当具备的四项基础工作：划定必要保护范围，作出标志说明，建立记录档案，并区别情况分别设立专门机构或者专人负责管理。	Four Haves	The four legal prerequisites for designated Protected Units of Cultural Relics (PUCRs) in China, which require each site to have: demarcated boundaries; an official plaque stating its name, its level and date of designation; an archive cataloguing its protected elements and activities; a dedicated organization or person(s) responsible for its daily management.

续表 Continued

Original Chinese (Hanzi and Pinyin) 中文原文（加拼音标注）	Meaning in Chinese 中文释义	(Recommended) English translation 英文翻译	Meaning / Description in English 英文释义
长城 各时代长城 各段长城 Changcheng Geshidai changcheng Geduan changcheng	分布于全国 15 个省、市、自治区、直辖市，由不同朝代建立的长城防御体系的统称。既可作为通用术语，也可作为特指用语，指特定时期（如楚长城，指由楚国建造的长城），或特定点段（如金山岭长城，指金山岭段长城），或特定地区（如北京长城，指北京市境内长城段落和相关设施）。	Great Wall	A collective term for each of the Great Wall defence systems built by different kingdoms and dynasties across 15 present day Provinces, Autonomous Regions and Direct Municipalities in China. It is used either as a general term, or a specific term for a specific time (the Chu Great Wall which means the Great Wall of the Chu State), or for a specific section or site (the Jinshanling Great Wall which means the Jinshanling section of the Great Wall) or a specific region (the Beijing Great Wall which means the sections and related facilities of the Great Wall within Beijing Direct Municipality).
长城地带 Changcheng didai	指长城及其附属设施所分布的宽阔地域。	Great Wall Zone / Corridor	The broad band of territory across which each of the different Great Wall systems were built.
长城保护管理工程（2005-2014） Changcheng baohu guanli gongcheng	由国务院批准，国家文物局组织实施的 10 年项目，旨在提升长城保护和管理。	Great Wall Conservation Programme (2005-2014)	A 10 year programme launched by the State Administration for Cultural Heritage (SACH) under the support of the State Council in 2006 to strengthen conservation and management of the Great Wall.
长城保护员 Changcheng baohuyuan	受各地政府聘用的兼职人员，职责包括巡视长城保护状况及向有关部门上报长城损坏情况。	Great Wall Patrollers	Part-time workers recruited by local authorities who monitor the condition of the Great Wall and report any damage or destruction to its fabric to the authorities.
长城保护条例 Changcheng baohu tiaoli	2006 年由国务院颁布，是中国为专门文物颁发的最高法规。	Great Wall Protection Regulation	A regulation promulgated by the State Council in 2006, the only one in China for a specific cultural heritage site.
长城资源调查 Changcheng ziyuan diaocha	2006-2012 年间，由国家文物局组织实施的对长城全线的首次调查，属于"长城保护工程（2005-2014 年）总体工作方案"一部分。	Great Wall Resource Survey	The first ever national-level Wall-wide survey of all surviving elements of the Great Walls in China, organized by SACH between 2006-2012, as part of tasks provided in the Great Wall Conservation Programme (2005-2014).

续表 Continued

Original Chinese (Hanzi and Pinyin) 中文原文（加拼音标注）	Meaning in Chinese 中文释义	(Recommended) English translation 英文翻译	Meaning / Description in English 英文释义
IP	中国国内最新流行的概念，指一个符号、品牌、或想法有市场营销和商业化的创意产业潜力，利于新品牌产品的开发，如手机 app、游戏、卡通、电影、纪念品以及其他商品。	IP Branding	A very popular new concept now in China which means a symbol, brand, or an idea that has marketing and commercialization potential for creative industries for the development of new branded products such as mobile apps, games, cartoons and movies, as well as souvenirs and other merchandise.
国家文物局 Guojia wenwujv	国家政府机构，全面负责文物管理和保护。2018 年前英文名称为 SACH。	National Cultural Heritage Administration (NCHA)	The national government body with overall responsibility for the regulation and conservation of cultural relics. Until 2018 it was called the 'State Administration for Cultural Heritage' (SACH).
文物保护单位 Wenwu baohu danwei	根据中华人民共和国文物保护法，不可移动文物根据其价值，可以公布为国家、省、市、县级文物保护单位。中国已公布 7 批国家重点文物保护单位，共 4296 个。文物保护单位约相当于英国登陆古迹。	Protected Units of Cultural Relics (PUCR)	According to CRPL, immovable cultural relics can be designated, according to their significance, as national, provincial, municipal and county levels of Protected Units of Cultural Relics. There have been designated seven batches of National Key Protected Units of Cultural Relics (NKPUCR) with a total of 4296 in China. PUCRs are approximately the equivalent of Scheduled Monuments in the UK.
社会组织 Shehui zuzhi	根据中国相关法规，社会组织指在不同级别的政府民政部门注册的社会团体、基金会、民办非企业实体三类公益组织。	Social Organizations	Social Organizations, according to Chinese regulations, refer to three types of organizations, i.e. social groups, foundations, and private non−enterprise entities registered with government civil affairs departments of different levels.
国家文物局 (SACH) Guojia wenwujv	2018 年前的英文译名，之后改为 NCHA。	State Administration of Cultural Heritage (SACH)	The body which became the National Cultural Heritage Administration (NCHA) in 2018.
国务院 Guowuyuan	中国中央政府最高国家权力的执行机关。	State Council	The highest executive body of China's central government.

续表 Continued

Original Chinese (Hanzi and Pinyin) 中文原文（加拼音标注）	Meaning in Chinese 中文释义	(Recommended) English translation 英文翻译	Meaning / Description in English 英文释义
公益组织 Gongyi zuzhi	非政府、非营利性质的提供公益性服务的机构。	Third Sector	Often literally translated as 'public interest' organizations which are neither government led nor for-profit organisations and provide services for public purposes and benefits.
文物保护工程 Wenwu baohu gongcheng	根据中国相关文物保护工程管理办法，包括保养维护工程、抢险加固工程、修缮工程、保护性设施建设工程、迁移工程等类型	Cultural Relics Conservation Project	The term used in related Chinese regulations, to refer to conservation projects in the following categories: maintenance; emergency stabilisation and consolidation; restoration; protective facility construction; and relocation of cultural relics.
保养维护 Baoyang weihu	对文物的轻微损害所作的日常性、季节性的养护	Maintenance	Routine and daily repair to minor damages.
抢险加固 Qiangxian jiagu	指文物突发严重危险时，由于时间、技术、经费等条件的限制，不能进行彻底修缮而对文物采取具有可逆性的临时抢险加固措施的工程。	Emergency Stabilisation And Consolidation	Refers to reversible and temporary measures taken to rescue and reinforce those cultural relics in serious dangerwhich cannot be restored due to time, technical issues, funding and other constraints.
修缮 Xiushan	指为保护文物本体所必需的结构加固处理和维修，包括结合结构加固而进行的局部复原工程。	Restoration	Refers to the structural consolidation and repair measures necessary to protect the fabric of the cultural relic, including partial restoration in conjunction with structural consolidation.
考古清理 Kaogu qingli	以专业考古学家为主导进行的考古发掘和现场清理。	Archaeologically Led Site Clearance	Work by professional archaeological organisations to identify the original archaeological remains and direct the clearance of debris and site preparation prior to restoration.

2. 英文术语的中文对照表
2. CHINESE GLOSSARY OF ENGLISH TERMINOLOGY

2.1 与哈德良长城相关的专用术语与词汇
Section 2.1 Hadrian's Wall specific terminology and vocabulary

English 英文原文	Meaning / Description in English 英文释义	(Recommended) Translation in Chinese (Hanzi and Pinyin) 中文翻译（加拼音标注）	Description in Chinese 中文释义
Broad Wall	The original specification for Hadrian's Wall, only partly completed, measuring approximately 3m wide.	宽墙 Kuanqiang	哈德良长城最初规格，仅部分建成，宽约 3 米。
Clayton Wall	The stretches of the Wall purchased and partly rebuilt by antiquarian John Clayton in the 19th century.	克莱顿长城 Kelaidun changcheng	由古物研究者约翰·克莱顿购买并部分重建的哈德良长城部分。
Earthworks	A generic term to describe archaeological features made from earth or turf.	土质工事 Tumu (fangyu gongshi)/ guimo	用于描述用土或草皮建成的考古遗址的统称。
Fort	Defended Roman military constructions for infantry and cavalry garrisons. They were built to standardised designs throughout the Roman Empire, although their sizes varied.	要塞 Yaosai	为罗马步兵和骑兵提供防御的军事建筑。在罗马帝国内其建筑设计标准统一，而规模有所不同。
Fortlet	A small fort.	小要塞 Xiaoyaosai	小型要塞。
Hadrian's Wall	The continuous linear barrier (and its associated infrastructure) built across the north of England upon the orders of the Emperor Hadrian from AD122.	哈德良长城 Hadeliang changcheng	始建于公元 122 年罗马哈德良皇帝时期，建于英格兰北部的防御工事（及其附属设施）。
Limes	A generic Latin term for the Roman imperial frontier system.	界墙 Jieqiang	罗马帝国边疆防御体系的拉丁语通称。
Milecastle	A fortlet that provided a gate through Hadrian's Wall, and which housed 15 to 30 soldiers. Milecastles were built at intervals of approximately 1 Roman mile, and each one has been numbered by archaeologists sequentially from east to west.	里堡 Libao	城墙上每隔大约 1 罗马里（1479 米）修建的小要塞，设出入口，能容纳 15–30 名士兵，每处里堡均由考古学家从东至西依次编号。
Military Way	The Roman military road, usually built between the Wall and the Vallum, that linked the forts.	军道 Jundao	罗马帝国的军事道路，常建于哈德良长城墙体和南部壕沟之间，沟通各要塞。
Narrow Wall	The second specification for Hadrian's Wall measuring approximately 2 to 2.5m wide – an economy measure.	窄墙 Zhaiqiang	出于节约成本考虑，哈德良长城采用的第二种建设规格，宽约 2–2.5 米。

续表 Continued

English 英文原文	Meaning / Description in English 英文释义	(Recommended) Translation in Chinese (Hanzi and Pinyin) 中文翻译（加拼音标注）	Description in Chinese 中文释义
Stanegate	The Roman road which ran east – west between the Roman towns at Corbridge and Carlisle, south of Hadrian's Wall. The road and the Roman forts built along it pre–date the construction of Hadrian's Wall.	石路 Shilu	考布里奇和卡莱尔罗马城镇之间，哈德良长城以南东西走向的罗马道路。该道路及其沿线的罗马要塞比哈德良长城建设时间更早。
Temporary Camp	A Roman military earthwork enclosing a unit of soldiers when they were on the move or while they were constructing more permanent features such as roads, forts and Hadrian's Wall itself.	临时营地 Linshi yingdi	罗马军团行军时，或建设长期设施如道路、要塞、哈德良长城墙体时，保护部队的临时土质防御工事。
Turf Wall	The early form of Hadrian's Wall in the west, running from the Irthing river to the Solway Firth. It was built from cut blocks of turf, and measured approximately 6m wide and 3.5m high. It was subsequently rebuilt in stone.	草被长城 Caobei changcheng	哈德良长城西段的早期形态，从厄辛河延伸到索尔维狭湾。由切割好的草皮块建成，宽约6米，高3米，之后改用石块重建。
Turret	Small observation and signalling towers built into the Wall at regular intervals of approximately 1/3 of a Roman mile. The two turrets between each Milecastle are numbered according to their Wall–mile, sequentially A and B, east to west. Similar to the defence towers of the Great Wall in function.	塔楼 Talou	小型观察塔和信号塔，在墙体上每1/3罗马里等距修建。每个里堡之间的两个塔楼根据其区段，从A和B顺序编号。功能类似中国长城的敌台。
Vallum	A broad ditch, flanked by banks, forming an additional barrier on the interior side of the Wall. Translated here as "southern ditch" to differentiate from "ditch", which is on the northern (exterior) side of the Wall.	南部壕沟 Nanbu haogou	宽阔的壕沟，两侧为堤岸，从而在城墙内侧形成一道额外的障碍。为区别于墙体北侧（外侧）的ditch，特译为南侧壕沟。
Vicus	A civilian settlement outside a Roman fort.	平民聚落 Pingmin jvluo	罗马要塞外围的居民居住点。
Wall–mile	The name given by archaeologists to identify sections of Hadrian's Wall between Milecastles. Each Wall–mile is numbered sequentially from east to west.	区段 Quduan	考古学家为辨识哈德良长城里堡之间墙体段落而起的指定名称，从东往西顺序编号。
Whin Sill	A distinctive geological feature of volcanic rock, forming ridges along which much of the central sector of Hadrian's Wall was constructed.	暗色岩床 Anse yanchuang	火山岩的独特地质特征，形成了哈德良长城中央部分沿线的山脊。

2.2 与哈德良长城相关的英国法规、行政管理、保护和管理机构相关的用语

Section 2.2 UK heritage organisations and related regulatory, administrative and conservation terminology related to Hadrian's Wall

English 英文原文	Meaning / Description in English 英文释义	(Recommended) Translation in Chinese (Hanzi and Pinyin) 中文翻译（加拼音标注）	Description in Chinese 中文释义
Antonine Wall	The section of the Frontiers of the Roman Empire World Heritage Site in Scotland. It runs from the Firth of Forth to the Firth of Clyde, north of Edinburgh and Glasgow respectively and was occupied for about 25 years in the mid 2nd century AD.	安东尼长城 Andongni changcheng	位于苏格兰的罗马帝国边疆世界遗产区段。从爱丁堡以北的福斯湾延伸到格拉斯哥以北的克莱德湾，在公元2世纪中期使用了约25年。
Area of Outstanding Natural Beauty (AONB)	A formal designation of natural heritage landscapes of particular beauty that are protected from development.	突出自然风景区 Jiechu ziran fengjingqu	正式公布的，具有特殊美学价值的自然遗产景观，以免受开发破坏。
Community Archaeology	Archaeological excavation and survey projects designed to involve volunteers from local communities working alongside professional archaeologists.	社区考古 Shequ kaogu	由当地社区志愿者与专业考古学家一起开展的考古发掘和调查项目。
Conserve as Found	The prevailing principle in UK archaeological conservation, through which surviving original archaeological remains are simply stabilised in the form in which they are discovered, rather than reconstructed or reassembled.	按发现时状态保护 An faxianshi zhuangtai baohu	英国考古遗址保护中的主要原则，即只将幸存的考古遗迹稳定在其被发现时的状态，而不进行重建或规整。
Conservation Principles, Policy and Guidance	The principal UK policy document concerning cultural heritage conservation, published by English Heritage in 2008.	保护原则、政策和指南 Baohu yuanze, zhengce he zhinan	英国文化遗产保护的主要政策文件，由英格兰遗产委员会于2008年出版。
Department of Digital, Culture, Media and Sport (DCMS)	The UK Government Department with ultimate responsibility for cultural heritage conservation and management policy.	英国数字、文化、媒体和体育部 Yingguo shuzi wenhua meiti he tiyu bu	对文化遗产保护和管理政策负有最终责任的英国政府部门。
English Heritage	The informal name for 'The English Heritage Trust', established in 2012 to manage historic sites in England in the care of the UK Government. Prior to 2012 English Heritage was a non-departmental public body which included the responsibilities of what is now Historic England.	英格兰遗产信托 Yinggelan yichan xintuo	"英格兰遗产信托"的简称，成立于2012年，负责经营管理英国政府拥有的英格兰历史古迹。2012年之前，指现在的非部门公共机构英国遗产委员会。

English 英文原文	Meaning / Description in English 英文释义	(Recommended) Translation in Chinese (Hanzi and Pinyin) 中文翻译（加拼音标注）	Description in Chinese 中文释义
Generic Consent	A scheme, first developed on Hadrian's Wall, through which minor routine maintenance and conservation work to Scheduled Monuments can be licenced without individual consent.	通用登录古迹许可 Tongyong denglu guji xuke	最初应用于哈德良长城的一种许可，可在未经单独批准的情况下对登录古迹开展一系列小型日常维护和保护工作。
Hadrian's Wall World Heritage Site	The protected elements of the Roman frontier defence system, inscribed in 1987. It is now a part of the Frontiers of the Roman Empire World Heritage Site.	哈德良长城世界遗产地 Hadeliang changcheng shijie yichandi	于 1987 年列为世界遗产的罗马边疆体系。现在是罗马帝国边疆世界遗产的一部分。
Hadrian's Wall Cycleway	One of a network of National Cycle Routes across the UK. Opened in 2007, it runs from Ravenglass on the Cumbrian coast to Wallsend.	哈德良长城自行车道 Hadeliang changcheng zixingche dao	英国国家自行车路线网络之一。于 2007 年开业，从坎布里亚海岸的雷文格拉斯延伸到沃森德。
Hadrian's Wall Path National Trail	One of a network of National Trails, it was opened in 2003 and follows the line of Hadrian's Wall from Wallsend in the east to Bowness-on-Solway in the west.	哈德良长城国家步道 Hadeliang changcheng guojia budao	国家步道网络之一，于 2003 年开放，沿哈德良长城尽东的沃森德延伸到西部的波尼斯 – 索尔维。
Hadrian's Wall Research Framework	An assessment of archaeological knowledge of Hadrian's Wall, published in 2009, which identifies academic priorities for further research. This assessment is currently being updated.	哈德良长城研究框架 Hadeliang changcheng yanjiu kuangjia	2009 年发表的对哈德良长城考古研究的评估，确定了进一步的学术研究重点，目前正在更新中。
Hadrian's Wall World Heritage Site Interpretation Framework	A set of principles and guidelines for the development of interpretation at sites and museums across Hadrian's Wall.	哈德良长城世界遗产地阐释框架 Hadeliang changcheng shijie yichandi chanshi kuangjia	为哈德良长城沿线遗址和博物馆开展遗产阐释制定的一系列原则和指南。
Hadrian's Wall World Heritage Site Management Plan	The document which sets out the priority issues facing the management of the World Heritage Site, and the agreed policies and actions necessary to address them. This document is reviewed and updated every 5 to 6 years.	哈德良长城世界遗产地管理规划 Hadeliang changcheng shijie yichandi guanli guihua	文件包括世界遗产管理所面临的优先问题，以及为解决这些问题而达成一致意见的政策和行动。每 5 至 6 年审核和更新。
Hadrian's Wall World Heritage Site Management Plan Co-ordinator	The individual responsible for co-ordinating the activities of partner organisations involved in managing and conserving the World Heritage Site.	哈德良长城世界遗产地管理规划协调员 Hadeliang changcheng shijie yichandi guanli guihua xietiaoyuan	负责协调参与管理和保护世界遗产地合作组织的活动的人。

续表 Continued

English 英文原文	Meaning / Description in English 英文释义	(Recommended) Translation in Chinese (Hanzi and Pinyin) 中文翻译（加拼音标注）	Description in Chinese 中文释义
Hadrian's Wall World Heritage Site Partnership Board	The body which oversees the policies, objectives and actions for the conservation and management of the World Heritage Site.	哈德良长城世界遗产合作委员会 Hadeliang changcheng shijie yichandi hezuo weiyuanhui	负责统筹世界遗产保护和管理的政策、目标和行动的机构。
Heritage at Risk Register	A list of heritage sites at risk of damage or destruction, compiled by Historic England in collaboration with Local Authorities.	濒危遗产名录 Binwei yichan minglu	由英格兰遗产委员会会同地方政府编制的有受损或毁坏风险的遗产地点清单。
Historic England	The informal name for 'Historic Buildings and Monuments of England' the national non-departmental public body responsible for advising national and local government about the conservation and management of heritage sites and historic buildings.	英格兰遗产委员会 Yinggelan yichan weiyuanhui	"英格兰历史建筑和古迹委员会"的简称，是负责向国家和地方政府提供有关遗产地和历史建筑的保护管理建议的国家非部门公共机构。
Local Authority	The general name given to municipal and county level local government.	地方政府 Difangzhengfu	对市、县级地方政府的统称。
National Planning Policy Framework (NPPF)	The national guidance document which sets out Planning policies and principles across England.	国家规划政策框架 Guojia guihua zhengce kuangjia	制定整个英格兰的规划政策和原则的国家指导文件。
Natural England	The national non-departmental public body responsible for advising national and local government about the conservation and management of the natural environment.	英格兰自然委员会 Yinggelan ziran weiyuanhui	国家非部门公共机构，负责向国家和地方政府提供有关自然环境保护和管理的建议。
Planning Authority	The generic name for local government which has specific responsibility for authorising new development.	规划部门 Guihua bumen	对负责审批新开发建设项目的地方政府部门的统称。
Scheduled Monument	Cultural heritage sites which are officially designated as protected by law.	登录古迹 Denglu guji	官方公布的受法律保护的文化遗产地。
Scheduled Monument Consent	The official authorisation required for any work on, or alterations to, a Scheduled Monument.	登录古迹许可 Denglu guji xuke	对登录古迹进行任何施工或变动所需的官方批准。
Site of Special Scientific Interest (SSSI)	A designated area protecting biological or geological sites of national importance.	具特殊科学价值地点 Jv teshu kexuejiazhi didian	为保护有国家级重要性的生物或地质遗址而设的指定区域。

续表 Continued

English 英文原文	Meaning / Description in English 英文释义	(Recommended) Translation in Chinese (Hanzi and Pinyin) 中文翻译（加拼音标注）	Description in Chinese 中文释义
Frontiers of Roman Empire	The collective term used to describe the border regions of the Roman Empire from the 2nd Century AD onwards.	罗马帝国边疆 Luomadiguo bianjiang	用于描述公元 2 世纪以来罗马帝国的边界地区的统称。
Frontiers of the Roman Empire World Heritage Site	The serial transnational World Heritage Site, first established in 2005, comprising Hadrian's Wall (inscribed in 1987) the Upper–German Raetian Limes (inscribed in 2005) and the Antonine Wall (inscribed in 2008).	罗马帝国边疆世界遗产地 Luomadiguo bianjiang shijie yichandi	系列跨国世界遗产，最初于 2005 年公布，包括哈德良长城（1987 年列入）、上日尔曼－雷蒂亚长城（2005 年列入）和安东尼长城（2008 年列入）。
National Trust	The third sector body responsible for the management of over 500 cultural and natural heritage sites within the UK (except Scotland) .	国家信托 Guojia xintuo	负责管理英国 500 多个文化和自然遗产地的第三部门机构。
Third Sector	The term used to describe all those organisations which are neither publicly owned nor privately owned. This includes not–for–profit organisations, charitable trusts, and other groups and associations.	公益组织 Gongyi zuzhi	用于描述所有非公共也非私有的组织，包括非营利组织，慈善信托以及其他团体和协会。
Upper–German Raetian Limes	The section of the Frontiers of the Roman Empire World Heritage Site in Germany which runs from the River Rhine to the upper Danube.	上日尔曼－雷蒂亚长城 / 界墙 Shangri'erman-leidiya changcheng / jieqiang	在德国部分的罗马帝国世界遗产边疆，从莱茵河延伸到多瑙河上游。

Chapter One
National Management Systems

宁夏明长城（摄影：王云刚）
Ming Great Wall in Ningxia (© Wang Yungang)

第一章
国家遗产管理体系

灰石护墙（版权：Roger Clegg）
Limestone Bank (© Roger Clegg)

HADRIAN'S WALL: AN INTRODUCTION

MATTHEW SYMONDS

Current World Archaeology - London - UK

Abstract

Hadrian's Wall is the most impressive archaeological relic of the Roman occupation of Britain. The ruins of this frontier system have attracted scholarly curiosity for 1,500 years, while over a century of scientific excavations has laid bare its core components. A shortage of written sources detailing the purpose of Hadrian's Wall leaves us dependent on the surviving archaeological evidence to understand it. This also requires looking beyond the Wall to consider the local communities populating the region, the vibrant 'civilian' settlements that grew up outside forts, and the wider network of frontiers encircling the Roman world. The various communities either separated or united by Hadrian's Wall evolved over a period of almost three centuries, ultimately laying the foundations for life following the collapse of Roman rule in Britain.

Keywords: Hadrian's Wall, Roman Britain, frontiers, military, archaeology, historiography.

INTRODUCTION

In modern parlance, the emperor Hadrian was a maverick (Fig. 1). He came to power following Trajan's death in AD 117 and was considered 'strange and baffling' by contemporaries[1], on account of an appetite for flouting convention. As well as becoming the first Roman emperor to cultivate a beard in the Greek style, Hadrian also eschewed the traditional path to imperial martial glory via territorial expansion in favour of securing the edges of the Roman world. One of his first acts as emperor was to abandon three provinces that Trajan had carved out of Mesopotamia, Assyria, and Ar-

Fig1
The emperor Hadrian, as represented by a bronze statue head found in the River Thames and now on display in the British Museum (© Matthew Symonds)
图1
哈德良皇帝，在泰晤士河畔发现的青铜头像，现在大英博物馆展出（摄影：马修·西蒙兹）

哈德良长城概览

马修·西蒙兹
(《当代世界考古》期刊，英国伦敦）

摘　要

哈德良长城是罗马占领不列颠时期留下的最令人印象深刻的考古遗迹。500 年来，这一边疆体系遗迹始终激发着学界的好奇心。同时，一个多世纪的考古发掘也揭示出若干长城核心部位。由于详细记载哈德良长城建造目的的史料稀缺，我们只能依靠现存的考古证据认知长城。这也要求我们放宽眼界，研究聚居于该地的当地社区，要塞外围充满活力的"平民"聚落，以及环绕罗马帝国的更广阔的边疆体系。三百年间时事变迁，许多聚落因哈德良长城而分裂，许多聚落因哈德良长城而统一，最终成为罗马统治崩溃后生活的根基。

关键词：哈德良长城　罗马不列颠　边疆　军事　考古学　编史学

引　言

用今天的话说，哈德良皇帝是个特立独行的人（图 1 ）。公元 117 年，图拉真皇帝驾崩，哈德良即位。时人因他喜欢不按常理出牌而觉得他"脾气古怪，捉摸不透"[1]。除了成为第一个蓄起希腊式胡须的罗马皇帝之外，他还摒弃了以领土扩张宣扬帝国军威的传统做法，而主张巩固罗马帝国边疆的安全。在他称帝后首先采取的若干举措中，就包括以无力保护为由，放弃图拉真收入帝国版图的美索不达米亚、亚述和亚美尼亚三个行省[1]。在后来的记载中，据说哈德良吹嘘"他通过和平所获得的比其他人通过战争得到的要多"，无疑是其治国方略的完美写照[2]。如今英格兰北部的这道长城仍冠以哈德良之名，使后人有机会验证他的豪言。

与中国长城相比，80 罗马英里（即 118 公里）长的哈德良长城就像是壁画上的一条小鱼微不足道。但是，哈德良长城只是公元 2 世纪围绕着罗马帝国建立起来的一系列罗马边疆体系中的一个而已。纵观整个体系，帝国为保卫边疆的投入令人叹为观止，其边疆工事横跨 20 个现代国家，总长达 7500 公里[2]。到公元 2 世纪中叶，演说家埃留斯·阿里斯提德斯（Aelius Aristides）可以有底气说"一支安营扎寨的军队，就像一堵城墙一样，将文明世界围合起来"[3]。这些说法，加上现代地图上描绘罗马边界通常使用的统一细线，给人以一致的印象。实际上，没有两个罗马边疆体系是完全相同的。他们巧妙利用了河流、山脉或沙漠等许多自然屏障，而不是完全修建人工屏障。哈德良长城凭借其庞大的规模从中脱颖而出。例如，大部分哈德良长城所设计的三米宽石砌城墙与当时伫立在上日耳曼边疆墙上的木栅栏有着天壤之别[4]。

与标准罗马防御体系相比，另一个不同之处是哈德良长城的腹地更为广阔。在欧洲的其他地方，守护边界和为罗马士兵提供住宿的军事哨所通常位于自然或人为屏障旁侧相对狭窄的地带。在不列颠，

menia, on the basis that they could not be protected[1]. In a later episode, Hadrian reputedly boasted that 'he had achieved more by peace than others by war', a line that certainly epitomises the emperor's approach[2]. The Wall in northern England that still bears Hadrian's name presents an opportunity to test this claim.

Compared to the Great Wall of China, the 80 Roman mile (118km) length of Hadrian's Wall could be seen as that of a mere mural minnow. The Wall is, though, only one in a series of Roman frontier systems that developed around the Roman world in the 2nd century AD. Taken together, the resources dedicated to securing the edge of the empire are impressive, with the frontier works stretching over 7,500km through 20 modern countries[2]. By the mid 2nd century the orator Aelius Aristides could declaim that 'an encamped army, like a rampart, encloses the civilised world in a ring'[3]. Such statements, coupled with the thin line that typically traces out the frontiers on modern maps, promote a sense of homogeneity. In reality, no two Roman frontier systems were identical, with many artfully augmenting natural obstacles such as rivers, mountains, or deserts rather than employing artificial barriers. Hadrian's Wall stands out among its peers by virtue of its sheer scale. The three metre-wide stone curtain planned for most of the Wall's length, for instance, is a far cry from the contemporary timber palisade erected on the Upper German frontier[4].

Another departure from standard practice concerns the wider hinterland of Hadrian's Wall. Elsewhere in Europe, the military posts securing the borders and accommodating Roman soldiers generally form a comparatively narrow band shadowing a natural or artificial barrier. In Britain, the military presence stretched deep into northern England, with forts and fortresses holding units ranging from under 500 to over 5,000 strong lying well to the south of the Wall. To its north, further forts established an outpost screen, while a cordon of posts continued beyond the terminus of Hadrian's Wall for at least 35km down the west coast of Britain. Seen this way, the Wall is simply the most elaborate element of a concentration of military force in northern England that is unusual in the wider context of Roman frontiers.

LONG DIVISION

Roman writers were notoriously coy about the scope of their frontiers, and a throwaway comment in a document written over 200 years after Hadrian's Wall was built provides the only clear statement of its role. The text tells us that '[Hadrian] was the first to construct a wall, 80 miles long, to separate the barbarians from the Romans'[5] (Historia Augusta, Hadrian, 11, 2). Taken at face value that seems clear enough, but closer scrutiny reveals plenty of ambiguity, especially concerning the word 'separate'. Should we envision a frontier that people could pass at military posts, after being searched and taxed, or does 'separate' imply a more closed border, with access restricted to the two points where major highways crossed the Wall? Attempting to answer this question requires meticulous study of the archaeological evidence.

The spectacular ruins of Hadrian's Wall have excited intellectual curiosity for 1,500 years. Barely a century after Roman control of Britain ended, the 6th-century monk Gildas seemingly distilled oral history and folklore

军队部署一直延伸至英格兰北部，并且在哈德良长城的南面设立了若干大小要塞，驻军人数从少于 500 到 5000 以上不等。在长城的北面，多个要塞建立起另一道前哨屏障。而在长城西端开外，则建立了一系列军事哨所，将其防御体系向英格兰西海岸延伸了 35 公里。由此可见，长城最能体现英格兰北部重兵把守的状态，这在更广阔的罗马边疆体系中也是不寻常的。

一、长期的分歧

古罗马时期的史家对边疆范围的界定是出了名的模糊。在一份于哈德良长城建成 200 多年后写就的文件里随口提到的一句话，成为了对哈德良长城的作用仅有的明确阐述。其中写道："[哈德良] 是下令修建长城的第一人。长城总长 80 罗马英里，将罗马人与野蛮人分隔开来 [5]"。这句话表面上看似解释得足够清楚，但再仔细一想却又觉得十分模棱两可，尤其是"分隔"这个词的使用。这究竟是一个怎样的边疆地带呢？人们在边哨接受搜查并交税后就可以通过吗；又或者"分隔"是指一个更封闭的边界，通道仅限于两条主要道路与长城相交的两点吗？想要回答这个问题，需要对考古证据展开细致入微的研究。

哈德良长城壮观的遗迹激发了学者的好奇心，持续 1500 年之久。在罗马结束对不列颠统治后不到一个世纪，公元 6 世纪的一位修道士吉尔达斯（Gildas）似乎从口述历史和民间传说提炼出一个关于哈德良长城起源的说法，尽管是人们想象出来的 [6][7]。最近几个世纪以来，人们试图根据遗迹实物来重塑其历史和作用。就保护而言，19 世纪的一位关键人物是当地土地所有者约翰·克莱顿（John Clayton）。他从 19 世纪 30 年代开始大量购买长城穿过的对外出售的土地。到 1890 年克莱顿去世时，其令人羡慕的不动产中共包括了五个罗马要塞。罗马遗迹的发掘行动经常会在克莱顿完成对土地的购买后开始。而对遗迹的后续处理方式则五花八门，从拆除到重建不等。尽管如此，他极大地延长了保护工作的周期，造福后世。科学发掘的起源众说不一，有些人认为可以追溯到 1892 年，当时 J·P·吉布森（J. P. Gibson）仔细记录一座塔楼内的地层堆积 [8]。越来越严谨的干预措施带来了关于哈德良长城信息的爆炸式增长，这种增长仍决定着当前的学术话语。

正如现代研究和保护不可能在真空中进行一样，罗马军队在公元 2 世纪 20 年代早期开始修筑长城时也不得不去了解当地早期的活动。罗马军队到来之前几个世纪，已有定居农业聚落在更广阔的范围内分布，特别是在长城东端及西端的沿海平原似乎分布更为密集。一些军事设施下方发现有多处犁痕，意味着当地农民可能遭到罗马军队驱逐。这一发现可以印证新边界建立初期产生的结果 [9]。哈德良统治初期的一场或若干战争可能加剧了占领者和被占领者之间的紧张关系 [10][11]。种种迹象表明，长城建造的意图是想堵住或改变当地已经存在的通道，从而引发冲突摩擦 [12]。当罗马军队进发苏格兰过程中，早在公元 1 世纪 70 年代就占领了英格兰北部地区，因此在修建哈德良长城时也既有军事设施也纳入考量。自公元 1 世纪晚期起，泰恩—索尔威地峡（Tyne‐Solway isthmus）所在的地区就已有要塞的存在。到了公元 105 年，这已经成为罗马撤出苏格兰之后的外部控制线。当时沿着一条罗马道路——如今被称之为"石路"（Stanegate）设有多处哨所，可能表明它本身已成为一道边界 [10]。无论修建哈德良长城利用的前期基础如何，哈德良长城最终确定的大部分线路似乎在寻求保持与石路上各罗马军事设施的视觉通道 [13][14]。

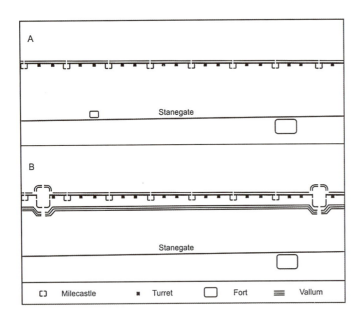

Fig. 2

Research has revealed evidence for a change in plan during construction, with a cordon of small posts (A), being augmented with forts and
the Vallum earthwork (B) (© Matthew Symonds)

图 2

研究发现了施工期间对设计进行修改的证据，原只有一系列小哨所（A），
后扩充了要塞和南部壕沟（B）[15]（制图：马修·西蒙兹）

to present an account - albeit fanciful - of the Wall's origin[6][7]. More recent centu-ries have seen attempts to reconstruct its history and role rooted in the fabric of the monument itself. A crucial 19th-century participant from a preservation perspective was the local landowner John Clayton, who - from the 1830s onwards - bought up land traversed by the Wall when it became available. By the time of his death in 1890, Clayton could count five Roman forts among his enviable property portfolio. Operations to unearth the Roman remains frequently followed Clayton's purchases, and although subsequent treatment of the structures varied considerably - ranging from removal to reconstruction - part of his legacy is an extraordinary longevity of conservation work. The dawn of scientific excavations arguably followed in 1892, when J P Gibson studiously recorded the stratigraphy within a turret[8]. Increasingly rigorous interventions triggered an explosion in knowledge about Hadrian's Wall, which still shapes current discourse.

Just as modern research and conservation does not occur in a vacuum, so too the Roman army was com-pelled to acknowledge earlier activity when construction of the Wall commenced in the early AD 120s. Settled farming communities had been living in the wider region for centuries, and appear to have been densely settled on the coastal plains at the eastern and western ends of the Wall. One early consequence of the new border is il-lustrated by the discovery of plough marks under some of the military infrastructure, suggesting that local farm-ers were dispossessed by the Roman army[9]. Tensions between the occupiers and occupied may have been ex-acerbated by a war or wars at the beginning of Hadrian's reign[10][11]. That friction existed is certainly implied by indications that the Wall's building programme was influenced by a desire to block or redirect traditional routes through the landscape[12]. As the region was initially conquered in the AD 70s, by Roman forces advancing north into Scotland, existing military bases were also a factor. Since the late 1st century AD, forts had existed in the area comprising the Tyne - Solway isthmus. By AD 105 this had become the outer line of control following Ro-man withdrawal from Scotland, and a proliferation of posts along a Roman road now known as the Stanegate

二、解读遗迹

借由一代又一代考古发掘者的辛勤努力，我们对哈德良长城组成部分的了解日渐增多。或许其最重要的发现就是证明哈德良长城的规划方案在施工期间发生了巨大的改动，这在文献中被称为"要塞决议（fort decision）"[5][15]。最初的"蓝图"似乎要求在墙体上等距设置一系列小哨所，而大量军事人员则驻扎在南侧石路的要塞中（图 2）。城墙北侧修建有一条护城壕沟，除非在部分段落现有自然地形条件不需要修建。而纽卡斯尔附近，由开发商资助的发掘现场发现在壕沟与墙体之间的狭道上建有木桩组成的防护设施，木桩顶部很可能呈现尖锥状[16]。在墙体上修建的驻军工事包括里堡和塔楼。顾名思义，里堡是城墙上每隔大约 1 罗马里（即 1479 米）修建的大型哨所。每两个里堡之间等距（间隔 495 米）建造一对塔楼。在这些军事工事的具体定位上是允许一定的灵活性的。然而军事设施部署往往要求精心规划其在大环境中的位置，使其军事功能最大化。而哈德良长城如此随意的定位体系极大背离了通常军事设施的建造习惯。这也不禁使人推测，这种边疆防御体系的新模式或许正是由哈德良亲手设计的。建造的里堡还设有相互贯通的城门，允许出入边境，这引发了争论，有观点认为其目的在于方便平民或军队的出入（图 3）。哈德良长城东部三分之二的墙体、塔楼和里堡都是用石头建造的，而对于西部的长城，

Fig. 3
The milecastles on Hadrian's Wall probably held garrisons of between 8 to 32 soldiers, and most contained a pair of gateways permitting passage through the frontier curtain. This example is known as Castle Nick, and is Milecastle 39 according to the convention of numbering the milecastles sequentially from east to west (© Matthew Symonds)

图 3
哈德良长城上的里堡或可容纳 8 到 32 名驻军，大部分建有一对门道，允许出入边境。图中示例被称为尼克堡，也即 39 号里堡。里堡编号惯例一般为从东向西顺序编号（摄影：马修·西蒙兹）

may indicate it became a frontier in its own right[10]. Either way, the precise course of much of Hadrian's Wall appears to have been dictated by a desire to retain a visual link to Roman military bases on the Stanegate[13][14].

READING THE RUINS

Our knowledge of the component parts that cumulatively comprise Hadrian's Wall has accrued thanks to the labours of generations of excavators. Perhaps the most important discovery from their work is evidence that the plan for Hadrian's Wall changed dramatically while construction was underway, a development referred to in the literature as the 'fort decision'[5][15]. The original 'blueprint' appears to have required a cordon of small posts arranged at regular intervals along the Wall curtain, while the bulk of the military manpower remained in the forts on the Stanegate road to the south (Fig. 2). A ditch lay to the north of Wall, except where the terrain rendered it redundant, while developer-funded excavations in the vicinity of Newcastle have revealed timber entanglements - probably with sharp spikes - on the berm between the ditch and the curtain[16]. The manned installations along the curtain consisted of a pair of turrets set at c495m intervals between larger posts known as milecastles, because they lie approximately one Roman mile (1,479m) apart. Some flexibility in positioning them was permitted, but implementing this arbitrary spacing system marks a radical departure from the usual military technique of placing such posts carefully within the landscape to maximise their impact. It is tempting to speculate that this novel solution to achieving frontier control was devised by Hadrian himself. The milecastles also contained gateways permitting passage through the frontier, prompting debate about whether they were intended to ease civilian or military access (Fig. 3). Along the eastern two thirds of Hadrian's Wall, the curtain, turrets, and milecastles were built of stone, while in the west only the turrets were originally masonry, with the remainder fashioned from turf and timber.

Before this version of Hadrian's Wall was complete a series of forts was added (Fig. 2), sometimes necessitating the demolition of elements that had already been constructed. In total, these forts housed approximately 9,090 soldiers[16], significantly increasing the number of troops available directly on the Wall curtain. An enigmatic earthwork known as the Vallum was also created to the south, and featured a ditch three metres deep by six metres wide, flanked by earth mounds creating an obstacle 36m wide. It is without parallel on a Roman frontier, and various roles have been proposed, including denying access to hostile, mobile groups on horseback[17]. By the time Hadrian died in AD 138, the turf stretch of Wall was being rebuilt in stone. Although Hadrian's successor Antoninus Pius decided to advance north, reconquering southern Scotland and building a new frontier running roughly between modern Edinburgh and Glasgow, Hadrian's Wall was being refurbished before Pius' death in AD 161. The abandonment of the Antonine Wall left Hadrian's Wall as the northern frontier of Roman Britain until imperial control collapsed in the early 5th century AD. Naturally, over the course of these centuries campaigns, expeditions, and diplomacy were still conducted to the north.

Both Hadrian's Wall and its hinterland changed over time. Remarkable new evidence from the Northum-

只有塔楼原本就是砖石结构，其余的是草被和木质结构。

在这期哈德良长城完工前，又增建了一系列要塞(图2)，因此有时就不得不拆除一些已经建好的部分。这些要塞总共容纳了约 9090 名士兵 [16]，大大增加了在长城上直接可以调用的军队人数。此外，在城墙南侧还修建了一个神秘的土木防御工事，即南部壕沟，底部 3 米深，6 米宽，两侧有巨大堆土，形成一个 36 米宽的屏障。这类南部壕沟在罗马边疆体系中是独一无二的，其发挥的作用有多种猜测，包括防御马背上的敌对机动势力的入侵 [17]。当哈德良于公元 138 年去世时，以石砌城墙替换草被城墙的工作正在进行。哈德良的继任者安东尼·庇护决定继续向北扩张，重新征服苏格兰南部，构筑新边界，位置大约横跨今天的爱丁堡到格拉斯哥之间，不过在庇护去世前，哈德良长城得到翻修。安东尼墙（Antonine Wall）被弃后，哈德良长城重新成为罗马不列颠的北部边界，直到公元 5 世纪初罗马帝国失去对不列颠的控制。当然，在这几百年间，针对北方的战役、远征和外交活动仍然正常开展。

随着时间的推移，哈德良长城及其腹地都发生了变化。诺森伯兰郡沿海平原发现的新证据表明，在哈德良长城投入使用期间，已有数个世纪历史的当地聚落被废弃了 [18]。相反，在要塞外围，充满活力的边疆平民聚落"vici"发展了起来（图 4 ），来自罗马帝国各地的士兵和平民和平共处 [19]。比如，

Fig. 4
Extensive 'civilian' settlements grew up outside the Roman forts, as at Housesteads, where the military base (centre) is less extensive than the earthworks of the vicus outside its defences (© Matthew Symonds)
图 4
大量"平民"定居点在罗马要塞周边发展起来，例如在豪塞斯特兹要塞，军事基地（中心）与其防御范围之外平民聚落的建设规模比相形见绌（摄影：马修·西蒙兹）

berland coastal plain indicates that local settlements, which had endured for centuries, were abandoned around the time Hadrian's Wall became operational[18]. Conversely, outside the forts, vibrant frontier settlements known as vici developed (Fig. 4), where soldiers and civilians from across the Roman Empire could rub shoulders[19]. A tombstone from South Shields, for instance, was erected in memory of Regina, a Catuvellaunian woman from south-east Britain, by Barates, a man from Palmyra in Syria[20]. Influential excavations within Birdoswald fort have demonstrated a shift from architecture reinforcing the imperial hierarchy to that projecting personal power during the 4th and 5th centuries AD. Eventually, a substantial timber hall was raised over the ruins of a fort granary. There was no break in occupation, though. Instead, a garrison loyal to distant emperors seemingly gradually mutated into a medieval-style warband led by its own chieftain[21][22]. In doing so, it set the scene for the next chapter in British history.

What can all of this tell us about the purpose of Hadrian's Wall? Modern scholarship is broadly split between two camps, one that sees the frontier as a way to regulate the peaceful movement of people, and the other as a means to repulse barbarian invasions[10][16]. Both sides generally view the Wall as an effective means to curtail undesirable activities such as raiding, and it would also be well suited to frustrate low-level violence perpetrated by groups referred to today as insurgents[23]. The collapse of a farming community on the Northumberland coastal plain could suggest that passage through the new frontier was far from straightforward, and a growing number of specialists agree that the milecastle gateways were intended for military rather than civilian use[24]. Despite signs of serious disruption to the north, the frontier probably did improve security for those living within its embrace. Villas were seemingly constructed within 22km of Hadrian's Wall, while rural settlement in Roman Britain as a whole expanded rapidly during the 2nd century AD. Clearly, the frontier changed different communities in profoundly different ways. These groups probably held conflicting views on whether Hadrian's model for peace truly brought progress.

在南希尔兹（South Shields）发现了一块墓碑，是来自叙利亚巴尔米拉的男子巴拉特斯（Barates）为纪念来自英格兰东南部的卡图维拉尼（Catuvellauni）部落的女子雷吉娜（Regina）而修建的[20]。博得瓦德（Birdoswald）要塞内重大考古发掘证明，公元4世纪到5世纪期间，建筑的作用经历了从强化帝国等级制度到突出个人权力的转变。最终，在要塞的一处粮仓遗迹的上面，建起了一座木结构大厅。不过，此地的人类活动却从未间断。事实上，效忠于遥远帝国皇帝的驻军似乎逐渐变成由酋长率领的中世纪战团[21][22]。这为书写英格兰历史的新篇章就此埋下了伏笔。

关于哈德良长城的目的，上文所述都能告诉我们些什么呢？现代学术研究大致分成两个阵营，一方将边界视作一种管理人口和平流动的方式，而另一方则认为是阻挡蛮族入侵的手段[10][16]。双方都认为哈德良长城是遏制袭击等不良活动的有效手段，而且它也非常适合阻碍低级别的暴力渗透活动，即在今天被称为叛乱分子组织的行动[23]。诺森伯兰郡沿海平原农业聚落的衰败可能表明，穿过新建边界并非易事；越来越多的专家认为，里堡城门的目的是军用而非民用[24]。尽管有对北方造成严重破坏的迹象，边界可能确实为那些生活在其保护范围内的人们提供了更安全的保障。罗马乡间别墅赫然建造在距离哈德良长城22公里的地方，而罗马不列颠的乡村聚落在公元2世纪期间整体得到迅速扩张。显然，罗马边疆体系以截然不同的方式深远地改变了不同地区的聚落。至于哈德良的和平方略是否真正带来进步，不同群体的观点或许截然不同。

参考文献
Bibliography

[1] Birley, A.R. Hadrian: The Restless Emperor. London: 1997.

A.R. 波利 . 哈德良：不安的帝王 [M]. 伦敦 :1997.

[2] Pichlmayr, F(ed). Epitome de Caesaribus: Sexti Aurelii Victoris liber de Caesaribus, Praecedunt Origo gentis Romanae, et liber de viris illustribus urbis Romae, subsequitur Epitome de Caesaribus. Leipzig: 1911.

F. 皮彻梅尔（编）.Epitome de Caesaribus: Sexti Aurelii Victoris liber de Caesaribus, Praecedunt Origo gentis Romanae, et liber de viris illustribus urbis Romae, subsequitur Epitome de Caesaribus[M]. 莱比锡 :1911.

[2] Breeze, D.J. The frontiers of Imperial Rome. Barnsley: 2011.

D.J. 布雷兹 . 罗马帝国边疆 [M]. 巴恩斯利 :2011.

[3] Oliver, J.H(trans). Roman Oration: The ruling power: a study of the Roman Empire in the second century after Christ through the Roman oration of Aelius Aristides. Philadelphia: 1953.

J.H. 奥利弗（译）. 罗马演说 : 执政权力 : 通过阿里斯蒂德的罗马演讲进行的基督后公元二世纪罗马帝国的研究 [M]. 费城 :1953.

[4] Crow, J.G. "The northern frontier of Britain from Trajan to Antoninus Pius: Roman builders and native Britons." in A Companion to Roman Britain, edited by M. Todd. Oxford: 2004: 114-135.

J.G. 克劳 . 从图拉真到安东尼庇护的不列颠北部边界 : 罗马建造者和当地的不列颠人 [J].M·托德编，不列颠尼亚史伴侣 [M], 牛津 :2004:114-135.

[5] Magie, D(trans). Historia Augusta: Scriptores Historiae Augustae: Volume 1. Loeb Classical Library, Cambridge MA/London: 1991.

D. 马吉（译）. 罗马君王传：卷一 [M]. 洛布古典图书馆 . 剑桥 MA/ 伦敦 :1991.

[6] Winterbottom, M (trans.and ed). De Excidio Britanniae: The Ruin of Britain and other works. London: 1978.

M. 温特博特姆（编译）. 不列颠的废墟及其他作品 [M]. 伦敦 :1978.

[7] Hingley, R. Hadrian's Wall: A Life. Oxford: 2012.

R. 欣利 . 哈德良长城：一个生命 [M]. 牛津 :2012.

[8] Breeze, D.J. Hadrian's Wall: A History of Archaeological Thought. Kendal: 2014.

D.J. 布雷兹 . 哈德良长城：考古思想史 [M]. 肯德尔 :2014.

[9] Hodgson, N. Hadrian's Wall: Archaeology and History at the limit of Rome's Empire. Ramsbury: 2017.

N. 霍奇森 . 哈德良长城：在罗马帝国边界的考古和历史 [M]. 拉姆斯伯里 :2017.

[10] Breeze, D.J. "Warfare in Britain and the building of Hadrian's Wall." Archaeologia Aeliana, 2003, 5(32): 13-16.

D.J. 布雷兹 . 不列颠的战争和哈德良长城的修建 [J].Archaeologia Aeliana,2003,5(32): 13-16.

[11] Birley, A.R. "Two governors of Dacia Superior and Britain." In Graecia, Roma, Barbaricum. In memoriam Vasile Lica, edited by V. Iliescu et al. Galaţi: 2014: 241-259.

A.R. 波利 . 上达契亚和不列颠的两位统治者 [A]. V·斯库编 , Graecia, Roma,Barbaricum. In memoriam Vasile Lica[M], 加拉茨 :2014:241-259.

[12] Symonds, M.F.A. Protecting the Roman Empire: fortlets, frontiers, and the quest for post-conquest security. Cambridge: 2017.

M.F.A. 西蒙兹 . 保护罗马帝国：要塞、边疆 , 和追求征服后的安全 [M]. 剑桥 :2017.

[13] Woolliscroft, D.J. "Signalling and the design of Hadrian's Wall." Archaeologia Aeliana, 1989, 5(17): 5-19.

D.J. 沃利斯克罗夫特 . 哈德良长城的信号和设计 [J].Archaeologia Aeliana,1989,5(17): 5-19.

[14] Poulter, J. "Surveying Roman Military Landscapes across Northern Britain." BAR British Series 492, Oxford: 2009.

J. 博尔特 . 不列颠北部的罗马军事景观调查 [J].BAR 不列颠卷 492, 牛津 :2009.

[15] Breeze, D.J., and Dobson, B. Hadrian's Wall. London: 2000.

D.J. 布雷兹 , B·多布森 . 哈德良长城 [M]. 伦敦 :2000.

[16] Bidwell, P.T. "The system of obstacles on Hadrian's Wall: their extent, date, and purpose." Arbeia Journal, 2005(8): 53-75.

P.T. 彼得威尔 . 哈德良长城上的障碍物体系：其范围、日期及目的 [J]. 阿伯亚期刊， 2005(8): 53-75.

[17] Woolliscroft, D.J. "More thoughts on the Vallum." In Transactions of the Cumberland and Westmorland Antiquarian and Archaeological society, 1999, 2(99): 53-65.

D.J. 沃利斯克罗夫特 . 有关南部壕沟的更多思考 [J]. 坎伯兰郡和威斯特摩兰郡古文物和考古协会会报 ,1999,2(99):53-65.

[18] Hodgson, N. et al. The Iron Age on the Northumberland Coastal Plain. Newcastle upon Tyne: 2012.

N. 霍奇森等 . 诺森伯兰郡沿海平原的铁器时代 [M]. 泰恩河畔纽卡斯尔 :2012.

[19] Nesbitt, C. "Multiculturalism on Hadrian's Wall." In The Oxford Handbook of Roman Britain, edited by Millett, M. et al. Oxford: 2016: 224-244.

C. 内斯比特 . 哈德良长城的多元文化论 [A].M·米利特等编 , 不列颠尼亚牛津指南 [C]. 牛津 : 2016:224-244.

[20] Collingwood, R.G., and Wright, R.P(eds). RIB: The Roman Inscriptions of Britain: Volume 1 Inscriptions on Stone. Oxford: 1965.

R.G. 科林伍德， R.P. 赖特 . 不列颠罗马铭文集：卷一 石头上的铭文 [M]. 牛津 :1965.

[21] Wilmott, T. Birdoswald: Excavations of a Roman fort on Hadrian's Wall and its successor settlements: 1987-92. London: 1997.

T. 威尔莫特 . 博得瓦德 , 哈德良长城罗马要塞和晚期聚落的发掘 :1987-92[M]. 伦敦 :1997.

[22] Collins, R. Hadrian's Wall and the end of empire: the Roman frontier in the 4th and 5th centuries. New York: 2012.

R. 柯林斯 . 哈德良长城和帝国的终结：公元四五世纪的罗马边疆 [M]. 纽约 :2012.

[23] Symonds, M.F.A. "The purpose of Hadrian's Wall: the Dorothy Charlesworth lecture delivered at the Shakespeare Centre, Kendal." In Transactions of the Cumberland and Westmorland Antiquarian and Archaeological society , November 6, 2017, 3(19), unpublished.

M.F.A. 西蒙兹 . 哈德良长城的目的：多萝西·查尔斯沃斯在肯德尔莎士比亚中心的演讲 . [J]. 坎伯兰郡和威斯特摩兰郡古文物和考古协会会报 ,2017,3(19), 未发表 .

[24] Welfare, H. "Causeways, at Milecastles, across the Ditch of Hadrian's Wall." Archaeologia Aeliana, 2000, 5(28): 13-25.

H. 维尔法 . 跨越哈德良长城壕沟的里堡堤道 [J].Archaeologia Aeliana, 2000, 5(28):13-25.

长城与中华帝国文明

段清波

（西北大学文化遗产学院，中国西安）

摘 要

帝国与长城相始终，长城的出现和发展伴随了帝国体制的构建、完善和衰败。战国时期是古代中国从王国体制到帝国社会治理体系转变的质变阶段，长城防御体系在城的基础上产生了。战国后期农业国家受到北方游牧势力南下的巨大压力，长城多修建于农牧交错地带，并成为了能给农业文明带来安全感的心理防线。随着帝国文明的兴盛，长城也从单一墙体发展为包含多种元素的巨型军事工程体系。长城分布区域的农牧交互带来了文明的互动碰撞，长城的修筑以军事需求为起点，以多民族融合为终结，见证了农牧双方发展的历史进程。农业民族与游牧民族在长城交互地带两千多年的交往，形成了农牧两大统一体，共同组成了中华文明的多元面貌，也因此成为中华民族的象征。

关键词：长城　帝国社会治理体系　中华民族　中国文明

城是文明形成过程中最为突出和最重要的一个标志[1]。战国时期，古代中国开始发生了从王国体制到帝国社会治理体系转变的质变过程[2]，与之相适应的、在城的基础上产生了长城这一新兴的防御体系，多数长城分布在农牧交错地带。长城的出现和发展伴随了帝国体制的构建、完善和衰败，因为两千五百年之间的农业文明和游牧文明的互动碰撞与融汇，才有了农业民族和游牧民族共同构建形成中国文明的历史进程。

一、长城的出现

在中国历史发展演变过程中，有一条重要的自然地理带深度影响着历史的进程，即长城地带。它自东北向西南呈带状绵延分布，东起西辽河流域，经燕山、阴山、贺兰山，到达湟水流域和河西走廊，包括了今天的内蒙古东南部、河北北部、山西北部、陕西北部、内蒙古中南部、宁夏、甘肃和青海的东北部[3]。长城地带两侧的气候环境、风土人情、文化风格等都呈现出显著的差异。

（一）、长城出现的背景

先秦时期拥有至高无上的政治地位和掌握大量社会财富的是王和各级贵族，他们一般居住在城邑中更为尊贵和安全的区域，尤其是王城和大型城市中，这也意味着社会财富主要集中在城市，正是出于这种原因，战国之前的战争主要是以攻取王城或大型城市为目标，目的是攻城掠取财富[4]。时至战国，战争的目标从攻城发展到攻城略地、略人，其目的是为获取更多的土地和役使更多的人口，广袤的土地和

THE GREAT WALL AND CHINESE IMPERIAL CIVILIZATION

Duan Qingbo

School of Cultural Heritage, Northwest University - Xi'an - China

Abstract

Empire and the Great Wall have always been linked. The Great Wall evolved in parallel with the construction, perfection and decline of the imperial system. During the Warring States Period, ancient China underwent a change from a system of separate kingdoms to a system of imperial social governance. The Great Wall defence system evolved from the earlier defensive systems of city walls. In the late Warring States period, agricultural states were under great pressure from the forces of nomadic peoples, who invaded from the north. The Great Wall was mostly built in the zone where agriculture and pastoralism converged, and it became a psychological defence line that brought security to the agricultural civilization. As the imperial civilization prospered, the Great Wall also developed from simply a series of walls to a huge military engineering system containing many different elements. The construction of the Great Wall reflected military needs initially, and ended with multi-ethnic integration, bearing witness to the historical process of the development of agriculture and nomadism. Agricultural and nomadic peoples have engaged with each other around the Great Wall for more than 2,000 years, integrating to form the characteristically diverse Chinese nation. The Great Wall has therefore become the symbol of Chinese civilization.

Keywords: The Great Wall; System of imperial governance;Chinese civilization;The Chinese nation

In the process of the formation of civilization, the city is the most prominent and important symbol[1]. During the Warring States Period, ancient China began to undergo a qualitative change from a system of kingdoms to an imperial social governance system[2]. Correspondingly, a new defence system of extended walls was formed from the basis of cities. Most of the Great Wall was distributed in the transition zone between agricultural and nomadic areas. The emergence and development of the Great Wall was accompanied by the construction, perfection and decline of the imperial system. The interaction, collision and fusion of agricultural and nomadic civilizations over 2,500 years, drove the historical process of agricultural and nomadic peoples jointly constructing and forming Chinese civilization.

THE EMERGENCE OF THE GREAT WALL

The natural and geographical characteristics of the Great Wall corridor[1] exerted a profound influence upon

---

1 This term is used to describe the broad band of territory in which the Great Wall is situated and across which the nomadic and agricultural civilisations intersected; elsewhere in this volume and in other academic literature it is described as 'the Great Wall zone'. (Editors' note)

众多的劳力可以创造出更多财富的认识获得人们的共识，这一阶段，土地的价值日益凸显，土地兼并愈加激烈。

与此社会背景相适应的是，此阶段的战争规模、模式和目的等都发生剧烈和根本的变化。首先，列国之间矛盾更加激烈、战争频繁，各国都需要建立常备军来进行作战或防御，从军人员的身份扩大到一般自由民，军队人数为之大增；其次，作战类型从春秋时期的车战变为步骑联合作战的形式；再次，作战目标转向了攻城略地以及获取人口资源，作战规模从城池的攻防转向大规模野战。

根据文献记载统计，春秋时期从公元前 722—公元前 464 年的 259 年间，只有 38 年没有发生战争，当时有 170 多个诸侯国；到了战国时期，从公元前 463 公元前 222 年的 242 年间，虽然有 89 年没有战争，诸侯国的数量却从 170 多个到战国后期只剩下七雄在彼此抗争，诸侯国数量惊人消失表明战争的规模和残酷程度匪夷所思。春秋时期的战争往往在一天之内解决，士兵由贵族子弟担任，以车战为主，参与的人数少，车辆也少，兵器以适应车战需要的长兵器为主；早期城濮之战时候，参战的车是 700 乘，鞍之战时，是 800 乘。齐桓公时齐国兵力仅有战车 800 乘、兵力 3 万人，到后期晋国竟达到战车 4900 乘、兵力 15 万人的规模，楚灵王时达到 4000 乘的兵力，春秋时战争的规模达到数万就已经相当可观了。

战国之名来源于此阶段战争的常态化和战争规模的扩大化，此时战争达到旷日持久的程度，规模大、参与的人数多，战争的形式演变成车、步、骑三兵种联合作战的形式，兵器以弓弩和常规兵器为主，秦赵之间的长平之战持续一年之久，这时候一场战争下来动辄数万人、数十万的军队裹挟其中。

战国后期列国的兵力和春秋相比，不仅是量上的差异，更是兵种、战争方式、兵员组成、兵器种类的差异，战争规模和战争目标也大相径庭。秦国带甲百万、车千乘、骑万匹；赵国带甲数十万、车千乘、骑万匹；公元前 293 年，白起破韩魏联军时，斩首 24 万；公元前 273 年，白起败魏军于华阳，斩首 15 万；公元前 260 年长平之战时，秦俘赵军 40 多万；公元前 251 年燕攻赵，起兵多至 60 万；公元前 224 年秦国派遣王翦带兵 60 万伐楚。从公元前 364 年至 234 年的 130 年间，秦国参与 15 次大的战争，给对方造成的伤亡达 148.9 万人。由于城墙的防御能力、防御方式与战国时期大规模军事兼并战争并不匹配，于是围合的矩形城邑——被展开，发展成为一道道边墙，布设在疆域边界，形成一种新的防御形式和防御思想体系，长城形态便应运而生。

长城防御思想防御形态脱胎于战国时期诸侯间大规模兼并战争，为了满足各诸侯国自身安全和发展的需要，各诸侯国尤其农业形态的诸侯国之间相互修筑长城防御对方，以期借助高大的墙体来寻求力量平衡或构建彼此的交往秩序，毫无疑问，修建长城的往往是处于弱势的一方。最早修建长城的是齐国，后来燕、韩、赵、魏、秦等国先后都修建了互相防御的长城，甚至有些较小的诸侯国也修建过长城，如鲜虞族建立的中山国也修建了防御赵国的长城[5]。

到了战国后期，中原农业民族在相互防御的同时，秦、赵、燕三国相继面临北方游牧邻居南下的强大压力，于是，由农业文明发明的长城理念与实践也运用到此时的农牧交错地带。

（二）长城地带的形成及特点

长城是冷兵器时代最为重要的军事防御设施，从战国至清代两千多年间，有 12 个朝代、24 个政治实体先后修建了规模不等、长短不同的长城，虽然各个时代长城的分布位置有所差别，但除战国时期外，

the development and evolution of Chinese history. The corridor stretches from northeast to southwest in a strip-line pattern. From the western arm of Liaohe river basin in the east, it passes through the Yanshan mountains, the Yinshan mountains and the Helan mountains and reaches the Huangshui river basin and Hexi corridor, including the southeast of inner Mongolia, the north of Hebei, the north of Shanxi, the north of Shaanxi, south-central inner Mongolia, Ningxia, Gansu and the northeast of Qinghai[3]. The climatic environment, customs and cultural characteristics on both sides of the Great Wall corridor show significant differences.

The Background of the Great Wall

In the Pre-Qin Dynasty, the aristocracy and nobility had supreme political status and possessed a large amount of social wealth. They generally lived in the more elite and secure city areas, and particularly in the royal cities and larger cities, resulting in social wealth being mainly concentrated in the cities. For this reason, before the Warring States Period, wars were mostly aimed at capturing royal cities or larger cities. The military objective was to seize and plunder the city[4]. In the Warring States Period, the aim of war became acquisition of more land and dominion over more people. This was driven by the emerging understanding that more land and more labour could create more wealth. In this period the value of land became increasingly significant and land annexation became more and more frequent.

Corresponding to this changing social context, the scale, modes and purposes of war in this period underwent fundamental changes. Firstly, the conflicts between different states became more intense and wars more frequent, so all countries needed to establish standing armies for either aggression or defence. The social identity of the people engaged in fighting also extended from the traditional noble classes towards greater participation by other sections of society, and the number of troops engaging in battles greatly increased. Secondly, the type of combat changed from chariot warfare in the Spring and Autumn Period to engagements of both infantry and cavalry. Thirdly, the combat objectives shifted from attacking cities to the acquisition of population, and military engagements shifted from the attack and defence of cities to large-scale field operations.

According to the statistics found in documents, there were only 38 years without war during the Spring and Autumn Period between 722 BC and 464 BC, a period during which there were more than 170 kingdoms. During the Warring States Period, from 463 BC to 222 BC, there were 89 years without war, but the number of kingdoms reduced sharply from 170 to seven. The disappearance of so many kingdoms hints at the unimaginable scale and ferocity of the wars. Wars in the Spring and Autumn Period often lasted no longer than one day of battle. Soldiers came from noble families, who were mainly involved in chariot warfare, with relatively few participants. Weapons were mainly longer - adapted to the needs of chariot warfare. In the early Chengpu War, the number of chariots participating was 700, while in the An War between Jin and Qi states, it was 800. In the Qihuan Gong period, the Qi State had only 800 chariots and 30,000 troops. While in the late Jin Dynasty, up to 4,900 chariots and 150,000 troops were mobilised. During the reign of the King Chu Ling, battles involved up to 4,000 chariots, while in the Spring and Autumn Period, armies in the tens of thousands were rare.

历代长城的大概走向却基本一致，自东北向西南呈带状绵延分布在"长城地带"，古来中原农业居民与北方游牧人群在此互相接触[6]。

长城地带的形成和自然地形以及气候环境的变化息息相关，中国历代长城大多分布在蒙古高原和华北平原、黄土高原的过渡区域，同时也和我国的400毫米等降水量线走势基本一致，长城地带除了东西两端分别位于半湿润和半干旱地区外，大部分地段是处于我国由半湿润气候向半干旱气候的过渡区，由于降水量、气候等因素的影响，这一地区也恰好处在我国农业和牧业的交汇处[7]。这个区域的经济形态自古以来时农时牧不断发生变化，农牧的界线空间也随之频繁摆动，在新石器时代晚期基本上是农业区，它之所以变为游牧人往来驰骋的地带，是文化、生态环境、族群等变动的因素交互作用下形成的一个复杂过程[8]。

二、历代长城

从公元前4世纪开始，战国时期的燕、赵、秦等诸侯国开始在北方农牧交错地带修建长城用以防御游牧民族的南侵。此后的秦、汉、隋、明等中原王朝及北魏、北齐、金等民族政权，为防御北方游牧政权而修筑规模不等的长城。此阶段长城修建的目的逐渐转变成为缓解农耕与游牧政权之间的冲突、维护长城内外社会经济秩序的目的。

多数时代的长城是农业民族为防御游牧民族南侵的产物，它历经战国（齐、楚、燕、赵、魏、秦、中山、鲁）、秦、汉、南北朝（北魏、东魏、北齐）、隋、唐（含渤海国、高句丽、吐谷浑）、北宋、西夏、辽、金、明、清等朝代两千多年的修建，至今存留21196.18千米，分布在黑龙江、辽宁、吉林、河北、天津、北京、山西、内蒙古、山东、河南、陕西、甘肃、青海、宁夏、新疆等15个省（市、自治区）的404个区（县）。

（一）战国时期长城

战国中期各农业诸侯国开始修建长城，这一时期的长城并非连续性的高墙，除秦国外，均未发现墙顶有覆瓦的现象[9]。战国长城一是各个诸侯国之间的相互防范，例如魏长城、赵南长城、燕南长城的修建；二是防范北方游牧民族的南下进攻，例如燕北长城、赵北长城以及秦昭王长城。公元前4世纪前后，齐国、中山国、燕国、赵国、魏国、秦国等也分别在其所属境内修建了长城。列国中，齐长城于公元前408年最早修建，分布在山东泰安、莱芜县境大横岭。魏长城有三道，分别是河西长城、河南长城及陕县长城[10]，均修建于魏惠王在位期间。中山长城于公元前369年修建，纵贯恒山，从太行山南下，到河北省邢台以南止。赵国在其南北界均修建了长城，赵南长城分布在河北临漳、磁县，修建于公元前333年；赵北长城即赵武灵王长城，分布在今内蒙古境大青山一带，于公元前300年修建。燕长城亦有两道，燕南长城自河北徐水县西太行山麓沿瀑河东行至安新县，修建于公元前311之前；燕北长城西起河北围场县东至辽宁朝阳，于公元前300年修建。秦昭王长城修建的最晚，起于今甘肃省临洮县，东南而行再转向东北，至宁夏固原，再向东北折而至陕西省神木县黄河西岸，修建于公元前272年。

历史上多数时代的长城并不是一次修建的，同一时代不同阶段因防御主方向的不同建造的长城路线也有所偏差，而且即使是同一时代也有先后修建多条长城的现象。同时，长城也不是简单的一道墙体，随着战争方式的不同、武器种类的差异，长城这一军事工程也存在从简单到复杂的发展过程。长城由单

The very name of the Warring States Period denotes the normalization of warfare and the enlargement of its scale in this period. Conflicts were prolonged, wide-ranging and involved a large number of combatants. The form of warfare evolved into joint operations involving chariots, infantry and cavalry. The weapons mainly consisted of bows and crossbows and other traditional weaponry. The battle between the Qin and Zhao states lasted for a year. Warfare continued throughout this time and tens of thousands of people were killed and sometimes hundreds of thousands of troops were engaged in warfare.

Compared with the Spring and Autumn Period, the military capability of those states in the late Warring States Period differed, not only in terms of the numbers of combatants involved, but also in the form of armour, the modes of war, the social composition of armies, and in the types of weapons used. The scale and objectives of war were also quite different. The Qin State had a million armed soldiers, and thousands of chariots, and over ten thousand cavalry; the Zhao State had hundreds of thousands of soldiers, thousands of chariots and over ten thousand cavalry. When Baiqi defeated the Han-Wei coalition forces in 293 BC, his army beheaded 240,000 enemy soldiers; and when Baiqi then defeated the Wei army in Huayang in 273 BC his army beheaded 150,000 enemy soldiers. The Qin captured more than 400,000 Zhao troops during the Changping War in 260 BC; the Yan set out with more than 600,000 troops to attack the Zhao in 251 BC; and the State of Qin sent Wang Ben at the head of 600,000 troops to attack the Chu in 224 BC. The State of Qin participated in 15 major wars which caused an estimated 1,489,000 casualties to other states during the 130 years from 364 BC to 234 BC. Because the defensive strength and form of the city wall were not sufficient to withstand attack in the large-scale military annexation wars in the Warring States Period, the enclosed rectangular cities were expanded and developed into a series of extended walls built along the borders of their territories. These created a new defensive form and ideological system. Thus, the Great Wall came into being as a result of the military necessities of this period.

The defensive ideology of the Great Wall originated from the wars of large-scale territorial annexation between princes during the Warring States Period. The feudal states built the Great Wall to defend themselves from each other and ensure their own security and prosperity. They sought to establish a balance of power or to build stable relations with each other by means of tall walls to define and secure their territories, especially in the agricultural regions. There is no doubt that it was states which were threatened by others who built the Great Wall. The first stretch of the Great Wall was built by the State of Qi[1]. Later, the Yan, Han, Zhao, Wei, Qin and other states built different elements of the Great Wall to defend themselves against each other. Even some smaller kingdoms built stretches of the Great Wall. For example, the State of Zhongshan, established by the Xianbei people, built the Great Wall as a defence against the State of Zhao[5].

In the late Warring States Period, the Three Kingdoms of Qin, Zhao and Yan were facing strong pressure from their nomadic neighbours who invaded from the north, whilst the agricultural states in the Central Plains had to defend themselves against each other. Therefore, the concept and practice of creating walls, which origi-

---

1 Academic debates continue regarding which was the earliest section of the Great Wall to be built. See Li Yipi in this volume. (Editors' note)

一的墙体，逐渐发展成以墙体为主线，以关隘为支撑点，包括马面、敌台、烽火台、营堡、道路在内的纵深梯次相贯、点线结合的巨型军事工程体系。

（二）帝国时期长城

帝国时期的长城是集墙体、壕、天险、障、道路、后勤等为一体的立体性防御体系，这一时期的长城几乎均分布在长城地带。

秦帝国为了解除匈奴对秦王朝的威胁和保障中原地区的安全，下令修建长城，"因地形，用制险塞，起临洮，至辽东，延袤万余里"[11]。西汉建立后，汉高祖刘邦下令修缮秦昭王所建长城，与匈奴于"故塞"为界；武帝时，数次北击匈奴使其退居漠北，同时修建汉内外长城；自元狩年间起，修筑了从今甘肃省永登县至酒泉的河西长城（图1）；公元前111年至前110年，将长城从酒泉向西延至玉门关；公元前104至前101年，从玉门关向西增筑烽燧至今新疆罗布泊，并且随后还在长城沿线增筑了很多亭障、列城等。魏晋南北朝时期，北魏、东魏、北齐政权为了防止柔然民族的南下均修建了长城，北魏长城有两段，一段东起今河北赤城县西至内蒙古五原县境内，另一段东起北京延庆县居庸关，向南至河北灵邱，再向西行经平型县、北楼县止于山西省河曲县，用以保卫首都。北齐、北周政权所修建的长城也均位于今山西至北京。隋代，曾七次修建长城，主要西起今宁夏灵武黄河边经陕西靖边、横山至绥德。

唐宋时期长城的修建几乎停滞，辽、金时期在内蒙古草原修建了界壕用以北防蒙古人南下。其中金界壕大规模修建是处于大定、明昌年间（1161~1195年），分为东北路、临潢路、西北路与西南路四段，分布在今黑龙江、内蒙古境内（图2）。

明长城的修建经过了两个阶段，前期（公元前1368~1447年），主要是对长城进行小规模的修缮，增加了若干防御设施；1449年以后，则大规模地构建长城；1471年修建了宁夏至陕西北部的长城，由内蒙伊克昭盟东部皇甫川延伸至定边境内，西接宁夏、固原两镇；1560年又造宣府、大同镇边墙千余里，并建造了大量的烽堠；1568年，戚继光主持北方军务，重修了东起山海关西到居庸关的蓟镇长城，并设计修建了空心敌台。此外，明朝还兴建了由甘肃省景泰县向南再折向西北，直抵嘉峪关的长城；永乐至成化年间还数次修建辽东长城，对即有长城屡次修缮或部分增筑。

清代于崇德三年（1638年）至康熙二十六年（1697年）间，在长达59年的时间里，陆续修建的一道北起法特哈（今吉林舒兰县西）、东至凤凰城（今辽宁凤城）、西至山海关的长达二千六百四十余里的"人字形"特殊防御工事，主要功能是防止内地居民出关垦殖，该工事的建筑方法为掘土为壕，壕内引水，以壕内之土堆为堤，堤上植柳并以绳结之，故称之为柳条边[12]。

三、长城与帝国社会治理体系

伴随着长城的兴起，古代社会的治理体系从战国开始出现质变，逐渐发生了从夏商西周以来以血缘宗法为基础的分封制向以地缘为基础的中央集权郡县制的转变。这一转变用时230多年，以公元前221年秦始皇统一中国为标志，意味着大一统理念下中央集权郡县制社会治理体系构建完成，也标志着中国文明完成从王国体制到帝国体制的转变。一个有趣的现象是，在秦帝国建立之前，北方草原的游牧民族

nated in an agricultural civilization, were also applied to the farming-pastoral ecotone at this time.

Formation and Characteristics of the Great Wall Corridor

The Great Wall was the most important military defence facility in the so-called 'Cold Weapons'[1] era of warfare. During the over 2,000 years from the Warring States Period to the Qing Dynasty, 12 dynasties and 24 different political entities successively built sections of the Great Wall of different scales and lengths. Although the geographical distribution of the Great Wall varied from time to time (apart from during the Warring States Period) the overall geographical distribution of the Great Wall in all dynasties was basically the same. The Great Wall corridor lay in a broad belt from northeast to southwest where the agricultural residents of the Central Plains and the nomadic people in the north came into contact with each other[6].

The formation of the Great Wall corridor was closely related to changes in landform and environment. The majority of the Great Wall in most dynasties was distributed through the transitional areas of the Mongolian Plateau, the North China Plain, and the Loess Plateau, each of which are on the line of 400mm annual precipitation. Except for the eastern and western ends of the Great Wall corridor, which are located in semi-humid and semi-arid regions respectively, most of the Great Wall corridor is in the semi-humid to semi-arid climate transitional area of China. Due to the influence of precipitation, climate, and other factors, this area also happens to be at the intersection of agriculture and animal husbandry[7]. Since ancient times, the economic form of this region has been constantly changing, and the boundary between farming and animal husbandry cultures has frequently fluctuated. In the late Neolithic, it was basically an agricultural area. It became a region into which nomadic peoples intruded through a complicated process of interaction between cultures, ecological changes and the rise and fall of different ethnic groups[8].

THE GREAT WALL IN DIFFERENT AGES

From the 4th century BC, the Yan, Zhao, Qin and other kingdoms began to build different stretches of the Great Wall in the northern farming-pastoral zone to defend themselves against the invasion of nomads from the north during the Warring State Period. The Qin, Han, Sui and Ming Dynasties, which were located in the central plains, and other ethnic regimes - such as the Northern Wei Dynasty, the Northern Qi Dynasty and the Jin Dynasty - built different parts of the Great Wall to defend themselves against the northern nomadic peoples. During that time, the purpose of wall-building gradually began to be focused on managing the conflict between farming and nomadic civilisations and on the maintenance of social and economic order, both outside and inside the Great Wall.

In most of that period, the Great Walls were built by agricultural societies to defend themselves against the invasion of nomads from the north. Today, 21,196 km of this system can be traced, across 404 districts (counties) in 15 provinces, direct municipalities, and autonomous regions: Heilongjiang, Liaoning, Jilin, Hebei, Tian-

---

1 This term refers to the period before gunpowder was used in warfare. (Editors' note)

图 1
汉代甘肃居延东大湾城（摄影：李国民）
Fig. 1
Dongdawan Fort of Han Great Wall, Juyan, Gansu (© Li Guomin)

jin, Beijing, Shanxi, Inner Mongolia, Shandong, Henan, Shaanxi, Gansu, Qinghai, Ningxia, and Xinjiang. This monument is the result of over two thousand years of construction from the Warring States Period (Qi, Chu, Yan, Han, Zhao, Wei, Qin, Zhongshan and Lu Dynasties), to the Qin, Han, Northern and Southern Dynasties (the Northern Wei, the Eastern Wei and the Northern Qi), the Sui, Tang Dynasties (including Bohai Country, Gaogouli, Tuguhun), the Northern Song, the Western Xia, Liao, Jin, Ming and Qing Dynasties.

The Great Wall in the Warring States Period

In the middle of the Warring States Period, those agricultural states began to build sections of wall, and the Great Wall was not one continuous standing structure. Apart from construction during the Qin Dynasty, there were no tiles on the top of the wall[9]. The objective of building the Great Wall in the Warring States Period was to defend states against each other, as evidenced by the construction of the Wei Great Wall, the Zhaonan (South Zhao) Great Wall, and the Yannan (South Yan) Great Wall. Other walls were built as defences against northern invasions, such as the Yanbei (North Yan) Great Wall, the Zhaonan (North Zhao) Great Wall, and the King Qinzhaowang Great Wall. Around the turn of the 4th century BC, the Qi, Zhongshan, Yan, Zhao, Wei, and Qin Dynasties respectively built Great Walls within their own territories. Among these, the Great Wall of the Qi Dynasty was the first to be built in 408 BC on the Daheng Mountain in Tai'an and Laiwu Counties in Shandong Province. The Great Wall of the Wei Dynasty had three sections - the Hexi (western Yellow River) Great Wall, the Henan (south Yellow River) Great Wall, and the Shanxian County Great Wall[10] - each of which were built during the reign of Emperor Wei Hui. The Zhongshan Great Wall was built in 369 BC and ran through the Hengshan Mountains southward from the Taihang Mountain to the south of Xingtai City, Hebei Province. The Zhao Dynasty built sections of the Great Wall along its northern and southern borders. The Zhaonan (South Zhao) Great Wall was built in 333 BC across Linzhang County and Cixian County in Hebei Province. The Zhaobei (North Zhao) Great Wall, also named the Zhaowulingwang Great Wall, was built in 300 BC through the Daqingshan Mountains, Inner Mongolia. The Yan Great Wall also had two sections: the Yannan (South Yan) Great Wall was built before 311 BC and ran eastward along the Baohe River from the west of

图 2
内蒙古多伦金界壕（摄影：于 冰）
Fig. 2
Jin Great Wall, Duolun, Inner Mogolia (© Yu Bing)

Taihang Mountain, Xushui County, Hebei Province, to Anxin County; the Yanbei (North Yan) Great Wall was built in 300 BC and stretched from Weichang County, Hebei Province, in the west, to Chaoyang City, Liaoning Province, in the east. The latest section of the Great Wall in this period is the King Qinzhao Great Wall, built in 272 BC, starting from Lintao County, Gansu Province, extending southeast first and then northeast to Guyuan city, Ningxia Autonomous Region, and then extended northeast and turned to the west bank of Yellow River in Shenmu County, Shaanxi Province.

Throughout history, none of the Great Walls was built in a single stage. The routes of the Great Walls differed even within a single period depending on the direction from which the threat was perceived, and states would build several lines of Great Wall, one after another. It is important to recognize that the Great Wall was not simply a wall. As the character of warfare and the weaponry changed, the military engineering of the Great Wall became increasingly complex. Over time the Great Wall evolved from simple wall lines into a sophisticated military engineering system with the Wall as the main line and the fortified strategic passes as the support points, with buttresses, defensive towers, beacon towers, forts and fortresses, and roads, as a huge military engineering system of great depth inwardly and outwardly.

The Great Wall during the Imperial Dynasties

The Great Wall during the imperial dynasties was a three-dimensional defence system which comprised walls, trenches, natural features, obstructions, fortified strategic passes, roads and supply lines. The Great Wall which was in use during that time was almost entirely situated within the Great Wall corridor.

In order to relieve the threat to the Qin Dynasty from the Xiongnu[1] and ensure the security of the central plain, the Qin Dynasty ordered the construction of a Great Wall, "following the terrain, putting up fortresses at strategic points. It begins at Lintao, and ends in the east of Liao, running for ten thousand li."[2] [11]. After the establishment of the Western Han Dynasty, the Emperor Liu Bang ordered the restoration of the Great Wall which had been built by King Qinzhao, and identified this former fortress as the border with the Xiongnu. During the reign of the Emperor Wu, the Han army attacked the Xiongnu many times, forcing them to retreat into the northern desert. The emperor ordered the building of Great Walls inside and outside the territory of the Han Dynasty. The Hexi (west of the Yellow River) Great Wall was built from the first year of the Yuanshou era onwards and ran from Yongdeng County, Gansu Province, to Jiuquan City (Fig. 1). Between 111 and 110 BC, the Great Wall was extended westward from Jiuquan City to Yumen Pass. Between 104 and 101 BC, beacons were set up westward along the Great Wall to Lop Nor, Xinjiang, and many 'pavilions', fortified strategic passes and border fortresses were built.

During the period of the Wei, Jin, and the Southern and Northern Dynasties, the Northern Wei and the Eastern Wei and the Northern Qi regimes respectively built Great Walls to defend against the invasion of the Rouran nation from the north. The Great Wall of the Northern Wei Dynasty had two sections. One ran from Chicheng County, Hebei Province, in the east to Wuyuan County, Inner Mongolia in the west. The other section was built to protect the capital and ran from the Juyong Pass, Yanqing County,

1 An ancient tribal confederation of nomadic peoples in China. (Editors' note)

2 A *li* is roughly 1/3 of a mile. (Editors' note)

也是部落林立、互不相属；秦帝国建立十年后，前所未见的统一的草原游牧帝国也横空出世[13]，从此开始直到近代热兵器流行，围绕长城开展的农耕民族和游牧民族之间各种形态的互动，一直是中国文明演变过程中的主旋律，农牧两大文明在中国文明形成过程中缺一不可。

（一）社会治理体系的转变与长城的修建

中国文明发展演化自有其独具特色的演变规律。

任何一种文明都是由社会治理体系、宇宙观与核心价值观三要素构成的。为使社会按照一定的模式有序运转，管理阶层通常会创造出一套有普遍约束力、能反映主要社会成员意志且行之有效的社会治理体系，为了保障这套社会治理体系能够有效实施，精英阶层会构建一套为社会治理体系提供合理性和合法性依据的宇宙观以及引导和约束全社会成员行为处事方式的核心价值观，而人类所创造的物质文化，就是在社会性因素的制约下形成的，也是不同时期宇宙观、政体观以及核心文化价值观三者共同作用的结果，反映了全社会的生产技术和思想文化[14]。

战国时期处在中国古代从王国制到帝国制的巨大转型时期。从夏商周以来形成的王国制社会治理体系已经不适合战国时期社会发展的需要，这种不适是全方位的，社会各个阶层都有这种认知，于是各个阶层都开始探索新的社会治理体系，"百家争鸣"本质上是不同学术流派对社会治理体系全方位思考这的概括。各国在迷茫中纷纷进行变法，郡县制的萌芽已经出现，直至秦帝国以及西汉晚期，以阴阳五行相克相生为宇宙观，以地缘大一统中央集权郡县制为社会治理体系，以规矩为核心文化价值观的汉文明彻底构建完成。

新的社会发展态势促成新的防御形式出现，于是乎打破春秋以前以城墙为主的防御模式，长城便成为新的防御方式，战国中期的长城主要修建在中原地区，是各农业经济国家之间相互防御的产物；战国后期，长城开始出现在农业民族和游牧民族交汇的地带（秦赵燕），并且几乎均是农业民族用来防御游牧民族而修建的，这也许正是秦汉以后在阴阳五行相克相生这一宇宙观下形成的对立思维方式的物化表现。幻想以一道长城就能为农业文明带来安全感的想法延续了两千多年，长城是农业民族的心理防线。

（二）长城与中华文明

长城分布区域是随着环境变化、农耕和游牧政权的此消彼长变化而有所不同。长城地区农业与游牧民族之间的碰撞与交流，不但是北方各游牧民族间交融的过程，也是农业文明与游牧文明之间的长期交流融合的过程，更是中国统一多民族国家的形成和发展的过程，长城的出现、长城地带的形成，是农业文明和游牧文明互动碰撞的结果。长城的历史证明，中国文明至少是由农业文明与游牧文明一起构建完成的，农业民族和游牧民族都是中华文明的创建者。长城这一伟大的军事工程见证了统一多民族国家的形成过程，长城的修筑，以军事需要为起点，以民族融合为终结。

长城地带的文化交流，主要体现在各民族多元文化不平衡发展的状态中，中原的农业文化向四周辐射，并且各民族文化的发展以中原定居文化为核心，共同发展，从而使长城地带的文化丰富多样、各放异彩。其中和亲及互市是农牧文化交流最直接的方式，汉初匈奴"常往来盗边"，西汉政权在处于劣势情况下，被迫"约结和亲、赂遗单于，冀以救安边境"，并且"奉宗室女为单于阏氏，岁奉匈奴絮、缯、酒、实物各有数"[15]。虽然被迫和亲，被迫奉赠，但是这样的政策对中原社会经济恢复与发展起到了积极的作用。

Beijing City in the east to Lingqiu County, Hebei Province, in the south, and then westward to Pingxing County, Beilou County, ending in Hequ County, Shanxi Province. The Great Wall built by the Northern Qi regime and the Great Wall built by the Northern Zhou regime were also situated between Shanxi Province and Beijing City. The Great Wall was built and repaired seven times by the Sui Dynasty. It ran from the banks of the Yellow River, Wuling City, Ningxia Province, in the west, and extended through Jingbian County, Hengshan District, Shaanxi Province, to Suide County.

During the Tang Dynasty and the Song Dynasty, the construction of the Great Wall almost stagnated. The Liao Dynasty and Jin Dynasty built boundary trenches in the Inner Mongolian grassland as a defence against the invasion of Mongols from the north. The extensive boundary trenches of the Jin Dynasty were built during the Dading and Mingchang years (1161-95). It was divided into four sections, named Dongbei (Northeast) Lu[1], Hengbin Lu, Xibei (Northwest) Lu, and Xinan (Southwest) Lu, which ran across present day Heilongjiang and Inner Mongolia (Fig. 2).

The construction of the Great Wall of the Ming Dynasty went through two stages. In the early stages (1368 to 1447), small-scale construction was carried out and some defensive components were added. After 1449, large-scale construction of the Great Wall began. In 1471, the Great Wall from Ningxia to the north of Shaanxi was built, extending from Huangfuchuan, in the east of the Yike region of Inner Mongolia, to Dingbian County, and connecting the Ningxia Zhen and the Guyuan Zhen[2] in the west. In 1560, the walls of the Xuanfu Town and Datong Town were extended more than 500km, and a lot of beacon towers were built. In 1568, Qi Jiguang took charge of the military affairs in the north, rebuilt the Ji Zhen Great Wall, which ran from the Shanhai Pass in the east to the Juyong Pass in the west, and he innovatively designed and built chambered towers.[3] In addition, the Ming Dynasty built a Great Wall which started from Jingtai County, Gansu Province, spread south and then northwest, and finally extended to the Jiayu Pass. Between the reign of Yongle to the reign of Chenghua, several constructions had been carried out on the Liaodong (east Liaoning) Great Wall, repairing and partly rebuilding, frequently on top of previously existing Walls.

During the Qing Dynasty, between the third year of the reign of the Emperor Chongde (1638) and the twenty-sixth year of the reign of the Emperor Kangxi (1697), a unique boundary system was constructed. It extended for more than 1,320km. It ran from Fateha (in the west of present day Shulan County, Jilin Province), in the north, to Fenghuang City (in present-day Feng City, Liaoning Province), in the east, and then extended westward to the Shanhai Pass. It was built to prevent peoples from the south cultivating the land to the north of this barrier. The construction process involved digging trenches, which were then flooded, then heaping the soil into dykes and planting willows along the dykes which were knotted together with rope. It was called 'the wicker edge'[12].

---

1 A *Lu* was a jurisdictional region in both administrative and military terms in the Jin Dynasty. (Editors' note)

2 A *Zhen* was where the headquarters of each *Bian* was located. There were nine *Bians,* or regional military frontier or boundary areas along the Great Wall. Sometimes *Zhen* is also used interchangeably with *Bian*, denoting a military region. (Editors' note)

3 Previously the defensive towers were built as solid structures without internal spaces. (Editors' note)

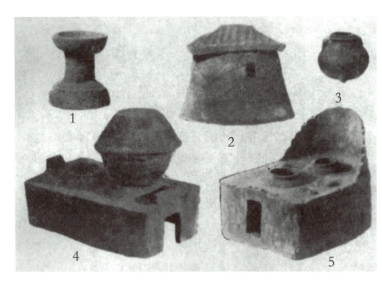

1   陶豆
     pottery food container

2   陶仓 I 式
     pottery warehouse I

3   陶鼎
     pottery cooking vessel

4   陶灶 I 式
     pottery kiln I

5   陶灶 II 式
     pottery kiln II

图 3
青海大通上孙家寨匈奴墓出土文物（版权：青海省文物管理处考古队）
Fig. 3
Archaeological finds at a tomb of Xiongnu, Datong, Qinghai Province (© Archaeological Institute of Qinghai Cultural Relics Administration)

而明代，汉蒙之间于隆庆五年（1571 年）开始互市，一改此前百十年来的战争局面，沿边"东起延永西抵嘉峪，"烽火不惊，三军晏眠，边圉之民，室家相保，弄狲于野，商贾夜行"，呈现出一派祥和的态势。

农业民族和游牧民族围绕着长城在两千多年的交往互动中，形成了中华文明独特的多元的文化面貌。以汉字为载体的中原汉语文对长城地带的游牧民族形成长期的影响，南下的游牧民族入主中原后纷纷学习汉语成为民族融合过程的必然。历年来长城地带历代墓葬发掘出来的随葬品，都显示出农牧交融、中原文明向长城地带辐射影响的现象。汉代长城沿线的墓葬中经常出土中原特色的文物[16]，如铁鐰、铁斧、绳纹陶器、各式刀剑、鎏金马具、铜镜、配饰、货币以及仓、灶、井等（图 3）[17]。

在中原农业文明向长城地带辐射的过程中，北方游牧民族文化也向中原汇聚，使得中原文化在发展中也受到各民族文化的强烈影响，而且衣、食、住、行无所不包。从赵武灵王提倡胡服到清代的旗袍、马褂，都反映出古代中原民族上衣下裳、宽领褒袖笨重服饰的重大转变；魏晋时期"胡床"南下农耕区，改变了中原民族席地而坐的习惯。

除此之外，沿长城南北而行的丝绸之路，也源源不断地将西亚、中亚的文明带到中原。棉花、油菜、芝麻等粮食作物和相关种植技术，都是通过丝绸之路从西域传入中原；小麦、大麦以及磨面方法从西域和其他民族地区的传入，中原汉族以五谷为饭的膳食种类得以改变；家用畜力中的马以及马车，主要是从蒙古高原引入长城以南的；在新疆阿拉沟、鱼儿沟等地西周至战国末期的墓葬中发现的骡子骨骼，应该是蒙古高原地区的游牧者培育出来的。在艺术文化方面，诸如笛、琵琶、箜篌、胡琴等乐器以及音乐音律、歌舞杂技等自南北朝时传入中原后，对中原的戏剧、宋词、元曲均产生了极大影响。现存的玉门昌马、酒泉的文殊山、洛阳的龙门（图 4）和大同的云冈等石窟艺术，敦煌的壁画艺术等，都是长城地

THE GREAT WALL AND THE IMPERIAL SOCIAL GOVERNANCE SYSTEM

With the rise of the Great Wall, the governance system of society began to change from the Warring States onwards. There was a gradual transition from the kinship-based patriarchal clan systems of the Xia, Shang and Zhou Dynasties to the geographically-based centralized county system based on prefectures and counties. This transformation took more than 230 years and was marked by the reunification of China by the Emperor Qin Shihuang in 221 BC. It represented the completion of a social governance system of centralized hierarchical prefectures and counties, which also marked the transformation of Chinese civilization from a royal system to an imperial system. An interesting phenomenon is that before the establishment of the Qin Empire, there were many ethnically unrelated tribes amongst the nomadic peoples of the northern grasslands. Ten years after the establishment of the Qin Empire, a unified grassland nomadic empire that had never been seen before was born[13]. From then on, until the advent of the modern 'hot weapon' era, the various forms of interaction between the farming and nomadic peoples around the Great Wall were the main theme in the evolution of Chinese civilization. The two civilizations - agricultural and nomadic - were indispensable to the process of the formation of Chinese civilization.

Transformation of the social governance system and construction of the Great Wall

The advance and development of Chinese civilization has its own unique law of evolution.

Any kind of civilization is composed of three elements: a social governance system, a philosophy or view of the universe, and a set of core cultural values. In order for society to operate in an orderly manner, rulers create systems of social governance that are universally binding, reflective of the prevailing will. To ensure the effective implementation of these systems, governing elites build a philosophy of the universe that provides rationality and legitimacy for the social governance system and establishes a set of core values to guide and constrain the behaviour of members of society. The material culture created by human beings is formed under the constraints of social factors, but it is also the result of the established philosophy, the prevailing political outlook and the core cultural values in different periods. Material culture also reflects both a society's production technology and its collective ideology[14].

The Warring States Period saw a great transformation from a system of kingdoms to imperialism in ancient China. Social governance through kingdoms which had formed during the Xia, Shang and Zhou eras was no longer tenable in the changing social environment of the Warring States Period. This dislocation between society and the governance system effected every aspect of life and was felt at all levels of society, and various classes began to explore new social governance systems. The "contention of a hundred schools of thought" was essentially a summary of all the thinking from different schools of thought about the social governance system. States were changing in the midst of this confusion, and the prefecture and county-based system began to emerge. From the Qin Dynasty to the late Western Han Dynasty, the mutually opposing and complementary precepts of Yin and Yang and the Five Elements[1] became

---

1 *Wu Xing*, or the Five Elements - wood, fire, earth, metal and water - is a central concept in ancient Chinese philosophy. (Editors' note)

图 4
河南龙门石窟（摄影：于 冰）
Fig. 4
Longmen Grotto, Luoyanag, Henan (© Yu Bing)

the basis of the prevailing philosophy, the geographically unified central government based on prefectures and counties became the new social governance system, and a structure of established rules became the cornerstone of society's core cultural values. The Han civilization completed these processes of transition.

These new societal developments led to new approaches to the question of defending the state. The defence philosophy based on city walls, which had been characteristic of the earlier Spring and Autumn Period, was replaced by the idea of the Great Wall. The Great Walls in the middle of the Warring States were mainly built in the central plains, as defences between the different agricultural states. In the late Warring States period, the Great Wall began to appear in the area where agricultural and nomadic peoples intersected. Almost all of them were built by the agricultural people to defend against the nomadic people. This may be a material embodiment of emerging different thinking from the concepts of Yin and Yang and the Five Elements. The belief that a Great Wall can bring a sense of security to an agricultural civilization was to endure for more than two thousand years. The Great Wall was both physically and psychologically significant in the defence of the agricultural nation.

The Great Wall and Chinese civilization

The geographical location of the Great Walls varied with changes in the environment, and with the rising and falling of agriculture and nomadic regimes. Collision and interaction in the areas of the Great Wall resulted in the blending together of different peoples, and their fusion through long-term trading and cultural exchanges. They also stimulated the development of a unified multinational country. The history of the Great Wall and the formation of the Great Wall corridor demonstrate that Chinese civilization was essentially constructed by the agricultural and nomadic civilizations together. This great military engineering project witnessed the formation of a unified multi-ethnic country. The construction of the Great Wall began from military necessity but ended with the integration of different ethnic groups.

Cultural exchanges in the Great Wall corridor were reflected in the different development of diverse cultures made up of various ethnic groups. The agricultural culture in the Central Plains influenced the surrounding areas, and various ethnic cultures adopted elements of the settled culture in the Central Plains as their core, creating the diverse and colourful cultures along the Great Wall corridor. At the beginning of the Han Dynasty, the Xiongnu people made frequent attacks on border areas. The Western Han regime was forced to make peace with the Huns and gave them plenty of food and money in return for peace[15]. Although these actions were forced upon the Western Han regime, they enabled social and economic recovery and development, which was ultimately beneficial. In the fifth year of the reign of Emperor Longqing (1571), in the Ming Dynasty, trading between the Han and Mongolian peoples was opened up and this brought to an end a hundred years of war. Along the border, the two sides traded frequently, and this provided stability and peace for the local population.

Through communication and interaction between the agricultural and nomadic peoples around the Great Wall, over more than two thousand years, the unique and diverse cultural features of Chinese civilization were formed. The Chinese language vested in Hanzi (Chinese characters) in the Central Plains had a long-term influence on the nomadic peoples along the Great Wall corridor, and the learning of Chinese by those nomadic people coming down to the south

带各民族乃至世界艺术的汇聚，使长城地带成为举世闻名的文化艺术宝库。

不论是农业民族政权还是游牧民族政权，当他们主导中原后，自觉不自觉地都希望能够统一中国，这种思想的形成，是长期以来民族融合的必然趋势，尤其是游牧民族政权入主中原后，想要稳定和谐发展，就必须与农业民族的思想文化进行融合，在政治、经济、文化等方方面面与汉民族达到契合，这种契合，正是农业民族与各民族不断融合，最后形成多元一体的中华民族的重要过程。

长城地带各民族的起源地域虽均不相同，但在几千年的民族融合相互交流、学习，这种"民族融合"，不是简单的"汉化"或者"胡化"，而是更深层次的诸如文化、思想等方面的交融。各民族文化"你中有我，我中有你"，在保有自己风俗习惯的同时，又兼具其他民族的文化特征，这才使得中华民族文化朝着多元化方向发展，促成了中华民族真正的繁荣，并体现出其特殊性和包容性。"中华民族作为一个自觉的民族实体，是近百年来中国和西方列强对抗中出现的，但作为一个自在的民族实体则是几千年的历史过程中所形成的"[18]。自从长城修建以来，长城内外逐渐形成了农牧两大统一体，两千多年来，长城内的农业民族通过屯垦移民和通商等方式在这里形成了一个巨大的网络，把长城内外各民族串联在一起，成为中华民族自在民族实体形成中重要的一部分，并取得了大一统的格局。长城，见证了农牧双方发展的历史进程，也因此成为中华民族的象征。

图 5
甘肃金塔明代烽燧（摄影：于 冰）
Fig. 5
Beacon tower, Jinta, Gansu (© Yu Bing)

to reign became an essential part of the process of ethnic integration. Grave goods excavated from tombs of various dynasties in the Great Wall area show the integration of farming and animal husbandry and the spread of central plains civilization along the Great Wall corridor. Han Dynasty tombs in regions along the Wall often contain artefacts characteristic of the central plains[16], such as iron knives, iron axes, jomon pottery, different kinds of swords, gold harnesses, bronze mirrors, accessories, currency and pottery warehouses, kilns and wells (Fig. 3) [17].

At the same time that the agricultural civilization of the Central plains spread to the Great Wall corridor, the nomadic cultures of the north moved to the Central Plains, so that the Central Plains culture was also strongly influenced by various ethnic cultures in its development, including clothing, food, housing and transportation. The foreign costume advocated by King Wuling of Zhao, and the cheongsam and mandarin jacket of the Qing Dynasty, reflected the significant changes, moving away from the heavy clothing of the ancient peoples in central China. During the Wei and Jin Dynasties, the 'hu chair' started appearing in the agricultural areas, replacing the habit of the Central Plains people to sit on the ground.

In addition, the Silk Road, which runs along either side of the Great Wall corridor, brought civilizations from Western Asia and Central Asia to the Central Plains. Cotton, rapeseed, sesame and other food crops, and the associated cultivation techniques, were all introduced into the Central Plains from the west along the Silk Road. New strains of wheat and barley and methods of milling were introduced from the west, changing the diet of the Han people of the Central Plains. Draught horses and workhorses for milling and lifting water were mainly introduced from the Mongolian Plateau to the area south of the Great Wall. Skeletons of mules found in the tombs from the Western Zhou Dynasty to the end of the Warring States period in the Alagou and Yuergou areas of Xinjiang were most probably bred by nomads in the Mongolian Plateau. In terms of art and culture, musical instruments such as the flute, the Chinese lute, the konghou and huqin, as well as styles of music, singing and acrobatics, were introduced to the Central Plains from the Northern and Southern Dynasties, and strongly influenced the drama and poetry of the Song Dynasty and the Yuan opera of the Central Plains. The grottoes in Yumen Changma, the Wenshu Mountain in Jiuquan, the Longmen Grottoes in Luoyang (Fig. 4) , the Yungang Grottoes in Datong, and the mural art in Dunhuang, represent a fusion of the art of various nationalities and cultures and contributes to the Great Wall corridor's status as a world-famous cultural and artistic treasure house.

Throughout history, the rulers of the Central Plains, from both the agricultural and the nomadic peoples, sought, consciously or unconsciously, to unify China. This mindset is a natural result of ethnic integration, and especially for those nomadic regimes who entered the Central Plains it was imperative for them to endeavour to achieve stable and harmonious development, through integration with the politics, economy and culture of the agricultural nation and the Han people. This continuous integration is the core process in the formation of the pluralistic Chinese nation.

Although the origins of the various ethnic groups in the Great Wall area are different, the ethnic integration over thousands of years produced a deep blending of cultures and ideas. Ethnic cultures have maintained their own customs and habits while absorbing the cultural characteristics of other ethnic groups; this has enabled the diverse national culture of China to develop. It has contributed to the prosperity of the Chinese nation and reflects its unique character and

结　语

　　文明始于城，帝国与长城相始终。农业文明与游牧文明一起缔造了中国文明，城和长城共同见证了中国文明的发展历程。中心城市出现在以血缘宗法分封制为社会治理体系的夏代，而长城出现在以分封制向中央集权郡县制转变的战国时期，从战国之后到大一统帝国时期的秦汉、隋唐、明代等时期，均修造有大量的长城，因此城和长城一起，共同见证了中国文明的形成与发展。

　　中国文明由农业文明和游牧文明共同构成，没有游牧文化的中国文化，是不可想象的。陈寅恪先生早就指出，"李唐一族之所以崛兴，盖取塞外野蛮精悍之血，注入中原文化颓废之躯，旧染既除，新机重启，扩大恢张，遂能别创空前之世局"[19]。自从长城修建以来，长城内外逐渐形成了农牧两大统一体，从修建形式上讲，长城似乎是一条有形屏障防御线把农耕社会与游牧社会分割开来，但实际上，长城作为防御体系也兼具一定的开放性，对内反映在长城的修建要与周围环境诸如地形、耕地、水源及前方、后方构成联系，而对外的开放性，则通过千万座联通长城内外的关隘，将农耕和游牧地区紧密地联系起来[20]。"农耕与游牧作为东亚大陆两种基本的经济类型，是中华文明的两个彼此不断交流的源泉，他们历经数千年相互融合、互为补充，汇成气象恢弘的中华文化"[21]。中华文明史中不但有以"耕"为核心的文化，也有以"牧"为核心的文化，两者的碰撞、交流、演进和共同发展，共同缔造了中华文明。

　　总之，整个长城地带农牧之间自史前时期就进行着持续的、规模日益扩大的文化交流。长城地带各民族对中国古代文化的发展做出的突出贡献，充分体现着以农业文化为主导向四周辐射，各族文化呈多元不平衡向中原文化汇聚的特征。农业和游牧文化经过相互交流碰撞、相互借鉴吸收创造出了中华民族绚丽多姿的文明。

its inclusiveness. "The Chinese nation, as a conscious national entity, has emerged in the confrontation between China and the Western powers in the past 100 years, but it has been formed as an independent national entity over the course of thousands of years of history."[18] Since the Great Wall was built, the pattern of the two unified cultures based on agriculture and animal husbandry formed gradually inside and outside the Great Wall. For more than two thousand years, agricultural people in the Great Wall corridor formed a network of migration and trade, connecting the various nationalities inside and outside the Great Wall and becoming the Chinese nation. The Great Wall corridor therefore played an important part in the formation of the nation, and the establishment of national unity. The Great Wall witnessed the process of development of both farmers and herdsmen, and has thus become a symbol of the Chinese nationality.

CONCLUSION

Civilization began in cities, and the empire and the Great Wall have always been linked. Agricultural civilization and nomadic civilization have created Chinese civilization. The city and the Great Wall have witnessed the development of Chinese civilization. 'Central cities'[1] appeared in the Xia Dynasty with a kinship-based clan system and feudalism as its social governance system, while the Great Wall appeared in the Warring States period when feudalism was transformed into a centralized county system. In the Warring States period to the Qin and Han Dynasties, the Sui and Tang Dynasties, the Ming and Qing Dynasties and other periods of the unified empire, a large number of Great Walls were built. Both the city and the Great Wall were formative in the development of Chinese civilization.

Chinese civilization originated from both agricultural and nomadic civilization. It is inconceivable that there could be no nomadic culture in Chinese culture. Mr. Chen Yinque has long pointed out that "the rise of the Tang Dynasty clan has taken the blood of barbarism and ferocity outside the Great Wall and injected it into the decadent body of the Central Plains culture. By removing the old stain, restarting the new machine and expanding, a new world can be created."[19] Since the construction of the Great Wall, the union of agricultural and pastoral societies has been gradually established on both sides of the Great Wall. "Whilst the Great Wall seems to be a closed physical barrier separating farming and nomadic societies, it had in fact a degree of openness. The construction of the Great Wall reflects its connection with the surrounding environmental features such as topography, arable land and water sources, on both sides of the Wall. The farming and nomadic areas were closely connected through thousands of passes." [20] "The two basic economic models of farming and nomadism in East Asia are the sources of continuous development of Chinese civilization. They have merged and supplemented each other for thousands of years to create a magnificent Chinese culture." [21]

The entire Great Wall corridor has experienced cultural exchanges between agriculture and animal husbandry since prehistoric times. The outstanding contributions made by all ethnic groups in the Great Wall corridor have created the colourful civilization of the Chinese nation through mutual exchange, collision, mutual learning and absorption.

---

1 A 'central city' is an archaeological term for historical cities of particular regional or sub-regional status and significance. (Editors' note)

参考文献
Bibliography

[1] 王震中 ."邦国—王国—帝国"说 [N]. 光明日报，2013 年 1 月 28 日 .

Wang, Z.Z. "State-Kingdom-Empire." Guangming Daily, January 28, 2013.

[2] a. 苏秉琦 . 中国文明起源新探 [M]. 北京：生活、读者、新知三联书社 .1999 年 .

b. 王震中 . 文明与国家起源的"聚落三形态演进"说和"邦国—王国—帝国"说 [J]. 黄河文明与可持续发展 .2013(1).

Su B.Q. A New Probe into the Origin of Chinese Civilization. Beijing: Sanlian Publishing House of Life, Reading and New Knowledge, 1999.

Wang Z.Z. "'The Evolution of Three Settlement Forms' and 'State-Kingdom-Empire' of Civilization and State Origin." Yellow River civilization and Sustainable Development, 2013(1).

[3] 夏明亮、童雪莲 ."长城地带"考古学术语属性探讨 [J]. 东北史地，2012(5):11-18.

Xia M.L., and Tong X.L. "Discussion on the Archaeological Terminology Attribute of the Great Wall Zone." Northeast China history and geography, 2012(5):11-18.

[4] 景爱 . 中国长城史 [M]. 上海：上海人民出版社 .2006 年 .

Jing A. History of the Great Wall of China. Shanghai: Shanghai People's Publishing House, 2006.

[5] 董耀会 . 长城——人类文明的标志（一）[N]. 中国文物报 .2016 年 1 月 26 日第 3 版 .

Dong Y.H. "The Great Wall-the symbol of human civilization(1)." Chinese Heritage, 3rd Edition, 2016.

[6] 林沄 . 夏至战国中国北方长城地带游牧文化带的形成 [J]. 燕京学报（新十四期），2003 年 5 月 .

Lin Y. "Formation of Nomadic Cultural Belt in the Great Wall Zone in the North of China from Xia Dynasty to the Warring States Period." Yanjing Journal, New 14th issue, 2003.

[7] 张子宇 . 历史地理学意义上的长城地带划分 [J]. 西安石油大学学报（哲学社会科学版），2013(2):107-112.

Zhang Z.Y. "Division of Great Wall Zones in Historical Geography." Journal of Xi'an Shiyou University (Philosophy and Social Science Edition), 2013(2):107-112.

[8] 林沄 . 夏至战国中国北方长城地带游牧文化带的形成 [J]. 燕京学报（新十四期），2003 年 5 月 .

Lin Y. "Formation of Nomadic Cultural Zone in the Great Wall Zone of Northern China from the Xia Dynasty to the Warring States Period." Journal of Yanjing, New 14th issue, 2003.

[9] 陕西省考古研究院、西北大学文化遗产学院 . 陕西省早期长城资源调查报告 [M]. 北京：文物出版社 .,2015.

Shaanxi Academy of Archaeology, Northwest University School of Cultural Heritage. Investigation Report of Early Great Wall Resources in Shaanxi Province. Beijing: Cultural Relics Press, 2015.

[10] 欧燕 . 中华文明史话——长城史话：现已消失的魏长城 [M]. 北京：中国大百科全书出版社 .1998:10.

Ou Y. Historical Tales of Chinese Civilization-Historical Tales of the Great Wall,the vanished Great Wall of the Wei Dynasty. Beijing: Encyclopedia of China Publishing House, 1998: 10.

[11] [汉] 司马迁 . 史记·卷八十八·蒙恬列传 [M]. 北京：中华书局，1959:2565.

[Han Dynasty] Sima Q. "Biography of Meng Tian." In Historical Records, Vol.88. Beijing: Zhonghua Book Company, 1959: 2565.

[12] 段清波，徐卫民 . 历代长城发现与研究 [M]. 北京：科学出版社 .2014.

Duan, Q.B., Xu, W.M. Discovery and Research of the Great Walls in the Past Dynasties. Beijing: China Science Publishing & Media Ltd,(CSPM). 2014.

[13] 林翰 . 匈奴史 [M]. 呼和浩特：内蒙古人民出版社，2007:21-23.

Lin H. History of Huns. Hohhot: Inner Mongolia People's Publishing House, 2007: 21-23.

[14] 段清波 . 论考古学学科目标和文化遗产的核心价值 [J]. 中原文化研究，2016(3):87-94.

Duan Q.B. "On Archaeological Subject Goals and Core Values of Cultural Heritage." Central Plains Cultural Research, 2016(3): 87-94.

[15] [汉] 班固 . 汉书·卷九四·匈奴传 [M]. 北京：中华书局 .1962:3754.

[Han Dynasty]Ban G. "Biography of Huns." Han Shu, Volume 94, Beijing: Zhonghua Book Company, 1962: 3754.

[16] 孙守道 . "匈奴西岔沟文化"古墓群发现 [J]. 文物，1960(8-9).

Sun S.D. "Discovery of Ancient Tombs of Xichagou Culture of Huns." Cultural Relics, 1980(8-9).

[17] 青海省文物管理处考古队 . 青海大通上孙家寨的匈奴墓 [J]. 文物，1979(4).

Archaeological Team of Qinghai Provincial Administration of Cultural Relics. "Xiongnu Tomb in Shangsunjiazhai, Datong, Qinghai." Cultural Relics, 1979(4).

[18] 费孝通 . 中华民族的多元一体格局 [J]. 北京大学学报，1989(4):1-19.

Fei X.T. "The Pattern of Diversification and Integration of the Chinese Nation." Journal of Peking University, 1989(4): 1-19.

[19] 陈寅恪 . 李唐氏族推测之后记 [A]. 历史语言研究所集刊·第叁本·第壹分 [C]，1931 年 8 月 .

Chen Y.Q. "The Postscript of the Tang Dynasty Clan Speculation." Journal of the Institute of Historical Languages, 3rd Edition, First Score, 1931.

[20] 董耀会 . 长城人类文明的标志（三）[N]. 中国文物报，2016-02-02，第 3 版 .

Dong Y.H. "Signs of Human Civilization on the Great Wall (III)." China Heritage News, 3rd Edition, February 2, 2016.

[21] 张岱年，方克立 . 中国文化概论 [M]. 北京：北京师范大学出版社 .2006 年 :28.

Zhang D.N., and Fang K.L. An Introduction to Chinese Culture. Beijing: Beijing Normal University Publishing House, 2006: 28.

ARCHAEOLOGICAL HERITAGE PROTECTION IN ENGLAND

Henry Owen-John

Historic England - Manchester - UK

Abstract

Archaeological heritage protection in England has evolved since the late 19th century and comprises both legislation and planning policy. In combination these measures provide a high level of protection for Hadrian's Wall as is evidenced by the current state of conservation of the Wall which is generally of a very high standard. Historic England plays an important role in advising national and local government on the protection and management of Hadrian's Wall. The proper application of heritage legislation and planning policy allows the UK to meet its obligations to the World Heritage Convention although one area of potential tension between the English system and the Convention in relation to the management of change within English World Heritage Sites is identified and discussed.

Keywords: Heritage, World Heritage Sites, scheduled monuments, protection, legislation, policy

Most land in England, including much of Hadrian's Wall, is privately owned and the conservation and management of heritage assets (archaeological sites, historic buildings and areas etc) is primarily the responsibility of these private owners. Where property is privately owned, national and local government needs to demonstrate that there is a public interest in any constraints that may be imposed on the rights of owners to manage their property as they see fit.

The public interest in protecting heritage assets in private as well as public and other ownership in England has long been accepted. The Ancient Monuments Protection Act came into force in 1882 and established a schedule of ancient monuments, together with an Inspectorate of Ancient Monuments to oversee the development and implementation of the schedule. This legislation offered a measure of protection for monuments such as the then privately-owned Castlerigg Stone Circle in the English Lake District. It is also noteworthy that over 130 years later Historic England, national government's adviser on the historic environment, still employs Inspectors of Ancient Monuments.

During the course of the 20th century the legislative powers to protect England's heritage were progressively strengthened and expanded from ancient monuments to historic buildings, while the planning powers and policies that were introduced in 1948 were extended 20 years later to allow for the protection of historic (usually urban) areas. In respect of archaeological remains one of the most significant pieces of legislation was introduced in the form of the 1979 Ancient Monuments and Archaeological Areas Act. Since the implementation of

英格兰的考古遗产保护

亨利·欧文·约翰

（英格兰遗产委员会，英国曼彻斯特）

摘　要

英格兰的考古遗产保护自十九世纪晚期开始得到逐步发展，主要包括立法以及规划政策两方面措施。这些综合措施使哈德良长城得到严格保护，长城现在保存状况总体上处于较高保护水准，证明措施的有效性。英格兰遗产委员会为国家和地方政府就哈德良长城的保护和管理方面提供建议，起到了重要的作用。遗产立法和规划政策的合理应用让英国能够履行《保护世界自然和文化遗产公约》中的义务，但英格兰体系和《公约》在英格兰世界遗产地的变化管理上存在潜在冲突，值得商榷。

关键词：遗产　世界遗产地　登录古迹　保护　立法　政策

在英国，包括在哈德良长城，大部分土地归私人所有。所以遗产（考古遗址、历史建筑和历史地区等）的保护和管理责任主要由私人承担。针对这些私人所有的遗产，中央政府和地方政府需要向所有者指明，在管理其财产时可能会因出于公共利益的需要而受到特定限制。

无论是私有财产还是公共财产或其他性质所有权，为公共利益而对其中的遗产进行保护在英格兰长久以来已为人们接受。《历史古迹保护法案》于 1882 年正式生效，确立了登录古迹名录制度，并设置古迹巡查官制度以督查登录古迹制度的进展和落实。该立法为古迹保护提供了有效手段，其中一个应用案例是位于英格兰湖区的卡斯尔里格石阵 (Castlerigg Stone Circle)，当时为私人所有[1]（图 1）。值得强调的是，英格兰遗产委员会作为中央政府历史环境顾问，在 130 年后的今天仍在执行古迹巡查官制度。

在 20 世纪，保护英格兰遗产的法律体系逐步加强，范围也由古迹扩展至历史建筑，而 1948 年颁布的规划权力和政策在 20 年后也扩展至保护历史（通常是城市）地段。关于考古遗迹，最重要的立法之一是《1979 年古迹及考古地区法案》。该法案实施后，想要对登录古迹（大概有 20000 处）作出变动的所有者需要先提交申请获得许可。基于英格兰遗产委员会的建议，如果中央政府认为方案会对古迹造成损坏，该申请会被拒绝。实际上，大多数申请都会得到批准，但通常要首先确保考古遗迹的保护措施已经落实到位。

哈德良长城大部分及其相关遗存（如南部壕沟）都作为登录古迹得到律法保护。"罗马帝国边界：哈德良长城世界遗产地"的构成仅包括已经列入登录古迹目录的罗马防御体系遗迹。这点十分重要，帮助英国履行身为《保护世界自然和文化遗产公约》的缔约国应尽的义务。在英格兰，世界遗产地身份并没有专门的法律保护，只能借助国家遗产立法和规划政策来真正落实。

---

1 在 1883 年，也就是法案颁布的第二年，英国政府将卡斯尔里格石阵征收为国有，由国家负责保护管理——译者注。

Fig. 1

Castlerigg Stone Circle in the north west of England: one of the first sites to be added to the schedule of monuments following the introduction of the 1882 Ancient Monuments Protection Act (© Henry Owen-John)

图1

英格兰西北部的卡斯尔里格石阵：1882 年《历史古迹保护法案》颁布后，首批列为登录古迹的遗址之一（摄影：亨利·欧文·约翰）

　　有部分残存的罗马帝国边界遗迹被埋在后来新建的区域之下（例如泰恩赛德和卡莱尔的考古发现），它们既没有被纳入登录古迹，也并非世界遗产地，但通过规划体系得到了保护（图2）。于2018年修订更新的《英格兰国家规划政策框架》（English National Planning Policy Framework，简称NPPF）是规划体系的核心法规之一。正如其名，它提供了管理英格兰境内建筑开发的框架。其旨在促进可持续发展，并专门有一章节对历史环境的保护和利用加以规定（《国家规划政策指南2018》[1]，详见。

　　NPPF制定的政策不仅涵盖所有遗产本体，包括那些未经法律认定的遗产，其历史环境章节还提出保护遗产周边环境的若干政策。这对于哈德良长城来说尤其重要，因为登录古迹的周边环境和世界遗产地因此都得到了保护。登录古迹制度只能对古迹和/或考古遗址遗迹的本体提供保护，而规划体系则对遗产的周边环境提供保护，防止不当的建设开发对古迹的历史价值造成损失。例如，大部分哈德良长城中段的高地地区和西端的沿海地区适合进行风力发电。有些情况下，风力发电机不会破坏世界遗产地的突出普遍价值；但另有些情况，它们可能会对哈德良长城的认知和鉴赏带来损害。在NPPF的框架下，如果带来的公共利益未能超过损害，后者的方案在必要时仍会被拒绝。

　　NPPF保护政策的另一关键要素是相称（proportionality）的原则。其第193条规定："遗产越重要，对其（加以保护的）权重就越应该越高（地进行保护）。"第194条继续规定，任何损害，包括在"具有最高历史价值的遗产，尤其是登录古迹，受保护的沉船遗址，注册战场，I级和II*级注册历史建筑[1]，I级和II*级注册公园和园林，和世界遗产地"的周围环境进行建设开发造成的损害，应当是罕见的特例"。

---

　　1 英国注册历史建筑（listed buildings）分为I级，II*级和II级三个级别。英国现有约50万处注册历史建筑，其中I级约占总数2.5%，II*级约占5.8%，II级约占91.7%——译者注。

this act owners wishing to make changes to schedule monuments (of which there are about 20,000) are required to submit applications for consent. If national government, advised by Historic England, believes that what is proposed would be harmful to the monument consent can be refused. In practice the majority of consent applications are approved but often after measures have been put in place to protect the archaeological remains.

Large parts of Hadrian's Wall and its associated features such as the Vallum have legal protection as scheduled monuments. The Frontiers of the Roman Empire: Hadrian's Wall World Heritage Site is comprised exclusively of the scheduled components of the frontier system. This is an important factor, which helps the UK State Party to the World Heritage Convention to meet its obligations to the Convention, as World Heritage Sites themselves do not have statutory protection in England and reliance is placed on the proper implementation of national heritage legislation and planning policy.

Parts of the Roman frontier that survive as archaeological remains beneath more recent built up areas, for example on Tyneside and in Carlisle, are not included in the schedule of monuments nor the World Heritage Site (WHS), but are nevertheless afforded protection through the planning system. The English National Planning Policy Framework (NPPF), which was revised and updated in 2018, is one of the key elements of the planning system and provides, as its name suggests, the framework within which development is managed in England. It aims to promote sustainable development and includes a section on the conservation and enhancement of the historic environment (National Planning Policy Guidance 2018, see https://assets.publishing.service.gov.uk/government/uploads/system/uploads/attachment_data/file/740441/National_Planning_Policy_Framework_web_accessible_version.pdf).

As well as providing policies for the physical protection of all heritage assets, including those which are not statutorily designated, the NPPF historic environment section sets out policies that protect the setting of heritage assets. This is particularly important in relation to Hadrian's Wall as it protects the setting of scheduled monuments and the WHS. While scheduling puts in place measures to protect the physical fabric of a monument and/or archaeological deposits it is the planning system that delivers protection from inappropriate development in the setting of a heritage asset which can detract from its significance. For example the open upland character of much of the central section of Hadrian's Wall and the coastal location of the frontier at its western end lend themselves to power generation by wind energy. While in some cases wind turbines will not cause harm to the Outstanding Universal Value of the World Heritage Site, in others they may harm the ability to understand and appreciate the frontier system. The NPPF provides the framework within which proposals in the latter category can, if necessary, be refused, should the public benefits fail to outweigh the harm.

Another important element of the NPPF's policies on conservation is the concept of proportionality. Paragraph 193 says that 'the more important the asset, the greater the weight [given to its conservation] should be.' Paragraph 194 goes on to say that any harm, including from development in the setting of 'assets of the highest significance, notably scheduled monuments, protected wreck sites, registered battlefields, grade I and II* listed buildings, grade I and II* registered parks and gardens, and World Heritage Sites, should be wholly exceptional.'

Most planning applications which may impact on the historic environment are decided by local planning au-

　　绝大部分可能对历史环境带来影响的规划申请都是由英格兰的地方规划部门（目前英格兰有 365 个）审定的。地方规划部门必须制订战略发展规划，以落实国家规划政策。这些地方规划中包括遗产政策并必须得到中央政府的批准，确保其符合国家规划政策。在地方规划中涉及到未来的土地使用时，地方规划部门不得提出有悖于遗产政策的遗址地开发方案。

　　英格兰遗产委员会发挥了重要的作用，既为地方规划部门就影响重要遗迹的建设开发方案提供顾问咨询，同时也向中央政府（数字文化媒体和体育部）就登录古迹许可的颁发提供顾问咨询。为履行与哈德良长城相关的这些职责，英格兰遗产委员会设置了一名专门的古迹巡查官。

　　英格兰的遗产法规和规划政策相结合，为遗产及其周边环境提供了高水平的保护。尽管世界遗产地未纳入英格兰法律认定的遗产，但事实上，整个"罗马帝国边界：哈德良长城世界遗产地"由一系列登录古迹构成，从而得到高水平的保护。并且当规划政策得到合理应用时，可以控制世界遗产地缓冲区内和更广阔的周边环境内的不当开发带来的损害，对遗产地实施保护。哈德良长城的整体保护状况大致上是很好的，证实了这些保护措施的效果。

　　然而，在英格兰规划体系中，有一个方面与《保护世界自然和文化遗产公约》的严格规定存在区别。NPPF 的原则认为，如果产生的公共利益足以抵消损害，则可能存在一些例外，即对世界

Fig. 2
Hadrian's Wall: with the exception of the parts of the Roman frontier that were built over during the urban development of Tyneside and Carlisle all the core elements of the frontier, such as this one at Cawfields, are protected through inclusion on the schedule of monuments (© Henry Owen-John)

图 2
哈德良长城：除部分遗迹在泰恩赛德和卡莱尔等城市发展中被埋压，哈德良长城所有核心部分，如位于考菲尔德斯的这段，因纳入登录古迹而受到保护（摄影：亨利·欧文·约翰）

thorities (LPAs) of which there are 365 in England. LPAs are required to have strategic development plans in place which reflect national planning policy. These local plans contain heritage policies and have to be approved by national government as being in conformity with national planning policies. In identifying future land use in local plans LPAs should not put forward proposals for the development of sites that conflict with the heritage policies.

Historic England plays an important role in advising LPAs on development proposals that affect significant heritage assets and also advises the national government (the Department for Digital, Culture, Media and Sport) on Scheduled Monument Consent applications. To discharge these duties in relation to Hadrian's Wall, Historic England employs an Inspector of Ancient Monuments.

The combination of heritage legislation and planning policy in England provides a significant level of protection for heritage assets and their settings. Although WHSs are not statutorily designated assets in England the fact that the entire Frontiers of the Roman Empire: Hadrian's Wall World Heritage site is comprised of scheduled monuments affords it a very high level of protection, while planning policy guidance, when properly applied, protects the WHS from harm through inappropriate development in the Buffer Zone of the WHS and its wider setting. The effectiveness of these measures is evidenced by the overall state of conservation of the Wall which is mainly very good.

There is however a distinction between one aspect of the English planning system and a rigid approach to the interpretation of the World Heritage Convention. The NPPF takes the view that there may be exceptional circumstances in which some harm to a WHS is permissible if the public benefit that will result is sufficient to offset the harm. Public benefit can include heritage benefits but also wider social and economic benefits. The World Heritage Convention takes a more absolute approach, especially Article 4, which requires States Parties to the Convention to use "the utmost of their own resources" in ensuring 'the identification, protection, conservation, presentation and transmission to future generations of the cultural and natural heritage' of Outstanding Universal Value.

It is arguable that the Convention could be interpreted in a way that does not allow any change that causes any harm to the OUV of a WHS and that if harm is unavoidable the change should not be allowed, regardless of any offsetting public benefits. ICOMOS, in its capacity as cultural heritage advisor to the World Heritage Committee, acknowledges at 2.1.5 of its 2011 Guidelines on Heritage Impact Assessment(available at https://www.icomos.org/world_heritage/HIA_20110201.pdf) that 'ultimately, however, it may be necessary to balance the public benefit of the proposed change against the harm to the place' but sometimes appears reluctant to adopt this approach in practice. There is therefore a potential tension between the English planning system and some current interpretations of the World Heritage Convention. This does however need to be seen in the context of a heritage protection system that has evolved over more than 130 years and which has proved very effective in safeguarding England's heritage for the benefit of this and future generations.

遗产地的有些损害是可以得到允许的。公共利益既包括遗产保护效益，也包括更广泛的社会和经济利益。《保护世界自然和文化遗产公约》则采用了一个更绝对的原则，尤其在第 4 条中要求缔约国"最大限度地利用自己的资源"以确保文化和自然遗产的突出普遍价值得到"认定，保护，保存，展示以及后代传承"。

争议之处在于，《公约》可以被理解为不允许对世界遗产地的突出普遍价值造成任何损害的任何改变发生，并且无论公共利益是否足以弥补损害，只要损害不可避免，就不允许对遗迹做出任何改变。作为世界遗产委员会的顾问，国际古迹遗址理事会在其发布《2011 遗产影响评估指南》（详见 https://www.icomos.org/world_heritage/HIA_20110201.pdf）的第 2.1.5 条中承认，"但最终，在改变方案所带来的公共利益和给该地造成的损害之间达到平衡是有必要的"，然而他们有时却显得并不情愿在实践中做到这一点。因此，在英格兰规划体系和《保护世界自然和文化遗产公约》的一些现有阐释之间存在着潜在冲突。但这需要在英国发展了 130 多年的遗产保护体系的大背景下审视，而这一体系已证明能够有效保护英格兰的遗产，造福当代和子孙后代。

参考文献
Bibliography

[1] 英国《国家规划政策指南 2018》

The UK. National Planning Policy Framework of 2018.

https://assets.publishing.service.gov.uk/government/uploads/system/uploads/attachment_data/file/740441/National_Planning_Policy_Framework_web_accessible_version.pdf)

THE MANAGEMENT OF HADRIAN'S WALL

Humphrey Welfare

Hadrian's Wall World Heritage Site Partnership Board - Carlisle - UK

Abstract

Although it is much shorter than the Great Wall, Hadrian's Wall is still a complex World Heritage Site: along its length there are great variations in landscape and in levels of archaeological survival. The large numbers of stakeholders mean that coordination of effort is essential. The long-established management system for the World Heritage Site is briefly described and the key documents are set out.

Keywords: World Heritage Site, records, Buffer Zone, stakeholders, Management Plan

Hadrian's Wall became a World Heritage Site (WHS) in 1987, the same year as the Great Wall. However, in 2005 a long stretch of the Roman frontier in Upper Germany also became a WHS, followed by the Antonine Wall, in Scotland, in 2008. Since then the three of them have formed the transnational Frontiers of the Roman Empire WHS. (This concept is now being further expanded, the intention being that all suitable sections of the Roman Imperial frontiers - throughout Europe, the Middle East, and North Africa - should become separate national or transnational WHSs.) In practice, visitors to Hadrian's Wall are hardly aware of the current partnership with Germany and Scotland; it is something that we need to strengthen and make better known.

On Hadrian's Wall, the WHS is the area protected by law as a scheduled monument: this is usually a very narrow strip, which measures as little as 40 metres wide in places (Fig. 1). For reference purposes the archaeological remains are divided up cartographically into short numbered sections so that they can be clearly and easily identified (https://hadrianswallcountry.co.uk/hadrians-wall-management-plan/supporting-information). The label on each section also contains an estimate of the area that is protected. Not all of the WHS is within the narrow strip; there are outlying sections - for example, the Roman fort and town at Corbridge which relate to an earlier road (the Stanegate) to the south of the Wall. Down the western coast (the 'Cumbrian coast') there is no continuous protected strip because there is no Wall: the string of forts, fortlets, and towers that formed the coastal defences are given separate individual protected zones. In the Historic England archives there is a parallel (but not identical) system of mapped records that contains the detailed archaeological descriptions. Most of this information is readily available online, especially through the Historic England Pastscape website (https://www. pastscape.org.uk/SearchResults.aspx?rational=q&criteria=Hadrians%20Wall&search=ALL&sort=4&record-sperpage=10). By and large, our records are good, having been built up over more than 300 years of research. In

哈德良长城的管理

汉佛瑞·维尔法
（哈德良长城世界遗产合作委员会，英国卡莱尔）

摘　要

虽然比中国长城短很多，但哈德良长城依旧是一处复杂的世界遗产地，沿线景观差异很大，考古遗址保存程度也各不相同。利益相关者的数量之多也意味着协调合作至关重要。本文简要介绍世界遗产地确立已久的管理体制，并列举一些关键性文件。

关键词：世界遗产地　记录　缓冲区　利益相关者　管理规划

哈德良长城于 1987 年成为世界遗产地（WHS），与中国长城同年入选。2005 年，位于上日尔曼的一段罗马帝国边界也成为世界遗产地，随后位于苏格兰的安东尼墙也于 2008 年入选。自此，这三段长城构成跨国的罗马帝国边疆世界遗产地。（此概念已进一步扩展，意图将所有罗马帝国边界中符合条件的区段——横跨欧洲、中东及北非——单独或跨国申报成为世界遗产地。）实际上，大多数哈德良长城的游客对其与德国和苏格兰的伙伴关系知之甚少；因此，我们需要加强伙伴关系并广泛宣传。

就哈德良长城而言，世界遗产地区域是作为登录古迹（scheduled monument）受法律保护，这个区域通常是相当窄的带状区域，某些区段仅 40 米宽（图 1）。为方便引述，我们将考古遗迹在地图上进行分区，便于清楚描述（https://hadrianswallcountry.co.uk/hadrians-wall-management-plan/supporting-information）。每个区段的标注也包含受保护范围的大致面积信息。并非所有世界遗产地都位于该窄长地带内，比如位于科布里奇（Corbridge）的罗马要塞就属于外围地带，它们与哈德良长城南面早期道路（石路，Stanegate）相连。在西海岸（坎布里亞海岸，Cumbrian coast）向南，因为不存在线性墙体，所以保护范围不是连续的带状。这里组成海岸防线一系列的大小要塞和塔楼各自划有独立的保护区。在英格兰遗产委员会的档案中，另外有一套（但不完全相同）的地图记录系统，其中包含详细的考古描述。大部分信息都可在线获取，特别是通过英格兰遗产委员会"昔日景观"网站（Historic England Pastscape website, https://www.pastscape.org.uk/SearchResults.aspx?rational=q&criteria=Hadrians%20Wall&search=ALL&sort=4&recordsperpage=10）。总体来说，我们的记录档案建立在超过 300 年的研究之上，相当完善。然而在个别区域，像是纽卡斯尔中心建成区，以及索尔维（Solway）边缘的西部沼泽等部分区域，我们尚不清楚防御形式的具体细节，甚至不清楚其确切位置。对不清楚的对象加以管理是相当困难的。

世界遗产地的窄长地带外是可横跨数千米的缓冲区（图 1）。1987 年时，缓冲区如此设置是为保护哈德良长城的视觉环境，控制新的开发建设不会侵害罗马帝国边界遗迹的审美鉴赏。然而，我们对缓冲区的想法有所改变：现在我们更加重视在这个东西海岸之间的区域之中当时罗马边疆体系是如何运行的，缓冲区的设置有助于对此的理解和认识不受影响。不过，在地方政府的规划管理体系中缓冲区仍然被用作管控

a few areas, however - such as the Newcastle conurbation, and the western marshes on the edge of the Solway - we do not yet know in any detail what form the defences took, or exactly where they were. It is difficult to manage what you do not know.

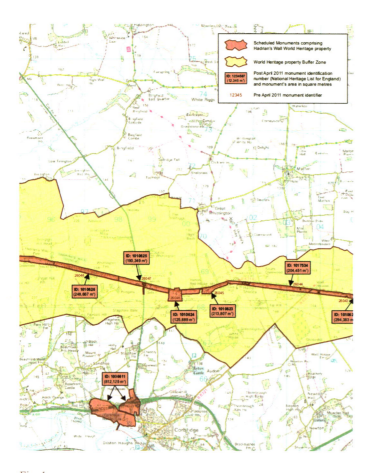

Fig. 1

A short section of the official map accompanying the WHS Management Plan, showing the narrow line of the WHS itself. The rectangular block (ID: 1010624) adjacent to the line in the centre of the image marks the site of the Roman fort at Haltonchesters. The much wider Buffer Zone was drawn up to protect the visual context of the Wall. A separate protected area to the south encompasses the Roman forts and the Roman town at Corbridge. Each grid square has a side of 1km (© Crown Copyright: Historic England)

图 1

哈德良长城世界遗产管理规划中官方地图局部，图中世界遗产地本身呈狭窄条状。图示位于红线中段的一处矩形区域 (ID: 1010624) 是霍尔顿切斯特罗马要塞的位置所在。设置更为宽阔的缓冲区则是为保护哈德良长城的视觉环境。南部有一个单独的保护区包括了科布里奇的罗马要塞和罗马城镇。每个网格方块的边长为 1 千米（皇家版权：英格兰遗产委员会）

Outside the narrow strip of the WHS is a Buffer Zone (Fig. 1) which can be several kilometres across. In 1987 this was designed to protect the visual setting of the Wall, so that new development would not intrude upon the aesthetic appreciation of the remains of the Roman frontier. However, our ideas on this have changed: we are now more concerned that appreciation and understanding of the operation of the frontier - along its line from east to west - is not compromised. Nevertheless, the Buffer Zone is still often used in the local government planning system as an area of constraint. Increasingly the management of the WHS is approached even more broadly, taking in the whole of the 'corridor' from Tyneside to the west coast. (The valleys of the Tyne and of the rivers that flow into the Solway have always provided a route through the hills at this, the narrowest point of the country, where it is only 80 miles across. This is where the settlements are, and the modern roads and the railway.)

Although very small in comparison to the Great Wall, this corridor is quite complicated: it passes through 10 local government areas; there are (for instance) different arrangements for the marketing of tourism on the east and the west; and there may be as many as 1000 private owners who have part of the WHS on their land. So there are huge numbers of stakeholders.

手段。另外，世界遗产地的管理考虑的范围越来越广，涵盖了从泰恩赛德到西部海岸的整个"走廊"。（泰恩河及流入索尔维湾的河流形成的河谷一直是穿过山丘的通道，是英国最窄的地方，只有80英里。此处也是聚落、现代道路和铁路聚集地。）

虽然比中国长城规模小很多，但是这条走廊却颇为复杂：它穿过10个地方政府管辖范围；举例来说，东边和西边便有不同的旅游营销规划；并且，哈德良长城坐落于多达1000个私有土地范围内。因此，利益相关者的数量众多。同时，罗马帝国边界遗迹经过的景观差别很大：部分地区为城市，区域范围内涉及很多组织和管理机构；其他地区则为乡村，压力来源虽然比较少却颇为不同。

遗迹保存现状也有所不同：哈德良长城只有很少区段已经过考古挖掘并得到加固展示，但于大部分的区段，哈德良长城遗迹依旧埋于地下或未明其踪；在中部及西部的许多区域，哈德良长城有很长的区段还未获得任何认真的考古关注（图2）。有些遗址现状或许较为稳定，可能也只需要加强监测及相对

Fig. 2
Hadrian's Wall near Lanercost. Here the remains of the Wall - the lower courses, the rubble core, and other archaeological information - survive under a field boundary. Almost everywhere along its course, the line of the Roman frontier had a profound affect on the later landscape (© Humphrey Welfare)

图 2
位于 Lanercost 附近的哈德良长城。此段长城遗迹—低矮的线路，碎石墙芯，以及其他考古信息—保留在当代农场围墙之下。哈德良长城这道罗马帝国防线，给它经过的所有区域景观都产生了深远影响（版权：汉佛瑞·维尔法）

Further, the landscapes through which the remains of the frontier run vary a great deal: some are urban, where there are very many organisations and authorities working across and around the sensitive areas; others are out in the countryside where there are fewer, but different, pressures.

States of conservation also vary: short stretches of the Wall have been excavated and consolidated for display, but for most of their course the remains of the frontier defences are still buried or obscured; in many parts of the centre and the west, long sections of the Wall itself have never received any significant archaeological attention (Fig. 2). This situation may be fairly stable and robust, and may need only monitoring and comparatively little maintenance, but in other places the sites are more vulnerable. For example, one of the features of the Wall corridor is the survival of many of the low earthwork enclosures that formed temporary camps for the soldiers; the remains are not easy for the non-specialist to appreciate but they are protected by law and in each case it is the farmer who is still responsible for the first level of management of the land. The maintenance of good relations with the farming industry, and mutual understanding, is therefore essential.

Much of the corridor is now managed largely for agriculture: sheep in the uplands of the central section (Fig. 3), cattle in the wetter lowlands to the west, and arable crops in the east where the climate is drier. Each of these farming systems poses a different level of threat to the surviving remains. The sheep can happily graze on the surviving earthworks and do little damage; the cattle can be superficially destructive to the grassland, and occasional light ploughing for the improvement of the pastures is considered to be necessary. In the east, deeper annual ploughing for cereal crops has levelled much of the Roman frontier, especially the earthworks of the Vallum. Nevertheless, the survival of archaeological information may still be quite good, especially in buried ditches. The selective excavation of a number of milecastles in arable areas revealed that - even in fields that have long been ploughed - preservation of the archaeological levels was sometimes better than expected[1]. Historic England plays the key role in ensuring that the legislation protecting the remains of the Roman frontier is adhered to, but a significant proportion of the monitoring and reporting of change is now done by volunteers.

In addition to their archaeological importance, some stretches of the Roman frontier are also managed and conserved explicitly for their geological and topographical importance (for example, for the crags formed by the dolerite of the Whin Sill - a classic geological type of international importance, Fig. 3), or for their wildlife: the marshes close to the western end of the Wall are especially attractive to large populations of migrating geese, so national and local natural environmental organisations also have to be involved.

Over and above these considerations of agriculture and the natural world, the Wall corridor is also managed for the people who come to enjoy all of these things: the history, the wildlife, and the landscape. Maximising free public access to all parts of the frontier - especially along the National Trail - has greatly increased the public's knowledge and appreciation of the Roman frontier, but even when the idea of a long-distance path along the Wall was first suggested - in 1976 - it was evident that access would probably bring conservation challenges. It has indeed turned out to be a classic case of visitor pressure on fragile remains, requiring constant care from various players. Where small changes to farming practice or to visitor behaviour are necessary these must be

Fig. 3
Peel Crags, in Wall-mile 39. This is sheep pasture, a farming regime that does little harm to the archaeological remains. The crags are formed by the Whin Sill, a classic landform of extruded volcanic lava, and have additional protection due to their geological importance. Hadrian's Wall can be seen along the crest as an unexcavated mound of rubble and, farther away, revealed and consolidated (© Humphrey Welfare)

图 3
区段 39 号处的皮尔峭壁。图中是一个牧羊场，这种农业方式对考古遗迹几无损伤。峭壁由暗色岩床形成，后者为一种受挤压而喷出的典型火山熔岩地貌，而峭壁也因其地质重要性而得到额外保护。沿着山脊可以看到哈德良长城，近处为保持原状的碎石堆，稍远处为经过发掘和加固的段落（摄影：汉佛瑞·维尔法）

较少的维护工作，但其他地方的遗址则相对脆弱得多。举例来说，哈德良长城走廊的其中一个特色是，留有许多曾作为士兵临时营地的低矮土木防御工事围地遗迹；非专业人员很难辨认出这些遗迹，但它们受法律保护，并且主要依赖农场主承担每处遗址的日常土地管理直接责任。因此，与农场保持良好关系并相互理解至关重要。

　　大部分的走廊地区如今都作农业用途；在中部区域的高地有绵羊（图 3），在西边更为潮湿的低地有牛群，并在东部较为干燥的地区有耕作物。每一个农业系统都对存留下来的遗迹带来不同程度的威胁。羊群可以在存留下来的防御工事遗迹上悠闲啃食青草而几乎不会带来任何伤害；牛群只会对草场表面造成破坏，偶尔也需浅耕来改善草地状况。在东边，每年为种谷物会进行深耕，破坏了许多罗马帝国边界遗迹，特别是南部壕沟的土木防御工事。不过，考古信息可能依旧得以存留，特别是那些地下壕沟。在耕种地区数个里堡的选择性挖掘显示，即使耕地已被长期反复耕犁，但考古遗迹的存留程度有时候比预期的还要好[1]。英格兰遗产委员会在确保罗马帝国边界遗迹依法受到保护中扮演关键角色，但如今，大部分的监测及变动报告都是由志愿者承担。

actively managed, by the landowner, by the tenant farmer, and by the partnership of highway authorities (part of local government) that looks after the Trail.

Even at sites which are open to the public as visitor attractions there may be complex arrangements in place: at Housesteads, within the most famous stretch of the Wall, the Roman fort is on land that is owned by the National Trust, but access to the fort, and its conservation, is managed by English Heritage; the car park is run by the National Park authorities, and the tenant farmer farms the surrounding land.

There are very many other stakeholders along the Wall corridor. The needs of the visitor to the World Heritage Site are provided by a large number of small businesses - village shops, pubs, hotels, specialist travel companies, and taxi firms - whose livelihood depends on the continuing attraction of the archaeology and of the landscape. Everyone wants the Wall to be well managed, but everyone has different interests, so how do we tackle the management of this complicated and extensive string of places?

All of this complexity is brought together in the Management Plan for the WHS (https://hadrianswallcountry.co.uk/hadrians-wall-management-plan). The initial edition of this Plan came out in 1996. It was the first Plan for a WHS in the UK and was largely experimental. Since then it has been revised every five to six years. Innovation has continued: the current edition was the first to be wholly digital and exclusively online. As it is not printed it can now be revised whenever necessary - not just at the end of each five-year period - so it has become a dynamic document. Any changes are, however, carefully recorded so that there can be no doubt about what the current version is.

The writing and revision of the Plan, and the progress towards its delivery, is overseen at a strategic level by the WHS Partnership Board. This is made up of representatives of the relevant local government areas, and the Chairs of the specialist Delivery Groups that report to the Board and who organise the work and activities that the Plan requires. Beyond the high-level international obligation established when the UK signed the World Heritage Convention, the Board itself has no legal status or authority; it simply works because those involved want the Management Plan to succeed. It is a very British arrangement.

The Plan contains the Statement of Outstanding Universal Value (https://hadrianswallcountry.co.uk/hadrians-wall-management-plan/hadrians-wall-significance) - which sets out what makes the Wall special - and the 30-year vision for the WHS. Below this, a series of Aims and Objectives are listed under some familiar headings: Conservation; Understanding; The Visitor Economy; and Management. Seventy short Policies cover everything from repair work to climate change, and from tourism to education. The idea is that these Policies can be adopted by local government and by other organisations, so that we are all working to the same ends. Shorter-term Objectives and Actions are set out for the five-year period of the Plan, but these can be altered as circumstances change. All of the work that the Plan requires is carried out or led by members of the Partnership rather than by a specific dedicated team. This is 'third-party delivery'.

Supporting information, available on the website alongside the Plan, includes the maps of the WHS, guidance on the relevant laws, the strategy for public interpretation, and information about the natural environment.

　　除了考古价值外，罗马帝国边界的部分区段还因其地理和地形价值而特别受到管理及维护（例如，由暗色岩床粒玄岩形成的峭壁，是具有国际重要价值的典型地理类型，图3），或因野生动物，如离哈德良长城西段不远的沼泽地特别吸引了大量迁徙中的大雁，所以国家及当地的自然环境组织也必须介入。

　　除对农业与自然环境的管理之外，哈德良长城走廊的管理还包括人的管理：大量人员来此地观赏历史、野生动物及自然景观。尽可能地向公众开放长城全线——特别是国家步道沿线——大幅提升了公众对罗马帝国边界的认识与鉴赏。但是，早在1976年首次提出沿哈德良长城旁开设长途步道的概念时，我们就明白开放很可能为遗迹维护带来挑战。确实，游客对脆弱的遗迹带来压力成为典型的风险因素，因此需要不同参与者持续关注。这不仅要求农业从业者和游客的行为做出调整，也要求对这些行为加以积极的管理，土地所有者、佃农和国家步道相关管理机构（和部分地方政府）都需要参与其中。

　　即便是作为对外开放的游客景点，有些管理体制也十分复杂：在豪塞斯特兹（Housesteads）这段哈德良长城最有名的区段，该处罗马要塞所在的土地所有权属于国家信托（National Trust），通往要塞的道路和要塞的古迹维护工作是由英格兰遗产信托负责；停车场是由国家公园管理局运营，遗址周围的土地由佃家耕种。

　　哈德良长城走廊沿线有很多其他的利益相关者。大量的小型商业服务于来世界遗产地参观的游客，如乡村商店、酒吧、旅馆、专题旅行社以及出租车公司，它们的生存也仰赖考古遗迹及景观对游客持续的吸引力。所有人都希望哈德良长城得到良好管理，但每个人都有不同的利害关系，那么我们应如何管理如此复杂且分布广泛的系列遗址呢？

　　所有的复杂性都体现在世界遗产地的管理规划中（Management Plan，https://hadrianswallcountry.co.uk/hadrians-wall-management-plan）。此计划的最初版本于1996年出台。这是英国第一份世界遗产地的管理规划，大多为实验性质。自那之后，每五到六年就会对规划进行修订。规划也在持续创新：最新版本首度完全数字化，且只在网上提供。因为不再有打印的版本，所以文件能随时更新——无需每五年才修改一次——成为一个动态文件。任何改变也都有详细记录，所以新旧版本不会混乱。

　　管理规划的编写和修订，从编制到发布都由哈德良长城世界遗产合作委员会全面监管。此合作委员会的成员包括相关地方政府代表、合作委员会下属的特别交付团队（Delivery Groups）负责人，和规划编制特别委托工作及活动的负责人。除了英国签署《保护世界自然与文化遗产公约》时承诺履行的高层级国际义务外，合作委员会本身并无任何法律地位或权威；它能成功运转是因为参与者都希望此管理规划获得成功。这是非常英式的体制。

　　哈德良长城管理规划包含突出普遍价值陈述（Statement of Outstanding Universal Value， https://hadrianswallcountry.co.uk/hadrians-wall-management-plan/hadrians-wall-significance），阐述哈德良长城的特别之处及世界遗产地的30年愿景。紧随其后是一系列宗旨和目标，熟悉的标题包括：保护，认知，游客经济，管理。七十条政策涵盖了从维修工作到气候变迁，从旅游业和教育各个领域。我们期望地方政府及其他组织能采用这些政策，这样所有相关方都可以共同迈向一致的目标。规划中列出了五年短期目标和行动计划，但可视情况而变。规划要求的所有工作都是由合作委员会的成员负责实施或牵头实施，

The strategy for research on the Wall has been published separately[2] and is being revised at present (2018).

The Plan sets out why public money should be spent on looking after the Wall, and has been greatly strengthened by consultation during its preparation: listening to what the public thinks should be done. People thus feel involved with the WHS and with its future. The consensus reached has encouraged the participation of volunteers in all sorts of roles: as guides, surveyors, researchers, and monitors. Very importantly, the Plan also promotes the UNESCO values of using knowledge to promote international understanding, non-violence, and peace.

Even with this extensive goodwill, the work that has to be done to deliver the aims of the Plan still has to be coordinated. The Coordinator, John Scott, works with all of the stakeholders, including the volunteers, to achieve the aims set out. An example of this - now well established - is the integration and marketing of the transport systems (buses and trains) along the full length of the Wall and across three local government areas. Separate companies provide the bus services - including a special one along the Wall during the summer - but the coordination puts this all together and therefore enables the visitor to understand how the full infrastructure can be used. Tourists are therefore able to plan how they can use public transport to get to most of the World Heritage Site.

Working alongside the Coordinator, the volunteers contribute a huge amount of effort throughout the WHS but, even so, there is not enough money to do all of the things that we would like to do. Most of the funding comes from local government but this is fragile. We are taking steps to make this stronger, and so to make the management of this special but complex place even more effective in the future.

而非由特定的专门团队负责实施。这是'第三方交付'（third-party delivery）。

规划的更多详细内容可在网站上获得，包括世界遗产地的地图、相关法律指引、公众阐释的策略，以及自然环境的信息。哈德良长城的研究策略已另外出版 [2]，如今（2018）正进行修订。

规划指出为何公众预算应用于哈德良长城保护，并在编制过程中通过公开咨询了解公众的意见，听取他们认为有哪些应该完成的任务，以此大大提高规划编制质量。人们因此觉得与世界遗产地同在，并为其未来付出一份心力。此共识的达成鼓励了志愿者发挥各种职能：导游、调查测绘、研究和监监测。特别重要的是，管理规划还推广了联合国教科文组织的价值，即运用知识来促进国际理解、非暴力，及和平。

即便有如此广泛的善意，我们仍需通过协调来达到计划的目标。协调员约翰·史考特（John Scott）与所有利益相关者（包括志愿者）合作，以达到设定的目标。举例来说，如今沿着哈德良长城全线及跨越三个地方政府范围的交通系统（公交和火车）已完善建立和整合。不同的公司提供各自的公交服务——其中包括暑期长城专线——但通过协调整合，游客能够了解所有基础建设的完整使用信息。游客因而能计划如何使用公共交通来探访哈德良长城世界遗产地的大部分区段。

志愿者与协调人员共事，也为世界遗产地整体付出很多努力，但即便如此，仍然没有足够的预算来完成我们想要达成的事项。大部分的资金都来自地方政府，但来源不稳固。我们正努力加强这一计划，进而能在未来更有效率的管理这个特殊却复杂的地方。

参考文献
Bibliography

[1] Wilmott, T. "The Hadrian's Wall Milecastles Project, in Hadrian's Wall." Archaeological Research by English Heritage 1976-2000, edited by T. Wilmott. Swindon: 2009: 137-202.

T. 威尔莫特 . 哈德良长城里堡计划 [J].T. 威尔莫特编 . 英格兰遗产信托 1976-2000 的考古研究，斯温顿 :2009:137-202.

[2] Symonds, M.F.A., and Mason D.J.P. Frontiers of Knowledge: A Research Framework for Hadrian's Wall. In Volume I: Resource Assessment, Volume II: Agenda and Strategy. Durham： 2009.

M.F.A. 西蒙兹，D.J.P. 麦森 . 知识的前沿 . 哈德良长城的研究框架 [M]. 第 I 部：资源评估 , 第 II 部：议程和策略 [M]，杜伦 :2009.

中国长城整体保护管理：挑战与探索[1]

于 冰

（中国文化遗产研究院，中国北京）

摘 要

中国长城整体保护是延续中华文明留给我们的宝贵机会，是长城价值体现和职责要求。应对长城差异性和分权挑战进行科学分析，才能理解其对长城整体价值和整体保护的影响。为应对这些挑战，近年国家在长城制度整体化、机构协调、重大项目实施和信息技术支撑等层面进行了有益探索创新。在新时代的新征程上，长城整体保护需要升级，打破学科偏见和行业壁垒。在新一轮改革中，长城保护管理应实施财政、土地和资产管理等方面重大政策调整，并在学术研究、技术攻关、区域协同和全民共享等方面组织实施考古长城、监测长城、生态长城和魅力长城国家行动。

关键词：长城 考古学 日常监测 公共政策 供给侧改革

引 言

开展双墙——英国哈德良长城与中国长城——对话，首先将罗马帝国边疆与中国长城作一宏观时空对比很有意义。

从规模来看，罗马帝国防御体系与中国汉代北部边疆防御体系大致相当，在世界范围内绝无仅有。

从持续时代来看，罗马防御体系修筑于公元前 3 世纪至公元 2 世纪，之后便废弃，英国哈德良长城仅为罗马帝国防御体系西北部极小一部分。中国长城自公元前 5 世纪起建，经秦汉时期大规模接筑后历代仍继续修筑，直至 17 世纪的明代，持续超过 2000 年。只有持续的中华文明，才需要持续修建强大的北方防御体系，或者说只有强大的北方防御体系，才保障了中华文明的持续，也才使这一庞大防御体系不断扩展和改建，形成总长超过 20000 千米的超级复杂巨系统。

从现代版图来看，罗马帝国的分布范围在现代 20 余个国家境内，其防御体系作为遗产整体保护难度极大。而中国长城的大部分仍位于当代中国境内，成为数千年多元一体中华文明延续的象征及伟大见证，整体保护历代长城遗产，是中国政府的历史荣耀。

从整体保护来看，虽然中国长城大部分位于中国境内，但某种程度而言，其面临的挑战并不亚于罗马帝国防御体系分散于数十个现代国家之中，考验着管理者的决心和智慧。

保护长城突出普遍价值真实性和完整性是长城管理的根本目标。整体保护是中国长城突出普遍价值所在，也是中国政府的神圣职责。作为巨型遗产，差异性和分权必然永远伴随着长城保护管理工作，这既是对整体协调之挑战，也是中国文化的丰厚资养之源。只有深入认清挑战，才可能有效应对，将其转

---

1 本文已在《中国文化遗产》2018 年第 3 期发表，本文有所删减修改。

INTEGRAL CONSERVATION AND MANAGEMENT OF THE GREAT WALL: CHALLENGES AND PRACTICES[1]

Yu Bing

China Academy of Cultural Heritage - Beijing - China

Abstract

It is a precious opportunity and obligation for the Chinese people to protect the Great Wall in an integrated manner. The challenges of heterogeneity and decentralization should be scientifically analysed to understand their real impact. Efforts and innovations have been made to address the challenges in national leadership and actions, supported by technological application. In the new journey of the 'New Era', the integrated conservation and management of the Great Wall will be upgraded to a new level, transcending path dependence of disciplinary bias and of sectors operating in isolation. In the course of this new round of reform, the conservation and management of the Great Wall should pursue a strategic direction in policy reform regarding fiscal, land and property management systems. Major initiatives in promoting academic research, technological advancement, regional collaboration and public enjoyment at the national level should be organized under the themes of the archaeology of the Wall, monitoring the Wall, the environment of the Wall, and promoting understanding of the Wall.

Key words: The Great Wall, heterogeneity, decentralization, integration

FOREWORD

For our Wall (Hadrian's Wall) to Wall (the Great Wall) dialogue, it is interesting to compare first the whole Roman Frontier and the Great Wall under a broad framework of time and space.

On a geographic scale, the Roman Empire and the Han Dynasty of China were of similar duration and size. The two massive defence systems built by the two powers in the east and west were unparalleled elsewhere in the world.

The Roman defence system was developed between the 3th century BC and 2nd century AD, with Hadrian's Wall constructed as its northwest frontier from the 2nd century AD, and discarded totally after the Roman Empire declined. The Great Wall was constructed in different phases for over 2000 years. The continuous Chinese civilization demanded a powerful defence system in the north. Some stretches were constructed as early as the 5th century BC; these were then connected and expanded in a unified way during the Qin and Han Dynasties for the first time, and strengthened and reconstructed in many dynasties until the last substantial development up to the 17th century in the Ming Dynasty. Only time allowed the Great Wall to be expanded into a mega-complex of over 20,000 km.

---

1 This paper is simplified and modified on the basis of what was published in the Chinese journal China Cultural Heritage, 2018(3)

化为机遇和发展动力。

一、长城整体保护面临的差异性挑战

长城及其管理面临的差异性，凭直觉就可以从长城资源多样性、环境复杂性方面论述很多。深入思考其带来的真正挑战，在于基础认知、形势变化和宏观政策上，我们还有太多的欠账。

（一）长城资源差异性对遗产研究认知的挑战

对于长城资源的差异性，现在得益于长城资源调查而可以有丰富的统计数据佐证其在时代、类型、材质、保存状况等方面的不同，还有更久远和浩瀚历史文献和研究成果介绍长城的方方面面。然而对于长城实物遗迹，对于不同地段长城的修建分期、形制、工艺，对于长城体系与不同自然环境的关系及变迁，乃至长城在中华文明进程中的多重功能作用与历史影响，我们缺少太多的实证研究。其中最关键的就是缺少考古学科在总体上的系统介入，以往考古学研究基本以普查性质为主，专项研究十分零散。

应该说，对明长城的研究和认知，或者说对明长城建筑设施的研究和认知，大大替代了对其他时代和类型的长城的研究和认知。我国长城始建于春秋战国时期，历经秦汉、魏晋南北朝、隋唐宋、直至明，2000 多年间有 20 多个诸侯国家和封建王朝都修筑过不同规模的长城。然而根据国家文物局组织长城资源调查认定，在各时期的长城遗存中，明长城资源占比超过 55%（表 1）。

长城在明代经过最后大规模修建，保存当然相对完整。上述长城资源调查结果中，明以前长城单体建筑、关堡和相关遗存所占比例普遍低于墙体，一方面是因为早期墙体可以根据走向计算消失段长度，

表 1 各时代长城遗存数量统计 ★
Table 1 Statistic of the Great Wall sites by historic times

时代 Dynasty	分布省份 Province （个）	墙壕 Wall and boundary trench （段）(stretches)	单体建筑 Individual structures （座）	关堡 Fortress and passes （座）	相关遗存 Auxiliary facilities （处）	合计 Total （段座 处）	长度 Length （千米） (kilometers)
春秋 Spring and Autumn (5th–3rd BC)	9	1795	1367	160	33	3355	3080.14
秦汉 Qin and Han (3rd BC – 3rd AD)	6	2143	2575	271	10	4999	3680.26

续表Continued

时代 Dynasty	分布省份 Province （个）	墙壕 Wall and boundary trench （段）(stretches)	单体建筑 Individual structures （座）	关堡 Fortress and passes （座）	相关遗存 Auxiliary facilities （处）	合计 Total （段座 处）	长度 Length （千米） (kilometers)
明 Ming (14th –17th AD)	10	5209	17449	1272	142	24072	8851.8
其他时代 ★★ Other	11[1]	1276	454	119	0	1849	未统计
金界壕 Jin (12th– 13th AD)	3	1392	7665	389	0	9446	4010.48
认定总数 Sum	15	11815	29510	2211	185	43721	21196.18
明代遗存 占比 % of Ming	–	44.1%	59.1%	57.5%	76.8%	55.1%	41.8%
明以前 占比 % of pre- Ming	–	55.9%	40.9%	42.5%	22.8%	44.9%	50.8%

★ 数据来源：国家文物局，2012，2016
Prepared on the basis of information from bibliography NCHA, 2012 and NCHA 2016
★★ 其他时代指北魏、北齐、隋、唐、五代、宋、西夏、辽
Other dynasties include North Wei, North Qi, Sui, Tang, the Five Dynasties, Song, Western Xia and Liao dynasties

On the contemporary world map, the remains of the Roman defence system are spread over about 20 modern countries, leaving conservation on an integrated scale difficult. In this sense it is easier for China to be able to conserve and manage, in a more holistic manner, the heritage of the Great Wall which is still mostly located within Chinese territory.

Integrated conservation and management is essential for the Great Wall World Heritage Site. The OUV represents a unique and prestigious testimony to the unified Chinese civilization and its multiple cultures. It is the glorious responsibility bestowed on the Chinese authorities and the Chinese people to safeguard this exceptional masterpiece of mankind. It is at the same time extremely challenging, probably no less than the whole Roman frontier now in different countries, to cope with the heterogeneity and decentralization faced by trans-regional heritage sites.

Heterogeneity and decentralization are not just challenges to the integrity of the Great Wall: they are also rich sources of cultural and spiritual significance. Only through clear understanding of these challenges can they be turned into opportunities and provide momentum to take forward understanding and conservation. The challenges come from at least three dimensions: research and academic capabilities; the overall natural and social environments; and trans-regional and decen-

---

1 根据国家文物局 2012 年发布《长城认定手册》内容统计。

另一方面由于考古工作滞后，有接近80%长城资源调查中的相关遗存由于性质不明和时代不明未予认定，还有大量位于长城墙体两侧1千米之外的长城资源未予调查。

考古工作薄弱还体现在长城保护维修中，从勘察设计到施工都以古建筑和文物科技保护从业者为主，考古工作者参与度极低。而即使是明代长城，也有大量处于遗址状态，或是在早期长城基础上加建的，或者是在明代不同时代多次修建的，需要借助考古学方法去研究，使长城保护维修展示中记录和体现更多的历史信息。

（二）长城社会自然环境差异性对行业管理的挑战

长城无论从精神文化意义，还是自然和社会发展影响，都具有更高远的议题格局，远远超出长城本体保护的行业层面。中国历代长城分布的区域，大致东起西辽河流域，经燕山、阴山、贺兰山，到达湟水流域和河西走廊，即"长城地带"。"长城地带的形成是生态环境、族群、文化等变动因素交互作用的复杂过程，与自然地形以及气候环境的变化息息相关"[2]。因此，长城地带社会自然历史环境本身就构成长城价值的实体见证，另一方面社会自然当代环境又是区域发展战略和长城保护管理环境要素及风险管理素的重要组成。

自然环境上，以长城墙体为例。长城墙体有84.6%修建于山地和丘陵地区。长城修建自然地理和地形条件，往往体现不同历史时期长城修建的不同背景和不同功能。例如研究表明，豫南楚长城人工墙体多紧贴山体或山间垭口外侧的崖边修建，具有明显军事防御特点。而燕、赵、秦修建的北方长城修建于自身疆界之外遥远的农牧分界线上，功能在于扩地广境，而不具备军事防御功能[3][4]。因此长城自然环境具有重要区域调查或景观考古价值。

社会环境上，长城分布于荒野、农村、城市，与农业、牧业、居民生活、基础设施建设关系密切。长城2000多座关堡中，有很多发展成为现代城乡聚落中心，如山海关、张家口堡内都是现代山海关区和张家口市市中心所在地。长城沿线地区经济发展差距极大。以2016年各地人均GDP统计，在长城沿线15个省（自治区、直辖市）中，既有排名全国前两位的天津和北京，也有排名最后的甘肃和山西。大量老、少、穷地区位于长城地带。与全国人均GDP的53817元相比，有10个省（自治区）人均GDP低于平均水平，属于经济欠发达地区（图1）。在长城沿线404个县域中，有112个属于国家级贫困县，156个属于少数民族自治地区。长城沿线旅游吸引力也特别能反映各地差异性。世界著名八达岭长城每年接待游客超过800万人次，而绝大部分长城无人问津，甚至当地人都不知道自己家乡有长城[5]。

（三）、长城保护利用需求多元化对保护管理供侧改革的挑战

将长城保护利用的供给侧和需求侧进行对照，长城保护利用的需求侧在国家改革开放的宏观背景下发生了巨大变化。以1990—2015年25年期间的统计为例，在经济发展、基础设施建设、社会结构和消费需求等各个方面的变化速度和变化规模都是惊人的（表2），需求侧在不同地区、不同领域、不同社会人群中也都越来越多元化。

作为长城保护利用管理的供给侧，受到体制机制的路径依赖约束，在相对滞后的供给侧改革与需求侧快速变革之间形成巨大反差。由于缺乏长城相关保护管理相关数据，暂以整个文物业统计来替代说明

tralized management systems.

CHALLENGES OF HETEROGENEITY TO INTEGRATED CONSERVATION

It is easier to imagine the difficulties of the diverse forms and varied environments represented by such a vast system over a continent and over millennia, than to undertake scientific analysis and understand its real impact. There has not been enough understanding of fundamental questions about the monument, the changing context in which it evolved, and the strategic functions of the Great Wall.

Research challenges arising from the diversity of the Great Wall

Substantial data resulting from large-scale general surveys such as the Great Wall Resource Survey (GWRS), launched in 2006 by the National Cultural Heritage Administration, provides us with tremendous information on the overall picture of the Great Wall system in terms of time, typology, surface material and preservation status (SACH, 2012). Great achievements in historical research have been accumulated since the mid-19th century by international and domestic academics and explorers. However, they can't replace empirical research and hard evidence from detailed investigation of specific sites along the Great Wall, including their construction phases, structure, building material, technique, relationship with the landscape, and their contribution to and profound impact on the evolution of Chinese civilization. Much work in this area remains to be done, especially the systematic involvement of archaeological specialists. Previously archaeological research was mainly focused on general survey projects for the Great Wall, while specialized research projects have been quite limited and fragmented.

Research on the later stage of the Great Wall built during the Ming Dynasty, and particularly on its architecture, has long overshadowed research on the Walls from other time periods and other types of heritage sites. Over 2000 years, more than twenty city states or dynasties built sections of the Great Wall of different sizes, starting from the Spring and Autumn period, through the Warring States period, Qin and Han dynasties, Northern and Southern Dynasties, Sui, Tang, the Five Dynasties, Song, Liao, Jin, Western Xia, up to the Ming Dynasty. Yet the Ming Wall accounts for more than 55% of surviving sites shown from the GWRS work (see Table 1).

As the most recent stage of large-scale construction, the Ming Dynasty Wall should, of course, be the best preserved. Yet looking more closely at the survey statistics we see that the individual structures, fortified passes, fortresses and auxiliary facilities from before the Ming Dynasty are generally under-represented compared to the Wall of that period. One reason is that the length of the Wall surveyed is calculated including the no longer visible stretches[1]. Another reason is that the date or nature of nearly 80% of the auxiliary facilities surveyed during GWRS have not been verified due to a lack of archaeological evidence. Moreover, most facilities and sites more than 1km away from the line of the Wall were not included in the survey.

The low level of archaeological activity is also reflected in restoration projects on the Great Wall. From exploration, design and implementation, architects and conservators dominate the process with little involvement of archaeologists.

---

1 No longer visible stretches account for 35.4% of total wall length before the Ming Dynasty (NCHA, 2012)

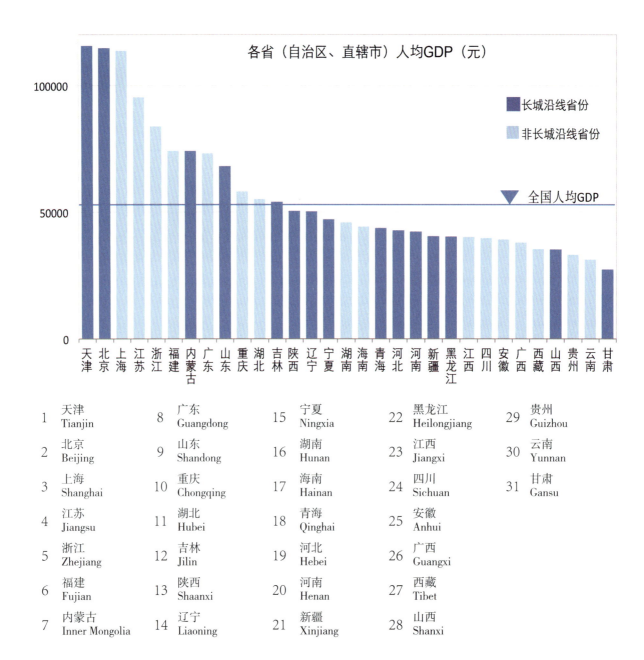

各省（自治区、直辖市）人均GDP（元）

图1

长城沿线 15 省（自治区、直辖市）2016 年人均 GDP 对比（单位：元）

Figure. 1

GDP per capita by province/AR/M in China (Unit: Yuan)

1	天津 Tianjin	8	广东 Guangdong	15	宁夏 Ningxia	22	黑龙江 Heilongjiang	29	贵州 Guizhou
2	北京 Beijing	9	山东 Shandong	16	湖南 Hunan	23	江西 Jiangxi	30	云南 Yunnan
3	上海 Shanghai	10	重庆 Chongqing	17	海南 Hainan	24	四川 Sichuan	31	甘肃 Gansu
4	江苏 Jiangsu	11	湖北 Hubei	18	青海 Qinghai	25	安徽 Anhui		
5	浙江 Zhejiang	12	吉林 Jilin	19	河北 Hebei	26	广西 Guangxi		
6	福建 Fujian	13	陕西 Shaanxi	20	河南 Henan	27	西藏 Tibet		
7	内蒙古 Inner Mongolia	14	辽宁 Liaoning	21	新疆 Xinjiang	28	山西 Shanxi		

供给侧在 1990—2015 年期间的变化情况（表3）。由表3可以看出，面对国家经济发展和消费需求的飞速发展，文物事业费的增长速度也得到快速提升。然而从文物行业开展的保护维修项目来看，仅仅增长了不到 1.86 倍；文物保护单位和博物馆接待参观人数增长较快，达到 6.7 倍，但与全国旅游总人数近

表 2 中国近 25 年代表性领域发展情况 ★
Table 2 Quarter-century change of representative fields in China

项目 Item	1990 年 (Year)	2015 年 (Year)	增长 Increase by	指标类型 Type of Index
中国 GDP 总量（万亿元） GDP（trillion RMB Yuan）	1.8873	68.91	增长 35.5 倍 35.5 times	经济 Economy
中国 GDP 世界排名 GDP world ranking	11	2	2010 年起世界第二 World No. 2 since 2010	
高速公路总里程（万公里） Highway mileage ('0000 km）	0.043	12.57	增长 291.3 倍，2014 年起世界第一 World No. 1 since 2014	基础设施 Infrastructure
高速铁路总里程（万公里） High speed railway mileage（'0000 km）	2008 年首条开通 First operation in 2008	1.9	占世界 60% Account for 60% world total	
中国城镇化率（%） Urbanisation rate (%)	26.4	56.1	2011 年起城镇人口超过农村人口 More urban population than rural since 2011	基础设施 社会结构 Infrastructure Social Structure
城镇人口总数（亿） Urban population (100 million)	3.0	7.7	增加 4.7 亿人，原住民大国 4.7	
旅游总人数（万人次） Tourists (10 thousand)	2,746	410,000	增长 148.3 倍 148.3 times	消费需求 Consumption
出境旅游人数（万人次） Outbound tourists (10 thousand)	300	12,000	增长 39 倍，2012 年起世界第一 39 times, No.1 since 2012	

★ 作者根据公开数据整理
Prepared by author according to publicized statistics

Even for the Ming Great Wall, archaeological expertise is essential to observe and record historic information: most sections are already designated archaeological sites, or have been reconstructed on top of earlier Walls.

Management challenges arising from the location of the Great Wall in different social and natural environments

The Great Wall has an incomparable significance in terms of its spiritual and symbolic, natural and social, historical and contemporary values for China. This far exceeds the traditional scope of the professional heritage sector. Historically, the Great Wall extended over a vast territory from the West Liao River system in the east, through Yan Mountain, Yin Mountain, Helan Mountain, to the Huangshui River system and Hexi Corridor in the west. This is collectively known as 'the Great Wall Zone'. "The formation of the Great Wall Zone was a complicated process of interaction between the environment, different ethnic groups, and changing cultural factors. It was closely interconnected with its natural geographical and climatic context"[2]. It is therefore essential to consider the historical, social and natural environments as material testimony to the OUV of the Great Wall, but also, the risks for conservation and management of the great variety of natural and social environments.

表 3 中国文物事业近 25 年代表性指标变化情况

Table 3 Quarter-century change of representative indices of China cultural heritage sector

	1990 年 (Year)*[1]	2015 年 (Year)[2]	增长倍数 Increase by	指标类型 Type of index
文物事业费（万元） Public input（10 thousand RMB yuan）	3.0049	323.03	107.50 倍 107.50 times	经费投入 Funding
文物机构数量（个） Number of institutions	3,065	8,676	2.83 倍 2.83 times	人员队伍 Human resources
文物从业人员（人） Number of employees	45,353	146,098	3.22 倍 3.22 times	
保护维修项目 （省保及以上，个） Number of restoration project （provincial KCRPU）	671	1,247	1.86 倍 1.86 times	文物保护 Heritage conservation
接待参观人数（万人次） Visitors（10 thousand）	13805.1	92508.306	6.70 倍 6.70 times	公共服务 Public Service

＊为保持口径一致，1990 年文物机构数量和文物从业人员数据分别加上文化（文物）厅（局）机关数量和事业编制人员

For consistency, the number of cultural (heritage) bureau institutions and government-affiliated employee are added to the number of institutions and number of employee in 1990

150 倍的增长速度仍不成比例。其中根本原因在于体制机制上的制约，这从文物业人员队伍的增长速度就可以看出，无论是机构数量还是从业人员数量 25 年间仅增长 3 倍左右，而且社会力量参与度低，没有能力承担更多的保护任务，也难以开展更丰富的公共服务满足民众参观游览需求。

二、长城整体保护面临的分权挑战

行政体制方面，中国政府拥有举世瞩目的巨大组织动员能力，但对于长城遗产这个开放的复杂巨系统，政府面临整体保护与经济发展、民生改善、社会管理等目标协调和公共资源配置的尖锐矛盾，这样的管理难题在世界上都绝无仅有。加之文物保护领域宏观决策和制度设计融合协调度较低，使长城整体保护面临较大的分权挑战。

（一）行政管理体制分权对顶层设计的挑战

长城管理体制是我国文物保护管理体制的典型代表。我国文物保护管理体制的基础特征是"属地管理"，即地方政府承担文物保护主要职责，城乡规划、机构建设、日常管理、经费预算等重大事项均由地方政府决策。中央政府主要协调、解决长城保护中的重大问题，负责文物建设控制地带内建设项目行政审批和全国重点文物保护单位本体保护维修项目经费补助职责。

对于点多线长域广的长城来说，日常监测维护是其保护工作的最主要职责，日常管理机构的缺失是严

Taking the linear Wall as an example, 84.6% of the Wall was constructed in mountainous and hilly areas. Different historical contexts and functions for the construction of the Wall at different times are mostly reflected in their geographic and topographic location. Research results show that the Wall of Chu State in the south of Henan Province was constructed at the edge of mountain ranges or at the mouth of valleys, showing a clear defensive purpose. Those Walls built by the Yan, Zhao, and Qin states in the north of Henan were located far beyond their boundaries, in the area where agricultural and nomadic territories met. These Walls were apparently for the purpose of expansion rather than defence[3][4]. The environment of the Great Wall is therefore of considerable significance for regional survey and landscape archaeology research.

The Great Wall is located in different social environments, from wild rural areas, closely associated with farming and grazing, to areas of extensive residential and urban development. Many of the more than 2000 fortified passes and fortresses have been developed into modern rural and urban settlements, such as Shanhai Pass and Zhangjiakou Fortress which are now centres of modern cities. Over the vast territory that the Great Wall covers, social development varies substantially. Regions such as Beijing and Tianjin, which rank in the top 2 for provincial GDP per capita, are developed and urban, while rural regions and vast wild areas such as in Shanxi and Gansu provinces, are among the lowest 4 regions for GDP nationwide (Fig. 1). Among the 404 counties along the Great Wall, there are 112 National Poverty Counties (2016 statistics) and 156 minority ethnic areas. This diversity could also be shown in the tourist attractions along the Great Wall: the world-famous Badaling site in Beijing receives over 8 million visitors annually, while most of the Great Wall remains obscure, and is even unknown to local residents[5].

Responding to changing demands on the Great Wall conservation management systems

Conservation and management capability can be seen as the supply side compared with the pressures of development and increasing tourism on the demand side. Taking economic development, infrastructure construction, social structure and cultural consumption as examples, the speed and scale of change is unimaginable (Table 2). The demand is also varied among different regions, fields and social groups.

On the supply side, a great gap has been formed due to relatively slower reform. The statistics of the whole cultural heritage sector are indicators for the management capacity for the Great Wall. Table 3 shows that with the fast growth of the overall economy in China, public investment in the cultural heritage sector has also grown, but this has not kept pace with the wider economy. The number of restoration projects has grown by only 1.86 times, and visitors by 6.7 times, but these are tiny proportions compared with the total tourist growth of nearly 150 times. The fundamental constraints come from the capacity of the sector. The size of institutions and number of their employees has grown by only 3 times. Together with the low social participation, there is lack of capability to cope with ever demanding conservation and public service workloads.

CHALLENGES OF DECENTRALIZATION TO HOLISTIC CONSERVATION

Even though the Chinese government has exceptional mobilization power, for such huge and open system as the Great Wall it is extremely challenging to balance resource allocation in a still developing country, between conflicting purposes of integrated conservation, economic development, improvement in standards of living and social progress. Decen-

重的体制缺失。长城沿线涉及 15 个省（自治区、直辖市），97 个地级市，404 个县（区、市）。据 2016 年统计，除各级文物行政部门外，共设置或指定 485 个保护管理机构负责长城日常管理工作，其中 43 个为长城专门管理机构[8]，占比仅为 8.9%。与我国其他世界遗产地大都设有专职管理机构不同，这也意味着大部分长城沿线地区没有专门长城管理机构。由于这属于地方政府的职责，国家文物局很难改善这一局面。

（二）基础制度设计加剧分权挑战

属地管理的分权挑战，因为现行两项基本制度——财政分税体制和国有资产体制不合理，而进一步加剧了分权对长城整体保护的威胁。

有大量文献讨论中国财政分权体制下中央和地方政府事权下放和财力上收之间的严重倒挂问题，这一现象在文物保护领域特别突出。在属地管理体制下，中央文物行政部门事权有限，却支配主要财政资源（曾接近 60%）。中央文物保护专项经费只能用于全国重点文物保护单位保护规划编制、本体维修等个别方向，土地征收、基础设施建设、日常管理、巡查、维护、研究和宣传工作等工作完全依赖地方财政，存在严重结构失衡。在中央与地方文物保护已经严重倒挂的财政制度基础上，地方各级文物保护管理机构事权与财力不匹配现象向基层逐级放大[9]，承担主要文物保护管理的县级及以下政府不仅在专门机构设置上严重缺失，而且在日常经费和工作条件上极为薄弱。

长城的情况特别说明问题。以长城在 2005 年至 2014 年经费统计为例，十年间用于长城日常保护管理的经费总计仅有 2639 万元，不足投入总额的 1.3%（图 2）。虽然这一统计数字并不准确，但无论是从日常保护管理经费数额之低，还是从该数字难以准确统计，以及长城日常保护管理险情不断的事实，都说明中央政府资金的巨大投入效果并未有效传导于基层和日常工作，资源配置决策精准度因分权体制下地方政府财力之薄弱而大打折扣。

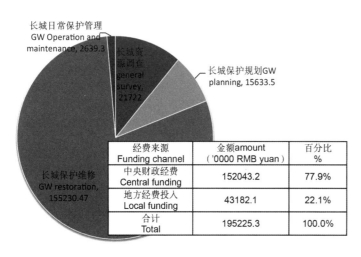

经费来源 Funding channel	金额amount （'0000 RMB yuan）	百分比 %
中央财政经费 Central funding	152043.2	77.9%
地方经费投入 Local funding	43182.1	22.1%
合计 Total	195225.3	100.0%

图 2
2005—2014 年长城保护经费投入统计 [10]
Figure. 2
Budgetary input to the Great Wall between year 2005-2014

在资产管理方面则存在重大法律缺陷。在中国，文物的资产属性仍备受争议。行政管理与资产管理混同，虽然法律规定大部分文物属于国家所有，但并未纳入国有资产管理体系，缺失登记、转让、出租或终止等各个环节的权利义务和程序规定。此外，文物所有权与其附着的土地所有权和使用权是分离的。因此国有文物长城大量分布于不同所有权和使用权的土地之上。在国有资产管理制度空白的现状下，国有文物保护与各类发展、建设、生产生活、交易等活动交融在一起，存在高度信息不对称和激励不相容，破坏风险面广、概率高，监管成本巨大[11]。

tralization is compounded by the problem of lack of coordination in decision-making and institutional systems.

Challenge of decentralized administrative system to holistic governance

The administration system of the Great Wall is typical of that of the whole cultural heritage sector in China. Its key feature can be summarized as 'localized management'. Local governments, mostly municipal and county-level ones, are charged with responsibilities for cultural heritage conservation. Major decisions such as regional planning, institution building, daily management and budgets are all at their discretion. The central government's responsibilities include coordination, licensing for construction work within National Key Protected Units of Cultural Relics (NKPUCR) buffer zones, and providing subsidies for NKPUCR restoration projects.

The shortage of daily management agencies is severe. According to 2016 statistics[8], of the 485 agencies involved in daily management across 404 counties along the Great Wall, only 43 of them are specialized, accounting for 8.9%. This means that for most stretches of the Great Wall there are not dedicated agencies for their daily care, which is quite unusual for World Heritage Sites in China. Since these sites are the responsibility of local authorities, there is little NCHA can do to improve the situation.

Decentralization challenge intensified by underlying policies

The challenges of decentralisation caused by the localized management system, are compounded by two fundamental (and underlying) systems: the fiscal system of tax sharing, and the state-owned property management system.

The reader can discover in the well-developed literature the asymmetry between tasks and resource allocation between national and local-level governments under China's fiscal decentralization system. We will focus on the greater impact on the heritage sector. Because of the localized management system, the centre has responsibility for only a minor percentage of the tasks, but it manages a substantial proportion (up to 60%) of resources (because of centralized taxation). This situation has important consequences. The central government directly finances expenditure for very limited work, including NKPUCR conservation planning and restoration, while the remaining costs such as land acquisition, infrastructure development, daily maintenance, research and public service are all funded by local government. Such asymmetry between tasks and resources increases the closer one gets to frontline management[9]. Those who take most of the day-to-day responsibilities are not only lacking institutional development, they also have small budgets and are under-staffed and under-equipped.

The situation for the Great Wall is telling. Between 2005-2012, the total daily operation and maintenance budget was 26.39 million RMB, accounting for only 1.3% of total input (Fig. 2). Even though these statistics may not be very accurate, they illustrate the largest problem which causes damage and risks to the Great Wall. The sharp increase in investment from the central government has not effectively improved the capacity at the grassroots level.

As for the property management system, there are several big loopholes in the legal framework. The concept of heritage property is still a controversial issue in China. Administrative management and property management tangle together. Though a large part of China's cultural heritage is state-owned, these sites are not included in the state-owned asset management system in relation to registration, transfer, lease, or termination obligations and processes. In addition to the lack of

对比英国哈德良长城，虽然也同样存在行政职能交叉的复杂政府管理部门和央地关系，但在英国，行政管理与资产管理是两套独立体系，英国政府拥有哈德良长城部分最重要的遗产地，并由国家级机构直接管理，起到关键示范和控制作用。例如英格兰遗产信托（English Heritage）代表英国政府直接管理 23 处哈德良长城遗产地，包括沿线 18 座地面尚存塔楼（Turrets）中的 16 座，国民信托（National Trust）也直接拥有并管理着哈德良长城中部约 1100 公顷土地，以及整个南部壕沟的绝大部分[12]，负责保护管理和开放服务。

三、长城整体保护的实践探索

长城的保护历来受到中国政府高度重视。从长城文物保护单位的公布，可以看出长城保护从单体保护走向整体保护的历程。早在 1961 年，山海关、八达岭和嘉峪关长城被公布为第一批全国重点文物保护单位。2001 年相关省（自治区、直辖市）的"长城"被首次整体公布为第五批全国重点文物保护单位。为加强长城整体保护和管理，国家文物局等中国政府部门通过法规和规划、机构建设、国家项目和技术应用等方面做出更有力度的探索。

（一）长城保护制度建设走向整体化

长城是目前为止颁布国家级法规和政策性文件最多的单项遗产。2006 年，国务院公布实施《长城保护条例》，是国务院首次就单项文化遗产保护制定专门性法规。为细化和落实《条例》，国家文物局还针对各地工作中出现的主要问题和实际需要，颁布实施了《长城保护维修工作指导意见》《长城"四有"工作指导意见》《长城保护员管理办法》和《长城执法巡查管理办法》等规范性文件和工作导则，在指导、检查、统一和规范长城沿线各地保护管理工作中发挥了重要作用。

国家文物局于 2006 年即启动长城保护规划编制工作。针对长城遗产的复杂性，长城规划体系包括三个层级：国家级长城保护总体规划，15 个省级（自治区、直辖市）区域规划和重要点段详细规划。规划编制过程也极为复杂，经历了从总到分、再从分到总的几轮整合，一方面确保各级规划目标和原则的统一，另一方面做到因地制宜符合各地针对不同社会自然条件制定不同的行动计划和措施。最终于 2019 年 1 月 24 日，在国务院批准下，国家文化和旅游部与国家文物局联合发布了《长城保护总体规划》。《规划》阐释了长城价值和长城精神，明确了其作为文化景观的属性。《规划》还界定了长城保护的原则、目标、重大任务和管理要求[13]。

（二）强化国家级指导和协调机构建设

为加强长城保护管理的整体协调，《长城保护条例》赋予国家文物局在长城保护管理中的更多职责，除同其他全国重点文物保护单位一样"负责长城整体保护工作，协调、解决长城保护中的重大问题，监督、检查长城所在地各地方的长城保护工作"外，还包括长城认定、会同国务院有关部门制定长城保护总体规划、建立全国长城档案、参观游览区备案等项职能[14]。

在国家文物局部署下，中国文化遗产研究院自 2006 年起设立长城保护研究专门机构和队伍（长城

property management, there is a separation of ownership of immovable cultural heritage in China from the land on which it sits. As a result, the state-owned Great Wall is located mostly on land in different ownership and land use right. This causes severe information asymmetries leading to weak control over conflicting uses, and to weak coordination between heritage management and decision-making processes regarding land-use planning for social and economic development[11].

In comparison with Hadrian's Wall, though the complexity is similar in terms of administrative responsibilities between central and local government, the property management system somehow counteracts the impact. The UK government, which controls many of the most important parts of Hadrian's Wall, and directly manages them, can play a key role in exemplary stewardship. For example, English Heritage, on behalf of the UK government, operates and maintains 23 sites along Hadrian's Wall, including 16 of the 18 visible turrets. The National Trust, empowered by act of Parliament (1907) to preserve natural or historic places for the nation, also directly owns and looks after around 1100 hectares of land, including the fort at Housesteads and 8km of the Wall, and considerable lengths of the Vallum[12].

BEST PRACTICE IN INTEGRATED CONSERVATION OF THE GREAT WALL

The Great Wall has always been a priority for protection and management by the Chinese government at all levels. A trend of integration can be seen through the designation of the Great Wall sites as NKPURCs. In 1961, three important fortifications and strategic passes (Shanhai Pass, Badaling, and Jiayu Pass) were listed as the first batch of NKPUs. In recent years, there has been a trend towards a more integrated vision. In 2001, the Great Wall was listed as a whole as one of the fifth batch of NKPUCRs. To unify conservation and protection of the Great Wall, the central government, including NCHA, has taken more powerful measures to lead integrated management, through legislation and planning, institutional mechanisms, national programmes and the application of technology.

Legislation and planning

Of all the cultural heritage sites in China, the Great Wall is the one that has the highest number of regulations and rules promulgated by the central authorities. In 2006, the State Council introduced the Great Wall Protection Regulation (GWPR). To implement the Regulation, NCHA issued a series of policies and guidelines, including the Guideline for the Four Basic Works of the Great Wall (2014), the Guideline for Restoration of the Great Wall (2014), the Management Rule for the Great Wall Patrollers (2016), and the Rule for the Great Wall Law Enforcement Inspections (2016).

NCHA initiated the Great Wall planning project in 2006. The planning system is designed to work at three-levels: the Master Plan at the national level, 15 regional plans at the provincial, autonomous regions and direct municipalities level, and specific plans for important stretches and areas at the site level. The process itself has also been extremely complicated. Since 2006, in parallel with the national survey, there have been several rounds of bottom-up and top-down coordination within the three-level planning system, to ensure, on the one hand, agreement on unified goals and principles and, on the other hand, differentiated actions catering to the specific needs of different natural, social and management conditions at a continental scale. Most recently, on 24 January 2019, the Great Wall Conservation Master Plan was published by the Ministry of Culture and Tourism (MCT) and NCHA with the approval of the State Council. The plan sets out the values and

项目组），协助国家文物局在专业层面促进和指导各地长城保护工作的开展。为单项文化遗产设置专门业务队伍在全国并不多见。通过多年努力，长城项目组已经初步发展成为长城保护专业管理中心，研究咨询中心和综合数据中心：

长城保护专业管理中心。长城项目组在长城的整体保护、分级管理体制中发挥了关键的承上启下专业作用。通过协助国家文物局开展长城保护规划编制协调、长城保护维修技术方案审核组织、工程现场检查指导组织、专项调研咨询与评估、长城信息系统建设运行、宣传教育、人员培训等工作，一方面为国家长城保护管理提供了有力的专业支持，另一方面同长城沿线各地建立起顺畅的工作机制和合作关系。目前长城项目组已经越来越多地起到了长城保管理工作组织协调的重要作用，全国长城保护专业管理中心的地位初步形成。为促进从事长城保护研究和日常管理机构的合作交流，2018 年成立了长城保护联盟。目前联盟共有 41 家成员单位，既包括中国文化遗产研究院等高校科研机构，八达岭旅游管理委员会等对外开放景区，也包括中国文物保护基金会等社会组织。联盟秘书处设在中国文化遗产研究院。联盟将致力于推动长城全线的旅游推广、文化活动和公众教育。

长城保护学术研究中心。长城项目组依托中国文化遗产研究院综合科研优势，将长城保护专业管理工作与研究相结合，通过开展持续多学科交叉的长城保护管理调研、咨询和研究，比较全面和深入地了解我国长城历史分布、保存现状、保护管理、工程技术特点，形成了不同于传统长城历史研究和专题研究的独特研究方向，重点开展以长城保护管理需求为中心的相关基础研究、应用研究和标准规范研究，取得了一系列长城保护管理研究成果，培养了一支热爱长城、了解长城的综合科研队伍，长城保护研究咨询中心的团队初步形成。

长城综合数据中心。通过长期对数据积累的重视，积累了较为全面、系统、综合的长城数据，包括全国长城历史文献、资源调查数据，长城资源认定数据和长城保护管理业务数据，这些数据全部与认定编码和地理数据挂接，具备查询、检索、统计、辅助决策功能，为国家长城保护管理循征决策、各级长城保护管理和科学研究提供了重要基础，全国长城综合数据中心的框架初步形成。

（三）国家级重大项目组织实施

"十一五"时期，国家文物局组织策划《长城保护工程（2005—2014 年）》。当时，鉴于长城"不可比拟"（方案语，本段同）的重大影响，鉴于长城持续受到"来势凶猛"的"毁灭性"破坏，国家文物局在现行"分段管理"的基础上，加强"整体保护""统一规划"和"科学安排"，得到国务院的认可和支持。前文提到的长城资源调查和认定、《长城保护条例》和长城保护规划制定等都属于该工程的重点内容。另一项重点内容是支持长城全线重要点段抢险修缮，减少长城损坏风险。在 2005 至 2014 年期间，共有 177 项长城保护维修项目立项和实施，分布在长城沿线 15 个省（自治区、直辖市）中的 14 个。这些重大行动得到 中央财政巨额财政资金保障，2005 至 2014 年间共投入中央财政资金 15 亿元。这一工程实施还极大促进了能力建设。除在中国文化遗产研究院设立长城项目组外，长城沿线各相关省（自治区、直辖市）文物行政管理部门负责落实国家文物局长城保护相关工作，组织协调本区域内的长城保护工作，并且通过组织实施长城资源调查、长城保护规划编制等任务，培养锻炼一大批长城保护研究和业务管理专业队伍，成为长城保护研究骨干力量。

significance of the Great Wall as a cultural landscape. It also defines the principles, goals, actions and management requirements of the Great Wall[13].

Strengthening guidance and institutional coordination at national level

To enhance coordination of the Great Wall conservation and management at the national level, NCHA is authorized, through GWPR, to take more responsibilities than it normally does for other KNPUCRs or World Heritage Sites in China. This includes identification, documentation, planning, tourism management, and law enforcement and inspection[14].

To support NCHA in these responsibilities, a dedicated office was established in 2006 within the Chinese Academy of Cultural Heritage (CACH) under the leadership of NCHA. It provides technical consultancy to NCHA, and professional advice to, and coordination among, the regions along the Wall at different levels. It is one of the few institutions that maintains a dedicated team for one specific heritage site at national level. Over the years, the office has developed into a national centre of expertise in co-ordination, academic interest and research, and documentation and information on the Great Wall:

Co-ordination. A Research Studio for the Great Wall (RSGW), developed through the dedicated office for the GWRS programme, has been set up within CACH. It plays a critical role in the integration of conservation under a framework of localized management through professional networks. It supports NCHA in coordination of master plan preparation, assessment of restoration programmes, site inspections, training and public awareness promotion. It also works closely with local agencies and social organizations along the Great Wall and establishes good connections to facilitate the smooth implementation of policies from central government. In order to promote cooperation and partnership working among institutions along the Wall and those involved in conservation, a Great Wall Conservation Alliance was formed in June 2018. There are now 41 members in the Alliance, ranging from public institutions such as CACH, several universities, tourist organizations of important sites open to public (such as the Badaling Tourism Agency), and third sector organisations such as the China Foundation for Cultural Heritage Conservation (CFCHC). Its secretariat is based at CACH. Joint tourist promotion, cultural activities and public education will be undertaken along the whole line of the Wall instead of at just a few famous sites.

Academic and research centre. To take advantage of the multidisciplinary strength of CACH, RSGW has consistently combined technical management work with academic research related to heritage conservation of the Great Wall. A distinctive approach of demand- or problem-oriented research has been developed, in contrast to traditional discipline-based research approaches. A series of consulting reports and guidelines have been published. A dedicated research team has been formed focused on heritage conservation of the Great Wall.

Documentation and information management centre. A comprehensive database for the Great Wall containing historic documents, GWRS data, the Great Wall Verification data and management information generated over 10 years has been accumulated by RSGW which operates a Great Wall Resource Information Management System on behalf NCHA.

Implementation of national programmes

Since the 11th Five-year-plan period, NCHA has launched several major national programmes for conservation and protection of the Great Wall as part of a long-term and integrated strategy.

为加强长城保护的绩效管理，国家文物局于 2016 年和 2017 年连续两次组织长城执法专项督察，重点督察长城沿线省级人民政府和文物行政部门履行长城保护法定职责情况。涉及长城的违法活动也纳入国家文物局 2016—2018 三年违法行动治理计划的重点。

（四）信息技术平台建设带动制度创新

对于长城这样规模巨大而又异常复杂的遗产，长城资源保护管理信息系统建设不仅作为管理工作必不可少，在推动制度建设和制度创新方面也发挥着关键作用。

基于这一考虑，信息技术应用贯穿于长城资源调查、长城资源认定、长城保护规划编制、长城保护工程十年评估、长城监测试点、长城专项督察等各项工作，通过统一长城认定编码关联关系，将长城调查数据、地理数据、长城认定数据和长城保护管理业务数据整合于长城保护管理数据库（图 3）。

目前的长城信息系统数据最为综合、全面、有效，为制度化建设和循证决策奠定基础。长城信息系统在制度创新方面的作用体现在几个方面：

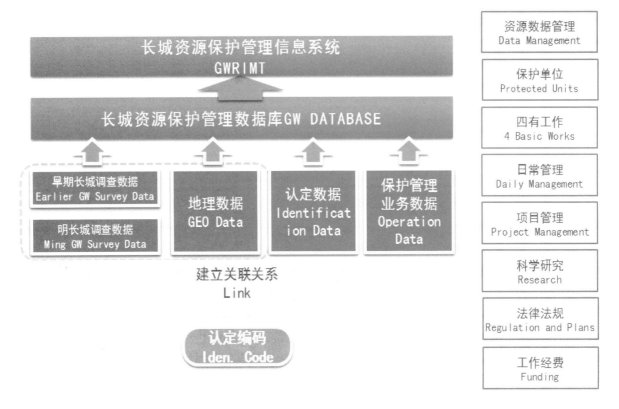

图 3
长城信息系统框架
Fig. 3
Data structure chart of GWRMIS

In 2005, a ten-year Great Wall Conservation Programme (2005-2014) was launched by NCHA supported by the State Council, to "coordinate actions and deploy resources for more integrated conservation on the basis of traditional localized management, in the face of serious threats to the exceptional masterpiece"[15]. It is within this Programme that the GWRS, the promulgation of the GWPR, and the development of the planning system, as mentioned above, were initiated and organized. Another major mission in the Programme is to implement major restoration work on those sections of the Great Wall which are in danger. Between 2005-2014, 177 restoration projects were licensed and implemented in 14 of the 15 provinces ,autonomous regions and direct municipalities. All these major projects were only possible with the support of central fiscal funding. Between 2005-2014 the central government invested 1.5 billion RMB, a substantial increase compared with previous Five-year-plan periods. Another legacy of the Programme is in capacity building. In addition to the RSGW within CACH, a large number of professional staff have been trained during the Programme. These now form the mainstay for daily management of the Great Wall, and for the management of cultural heritage more generally at local level in regions along the Great Wall.

To improve performance, NCHA organized two specialized inspections in 2016 and 2017 to check how the provincial governments were fulfilling their overall responsibilities prescribed by laws and regulations. Illegal activities related to the Great Wall were also identified as the priority during the three-year Law Violation Rectification Action (2016-2018) by NCHA.

Institutional innovation driven by the application of information technology

Given the scale and complexity of the Great Wall, the introduction of information technology in the management of the Great Wall is crucial, not just as a tool, but also as an innovative driving force for improved management.

Since the initiation of the national Great Wall general survey (GWRS), IT has been used throughout the process. A Great Wall Resources Management Information System (GWRMIS) was developed with functions of data (archaeological and geographical, text and multimedia) collection, storage and processing. The development of the GWRMIS continues, to integrate and update as much information as possible from the front-end work of daily management, restoration projects, research projects, and legislation (Fig. 3). The GWRMIS has developed into a comprehensive platform with functions of logging, storage, modification, retrieval, and statistics, to provide information for Great Wall conservation, use, management and research.

Now GWRMIS has the most comprehensive and up-to-date data about the Great Wall in China, providing a firm basis for institutional development and evidence-based decision-making. The role of the GWRMIS in the promotion of institutional innovation is explored in the following areas:

Enhancement of law enforcement and management. Through GWRMIS, the Great Wall Verification system is linked with Protected Units of Cultural Relics (PUCRs) of different levels through the Great Wall Verification Codes (GWVC). This allows better law enforcement and management. In the past, the listings of PUCRs were undertaken separately from Great Wall Verification, resulting in the inconsistent composition of PUCRs related to the Great Wall. This made law enforcement very difficult. During the process of GWRMIS development, under the organization of RSGW, a large amount of work has been undertaken by the IT agency and managers from regions along the Great Wall to define a clear relationship between each PUCR and GWVC. For example, the NKPUCR of the Great Wall on the 5th batch list includes 9883 km of

74

实现长城依法管理精细化。通过长城信息系统，长城认定编码将长城资源认定与文物保护单位挂接，成为长城依法管理精细化直接推力。过去，长城各级文物保护单位公布与长城资源认定独立开展，长城各级文物保护单位数量多、构成不明确，为长城执法带来极大困扰。长城信息系统建设过程中，在长城项目组组织下，经过技术公司和长城沿线各地长城管理人员大量细致工作，明确了每个长城保护单位与长城认定编码的对应关系。例如，第五批全国重点文物保护单位长城（包括第六、七批合并）共包括墙体 9883 千米，烽火台 2901 座，关堡 769 处，相关遗存 9 处，其他单体建筑 9182 处。

促进长城保护管理工作决策科学化。国家文物局在长城保护管理配套制度中，对长城保护维修项目申报、长城保护界桩设置等提出明确编码要求。通过长城信息系统平台，一方面可以帮助文物行政部门管理时通过编码快速查询相关长城本体和环境状况，另一方面实现长城保护管理业务数据的有效积累。这些业务数据积累实现了对长城全线保护管理状况的初步掌握。例如通过长城信息系统，定量分析出长城保护工程十年实施以来各方面工作的进展情况，指出在省级以上文物保护单位公布、"四有"工作、参观游览区管理等方面的不足 [15]，为近年国家文物局开展的长城专项督察工作中制定督察重点内容提供直接依据，初步实现局部循证决策。

推动长城保护管理工作报告制度建设。作为服务型政府，向社会报告文物保护工作成果义不容辞，也是文物工作由具体事务管理向目标和结果监督控制转变的体现。长城信息系统建设，实现对分布于15 个省域长城遗产各个方面工作整体掌握。2016 年底，国家文物局首次向社会发布《中国长城保护报告》，其中包含大量数据展示长城保护管理工作成果，长城信息系统功不可没。

结　语

长城整体保护的意义和使命，无比荣光。长城整体保护的困难与挑战，举世无双。对应挑战，中国各级政府和社会各界已经进行的大量探索只是万里征程的起步。

中国正在下决定实施全面深化体制改革，"更加注重改革的系统性、整体性、协同性，加快发展社会主义市场经济、民主政治、先进文化、和谐社会、生态文明" [16]。在开启新征程的新时代，长城整体保护管理也应打破学科偏见和行业局限的路径依赖，提升到一个崭新水平。在国家体制改革框架内，长城保护应当实施重大政策调整和国家战略行动部署。

在政策调整方面，长城作为北方长城地带的标志性地物，应当纳入区域经济、政治、文化、社会和生态建设"五位一体"总体布局，也应当为"五位一体"总体布局做出贡献。应当树立相互关联的三大主题目标：保护、共享和发展。这更好实现和平衡这三大目标，性格财政、土地和资产管理体制为当务之急。

在行动计划方面长城议题在学术研究、技术攻关、区域协同和全民共享等方面都具有重大国家战略意义和联合行动现实需求，建议国家实施以下重大行动计划：

考古长城。加强长城遗产实证研究和价值挖掘，对已有长城资源调查数据的挖掘分析，组织实施长城区域综合考古调查研究，配合长城保护维修工程开展考古清理研究，加强长城考古资料集成汇总研究

Wall, 2901 beacon towers, 769 fortified passes and fortress, 9 related facilities and 9182 other individual structures.

Improvement of decision-making in conservation of the Great Wall. GWVC information is required by NCHA when restoration programmes are submitted for approval and for funding. GWVC information also has to be marked on boundary poles. Through GWRMIS, the relevant Wall sites and their environmental conditions can be found quickly through GWVC, while further information such as restoration programmes and boundary poles can be documented into the system. The accumulation of operational data provides a basic overall picture of the whole Great Wall. For example, progress over the last 10 years in implementing the Great Wall Conservation Programme (2005-2014) has been analysed quantitatively through GWRMIS. Weaknesses found in the review, in PUCR listing above provincial level, in meeting the requirements of the '4 Haves'[1] and the management of tourist sites, are alerted to NCHA. These themes have subsequently become priorities for specialised inspections on the GWPR.

Enabling reporting mechanisms on conservation of the Great Wall. As a service- and performance-oriented government department, we have to report publicly the results of our work on cultural heritage conservation. The development of GWRMIS facilitates the documentation of work in 15 province-level regions along the Great Wall. At the end of 2016, NCHA issued, for the first time, a China Great Wall Conservation Report[15] to the public, including some quantitative data depicting achievements in conservation of the Great Wall. This would not have been possible without the support of GWRMIS.

GWRMIS plays an important role in the integrated management of the Great Wall. Most of the statistics in this paper would not be available without this powerful system. Now NCHA has access to a better overall picture of comprehensive and updated information from numerous sites along the huge span of the Wall, to enable it to issue licences, carry out inspections, and make reports in a more efficient way.

CONCLUDING REMARKS

The protection and conservation of the Great Wall, a gigantic, complex and evolving structure created over 2000 years of construction, is most challenging. Recent innovations in practices and approaches are just the beginning of a long journey.

China is determined to deepen reform, in a comprehensive systematic, integrated and coordinated way, promoting development of the socialist market economy, democratic politics, an advanced culture, a harmonious society and ecological progress[16]. On the journey of the 'New Era', the integrated conservation and management of the Great Wall will be upgraded to a new level, encouraging ever greater collaboration between different sectors and disciplines. In the course of this new round of reform, the conservation and management of the Great Wall will look strategically at policy reform, and the carrying out of major initiatives.

More widely, the Great Wall, a prominent landmark across a vast northern belt of China, should be considered

---

1 'The 4 Haves' are the four legal prerequisites for designated PUCRs in China as set out in the '1982 Law of the People's Republic of China on the Protection of Cultural Relics'. They require each site to have: demarcated boundaries; an official plaque stating its name, its level and date of designation; an archive cataloguing its protected elements and activities; a dedicated organization or person(s) responsible for its daily management. (Editors' note)

与典型点段微观研究结合，揭开长城悠久丰富历史中蕴含的巨大宝藏，为长城价值认知和保护维修展示传播提供科学支撑。

监测长城。继续推动技术创新带动制度创新，实施监测长城重大攻关计划。全面及时监控长城遗产变化状况与风险水平，是长城保护循证决策的基本依据，是从长城点段被动抢险向整体主动保护转型的基础工作，通过互联网、大数据、人工智能以及宏观、中观、微观技术手段，整合长城沿线文物保护管理力量和社会资源，提升长城保护日常监测、维护、记录、管理工作能力建设水平。

生态长城。长城是中华大地千百年形成的人与自然环境联合工程奇迹，对自然生态、人居环境、城乡格局演变产生深远影响。长城保护离不开生态保护，生态保护需要尊重历史环境。实施长城景观保护与修复，将长城保护与国家实施的生态文明建设、国土空间规划、区域协调发展、乡村振兴、国家公园体制改革等战略[17]统筹协调，以长城为主题，推动长城地带历史文化与自然环境生态相融合的综合发展模式，建设美丽长城家园。

魅力长城。长城是国际上认知度极高的遗产地[18]，也是外国人认知度最高的中国文化符号[19]。然而长城品牌影响力只集中于少数几处长城旅游景区，长城文化品牌和国家形象的深厚内涵和丰富资源远远没有得到有效发挥。实施长城文化旅游品牌国家工程，通过长城统一标识系统建设、国家长城步道建设、长城解说系统建设、互联网＋长城等丰富手段，促进考古长城、监测长城和生态长城工程成果转化和品牌扩散，让更多长城走近更多民众。

通过政策改革和组织实施重大行动计划，愿长城的差异性与分权不再是长城整体保护管理的威胁与挑战，而是长城丰富多彩生机焕发的动力与源泉，助国实现"传承弘扬长城精神，宣传推介长城文化，保护长城建筑遗产，延续长城文化景观"[20]。

holistically in relation to all regional economic, political, cultural, social and ecological policy and development. Three inter-linked goals have emerged through decades of learning about protection of the Great Wall and its changing context: protection, sharing, and development. To achieve and balance the goals better, it is imperative to reform policies and the institutional system, including the fiscal, land and property management systems.

Major initiatives in academic research, technological advancement, regional collaboration and public enjoyment at the national level should be developed, providing the momentum for comprehensive reform of conservation and management of the Great Wall.

The Archaeology of the Wall. A priority is to strengthen archaeological research on the material remains of the Great Wall and evidence-based analysis of their significance. There is also an opportunity for systematic archaeological research using existing survey data, regional comprehensive surveys, archaeological work during restoration projects, and recording of individual sites. Collating all this information into the central database will enable awareness raising, promotion, restoration and interpretation work.

Monitoring the Wall. A priority here is to promote technology-driven institutional innovation through major monitoring programmes. Monitoring the status and risk factors of the Great Wall in a timely and comprehensive manner is the basis for good conservation decision-making, and for a move from the reactive rescue of individual sites to proactive holistic preservation. Through the combined application of the internet, big data and artificial intelligence, professional staff and social resources along sections of the Great Wall should be better integrated, building capacity during daily inspection, maintenance, documentation and management.

The Environment of the Wall. The Great Wall is a masterpiece of the combined work of man and nature, which has evolved across a vast continent over the last two millennia. It affects, and is being affected by, the natural ecology, human habitats, and the development of rural-urban settlement patterns. The protection of the Great Wall cannot be achieved without the protection of its environment, and at the same time, ecological protection needs to respect the historic context of the Wall. Conservation of the Great Wall need to be integrated with national ecological initiative, national territory planning, regional coordinated development, rural regeneration and national park reform, as outlined in national policies[17]. In the Great Wall corridor regions, we should promote sustainable and comprehensive development, combining the historic environment with the natural and ecological environment, to build a beautiful landscape along the Great Wall.

Enabling learning about the Value the Wall. The Great Wall is one of the most recognized World Heritage Sites[18], and also the most recognized cultural symbol of China globally[19]. However, the brand perception is based on a few famous tourist sites. Its full meanings and rich historic evidence have not yet been fully explored and explained. We should implement a national programme of development of the cultural and tourist brand of the Great Wall to explain more widely what can be learned from archaeological research, monitoring and the wider environment. Our aim is to bring the Wall closer to more people through a unified branding, a national trail, an interpretation strategy, and internet platforms.

With policy reform and the implementation of major initiatives, it is hoped the complications of heterogeneity and decentralization will become the stimulus and inspiration for celebrating the rich culture and vitality of the Great Wall. Our aim is "to pass on and enrich the spirit of the Great Wall, promote and enhance the culture of the Great Wall, preserve the architectural heritage of the Great Wall, and Revitalize the landscape of the Great Wall"[20].

参考文献
Bibliography

[1] 国家文物局 . 长城认定手册 [Z].2012.

National Cultural Heritage Administration. The Great Wall Resource Verification Handbook. At the News Release Ceremony for the Great Wall Survey and Identification Results in Beijing，publicized on June 5, 2012.

[2] 段清波 . 城和长城：中华文明的见证 [N]. 光明日报，2017-03-26(7).

Duan, Q.B.　"Walls and the Great Wall: Testimony to the Chinese Civilization."　Guangming Daily, March 26, 2017(7).

[3] 白音查干 . 战国时期燕、赵、秦长城新论 . 内蒙古社会科学（汉文版）[J]，1999(9).

Baiyan Tsagaan.　"New Study on Yan, Zhao and Qin Walls during the Warring Period."　Inner Mongolia Social Science (Chinese Edition), 1999(9).

[4] 李一丕 . 河南楚长城研究 [J]. 文博，2014(5).

　　Li, Y.P.　"Research on Chu Great Wall in Henan."　Wenbo, 2014(5).

[5] 赵海东，李玉波 .9 成内蒙古人不知内蒙古有长城 万里长城如何保护 [N]. 中国青年报，2008-11-11(法制社会版).

Zhao, H.D., and Li, Y.B.　"90% of residents in the Inner Mongolia unaware of existence of the Great Wall in the region."　China Youth Daily, Nov 11, 2008.

[6] 国家文物局计财处 . 一九九〇年文物事业统计资料 [Z].1991.

National Cultural Heritage Administration Office. Cultural Heritage Sector Statistics 1990. 1991 internal report.

[7] 国家文物局办公室 . 文物事业统计资料 2015 年 [Z].2016.

　　National Cultural Heritage Administration Office. Cultural Heritage Sector Statistics 2015. 2016 internal report.

[8] 中国文化遗产研究院 . 爱我中华 护我长城——长城保护 2006-2016[M]. 北京：文物出版社，2017: 152.

Chinese Academy of Cultural Heritage. Love China Protect the Great Wall - Conservation of the Great Wall 2006-2016. Beijing: Cultural Relics Publishing, 2017: 152.

[9] 于冰 . 大遗址保护财政制度需求特征与现状问题分析 [J]. 中国文物科学研究，2015(1).

Yu, B.　"Demand and Supply Analysis for Large Archaeological Sites Conservation Fiscal System."　China Cultural Relics Scientific Research Journal, 2015(1).

[10] 中国文化遗产研究院 . 长城保护工程（2005-2014）总结评估报告 [R].2016.

National Cultural Heritage Administration. The Great Wall Conservation Program (2005-2014). 2016.

[11] 于冰 . 试析大遗址保护文物产权管理制度 [J]. 中国文物科学研究，2014(2).

Yu, B. "Analysis on the Property Right System of Large Archaeological Sites." China Cultural Relics Scientific Research Journal, 2014(2).

[12] Hadrian's Wall World Heritage Site Management Plan Committee. Frontier of the Roman Empire World Heritage Site Hadrian's Wall Management Plan 2008-2014. 2015:23.

哈德良长城世界遗产管理计划委员会 . 哈德良长城世界遗产地罗马边疆管理计划 2008-2014.2015:23.

[13] 文化和旅游部，国家文物局 . 长城保护总体规划 .2019 年 1 月 24 日发布 .

Ministry of Culture and Tourism, NCHA. The Great Wall Conservation Master Plan. Jan 24, 2019.

[14] 国务院 . 长城保护条例 [Z].2006-09-20.

The State Council. Regulations on the Protection of the Great Wall. Sep 20, 2006.

[15] 中国文化遗产研究院 . 长城保护工程（2005—2014）总结评估报告 [R].2016-11-30.

http://www.sach.gov.cn/art/2016/11/30/art_722_135294.html.

National Cultural Heritage Administration. China Great Wall Conservation Report. published on Nov 30, 2016.

http://www.sach.gov.cn/art/2016/11/30/art_722_135294.html.

[16] 中共中央关于全面深化改革若干重大问题的决定，2013 年 11 月 12 日中国共产党第十八届中央委员会第三次全体会议通过 .

Central Committee of the Communist Party of China on Some major Issues Concerning Comprehensively Deepening the Reform. Adopted at the Third Plenary Session of the 18th Central Committee of the Communist Party of China on November 12, 2013.

[17] 习近平 . 决胜全面建成小康社会 夺取新时代中国特色社会主义伟大胜利——在中国共产党第十九次全国代表大会上的报告，2017-10-18.

Xi, J.P. Secure a Decisive Victory in Building a Moderately Prosperous Society in All Respects and Strive for the Great Success of Socialism with Chinese Characteristics for a New Era. Delivered at the 19th National Congress of CP. October 18, 2017.

[18] Eurostat. Big data pilot project on the use of Wikipedia page views on World Heritage Sites[EB/OL].

欧洲统计局 . 关于世界遗产地维基百科页面浏览量使用的大数据试点项目 .

http://ec.europa.eu/eurostat/documents/7894008/8031877/Pages+from+KS-04-15-737-EN-N.pdf.

[19] 诸葛亚寒 . 长城是外国青年认知度最高的中国文化符号 [N]. 中国青年报，2016-6-20(4).

Zhuge, Y.H. "The Great Wall is the Most Recognized Cultural Symbol of China among Foreign Youngsters." China Youth Daily, June 20, 2016.

[20] 文化和旅游部，国家文物局 . 长城保护总体规划 [R].2019 年 1 月 24 日发布 .

Ministry of Culture and Tourism, NCHA. The Great Wall Conservation Master Plan. 2019.

HADRIAN'S WALL, THE UPPER GERMAN-RAETIAN LINES AND THE FRONTIERS OF THE ROMAN EMPIRE WORLD HERITAGE SITE(S)

C. Sebastian Sommer

Bayerisches Landesamt für Denkmalpflege - Munich - Germany

German Limes Commission - Bad Homburg/Saalburg - Germany

Abstract

The original concept of the Frontiers of the Roman Empire World Heritage Site was that of a transnational serial nomination. Based on the 1987 inscription of Hadrian's Wall, the Upper German-Raetian Limes in Germany and the Antonine Wall in Scotland were inscribed 2005 and 2008 respectively as components of the WHS. However, this concept is not feasible for further extensions. After a Thematic Study the fragmentation of the European Roman frontiers into separate parts had to be accepted. At present a nomination of 'Frontiers of the Roman Empire - The Danube Limes' is under evaluation. The paper also gives a short description of the Upper German-Raetian Limes.

Keywords: Frontiers of the Roman Empire, Upper German-Raetian Limes, The Danube Limes, Thematic Study

Since 2005 Hadrian's Wall in England is no longer the only Roman frontier installation on the UNESCO World Heritage List. In that summer the Upper German-Raetian Limes in Germany was added to the list. However, that was not a national inscription, but rather - after a lot of international communication - an international approach. In this context the World Heritage Committee recommended 'that the nomination (of the Upper German-Raetian Limes) be seen as the second phase of a possible wider, phased, serial transboundary nomination to encompass remains of the Roman frontiers around the Mediterranean Region'[1] of which Hadrian's Wall was the first component and the Upper German-Raetian Limes the second. In 2008 the Antonine Wall in Scotland was added as the third, resulting in the site number 430ter[2].

The Upper German-Raetian Limes could also be called the great wall of Germany. It connects the rivers Rhine and Danube in a line 550km long. In its last phase in the Roman province of Upper Germany a wall and a ditch formed a continuous barrier, whereas in the province of Raetia that function was taken by a wall approximately four feet wide and 10 feet high. Timber towers, later replaced by stone towers visible from one another at distances of 500-900m apart monitored the line. Regularly spaced forts with a garrison of 500 to 800 men, sometimes mounted, provided the soldiers for that supervision and for potential conflicts[3]. However, Germans as possible enemies settled more than 60km away from the Limes and at least

哈德良长城、上日耳曼—雷蒂亚界墙及世界遗产地"罗马帝国边界"
HADRIAN'S WALL, THE UPPER GERMAN-RAETIAN LINES AND THE FRONTIERS OF THE ROMAN EMPIRE WORLD HERITAGE SITE(S)

81

哈德良长城、上日耳曼—雷蒂亚界墙及世界遗产地"罗马帝国边界"

C. 塞巴斯蒂安·索默

（巴伐利亚州遗产保护办公室，德国慕尼黑；德国界墙委员会，德国巴特洪堡及萨尔堡）

摘　要

"罗马帝国边界"世界遗产地的最初构想是形成一个统一的系列跨国界遗产。1987 年哈德良长城列入世界遗产名录，随后德国上日耳曼—雷蒂亚界墙和安东尼墙分别于 2005 年与 2008 年列入名录。然而，这种构想对于遗产的后续扩展申报缺乏可操作性。通过专题研究表明，对欧洲古罗马边界只能采取分段单独申报方式。当前，"罗马帝国边界——多瑙河界墙"正在接受评估。本文亦将简要介绍上日耳曼—雷蒂亚界墙。

关键词：世界遗产地"罗马帝国边界"　上日耳曼—雷蒂亚界墙　多瑙河界墙　专题研究

自 2005 年起，英格兰哈德良长城不再是唯一列入联合国教科文组织世界遗产名录（the UNESCO World Heritage List）的罗马边界建筑遗存。那年夏天，德国上日耳曼—雷蒂亚界墙（the Upper German-Raetian Limes）加入其中。然而，这次申报并非单独的国家行动，而是经过多次国际协商，更具有国际性质。在此背景下，世界遗产委员会（the World Heritage Committee）建议"将上日耳曼—雷蒂亚界墙视作范围更广的、系列性和阶段性跨国申报的第二阶段，该跨国申报还将包括环地中海地区所有罗马边界遗迹"[1]，其中哈德良长城属于第一阶段，上日耳曼—雷蒂亚界墙属于第二阶段。2008 年，苏格兰安东尼长城（the Antonine Wall）作为第三阶段列入世界遗产，遗址编号 430ter[2]。

上日耳曼—雷蒂亚界墙全长 550 公里，连接莱茵河和多瑙河，可谓德国的长城。建成后，古罗马上日耳曼行省境内，长城由一道墙与一道壕沟组成了绵延的屏障；在雷蒂亚行省，屏障则是由宽 1.2192 米，高 3.048 米的墙构成 1。长城沿线每隔 500—900 米建木质塔楼（tower），处于彼此可视范围，对墙体防线实施监察，后木塔改建为石塔。在等距离间隔还建有要塞，每座要塞驻扎 500 到 800 士兵或骑兵负责监察，并为可能发生的冲突提供保障 [3]。然而，潜在敌人日耳曼人的定居点距离界墙有 60 公里之多，至少在界墙筑成后的头 100 年（即公元 2 世纪），没有武装摩擦的记录。因此，精心构筑的长城真实功能为何，多年来争论不断。最近我提出，根据今日罗马市马可柱（Marcus'2 Column）底部图案所表现的雷蒂亚界墙，其最初形式为木质栅栏，因此界墙的功能更可能是保护（比如罗马子民或罗马帝国）而非防御。这种现象至今仍与民族主义方式相类似：在极度夸大外部威胁

1　宽约 1.2 米，高约 3 米——译者注。

2　马可·奥勒留，Marcus Aurelius （公元 161-180 年），罗马帝国皇帝，其中公元 161-169 年与维鲁斯皇帝共治——译者注。

through the first 100 years of the Limes' existence, in the 2nd century AD, there are no indications of skirmishes. Therefore, there is a long debate about the function of these elaborate installations. Fairly recently, I proposed that at least the Raetian Limes, which originated with a continuous palisade, is shown at the base of Marcus' Column in Rome, indicating that it was less built against someone, but rather for someone, i.e. the people of Rome (and the Roman Empire). This would be comparable with a number of modern nationalistic approaches, where the external threat is exaggerated vastly and measures proposed and taken primarily aim at internal affairs[4].

Der Zerstörungsprozess durch Zerfall, Erosion und Eingriffe des Menschen am Beispiel einer Kastellumwehrung.

Fig. 1

Fig. 1 Use, deterioration, recycling and reuse of archaeological monuments, here the example of a Roman fort (© Becker et al. 2001, p. 30).

图1

对考古遗址的使用、损毁、循环使用和再利用，图中示例为一罗马要塞（版权：Becker et al. 2001, p. 30[5]）

At present a good part of the Limes and its installations are in a ruinous state above ground. Others have been 'recycled' and the land used differently - with the result that nothing is now visible (Fig. 1). With the goal of a maximum preservation in the last decades, primarily non-destructive methods - aerial photography in arable land, geophysics and in recent years airborne laser scanning (Fig. 2) - have been used as means of scientific research. Excavations have been kept to a minimum and are usually only executed where unavoidable construction threatens parts of the monument.

Our main concern these days is the management of the monument and its elements. Besides the general problem of preservation we are dealing with accessibility for the general public, information about the sites and dissemination of knowledge (Fig. 3). A major achievement is the German Limes Road, a tourist route that connects all the major places along the Limes. It was followed many years ago by a bicycle route even closer to the line of the Limes, and in the last few years we have established a

哈德良长城、上日耳曼—雷蒂亚界墙及世界遗产地 "罗马帝国边界"
HADRIAN'S WALL, THE UPPER GERMAN-RAETIAN LINES AND THE FRONTIERS OF THE ROMAN EMPIRE WORLD HERITAGE SITE(S)

83

的同时，所提出并采取的举措则主要针对内部事务 [4]。

当前，上日耳曼—雷蒂亚界墙及其建筑的地面以上有相当部分处于废墟状态。其余部分被"再利用"，土地被用于不同功能，导致遗址已经不可见（图1）。过去几十年，专家已采用非破坏性手段为主的多种方式进行科学研究，包括对耕地进行航空摄影（aerial photography in arable land）、地球物理学手段（geophysics）等，近年来还启用机载激光扫描（airborne laser scanning，图2），目标是实现最大程度的保护。考古发掘则被降到最低限度，一般而言只有必须实施建设项目危及界墙遗迹的情况下才进行发掘。

近年来，我们的工作重心在于古迹及其构成要素的管理。除了常规的保护工作外，我们也开展提高公众参观便利性、遗产地信息研究和知识传播方面的工作（图3）。一项重大成果当属"德国界墙之路"（the German Limes Road），这是一条旅游线路，连接界墙沿线所有重要节点。设立"界墙之路"后，多年前还开辟了一条自行车线路，距离墙体更近；前几年，还沿界墙全线修建了步道，往往紧靠遗迹，有时甚至直接设在墙体上。其主要目标曾经是，现在仍然是增加当地公众参与度。理想是希望各地居民都以主人翁心态对待遗迹。然而，这样也会对遗迹带来特殊压力。为适应旅游业需要，我们需要重建或部分重建多处塔楼、城门和墙体——实为新建。因此古迹真实性和完整性存在突出问题（图4）。

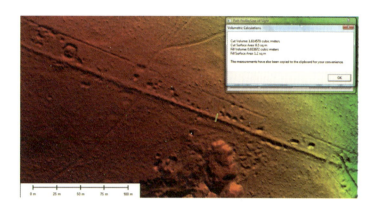

Fig. 2
Airborne laser scan of the Raetian Wall east of Zandt. Visible are the thin line of the earlier palisade, the remains of the stone wall, accompanied by small quarry pits, traces of a timber tower with its sub-rectangular ditch and the irregular traces of the lower parts of a later stone tower (© Bayerisches Landesamt für Denkmalpflege/H. Kerscher).
图 2
对赞特以东雷蒂亚界墙的机载激光扫描。图中可见早期木栅栏的细线，石墙遗迹，周边小型采石坑遗迹，一座木哨楼及其圆角矩形壕沟的痕迹，和一处形状不规则的晚期石哨楼底部的痕迹（巴伐利亚州遗产保护办公室: H. Kerscher 提供）

Fig. 3
Presentation of the Roman fort Ruffenhofen and its surroundings as non-destructive plantation (© Bayerisches Landesamt für Denkmalpflege: K. Leidorf)
图 3
罗马要塞鲁芬霍芬及其周边非破坏性的种植园（巴伐利亚州遗产保护办公室: K. Leidorf 提供）

continuous footpath over the whole length of the Limes, often next to the remains, sometimes even directly on them. A major goal was, and is, engagement of the local population. Ideally, they should consider the monument as their own everywhere. However, this may lead to a particular kind of pressure on the monument. Due to specific tourist demands we now have to deal with a number of (partial) reconstructions of towers, gates and sections of wall (which are in fact new buildings). Here the question of authenticity and integrity arises prominently (Fig. 4).

Following the proposal of the World Heritage Committee with the inscription of the Upper German Raetian Limes, the intention of not only the British and German colleagues but also archaeologists and heritage managers in the whole of Europe was to gradually inscribe all the frontiers of the Roman Empire in Europe and eventually in the Near East and North Africa as parts of the 'Frontiers of the Roman Empire World Heritage Site'.

This was proposed to be defined as consisting of the line(s) of the frontier at the height of the Empire from Trajan to Septimius Severus (about AD 100 to 200), and the military installations of different periods which are on that line. The installations include fortresses, forts, towers, the limes road, artificial barriers and immediately associated civil structures'[6]. Most States Parties in Europe included their elements on their Tentative Lists, followed in 2012 by Tunisia with the 'Limes du Sud tunisien'. The intriguing idea behind this was a final World Heritage Site covering three continents, based on intensive transnational cooperation, dealing with the monuments under common management principles, promoting coordinated development and advancing international research.

However, times are changing and with this come different rules and regulations. Following the Ittingen Report[7] the multiple addition of national or binational components for serial sites seems not acceptable any more. Instead, a fragmentation of the Frontiers of the Roman Empire was proposed and a Thematic Study suggested, in line with the 'Silk Road approach'. This Thematic Study was written by a small international writing team within nine months, after incredibly fast provision of data on all potential sites from colleagues of all relevant States Parties in Europe[8]. The Thematic Study dealt with the different elements in North Africa, the Near East and in Europe, but concentrated for the time being on the European sites in detail, due to the present challenges and unrest in the other parts. In particular, the study looked at which types of ancient structures the potential sites may represent and their contribution to an overall picture. Importantly, the sites were selected according to their preservation and management possibilities. Additionally, within the nomination strategy different sections of the European Limes were considered in relation to potential statements of Outstanding Universal Value. In the 2017 meeting of the World Heritage Committee the Thematic Study with its nomination strategy was acclaimed and considered a good example for complex transnational World Heritage approaches[9].

Relying on the Thematic Study and its nomination strategy, in 2017 we wrote a nomination dossier for a new World Heritage Site 'Frontiers of the Roman Empire - The Danube Limes' under the lead of Austria, comprising a length of Roman frontier of almost 1000km along the western part of

哈德良长城、上日耳曼—雷蒂亚界墙及世界遗产地"罗马帝国边界"
HADRIAN'S WALL, THE UPPER GERMAN-RAETIAN LINES AND THE FRONTIERS OF THE ROMAN EMPIRE WORLD HERITAGE SITE(S)

85

世界遗产委员会将上日耳曼—雷蒂亚界墙列为遗产之后，不仅是英国和德国同行，全欧洲的考古学家与遗产管理者都有意渐次将整个欧洲的罗马帝国边界列为"罗马帝国边界世界遗产地"（the frontiers of the Roman Empire），并最终扩展至近东及北非。

在原来的方案中，"包括帝国鼎盛期从图拉真皇帝（Trajan）到塞维鲁皇帝（Septimius Severus）（年代跨度为约公元 100 年到 200 年）期间的各地界墙及沿线不同时期修筑的军事建筑。这些建筑包括大小要塞（fortresses and forts）、塔楼、边界道路（limes road）、人工篱障（aritificial barriers）以及直接相关的民用设施"[6]。欧洲成员国大多都将各自的边界遗址纳入本国《世界文化遗产预备名单》，之后在 2012 年，突尼斯也将"南突尼斯界墙"（Limes du Sud tunisien）纳入预备名单。其最终设想的世界遗产地将横跨三大洲，各国间紧密合作，在共同管理原则下管理遗迹，推进联合开发，增强国际研究。

然而，时代在改变，很多规则制度也在改变。《伊廷根报告》[7] 之后，由多国或两国多次对系列遗产地进行扩展申报的模式似乎行不通了。相反，报告建议采用"丝绸之路模式"，对罗马帝国边界进行拆分申报，并建议开展专题研究（the Thematic Study）。专题研究由一支小规模国际团队历时九个月编成，期间欧洲相关成员国的同行以惊人速度贡献出所有潜在遗产地数据[8]。专题研究涉及北非、近东及欧洲的不同遗迹，但限于当前面临的种种限制，加之部分地区局势动荡，研究仍只重点详述欧洲的遗产地。研究特别关注潜在遗产地代表哪种类型的古代建筑，以及在整体中发挥的作用。值得一提的是挑选遗产地的标准在于它们的保护和管理潜力。另外，对欧洲界墙不同段的申报策略以其潜在"突出普遍价值"为基准。2017 年世界遗产委员会会议上，该专

Fig. 4

Raetian Wall at Erkertshofen. 'Reconstruction' of a Roman watchtower and parts of the wall (© Bayerisches Landesamt für Denkmalpflege: C. S. Sommer)

图 4

赖谢茨霍芬的雷蒂亚界墙"重建"的罗马瞭望塔和部分界墙墙体（巴伐利亚州遗产保护办公室：C. 塞巴斯蒂安·索默 提供）

the river Danube, with 164 Component Parts in 98 Clusters in the territories of Germany (Bavaria), Austria, Slovakia and Hungary. The nomination was submitted by Hungary in January 2018 and is currently under evaluation. According to the nomination strategy it is intended that, after inscription, the nomination is followed by a significant extension (including an extension of the OUV) through the elements of the eastern Danube Limes within the territories of Croatia, Serbia, Bulgaria and Romania. Separate nominations of the Lower German Limes in The Netherlands and Germany and the Dacian Limes in Romania are presently also under preparation.

As if this is not 'crazy' enough we still believe in an all-embracing Frontiers of the Roman Empire World Heritage Site. To keep this idea alive, we intend to organize the international management of each of the different World Heritage Sites in similar ways following the system established for the existing World Heritage Site. For official affairs there is an Intergovernmental Committee, with representatives from each State Party, while management will be overseen by a Management Group. Here the site supervisors and others responsible for the management of the sites will come together annually at different parts of the respective World Heritage Site to see examples of, and to exchange best practice. In case of the inscription of several WHS 'Frontiers of the Roman Empire' a 'World Heritage Cluster' is proposed to form the basis for exchange across those different World Heritage Sites.

哈德良长城、上日耳曼—雷蒂亚界墙及世界遗产地"罗马帝国边界"
HADRIAN'S WALL, THE UPPER GERMAN-RAETIAN LINES AND THE FRONTIERS OF THE ROMAN EMPIRE WORLD HERITAGE SITE(S)

87

题研究及所提出的申报策略得到赞同，并列为处理复杂跨国世界遗产的优秀范例[9]。

在该专题研究与申报策略基础上，由奥地利牵头，我们为新世界遗产地"罗马帝国边界——多瑙河界墙"编写了申报文本。罗马帝国边界——多瑙河界墙全长近1000公里，绵延多瑙河西段，有164个组成部分，形成98个片区，分布于德国（巴伐利亚）、奥地利、斯洛伐克和匈牙利。申请于2018年1月由匈牙利提交，目前正在评估当中。根据申报策略，在该遗产申报成功后，将进行大规模扩展（其"突出普遍价值"也将扩展），以涵盖克罗地亚、塞尔维亚、保加利亚和罗马尼亚境内的多瑙河界墙东段。荷兰和德国境内的下日耳曼界墙（the Lower German Limes）、罗马尼亚境内的大夏界墙（the Dacian Limes）也在进行筹备，将分别申报。

好象这些工作还不够"疯狂"，我们仍然憧憬一个包括所有遗迹的世界遗产地"罗马帝国边界"。为推进这一理想，我们准备仿照现有世界遗产地体系，联络各个罗马帝国世界遗产地组建国际管理组织。该组织中，"政府间委员会"与各成员国代表将负责官方事务，而实际管理由"管理组"执行。遗产地管理人员及其他遗产地管理负责人每年都将各地轮流汇聚，观摩优秀范例，交流最佳实践。鉴于"罗马帝国边界"将由多个世界遗产地组成，提议组建"世界遗产片区"（World Heritage Cluster），为不同世界遗产地之间的交流奠定基础。

参考文献
Bibliography

[1] WHC. WHC-05/29.COM/22, Decision 29 COM 8B.46. 2005.

世界遗产中心 .WHC-05/29.COM/22, 29 号决议 COM 8B.46[Z].2005. http://whc.unesco.org/archive/2005/whc05-29com-22e.pdf.

[2] WHC. WHC-08/32.COM/24Rev, Decision 32 COM 8B.40. 2009.

世界遗产中心 .WHC-08/32.COM/24Rev,32 号决议 COM 8B.40[Z].2009.

http://whc.unesco.org/archive/2008/whc08-32com-24reve.pdf.

[3] Sommer C. S., and Matešić, S. "The Limes in Southern Germany - The History of a Roman Frontier." In At the Edge of the Roman Empire - Tours to the Limes in Southern Germany, edited by S. Matešić, C. S. Sommer. World Heritage Site Limes Special Volume 3, Bad Homburg, München: 2015: 14-25.

C.S. 索默 . 马特斯奇 . 南德界墙：古罗马边境史 [A].S·马特斯奇 ,C·S·索默 . 罗马帝国的边缘：南德界墙之旅 [M]. 世界遗产地界墙特别卷 3，巴德 - 洪堡，慕尼黑 :2015:14-25.

[4] Sommer C. S. "Questions, Questions and More Questions for Research on the Raetian Limes." in At the Edge of the Roman Empire - Tours to the Limes in Southern Germany, edited by S. Matešić, C. S. Sommer. World Heritage Site Limes Special Volume 3, Bad Homburg, München: 2015: 26-33.

C.S. 索默 . 雷蒂亚界墙研究产生的疑问、疑问及更多疑问 [A].S·马特斯奇 , C·S·索默 . 罗马帝国的边缘：南德界墙之旅 [M]. 世界遗产地界墙特别卷 3，巴德 - 洪堡，慕尼黑 :2015:26-33.

[5] Becker, Th. et al. "Der Limes zwischen Rhein und Donau." in Archäologische Informationen aus Baden-Württemberg. Stuttgart: 2001: 444.

Th. 贝克尔，等 . 莱茵河与多瑙河之间的界墙 [J]. 巴登 - 符腾堡州考古信息。斯图加特：2001: 444.

[6] WHC. WHC-08/32.COM/10B. 2008.

世界遗产中心 .WHC-08/32.COM/10B[Z].2008.

http://whc.unesco.org/archive/2008/whc08-32com-10Be.pdf.

[7] WHC. WHC-10/34.COM/9B .

世界遗产中心 .WHC-10/34.COM/9B[Z].

https://whc.unesco.org/archive/2010/whc10-34Com-9Be.pdf. with Decision 34, COM 9B. 连同 34 号决议 .

https://whc.unesco.org/en/decisions/4249. 2010.

[8] Ployer, R., Polak, M., and Schmidt, R. The Frontiers of the Roman Empire: A thematic Study and proposed World Heritage Nomination Strategy. Advised by ICOMOS - International and commissioned by the Intergovernmental Committee of the "Frontiers of the Roman Empire" World Heritage Site (UK, DE) and the Bratislava Group. Wien, Nijmegen, München: 2017.

R. 施密特，R. 波莱耶，M. 珀拉克 . 罗马帝国边界专题研究及世界遗产申报策略方案 [R]. 国际

哈德良长城、上日耳曼—雷蒂亚界墙及世界遗产地"罗马帝国边界"
HADRIAN'S WALL, THE UPPER GERMAN-RAETIAN LINES AND THE FRONTIERS OF THE ROMAN EMPIRE WORLD HERITAGE SITE(S)

89

ICOMOS 提供咨询，罗马边界遗产地政府间委员会（英国，德国）及布拉迪斯拉法项目组共同委托. 维也纳，奈梅亨，慕尼黑：2017.

https://www.limeswerelderfgoed.nl/wp-content/uploads/2017/09/FRE-TS_FinalVersion_rapport_1.pdf.

[9] WHC. WHC/17/41.COM/8B. with Decision 41 COM 8B.50. 2017.

世界遗产中心 .WHC/17/41.COM/8B. 附加项连同 41 号决议 COM 8B.50[Z]. 2017.

http://whc.unesco.org/archive/2017/whc17-41com-8B-Add-en.pdf.

Chapter Two
Conservation Principles and Practices

山东齐长城（摄影：于 冰）
Qi Great Wall in Shandong (© Yu Bing)

第二章
长城保护理念和实践

皮尔峭壁（版权：英格兰遗产委员会）

Peel Crags (© Historic England)

UK CONSERVATION PHILOSOPHIES AND PRINCIPLES

Rebecca H Jones

Historic Environment Scotland - Edinburgh - Scotland, UK

Abstract

This paper presents a general overview of UK conservation philosophies and principles with particular relevance to Scotland, a nation within the UK. Examples are from the Antonine Wall in Scotland, part of the same Frontiers of the Roman Empire World Heritage Site as Hadrian's Wall. Statutory protection as well as undesignated assets and significance are considered. The heritage cycle is important: understanding leads to valuing; valuing leads to caring; caring and protecting helps enjoyment; from enjoying comes a thirst to understand. This impacts on our approach to authenticity, repair and replication. Finally, the importance of public involvement and public benefit is highlighted.

Keywords: Antonine Wall, conservation, Scotland, guidance, Stirling Charter, heritage cycle, gaming.

BACKGROUND

The UK is made up of four countries: England, Scotland, Wales and Northern Ireland. Hadrian's Wall, the subject of many of the papers in this seminar, is in England. But the Hadrian's Wall World Heritage Site is part of a wider World Heritage Site (the Frontiers of the Roman Empire) which also includes the Antonine Wall in Scotland (Fig. 1). The case studies and examples presented in this paper are from Scotland but are applicable across the four nations that make up the UK.

PRINCIPLES, POLICIES AND GUIDANCE GUIDANCE

All four countries produce documentation and guidance in their jurisdictions. Most are derived from the same principles - many of which are international - so there are broad synergies in our work and in our approaches to conservation philosophy. Many of our approaches started in a UK piece of legislation - the 1882 Ancient Monuments Protection Act - which recognised the need for the government to safeguard the nation's heritage. In Scotland we also have a national charter for Conserving Scotland's Built Heritage, created in 2000 and known as the Stirling Charter. The Charter consists of six articles, the first four of which are as follows:

- actions taken in respect of Scotland's built heritage should secure its conservation for the benefit and enjoyment of present and future generations;

英国文化遗产保护理念和原则

蕾贝卡·H·琼斯

（苏格兰遗产委员会，英国苏格兰爱丁堡）

摘　要

本文概要介绍英国文化遗产保护理念和原则，特别是与其成员国苏格兰相关的内容。文中案例来自苏格兰境内的安东尼墙，它与哈德良长城都是罗马帝国边疆世界遗产地的一部分。本文论及法规保护，非指定资产及历史价值。历史遗产循环（heritage cycle）至关重要：通过了解才能认识其价值，认识价值则带来关注，关注和保护能提升鉴赏，鉴赏能激发继续了解的动力。这也影响我们对待真实性、修复和复制上的态度。本文最后重点呈现公众参与和公共利益的重要性。

关键词：安东尼长城　保护　苏格兰　指南　斯特灵宪章　历史遗产循环　游戏

一、背　景

大不列颠和北爱尔兰联合王国（英国）由四个王国组成：英格兰、苏格兰、威尔士和北爱尔兰。本文集的主题哈德良长城位于英格兰。但哈德良长城世界遗产地是更广大的世界遗产地（罗马帝国边疆）构成之一，另外还包含苏格兰的安东尼长城（图1）。本文论及的案例研究和示例皆位于苏格兰，但也适用于英国所有四个成员国。

二、原则，政策和指南

四个成员国皆于各自的司法管辖区内制定官方文件和指南。这些文件采用的原则大致相同——多为国际通用原则——所以在各项工作和遗产保护理念方面有着广泛的一致性。我们大部分的理念起源于英国1882年的《历史遗迹保护法案》（Ancient Monuments Protection Act），指出有必要由政府承担保护国家遗产的责任。在苏格兰，2000年颁布了《保护苏格兰建成遗产》国家宪章，又被称作《斯特灵宪章》（Stirling Charter）。该章程包括六项条款，前面四条如下：

·就苏格兰建成遗产（built heritage）采取的行动应着重保护，确保当代和后代从遗产获得的利益和享受；

·应坚持有利于遗产保护的普遍前提：未经充分认真地考察建成遗产的历史价值及所有可行的保护方法，不得对任何遗产构成要素造成损害；

·苏格兰的建成遗产应以可持续的方式进行管理，并将其视为不可替代的资源；

·应采取不会牺牲文化价值的适当措施，包括以访问、研究、信息共享和教育等，促使所有人得以

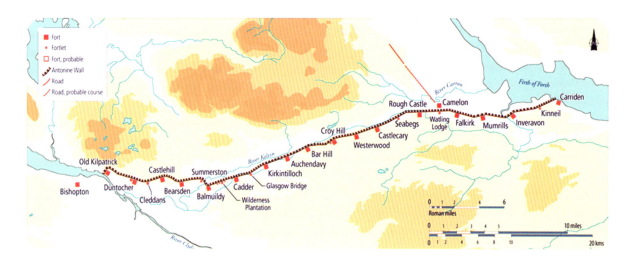

Fig. 1

Map of the Antonine Wall in Scotland which runs east - west north of the cities of Edinburgh and Glasgow (courtesy: Prof. D. Breeze)

图1

苏格兰安东尼长城地图，墙体呈东—西走向，在爱丁堡和格拉斯哥北侧经过（感谢：D·布雷兹教授）

· there should be a general presumption in favour of preservation: no element of the built heritage should be lost without adequate and careful consideration of its significance and of all the means available to conserve it;

· Scotland's built heritage should be managed in a sustainable way, recognising that it is an irreplaceable resource;

· appropriate measures, which do not compromise cultural significance, should be taken, including through access, research, information and education, to assist all people to enjoy, appreciate, learn from, and understand Scotland's built heritage.

Articles five and six are lengthy, but set out the principles which should be adopted by those with a role and responsibility to ensure effective conservation (five) and how works should be carried out (six). This includes the need for full knowledge and understanding of the heritage resource; adequate recording; minimum intervention; the need for appropriate materials, skills and knowledge; and effective monitoring of the condition of the built heritage resource to ensure adequate maintenance[1].

A range of international charters adopted by ICOMOS and others set guiding principles, from which many of which our principles are derived. These include the Venice Charter[2] and the Burra Charter, originally created in 1979 with the latest revision in 2013[3].

Significance and designation

Key to many of these is the importance of our understanding of the significance of places - we should understand and articulate their values and significance before making decisions about their future. This

享受、欣赏、学习并认识苏格兰的建成遗产。

宪章第五条和第六条条款的内容很多，第五条主要规定哪些在遗产保护中负有责任和义务的相关方应当遵循的原则，第六条主要规定相应的工作程序。规定包括应当全面理解认识遗产资源；充分记录；最小干预；对材料、技能和知识的要求；以及有效监测建成遗产资源状况，以确保开展充分的维护工作[1]。

国际古迹遗址理事会（ICOMOS）及其他组织发布了一系列国际章程作为指导原则，我们的许多原则也是源自于此。其中包括《威尼斯章程》[2]，（还有《巴拉章程》，原于 1979 年制定，后于 2013 年进行最新修订[3]。

（一）价值和认定

许多原则的关键在于我们是否理解遗产的价值，而这至关重要。我们应在对它们的未来做出决策前认识并明确陈述其重要性和价值。这些价值包括物质和非物质，而且我们承认对于历史价值的认识会随着时间改变，因此我们应确保决策是建立在现有的最佳证据上。价值是集合性词汇，意指某处附加的所有遗产价值，无论该遗产是建筑、考古遗址，或是一整座村落或景观这样的大型历史区域。理解价值应能帮助：

· 认识一个地方的发展及该发展的背景；

· 识别造成破坏的因素，以及遗产破坏因素相关的风险；

· 阐明风险因素会如何影响遗产价值、完整性和真实性；

· 指导保护价值所需要采取的行动和限制措施。

确实，保护的目标是长久延续文化价值，因此应当妥善管理遗产地，以保护其价值，而且要考虑遗产地各种不同的文化价值。

作为成员国的中央机构，我们有遗产地认定体系，有时将其意义区分为国家级、郡级（regionally）和地方级。遗产地类型涵盖甚广，其中还有海洋保护区（Marine Protected Areas）。大部分的哈德良长城和安东尼长城都被公布为登录古迹，都是具有国家级意义的古迹。登录的目标为保存意义重大的遗产地和古迹，并尽可能地维护它们从历史上存留下来的形态。

安东尼长城横跨苏格兰部分人口最稠密的地区，因此也穿过了相当多样的城市景观，但在部分乡村地方也有保存良好的城墙遗迹（图 2）。同时，也有一些长城区段的古迹状态并不完好。哈德良长城及安东尼长城世界遗产地中已知或被推测存在的地下遗迹，大多会通过公布为登录古迹的方式加以保护。

除认定体系外，苏格兰遗产委员会也管理国家历史环境档案（National Record of the Historic Environment）。在全英国，各地方政府也有各自的当地历史环境档案，可运用于各种活动，特别是用以管理对历史环境造成的改变。同时，法规保护的遗址和非指定资产记录都用于提供信息支撑决策。与所有好的决策过程一样，关键在于以古迹价值的认知。

我们同时也有多样的规划政策和辅助规划指南，所有都会在决策过程的不同阶段中得到审核。这使得关于改变的决策能信息充分、合理、一致并透明化。

除上述这些的实际操作程序外，我们也须考量气候变化的影响，它对脆弱土遗址和遗产本体保护的影响也日益显著。

includes tangible and intangible significance, and we acknowledge that our understanding of significance changes over time and we should therefore ensure that decisions are made on the best available evidence. Significance is a collective term for the sum of all the heritage values attached to a place, be it a building, an archaeological site, or a larger historic area such as a whole village or landscape. Understanding significance should help to:

· understand the development of a place and the context to that development;

· identify the drivers of decay and the risk associated with these to historic fabric;

· illustrate how this will impact on significance, integrity and authenticity;

· guide the actions and constraints required to sustain that significance.

Indeed, the purpose of conservation is to perpetuate cultural significance and such places should be managed to sustain their values, recognising that there will be different cultural values.

As state bodies within our respective countries, we have designation regimes recognising sites, sometimes separating what is nationally significant, regionally significant and locally significant. This can include a wide range of site types, and we also have Marine Protected Areas. Most of Hadrian's Wall and the Antonine Wall are classed as scheduled monuments, and these are our lists of monuments of national importance. The aim of scheduling is to preserve our most significant sites and monuments as far as possible in the form in which they have been passed down to us today.

Scotland's Antonine Wall runs through some of the most densely populated parts of Scotland and so through a very varied urban landscape in places, but there are also some rural stretches where the remains of the Wall can be well preserved (Fig. 2). There are also sections of the Wall which do not survive as clearly. If it is known or thought that there are buried remains surviving, then those parts of our World Heritage Sites such as Hadrian's Wall and the Antonine Wall are largely protected through scheduling.

In addition to the designation regime, a National Record of the Historic Environment is maintained by Historic Environment Scotland, and local authorities have their own local Historic Environment Records across the UK, used for various activities, but particularly when managing change to the historic environment. Together, the statutory protected sites and records of undesignated assets are used to inform and guide decision making. As with all good decision making, at its core lies our understanding of a monument's significance.

We also have various planning policies and Supplementary Planning Guidance, all of which are reviewed at various points. These enable decisions about change to be informed, reasonable, consistent and transparent.

In addition to the pragmatic approach outlined, we also need to take account of climate change, the impact of which is becoming increasingly apparent as we assess the vulnerability of fragile earthen monuments and consider the maintenance of historic fabrics.

Fig. 2
Aerial view of the Roman fort of Rough Castle and the Antonine Wall (© Crown Copyright: DP014299, Historic Environment Scotland)
图 2
拉夫堡罗马要塞和安东尼墙的鸟瞰图（皇家版权：DP014299，苏格兰历史环境委员会）

（二）历史遗产循环

以上所有皆构成历史遗产循环之一环：通过了解才能认识其价值，认识价值则带来关注，关注和保护能提升鉴赏，鉴赏能激发继续了解的动力。

价值可分为不同种类：

· 证据价值——一个地方能提供佐证过去人类活动的潜力；

· 历史价值——过去的人、事及生活的方方面面能够通过遗产与当代产生的各种联系；

· 美学价值——人们能从一处遗产获得启发；

· 社群价值——一个地方对于相关人们的意义，或人们在此处拥有共同的经验或回忆。

若要保护并促进历史遗产循环、认知价值并传承价值，我们须尊重其背景和真实性，并避免将遗产

The heritage cycle

All of this has a role in the heritage cycle: that by understanding, we will value a site; by valuing, we will want to care for it; by caring and protecting, it will help us to enjoy it, and from enjoying comes a thirst to understand.

In terms of values, there are different types:

· Evidential - the potential of a place to yield evidence about past human activity;

· Historical - the ways in which past people, events and aspects of life can be connected through a place to the present;

· Aesthetic - the ways in which people draw stimulation from a place;

· Communal - the meanings of a place for the people who relate to it, or for whom it figures in their collective experience or memory.

In order to maintain and promote the heritage cycle, understand significance and sustain values, we need to respect context and authenticity and avoid dislocation of historic fabric from its setting.

Sites derive significance from their contexts. Whilst it may be technically possible to move structures and objects from their original site, significance and context will be diminished. Where possible, we avoid moving structures, objects or fabric components from sites to extend their lifespan. We try and document sites subject to change for future study. If we choose to replace a feature, this will be done only using traditional materials and skills in order that the intangible value in skills and materials will be nurtured, and we will be honest in presentation in this scenario. Where necessary, items may be taken off-site for conservation work but only when there is an agreed plan for re-instatement.

We see authenticity as being true in substance: without authenticity, the worth of a monument is compromised.

We also have a tradition of replicas in Scotland, particularly for carved stones[4]. In 2012, the local community raised funds for a full-scale replica of one of the most significant pieces of monumental sculpture, known as the Bridgeness Distance Slab (Fig. 3). This stone, now housed in the National Museum of Scotland in Edinburgh, has high quality carvings including a Roman cavalry man riding over four naked Britons, the cavalry man now serving as the logo for the Antonine Wall World Heritage Site. The stone also contains an inscription stating how much of the Wall was built in this area by one of the Roman Legions. Recent work using non-destructive portable X-ray fluorescence and Raman Spectrometry has identified some of the colours that were used on the stones, bringing them to life with a level of realistic detail which includes blood-red around the decapitated heads of the Britons[5]. In the case of this new replica, it is mounted in an attractive stone setting and accompanied by a detailed information board, all sited close to where the original stone was found in the 19th century. This accurate replica was created using the non-damaging technique of laser scanning the original and recreating it in sandstone.

本身及其环境错置割裂。

遗址的价值产生于自背景环境。就技术而言，将遗址的结构和物体移出原址或许可行，但其价值和环境将受到减损。只要可能，我们就应当避免将结构、器物或遗迹构件从原址迁移，以延长它们的寿命。我们尽力记录遗址的变化以供未来研究。如果决定替换某一元素，则必须使用传统材料和传统工艺，以保存技艺和材料中蕴涵的非物质价值，并对此情况做出如实说明。必要时，构件可能会被移出原址以进行维护工作，但归位方案应事先得到同意。

我们视真实性为在实质上的真实：若无真实性，古迹的价值便会受到损害。

在苏格兰也有制作复制品的传统，特别是石雕 [4]。在 2012 年时，当地社区募集资金复制了一座原大的重要雕塑，名为布奇尼斯警示牌（Bridgeness Distance Slab，图 3）。此石雕现藏于爱丁堡的苏格兰国家博物馆，上有精美雕刻，其中有一名罗马骑兵，骑马踏在四个裸体布列颠人身上，该骑兵形象如今用于安东尼长城世界遗产地的标志。此石雕也含有铭文，记叙罗马军团的番号和在此地修建城墙的长度。最近使用非损伤性便携 X 射线荧光（X-ray fluorescence）和拉曼光谱仪（Raman Spectrometry），揭示石雕上曾经使用过颜色，使雕刻栩栩如生，比如在布列颠人被砍头颅周围呈血红色 [5]。这件新复制石雕立于精美石座之上，旁边设置有详细的信息说明板，放置在 19 世纪原石出土的位置附近。此精准的复制品是依照非损伤激光技术扫描原石并用砂岩制成。

（三）环境（Setting）

保护管理的一个关键方面是古迹的环境：管理环境如何提升古迹价值，如何促进人们了解、欣赏和体验古迹。遗址建于景观中，虽然景观会随着时间而变，但仍可能会有关键视野和背景，与古迹价值密不可分。

在对变化的管理中，环境也很重要。此流程共有三个阶段：

·识别历史资产；

·调查和分析背景环境，看其如何帮助理解、欣赏和体验历史资产或历史区域；

·评估改变活动对环境带来的潜在影响，及其负面影响能得到控制的程度。

为了提高管理效率，我们制定了一系列管理改变的指南，其中一项专门针对世界遗产地 [6]。

英格兰遗产委员会也编制了一系列完善的指南，包括《保护原则、政策和指南》，可供英国其他成员国自由参考 [7]。

三、公共利益

然而，如果我们无法激发那些在遗址附近生活、工作和游玩的人来关注珍惜古迹的话，那么政府试图立法保护遗址是毫无意义的。事实上，只有当地人也在乎古迹时，许多遗址才能得到有效保护。在苏格兰，我们一直在考虑如何提高公众参与遗产保护的程度。如果我们声称为公共利益而行，则我们需要确保公众确实与我们的想法一致。在 2016—2017 年间，我们开展一个叫做'你的文化遗产是什么'（What's Your Heritage）的活动，试图找出苏格兰哪些地方、建筑及古迹最著名、最受喜爱，且对公众

Setting

A key aspect of conservation management is the setting of a monument: how its surroundings contribute to significance and how it is understood, appreciated and experienced. Sites were built in their landscapes and although those landscapes have changed over time, there may be key views and contexts which significantly contribute to the importance of a monument.

Setting is also important when managing change. This is a three-stage process:

- **identify** the historic assets;
- **define** and analyse the setting by establishing how the surroundings contribute to the ways in which the historic asset or place is understood, appreciated and experienced;
- **evaluate the potential impact** of the proposed changes on the setting, and the extent to which any negative impacts can be mitigated.

In order to do this effectively, we have created a range of guidance on managing change, one in particular on World Heritage Sites[6].

Historic England, as well as their Conservation Principles, Policies and Guidance, also have a suite of well-developed guidance from which the other UK nations freely borrow[7].

PUBLIC BENEFIT

But there is no point in the government trying to legislate to protect sites if we cannot inspire those who live, work and play near these sites to value them. In reality, we can only protect many sites if those who live locally care about them as well. In Scotland, we have been looking at how we can involve the public more in our conservation practices. If we claim to be doing our work for public benefit then we need to try and ensure that they actually want us to do so. In 2016-17 we ran a campaign entitled What's Your Heritage, to try and find out which of Scotland's places, buildings and monuments should be recognised, celebrated and mean the most to the public. The resulting report[8] has fed into our forthcoming policy statement on the historic environment as well as new criteria for designations.

Part of involving the public is also being transparent, so we publish all of our decision making online through our heritage portal. Having all our decision making online is relatively new but has been well received.

Our final principles are that:

- The historic environment is a shared resource;
- Everyone should be able to participate in sustaining the historic environment.

We have recently run a project along the Antonine Wall asking the public what they want to see and what would help them to understand and value the Wall. Through this project, we will create five more replica distance slabs, building on the success of the example in Bridgeness (Fig. 3) together with Roman-themed play-

而言最有意义。调查结果 [8] 已反映到我们即将发布的历史环境政策声明及遗产认定的新标准中。

信息透明也是公众参与的一部分，所以我们将所有的决策过程公布在遗产官方网站上。将所有的决策过程放在网上是较新的方式，但反响极佳。

我们的最终原则为：

·历史环境是共享的资源；

·每个人都应该能够参与到历史环境保护中。

我们最近沿着安东尼长城开展了一个项目，调查大众他们想要看到什么，怎样才能帮助他们了解并珍惜安东尼长城。通过此项目，我们会在布奇尼斯案例（图3）的成功基础上再竖立五个警示牌复制品，配以罗马主题游乐场让儿童能身历罗马历史。

Fig. 3
Replica of the Bridgeness Distance Slab, erected in Bridgeness, near the eastern end of the Antonine Wall, in 2012 (© Crown Copyright: Historic Environment Scotland)
图 3
布奇尼斯警示牌复制件，2012 年立于布奇尼斯，临近安东尼长城东端（皇家版权：苏格兰历史环境委员会）

2018 年早些时候，我们发布了一款根据长城要塞上真实证据开发的游戏，叫做‘出发吧罗马人’（Go Roman），人们可免费下载此应用程序至移动设备上 (https://itunes.apple.com/gb/app/goroman/id1251988769?mt=8https://play.google.com/store/apps/details?id=com.dds.barhillgame&hl=en_GB)。虽然让来自各方面研究古罗马考古学家认可数字重建是个挑战，但游戏本身是具有娱乐性的探索，玩家能扮演历史记载中安东尼长城附近的罗马士兵或奴隶女孩，完成一系列的挑战。

通过提供娱乐内容，我们希望能增加人们对古迹的认识和理解，进而能够珍惜并保护古迹。我们的最终目标是为了鼓励公众在不知不觉中实践文化遗产保护理念及原则。

parks enabling the very young to be engaged with their Roman past.

Earlier in 2018, we launched a game based on authentic evidence from the forts on the Wall , called 'Go Roman' and freely available for download as an app onto mobile devices (https://itunes.apple.com/gb/app/go-roman/id1251988769?mt=8 https://play.google.com/store/apps/details?id=com.dds.barhillgame&hl=en_GB). Although getting various Roman archaeologists to agree on digital reconstructions was a challenge, the game itself is an entertaining quest where the user completes a series of challenges either as a Roman soldier or a slave girl documented from near the Antonine Wall.

By providing enjoyment we hope to increase knowledge and understanding, leading to valuing and protection. Our ultimate aim is to encourage the public to implement the conservation philosophies and principles without realising that they are doing so.

参考文献
Bibliography

[1] Historic Scotland. The Stirling Charter for the Conservation of Scotland's Built Heritage. Edinburgh：2000.

苏格兰遗产委员会 . 保护苏格兰建成遗产的斯特灵宪章 [Z]. 爱丁堡 :2000.

[2] ICOMOS. International Charter for the Conservation and Restoration of Monuments and Sites (the Venice Charter 1964). 1964.

国际古迹遗址理事会 . 保护及修复古迹和遗址的国际宪章（威尼斯章程 1964）[Z].1964.

https://www.icomos.org/charters/venice_e.pdf.

3 Australia ICOMOS. The Burra Charter. The Australia ICOMOS Charter for Places of Cultural Significance. 2013.

澳大利亚国际古迹遗址理事会 . 布拉章程 . 澳大利亚国际古迹遗址理事会的《文化价值地方章程》[Z].2013.

https://australia.icomos.org/wp-content/uploads/The-Burra-Charter-2013-Adopted-31.10.2013.pdf.

[4] Foster, S. "Circulating agency: the V&A, Scotland and the multiplication of plaster casts of 'Celtic crosses'." Journal of the History of Collections, 2015, 27(1): 73-96.

S. 福斯特 . 流通机构：V&A，苏格兰以及'凯尔特十字'石膏模型数量的增加 [J]. 收藏品历史期刊，2015，27（1）：73-96.

[5] Campbell, L. Decorating the Distance Stones: pXRF and Portable Raman Spectroscopic Analysis of Pigments on the Antonine Wall Distance Stones. University of Glasgow unpublished report for Historic Environment Scotland, 2018.

L. 坎贝尔 . 装饰距离标示石板：对安东尼长城距离标示石板的可携带 X 射线荧光和可携带拉曼光谱分析 [R]. 格拉斯哥大学为苏格兰遗产委员会产生的未出版报告，2018.

[6] Historic Environment Scotland. Managing Change in the Historic Environment. 2016.

苏格兰遗产委员会 . 管理历史环境的改变 [R].2016.

https://www.historicenvironment.scot/advice-and-support/planning-and-guidance/legislation-and-guidance/managing-change-in-the-historic-environment-guidance-notes/.

[7] English Heritage. Conservation Principles, Policies and Guidance. 2008.

英格兰遗产信托 . 保护原则、政策和指南 [R].2008.

https://content.historicengland.org.uk/images-books/publications/conservation-principles-sustainable-management-historic-environment/conservationprinciplespoliciesguidanceapr08web.pdf/.

[8] Historic Environment Scotland. What's Your Heritage? Past Places and Traditions. 2017.

苏格兰遗产委员会 . 你的文化遗产是什么？过去的地方和传统 [R].2017.

https://www.historicenvironment.scot/archives-and-https://www.historicenvironment.scot/archives-and-research/publications/publication/?publicationId=cef9fd83-0923-4c03-aeb1-a79700daf9c1.

HADRIAN'S WALL - CONSERVATION PRACTICE

MIKE COLLINS

Historic England - Newcastle upon Tyne - UK

Abstract

This paper explores current management practice on the Hadrian's Wall Roman frontier. A complex site with many stakeholders, successful management of Hadrian's Wall involves not only the protection of the significance of its Roman archaeology and its setting, but also an appreciation of the needs and aspirations of these stakeholders, and the wider economic and social role that the Wall must play. The paper goes on to look at the principles underlying conservation work on the Wall, some successes and failures of management over the last hundred years, and key challenges for Hadrian's Wall into the future.

Keywords: Hadrian's Wall; Roman; frontier; heritage; management; conservation.

OWNERSHIP, ROLES AND RESPONSIBILITIES

Hadrian's Wall runs for approximately 118km across the north of England. Along this length its context and management issues vary hugely, taking in two major cities, agricultural, coastal and industrial land. The vast majority of this land lies in private ownership, with sections owned or occupied by up to 1000 individuals, charitable trusts and local councils.

Many key sites along the Wall, including those in State guardianship, are presented to the public as heritage visitor attractions. This use provides significant economic benefits to the Hadrian's Wall area. However, for other owners the Wall is incidental to their property, and indeed places some restriction on free use of their land.

Successful management of Hadrian's Wall is not therefore the responsibility purely of central or local government, but requires cooperation between many interested parties. This requires an appreciation of the archaeological significance of the Wall, and must take into account the other needs of landowners and the public value that the Wall can deliver. Historic England's role in this process is not only to advise the UK government, but to advise and work in partnership with others along the Wall to protect its significance as part of a living, working landscape.

SCHEDULED AND NON-SCHEDULED ARCHAEOLOGICAL REMAINS

The majority of the surviving remains of the Hadrian's Wall frontier are protected under UK law as 'scheduled monuments'. This requires anyone wanting to carry out works to the monument to obtain special permis-

哈德良长城——保护管理实践

麦克·考林斯

（英格兰遗产委员会，英国纽卡斯尔）

摘　要

本文探讨现今哈德良长城罗马帝国边疆的管理措施。哈德良长城这一复杂遗址有许多利益相关者，其成功的管理不仅是要保护罗马考古遗址及其周边环境的价值，更需考虑利益相关者的需求和意愿，以及长城对宏观经济和社会贡献。本文还介绍了哈德良长城保护工作的基本原则、数百年来一些成功和失败的管理案例，以及未来主要的挑战。

关键词：哈德良长城　罗马　边疆　遗产　管理　保护

一、所有权，角色和责任

哈德良长城横跨北英格兰，全长约 118 公里。其沿线环境和管理问题差别很大，涉及两大城市、沿海地区，以及农业、沿海和工业用地。遗址大多处于私有土地，长城各段的所有者或占用者包括多达 1000 个私人拥有者、慈善信托和地方政府。

长城沿线许多重要遗址，包括受国家监管的遗址，以遗产观光景点的模式向公众开放，为哈德良长城区域带来显著经济利益。然而，私有土地上有长城遗迹肯定限制了其所有者的土地利用自由。

因此，成功管理哈德良长城不能完全仰赖中央政府或地方政府，而是需要许多利益相关者一同合作。这既需要认识长城的考古价值，同时也需考量土地所有者的需求和长城能带来的公共价值等其他因素。在此过程中，英格兰遗产委员会不仅会向英国政府提供咨询意见，同时也与长城沿线的利益相关者合作并提供咨询建议，使长城价值融入活态景观加以保护。

二、认定与非认定考古遗迹

大部分尚存的哈德良长城边疆遗迹是作为'登录古迹'（scheduled monuments）受英国法律保护。任何人要在古迹范围内开展任何工程都必须从政府获得特殊许可，称为登录古迹许可（SMC）。英格兰遗产委员会作为此类申请的地方顾问，与土地所有者及申请者进行联系协调，然后向政府提出建议。

哈德良长城区域内也有其他罗马帝国边疆的考古遗迹并非均以此方式加以保护。部分是因为我们对长城考古的认识还不完全，常常发现新的遗址和遗迹。其他原因是遗迹残存状况尚不明确，因此将其列入"登录古迹"的理由还不充分。还有部分遗址，特别是那些位于繁华城市区的长城区段，则通过评估

sion, known as scheduled monument consent or SMC, from the government. Historic England acts as local advisor on such applications, liaising with owners and applicants before making recommendations to the government.

The Hadrian's Wall area also contains further archaeological remains from the Roman frontier which are not protected in this way. In part this is because our understanding of the archaeology of the Wall is partial, with new sites and remains always being found, whilst in others uncertainty about the level of survival of remains means that it is not justified to include them in the schedule. There are also sites, particularly in the busy urban areas on the Wall, where the judgment has been taken to manage risk to the archaeological remains through the more general planning system that applies to development (Fig. 1).

THE MANAGEMENT OF CHANGE

The Hadrian's Wall area is, then, not an archaeological theme-park but a living landscape. Protection of its remains ultimately relies on broad support both from individual landowners and at local and national government level. Sustaining this support requires us to take account of the needs and aspirations of all stakeholders, so that Hadrian's Wall is both protected and delivers economic and wider public benefits. Its management is therefore not about trying to prevent any change to the monument occurring, but about managing this change in a way that protects what is significant about the site.

Activities requiring planning or other statutory permissions

Most forms of development in the UK require planning permission, generally obtained from the local planning authority (LPA), who make their decision taking into account a broad range of priorities set by central government. These priorities, contained in the National Planning Policy Framework (NPPF), set out how development on or near sites like Hadrian's Wall needs to be approached. This includes the need to protect nationally-significant archaeological remains, and for any harm to such remains to be carefully balanced against the public benefits of the development proposed.

This broad approach is also the one taken to research excavation on the Wall, with the harm (in this case the loss of the archaeological remains that are investigated) balanced against the benefits (in this case the knowledge, preferably focused on agreed research priorities) (Fig. 2).

In practice on Hadrian's Wall there is often a need for further information, in the form of geophysical or archaeological trial trenching, to understand what the impact of a proposal is going to be before such a balancing exercise can be carried out. Where this is necessary the applicant will be responsible for commissioning further work, using suitable professional archaeologists.

This approach allows an informed decision to be taken that emphasises the protection of Hadrian's Wall, but also provides a framework in which this is considered alongside the needs of landowners and wider society.

认为可以通过适用于建设项目的规划管理体系对考古遗迹风险加以控制（图1）。

三、变化管理

哈德良长城区域并非考古主题公园，而是活态景观。保护遗迹最终还是要仰赖私人土地所有者、地方政府和中央政府的广泛支持。若要持续得到支持，就必须考量到所有利益相关者的需求和意愿，哈德良长城也才能既得到妥善保护，同时又为经济和公共利益做出贡献。所以，管理并不是要阻止遗迹改变的发生，而是对变化加以管理，从而使遗址的价值得到保护。

Fig. 1

Excavation of newly discovered bathhouse, Segedunum, North Tyneside (© Historic England)

图 1

新发现浴室的发掘现场，北泰恩赛德，塞格杜努姆要塞（版权：英格兰遗产委员会）

（一）需要规划许可或其他法定许可的活动

在英国，大多数开发都需要规划许可，许可通常是由地方规划部门（LPA）发放。规划部门会按照中央政府规定的一系列优先事项来做出决策。优先事项在《国家规划政策框架》（National Planning Policy Framework，NPPF）中给予了明确，规定了对象哈德良长城这样的遗迹本体或对其周边的建设开发该如何进行。规定中考虑的因素包括需要保护具有国家价值的考古遗迹，需要认真平衡任何破坏遗迹的活动与建设方案带来的公共效益孰轻孰重。

此规定的程序同样也适用于长城的研究性考古发掘，也需要在对遗迹造成的损害（此指在调查发掘中对考古遗迹造成的损失）以及收益（此指获得的信息和认知，最好集中于事先批准的研究方向）中取得平衡（图2）。

在哈德良长城实际工作中，在做出平衡决策之前常常需要更多的信息依据，通过地理勘探或考古试掘的方式来评估活动方案可能会产生什么影响。这种情况下活动方案的申请者有责任聘用合适的考古专家实施这项工作。

以此方法，决策者能做出具有充分依据的决定，既确保哈德良长城得到保护，同时能在规范的框架下兼顾土地所有者和宏观的社会需求。如若不得不批准将伤及遗迹的建设开发项目，则必须提出开展考古工作的要求，尽可能使不可避免的影响产生最大化的知识收获。

（二）无需法定许可的活动

大多数开发都是由核发法定许可来管控，但有些工程，尤其是与公共基础设施建设相关的项目（如

Where harmful development is to be allowed, this will be subject to conditions requiring implementation of a programme of archaeological work, designed to maximise the knowledge gained from this unavoidable impact.

Activities not requiring statutory permissions

While most developments are controlled through statutory permissions, there are activities, particularly relating to the provision of utilities (water, gas, telecommunications) which do not require planning permission, but which could have a significant archaeological impacts.

These issues are particularly acute in the urban areas of Newcastle and Carlisle, and we are again in a position where the aim is to secure this important infrastructure with the minimum impact on the archaeology of Hadrian's Wall.

A balanced approach is particularly important because in these cases we rely either on non-statutory requirements in the relevant industry codes of conduct for or, more usually, on the determination of individual companies to behave responsibly even where this is not a legal necessity.

Protection of the setting of Hadrian's Wall

In addition to the archaeological remains themselves, the area around Hadrian's Wall often plays a role in its significance. This arises where the surroundings allow an understanding and appreciation of the Roman military planning and land use involved in the creation and operation of Hadrian's Wall. This is more usually referred to as the 'setting' of Hadrian's Wall.

Clearly not every development visible from the Wall will harm this setting. However, aspects such as the ability to understand how the local topography and landscape impacted on the detailed design and line of the frontier, or how individual Roman installations communicated visually with each other, are an important part of the frontier's significance.

As with direct physical impacts, impacts on this understanding and appreciation are carefully considered as part of the statutory permission process, with the aim being to protect the frontier from development harmful to its setting, and for any such harm to be explicitly balanced in the decision-making process against the public benefits of the development.

Natural Processes

The final major category of change on Hadrian's Wall with a potential to cause harm to the site is that of natural processes. Given the likely impact of climate change we will probably see increasing direct impacts from these, and also from indirect impacts such as increases in rainfall along the Wall making the archaeological remains more vulnerable to stock and visitor erosion (Fig. 3).

Whilst some issues, like climate change, will take time for their impacts to be fully understood, Hadrian's Wall already faces some significant harm from natural processes, particularly from coastal and river erosion. Given the

供水、供气和通讯）无需取得规划许可，然而它们实际上会对考古遗迹带来重大影响。

这类问题在纽卡斯尔和卡莱尔（Carlisle）的市区特别严峻，在这些情况下我们的目标仍是既要确保这些重要基础建设，又要尽可能地减少对哈德良长城考古遗迹的影响。

这时，能制订出平衡各方需求的方案至关重要。在这些情况下我们要么仰赖相关行业的非法定行为准则，要么（在大多数情况下）仰赖具体的建设单位承担起相应的保护责任，即便没有硬性法律要求。

Fig.2
Research excavation of a Roman temple, Maryport, Cumbria (© Historic England)
图 2
一座罗马神庙的研究发掘，坎布里亚郡，玛丽波特（版权：英格兰遗产委员会）

（三）保护哈德良长城的周边环境

除了考古遗迹本身，哈德良长城的附近区域通常也有重要的历史价值。周边环境能帮助我们更好地认识和理解建造及营运哈德良长城时的罗马军事战略和土地利用方式。这通常被称为哈德良长城的'周边环境'（setting）。

显而易见的，并非从长城上可见的所有建设开发都会危害到周边环境。然而，应该考虑当地地形和景观如何影响边疆防御体系的细节设计和选线，或各处古罗马的驻军营地之间如何传递视觉信息等等，这些方面都是哈德良长城价值的重要组成部分。

核发法定许可时，除了直接的本体影响外，对周边环境的影响和认识也会被纳入考量，目的在于保护哈德良长城周边环境免受开发威胁。在决策过程中，也需要在遗产保护及建设开发的公共利益间取得明确的平衡。

（四）自然过程

最后一个可能会对哈德良长城带来伤害的变化因素是自然过程。因为气候变化的影响，自然过程带来的直接影响可能会日益增加，而其间接影响也会增加，如长城沿线的降雨量增加也会使得考古遗迹更容易受牲畜和游客侵蚀（图3）。

如果说有些因素（如气候变化）对哈德良长城造成的影响需经一段时间才能完全显现出来，而有些因素已经在切实严重危及长城，特别是海岸侵蚀及河流侵蚀。若要防范此种侵蚀，所要采取的工程措施极为复杂，高额的资金成本和融资渠道也难以解决。因此，我们已经接受终有部分遗址会毁于自然因素破坏的现实。对于哈德良长城，既然这类损失不可避免，我们便转向做好记录和发掘工作，在损失形成

considerable engineering challenges in trying to stop this kind of erosion, and the costs and challenges faced in trying to access funding, it is accepted that there will always be sites where this kind of damage will occur. On Hadrian's Wall, where the inevitability of loss has been established, our efforts on such sites have focused on recording and excavation, to gain the maximum amount of information and understanding before loss occurs.

PUBLICATION AND ARCHIVING

Wherever archaeological excavation before development, or other research, takes place on Hadrian's Wall there is an accepted need to make the results of this work available for future researchers. This requires a proper academic publication of the results, and the creation of an archive, to allow integration of this knowledge into our understanding of the Wall and even to allow reassessment of sites in years to come.

In common with much of British archaeology, Hadrian's Wall has a number of 20th century excavations which have yet to be published. Over the last 20 years considerable progress on this excavation backlog has been made by individual researchers, leading to publication of major works on sites such as the forts at Haltonchesters, Housesteads, Segedunum and Arbeia.

Recent years have also seen a resurgence in the amount of research on the Wall, alongside the ongoing work of the Vindolanda Trust. In each case robust plans for publication and archiving have been a part of the project planning, with publication now either complete or on track. The next challenge is likely to be the publication of synthetic works, which bring together the results from individual sites, particularly in a form that addresses the increasing interest from the general public in archaeological discovery on the Wall.

CONSERVATION WORKS

The upstanding remains of Hadrian's Wall are a hugely important archaeological and historic resource. Most of these remains are in good condition, particularly those in the guardianship of English Heritage, or cared for by independent bodies such as the National Trust, the Vindolanda Trust, Tyne & Wear Archives and Museums and others. These upstanding remains require significant investment in repair and maintenance if they are to be maintained.

The approach taken to this maintenance, as well as consolidation of remains unearthed by excavation and to be displayed to the public, has evolved considerably over the last hundred years. What is applied today has drawn on the development of conservation philosophy across the wider UK during this period, tailored to the particularly exposed upland nature of much of the visible remains of the Wall.

Three key principles are applied to conservation on Hadrian's Wall today:

Minimal intervention
The aim is for the remains of Hadrian's Wall presented to the public to be as authentically Roman as pos-

前尽可能地取得信息并加深我们对它的认识。

四、出版和档案建设

无论是开展配合建设开发项目的考古发掘或是其他性质的考古研究，都必须分享发掘成果以供未来研究人员使用。这就要求以学术成果的形式加以出版，并建立档案，使这些成果整合进长城现有的知识体系，也使在未来需要时能对遗址进行重新评估。

与大部分英国考古研究相同，哈德良长城有一些20世纪的发掘成果尚未出版。过去20年来研究学者在这些成果整理方面取得重大进展，促成若干重要遗址发掘成果的出版，如霍尔顿切斯特（Haltonchesters）、豪塞斯特兹（Housesteads）、塞格杜努姆（Segedunum）和阿尔比亚（Arbeia）等罗马要塞。

Fig. 3
Coastal erosion at the Roman cemetery at Beckfoot, Cumbria (© Historic England)
图 3
罗马火葬墓地处发生的海岸侵蚀，坎布里亚郡，贝克夫特（版权：英格兰遗产委员会）

近年来，长城的研究数量也与日俱增，特别是文多兰达信托（Vindolanda Trust）正在开展的工作。在这些项目中，详细出版计划及档案建设工作早在项目规划阶段就已经列入其中，目前项目成果有些已经出版，有些正在出版过程中。下一步的挑战将是整合不同遗址的发掘成果推出综合性出版物，特别是要满足公众对长城考古发现日益增长的兴趣。

五、保护工作

哈德良长城依旧矗立的遗迹是极为重要的考古和历史资源。大部分的遗迹保存状况良好，特别是那些由英格兰遗产信托（English Heritage）监管的遗址，或由国家信托（National Trust）、文多兰达信托、泰恩·威尔地区档案及博物馆（Tyne & Wear Archives and Museums）等独立机构管理的遗址。若要保持这些遗迹的良好状态，则需投入大笔资金来维修和维护。

在过去一百年来，维护所采取的方法，以及遗址发掘出土后的加固方法和开放展示的方法经历了巨大演变过程。现在阶段采取的方法汲取了英国在此过程中保护理念发展进步的经验，同时结合长城可见遗迹所处的高地环境量身打造。

sible. Although this needs to be balanced with providing conservation which will survive a sometimes harsh environment, the general approach is therefore is to do the minimum necessary to secure the Wall from loss. In practice this means repairing masonry in-situ and not taking down and rebuilding stonework unless this cannot be avoided (Fig. 4).

Conserve as found

For the same reasons of authenticity, the approach generally taken is to conserve what has come down to us from the past as it was found. This means generally avoiding adding material into Roman masonry, and particularly avoiding the restoration or reconstruction of lost elements. The main exception to this would be where additional masonry is necessary to secure authentic Roman remains above. In these cases, with alternative approaches to support ruled out, small amounts of introduced masonry, usually subtly differentiated from the original, have been used.

Recording

In all cases making a detailed record of the work that has taken place is vital to allow future heritage managers and archaeologists to understand the changes that have been made to the remains of Hadrian's Wall, but also so that we can evaluate the effectiveness of conservation works carried out and learn from this for the future.

Funding and Heritage at Risk

As discussed above, the majority of the remains of Hadrian's Wall are in private ownership. Significant funding has been put into maintenance and repair by many of these owners, particularly the independent trusts and museums with a conservation remit. Others, particularly owners for whom the Wall adds little directly to their business, understandably find it much harder to fund the cost of conservation works. In this context three further sources of funding have allowed important conservation works in recent years.

Historic England has funded important conservation works via grants to owners. These are prioritised to those parts of the frontier which appear on our national Heritage at Risk Register. Other works have been undertaken using funding from the UK's National Lottery. However, the greatest amount of work over the last 15 years, particularly on major sites like Great Chesters and Caw Gap has been funded through farm support payments, the future of which is unclear with the UK's withdrawal from the European Union.

FAILURES AND SUCCESSES

Quarrying on the Wall

Perhaps the most significant conservation challenge on Hadrian's Wall in the last century has been the

如今哈德良长城保护中主要适用三大原则：

（一）最小干预

保护目标是让哈德良长城遗迹以尽可能真实的形态展现给大众。虽有时因环境严峻而需多加干预才能保护遗迹，但基本原则还是以最小干预手段来保护长城免受损失，并从中找到平衡。在实际工作就是要原址进行石质墙体的修缮，不得拆除或添加石块，除非万不得已（图4）。

（二）保存遗迹被发现时的状态

同样为保护遗址真实性，通常采取的方法是保持遗迹历经时代流传至今被我们发现时的状态。这意味着避免对罗马石质墙体进行补砌，尤其避免对已经缺失的部分加以修复或重建。例外的情

Fig. 4
The remains of Hadrian's Wall after "minimal intervention" repair at Burtholme Beck, Cumbria (© Historic England)
图 4
经"最小干预"修复后的哈德良长城遗迹，坎布里亚郡，波索姆贝（版权：英格兰遗产委员会）

况是为保证上部罗马遗迹结构安全而必须在下部进行补砌，以保护上部遗址的真实性。在这种情况下，当排除了其他所有支撑方法，才能够采取新补少量石块的方法，而且补砌方式通常会与原工艺形成微小的差异。

（三）记录

所有保护维修项目都必须详细记录开展的每一步工作，这一点至关重要。如此，未来遗产管理人员及考古学家不仅能掌握哈德良长城遗迹的变化情况，并对采取的保护措施加以评估，为以后的保护维修提供借鉴经验。

（四）资金来源和濒危遗产名录

如上所述，大部分哈德良长城遗迹都处于私有领地。这些私人所有者投入了大笔资金来维护及修复遗迹，那些有责任保护遗迹的独立信托和博物馆更是如此。而对于另外一些所有者而言，哈德良长城并不能对其产业带来额外收益，因而他们不愿投入过多资金来承担保护工作是可以理解的。在这种情况下，近年来有三个额外的资金渠道推动重要保护工作的进行。

英格兰遗产委员会一直以来发放补助金给土地所有者，资助重要保护工作。补助金优先发放给列入英国濒危遗产名录（Heritage at Risk Register）的长城区段。还有一些保护工作利用来自英国国家

quarrying of significant parts of the Wall and its surroundings at Walltown and Cawfields for stone, an important source of local employment. The successful campaign to preserve the Wall, which eventually in the 1950's succeeded in halting the destruction following the purchase of the quarrying rights, represented an important change in the UK's attitude to conservation of the historic environment.

The Ministry of Works Consolidation Programme

Many of the remains of the Wall presented to the public today as part of the national collection are the result of the programme of consolidation carried out by staff from the government's Ministry of Works. This is a magnificent legacy, from which millions of visitors have gained enjoyment and an understanding of our Roman heritage, and which is still in good condition 80 or more years after work was undertaken.

With the benefit of hindsight, however, the legacy of this work is mixed - clearance of the Wall was largely carried out without archaeological supervision or recording and significant rebuilding was undertaken. This has left us with a magnificent monument, but at the expense of loss of understanding of the relationship between the Wall and its surrounding archaeology and questions about the degree to which some of these sites are genuinely and authentically Roman.

Recent Success

In addition to major conservation works at Great Chesters, Caw Gap and Burtholme Beck, and the current resurgence in research and publication on the Wall, recent years have seen major successes for Hadrian's Wall and its management. These have included:

- Three iterations of the management plan for the Hadrian's Wall World Heritage Site, and the successful integration with the Antonine Wall and Upper Raetian German Limes as part of the Frontiers of the Roman Empire World Heritage Site
- The successful planning and sustainable management of the Hadrian's Wall Path National Trail, a major step-change in public access and enjoyment of the Wall
- The publication of an archaeological map for Hadrian's Wall, fully revised and taking into account the more than 30 years of discoveries since the last edition.

CHALLENGES FOR THE 21ST CENTURY

Hadrian's Wall remains in good health and good condition; it is a major economic driver and a source of local and national pride and identity. Nevertheless, challenges remain, with principle issues being the sustainable resourcing for management and co-ordination, and for maintenance of the National Trail, and as well as uncertainty about future farm support which does so much to safeguard the Wall.

彩票（National Lottery）的资金。然而，过去 15 年来大多数的保护工作，特别是在大切斯特（Great Chesters）和科盖普（Caw Gap）等大型遗址的项目，资金来源都是农业支持款项，其未来因英国脱欧而尚未明朗。

六、失败与成功

（一）在长城上采石

在过去的一个世纪，哈德良长城保护面临最大的挑战或许可以说是沃尔敦和考菲尔德地区在长城绝大部分墙体及其周边发展的采石业，该产业为当地就业的主要来源。最终，保护长城的斗争取得成功，在 20 世纪 50 年代政府以购买采石权方式遏制住对墙体的毁坏，这也标志着英国对保护历史环境态度的重大转变。

（二）建设部（Ministry of Works）的加固项目

今天面向公众开放的国有长城遗迹，大部分是当年由英国建设部员工实施的加固工程。其成效十分突出，数百万名游客得以享受并认识哈德良长城罗马遗产，且加固工作完成 80 多年后仍然状况良好。

然而，即便成效明显，加固工作带来的影响却有好有坏。大部分长城清理工作并没有考古专家的监督或记录，而且实施了大量重建。工程给后人留下了一处壮观的遗迹，代价却是丧失了了解长城与其周边环境关系的考古学研究机会，对于遗址哪些部分保留了罗马原始状态也无法回答。

（三）近期成果

这几年来，大切斯特、科盖普和波索姆贝（Burtholme Beck）等地区开展的大规模保护工作，长城的研究及出版数量也有所上升。除了上述成就外，还涌现出许多哈德良长城及其管理的成功案例，其中包括：

· 哈德良长城世界遗产地管理计划的三次修订，以及其与安东尼长城和上雷蒂亚—日尔曼长城成功合作，列入罗马帝国边疆世界遗产地。

· 哈德良长城国家步道的成功规划和持续管理，是公众接触并享受长城的一大突破。

· 哈德良长城考古地图的出版，进行了全面修订并将超过 30 年的发现成果纳入最新版本中。

七、21 世纪的挑战

哈德良长城处于健康良好状况，不仅是经济发展的重要引擎，也是地方和国家骄傲及身份认同的来源。然而，挑战依旧存在，主要问题包括管理和合作所需的可持续资源，国家步道的维护，以及未来农场资金的不确定性，该资金目前是长城保护的主要来源。

金山岭长城维修、保护与利用

贾海麟
（金山岭长城文物管理处，中国承德）

摘　要

河北省人民委员会在 1956 年将滦平县境内长城列为"河北省重点文物保护单位"。1984 至 1986 年间，国家文物局对金山岭长城段实施第一次大规模维修后，即正式对外开放。滦平县金山岭长城管理处作为金山岭长城的主管单位，全面负责金山岭长城文物保护与旅游开发的各项工作。历经 30 余年的发展，金山岭在长城维修、保护与旅游展示利用方面取得了可喜的成绩。对这些成绩经验的概括总结，有利于把握金山岭长城的发展脉络，有利于金山岭长城在修缮保养过程中避免不必要的失误，有利于金山岭长城在今后的大旅游大建设中保持自身独特的发展方向。[1] [2] [3]

关键词：世界文化遗产　长城　金山岭长城

河北省承德市滦平县位于燕山山脉与河北平原交汇处，县域东西长南北窄，形成以山地丘陵与河谷沟壑并存的自然环境。境内最高峰为白草洼国家森林公园主峰，海拔 1768 米，最低处为古北口长城北侧潮河川湿地，海拔 210 米。山体地层多由火成岩构成，距县城西南 7.5 千米处东营村的碧霞山为侏逻纪地貌，怪石奇峰林立。

境内以南北走向的拉海岭山山脉为界，东部属于滦河水系，有滦河、伊逊河、兴洲河。西部属于潮河水系流经古北口，潮河流程 60 千米。

县域属大陆季风型山区气候，春秋季风大，多西北、西南风，年平均气温 7.6 摄氏度，无霜期 150 天，年平均降雨量 500 毫米左右。

滦平县内长城主要位于西南部山区的涝洼乡和巴克什营镇，长城东起涝洼乡"回头残楼"，西抵营盘乡高楼子，全长 64 华里，驰名中外的金山岭长城为其间的主要段落。

金山岭长城，南与北京市密云区相邻，距北京城区 130 千米，北与承德市相接，距清皇家园林"避暑山庄"87 千米，木兰围场草原 280 千米。有京承高速公路及 101 国道穿越长城通过。此处长城始建于明代洪武年间，隆庆至万历年间在戚继光任蓟镇总兵官时期增筑。明代属于蓟镇古北口路管理，是明朝与北方势力的军事疆界，形成当时南控幽燕，北捍朔漠，守卫着华北平原通往内蒙古草原的交通要道。清康熙皇帝在《回銮抵古北口》中称此地为 "地扼襟喉趋朔漠、天留锁钥枕雄关"。

金山岭长城西起龙峪口，东至望京楼，全长 10.5 公里。其间有敌楼 67 座，通关隘口 5 处，烽火台 3 座。因属地管理及习惯上称谓，又将辖区内长城划分为四部分：一是西部龙峪口至六眼楼现为军管区，习惯上称为金山岭长城西段；二是东部四眼楼至望京楼 现作为司马台景区经营管理，称为司马台；三是依国家文物局保护要求，将小狐顶楼（麒麟楼）、大狐顶楼、碾子沟楼（司马台称为"13 号楼、12 号楼、

RESTORATION, PROTECTION AND UTILIZATION OF JINSHANLING GREAT WALL

Jia Hailin

Jinshanling Great Wall Cultural Relics Management Office - Chengde - China

Abstract

The Great Wall in Luanping County was listed as a provincial level Protected Unit of Cultural Relics (PUCR) by the People's Committee of Hebei Province in 1956. This section of Jinshanling Great Wall, located in Luanping County, was officially opened to the public after the first large-scale maintenance project was undertaken between 1984 and 1986, supported by the State Administration of Cultural Heritage. As the designated administrative body, the Jinshanling Great Wall Management Office of Luanping County is responsible for comprehensive work on the site, including conservation and tourism development. Great achievements have been made over 30 years of maintenance, protection and tourism interpretation. Review of these successful experiences helps us to understand different stages of development, to avoid unnecessary mistakes in future maintenance and repair, and to preserve its uniqueness in the future, especially in the context of the large-scale development of a Grand Tourism City of Luanping.

Keywords: World Heritage; Great Wall; Jinshanling Great Wall

Luanping County, Chengde City, Hebei Province, is located at the intersection of the Yanshan Mountains and the Hebei Plain. The county is long and narrow, stretching from north to south, forming a natural environment where mountains, hills and river valleys coexist. The highest peak is in the Baicaoyu National Forest Park, with an altitude of 1,768m. The lowest point is the Chaohe River wetland on the north side of the Great Wall at Gubeikou, with an elevation of 210m. The mountain strata are mostly composed of igneous rocks. The Bixia Mountain in Dongying Village, 7.5 km southwest of the county town, is of Jurassic geomorphology, full of picturesque peaks and rocky outcrops.

The territory is bounded by the Lahailing Mountains which run north-south. The eastern part lies in the Luanhe River system, including the Luanhe River, the Yixun River and the Xingzhou River. The western part is situated in the Chaohe River system flowing through Gubeikou; the Chaohe River flows for 60 km in the County.

The county is located in the continental monsoon mountainous climatic region. It has strong northwesterly and southwesterly winds in spring and autumn. The annual average temperature is 7.6 degrees Celsius, the frost-free period is 150 days, and the annual average rainfall is about 500 mm.

The Great Wall in Luanping County is mainly located in the southwestern part of Laowaxiang township and

11 号楼"），设为金山岭与司马台双方公共管理区域，习惯称为公共段；四是金山岭长城景区开放段。

金山岭长城开放区域为西六眼楼至东五眼楼，长 4658 米，有敌楼 30 座，自西向东分别是六眼楼、桃春楼、桃春东楼、西岔沟楼、西五眼楼、西梁砖垛楼、砖垛口西方台、砖垛楼、砖垛口东方台、支墙敞楼、支墙四方台、将军楼、西域楼、沙岭口西方台、沙岭口东方台、黑姑楼、一号敞楼、二号敞楼、小金山楼、大金山楼、窑沟楼、高尖楼、后川楼、沙子沟楼、花楼、拐角楼、冰道沟楼、黑楼、车道沟楼、东五眼楼。其中砖石空心敌台 9 座，战台 1 座，基础平台 4 座，木结构敌台 16 座（木构件缺失，仅存砖墙体）。

通关隘口自西向东为龙峪口、桃春口、砖垛口、沙岭口、后川口。

烽火台有沙岭口东山砖石混筑圆形烽火台 1 处、砖垛口西山砖石混筑圆形烽火台 1 处、龙峪口东侧残存石砌方形烽火台 1 处（图 1）。

作为明代长城的代表段落金山岭，1986 年 12 月正式对外开放，1982 年与承德"避暑山庄"一同批准为国家级风景名胜区，1987 年长城列入世界文化遗产名录，1988 年公布为第三批全国重点文物保护单位，2016 年通过国家 5A 级旅游景区质量景观评定。

图 1

雾漫金山（摄影：郭中兴）

Fig. 1

Jinshanling Great Wall in the Fog (© Guo Zhongxing)

Bakshiying town. The Great Wall runs west from Laowaxiang's Hui Tou Can Lou tower, to the Gaolouzi tower in Yingpan township, totaling 64 miles long. The well-known Jinshanling Great Wall is a major part of this section.

The Jinshanling Great Wall, adjacent to Beijing's Miyun District in the south, is 130 km away from Beijing's urban area. To the north it borders Chengde City and is 87 km away from the Summer Mountain Resort of the royal Qing family and 280 km from the Mulanweichang Grassland. The Jingcheng Expressway and 101 National Road each cross the Great Wall in Luanping County. This section of the Great Wall dates originally from the Hongwu Period of the Ming Dynasty. During the period from Longqing to Wanli, further sections of the Great Wall were built when Qi Jiguang acted as the general commander of Ji Zhen. The Jinshanling Great Wall was under the jurisdiction of the Gubeikou Lu under Ji Zhen during the Ming Dynasty. It constituted the military boundary between the Ming Dynasty and the tribes to the north, and guarded the route leading to the Inner Mongolian grassland from the North China Plain.

Jinshanling Great Wall starts from Longyukou in the west and Wangjing Tower in the east, with a total length of 10.5 km. There are 67 defensive towers, 5 fortified passes and 3 beacon towers. Through the Chinese system of localised management of heritage sites, responsibility for the Great Wall in this region is divided between four administrative areas. The Western section from Longyukou to Liuyanlou Tower is now a military administrative area, which is customarily called the Jinshanling Great Wall West Section. The Eastern section from Siyanlou Tower to Wangjing Tower, is now operated as the Simatai Scenic Area, known as Simatai Great Wall. According to the requirements of NCHA, Xiaohuding Tower (Qilin Tower), Dahuding Tower and Nianzigou Tower (referred to as Tower 13, Tower 12 and Tower 11 respectively by Simatai) are designated as a section jointly managed by both Simatai and Jinshanling. The fourth administrative area is the open section of the Jinshanling Great Wall Scenic Area.

The open area of the Jinshanling Great Wall runs from the West Liuyanlou Tower to the East Wuyanlou Tower. It is 4,658m long and has 30 defensive towers. From west to east, these are Liuyanlou, Taochunlou, Taochundonglou, Xichagoulou and west Wuyanlou, Xiliang Brick Tower, Zhuanduokou, Xifangtai, Zhuanduolou, Zhuanduokou Dongfangtai, Zhiqiangchanglou, Zhiqiang Sifangtai, General Tower, Xiyu Tower, Shalingkou Dongfangtai, Shalingkou Xifangtai, Hegulou, No.1 Changlou, No.2 Changlou, Xiaojinshan Tower, Dajinshan Tower, Yaogou Tower, Gaojian Tower, Houchuan Tower, Shazigou Tower, Hualou, Corner Tower, Bingdaogou Tower , Heilou, Chedaogoulou, east Wuyanlou Tower. Among them, there are 9 masonry and brick chambered towers, 1 battle platform, 4 base platforms, and 16 wooden defensive platforms. (The wooden components are missing; only the brick walls remain.)

From the west to the east, the fortified passes are Longyukou, Taochunkou, Zhuanduokou, Shalingkou and Houchuankou.

The beacon towers include a circular masonry and brick tower constructed on the eastern mountain at Shalingkou, a circular masonry and brick beacon tower constructed on the western mountain, and the remains of a

为加强对金山岭长城及其周边环境的保护。河北省文物事业管理局在 1992 年 3 月 10 日公布河北省人民政府 [1992] 9 号文件《河北省人民政府关于印发〈河北省国家级、省级文物保护单位保护范围及建设控制地带〉的通知》中，确定了金山岭长城的保护范围及建设控制地带。

保护范围：以长城基础两侧为边线，分别向两侧外扩水平距离 300 米；

建设控制地带：以保护范围边线为基线，再分别向两侧外扩 300 米（图 2）。

河北省对长城的保护与管理起步较早。1956 年，河北省人民委员会即将金山岭一带长城列为省级重点文物保护单位（图 3）。

图 2
金山岭长城保护区域图（制图：贾海麟）
Fig. 2
Jinshanling Great Wall Protection Area Map
Yellow: Core Zone Gray: Buffer Zone (© Jia Hailin)

图 3
1956 年设立的长城保护标志（摄影：贾海麟）
Fig. 3
Great Wall Protection Sign erected in 1956 (© Jia Hailin)

1977 年，滦平县民办教师贾云峰向国务院领导写信，呼吁加强长城保护。此信被时任中央委员会副主席、政治局常委、国务院副总理李先念批示"长城不能毁，要保护好"（图 4）。

1978 年，滦平县文管所首次对辖区内明长城进行实地考察，根据考察结果撰写了《滦平县长城调查报告》。

1979 年，在内蒙古呼和浩特市召开的"全国长城保护研究座谈会"上。滦平县文化局局长苗济田在大会上介绍了后来被称为"金山岭长城"的这段明长城，随即引起参会专家、学者的高度重视。会议结束后在国家文物局文物处处长陈滋德的带领下对滦平县长城进行实地察看。这次考察活动经新华社播发，中国国际广播电台以十几种语言进行播报后，河北省滦平县存在雄伟壮美长城的消息立即传遍世界各地（图 5）。

为什么金山岭长城的一次考察新闻稿能引起如此大的轰动呢？这里除了保护完好的长城，还有万里长城中存在的唯一的"麒麟影壁"；还有无数的印有"文字"的长城砖。

金山岭长城小狐顶楼（麒麟楼）楼橹上，保存着一幅青砖拼接砌筑的麒麟影壁，影壁上一只腾云驾雾的麒麟浮雕

masonry square beacon tower to the east side of Longyukou. (Figure 1)

As an outstanding example of the Great Wall of the Ming Dynasty, Jinshanling was officially opened to the public in December 1986. In 1982, it was approved as a National-Level Scenic Area together with Chengde Summer Mountain Resort. In 1987, the Great Wall was inscribed as a Cultural World Heritage Site and was designated in the third batch of NKPUCRs in 1988. It passed the national 5A level Scenic Area accreditation in 2016.

To strengthen the protection of the Jinshanling Great Wall and its surrounding environment, on 10 March 1992 the Hebei Provincial Cultural Relics Administration Bureau promulgated 'The People's Government of Hebei Province [1992] No. 9 document', which defined the "protection boundaries and construction control zone for national and provincial PUCRs in Hebei Province". For Jinshanling, the protected area extends 300m on either side of the Great Wall, and the construction control zone extends a further 300m from the outer limits of the protected areas (Fig. 2)

图 4
修复前的金山岭长城（摄影：成大林 .1979）
Fig. 4
Jinshanling Great Wall before restoration (© Cheng Dalin, 1979)

The protection and management of the Great Wall started early in Hebei Province. In 1956, the Hebei Province People's Committee listed stretches of the Great Wall, including Jinshanling as a provincial level PUCR. (Fig. 3)

In 1977, Li Xianzhang, a village teacher from Luanping County, wrote a letter to State Council leaders calling for strengthened protection for the Great Wall. The letter was signed by Li Xiannian, then vice chairman of the central committee, member of the standing committee of the political bureau and vice premier of the state council, who stated that "the Great Wall must not be destroyed but must be well protected". (Fig. 4)

In 1978, Luanping County Cultural Management Institute conducted the first field investigation of the Ming Dynasty Great Wall within its jurisdiction. The results were published in the "Report on the Great Wall Survey

图案，是迄今保存最完整、最壮观，且是唯一镶嵌在长城影壁上的一幅麒麟图（图6）。

"麒麟影壁"图案长184厘米，高110厘米。由竖排3块，横排5块大小相同的15块长城方砖砌筑组成。

麒麟图案是预先在泥坯上捏制、雕塑，然后经砖窑烧制完成。如果没有高超的制作与烧制工艺，是不可能用薄厚不均的泥坯砖块烧制出如此精美的麒麟图案的。这充分体现金山岭长城的修建，已达明代长城修建技术的顶峰（图7）。

图5
修复前的金山岭长城（摄影：成大林 .1979）
Fig. 5
Jinshanling Great Wall before restoration (© Cheng Dalin, 1979)

金山岭东部及西部长城敌台、墙体上，多是用带有"文字"的长城砖砌筑，这种砖的用量在长城修建史上极为罕见。砖上文字内容有"万历五年山东左营造""万历五年镇虏奇兵营造""万历六年振武营右造""万历六年延绥营造""镇虏奇兵营万历七年造"等多达近十种，记录着当时修建长城部队的番号和施工年代。这些文字砖的遗存，除了具有较高的史学研究价值，也成为万里长城上的一处奇观（图8）。

在谭伦、张居正的支持下，戚继光"因地形，用险制塞"，通过对蓟镇原有一千二百里的长城进行改建和重建，增加空心敌台等方式，形成金山岭长城健全、缜密并且具有一定纵深的、完整的长城军事防御体系。

金山岭区域平均海拔约500米，长城俯卧盘旋于山巅之上，起伏跌宕于沟壑之间，气势磅礴，雄伟壮观。其由远及近分别设置的烽火台、劈山墙、挡马墙、支墙、坞墙、障墙、炮台、战台、敌台、指挥所等，是明代长城军事建筑的典范。而其视野开阔、敌楼密集、景观奇特、建筑艺术精美、保存完好又被赞誉为中国万里长城中的精粹。

1983年国家文物局在滦平县召开"全国长城保护工作会议"。会议上对金山岭长城维修价值进行了学术论证，

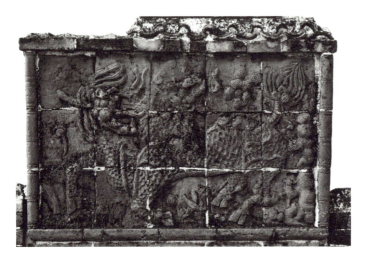

图6
麒麟影壁（摄影：贾海麟）
Fig. 6
Qilin moulded brick panel picture (© Jia Hailin)

of Luanping County".

In 1979, a National Great Wall Protection Research Symposium was held in Hohhot, Inner Mongolia. Miao Jitian, director of the Culture Bureau of Luanping County, gave a presentation on the section of Ming Dynasty Great Wall (later called the 'Jinshanling Great Wall'), and immediately attracted the attention of experts and scholars. After the meeting, under the leadership of Chen Zide, director of the Cultural Relics Department of the State Administration of Cultural Heritage, a field investigation on the Great Wall was carried out in Luanping County. This investigation was broadcast by Xinhua News Agency and China Radio International aired the news in more than a dozen languages. Awareness of the majestic and magnificent Great Wall in Luanping County of Hebei Province was immediately spread around the world. [2]

Why did a press release on an field tour on the Jinshanling Great Wall cause such a stir? In addition to the well-preserved Great Wall, it also features the only surviving moulded brick panel picture of a Qilin[1] along the Great Wall, and includes countless Great Wall inscribed bricks.

The panel picture, which is made of black bricks, can be seen on the platform of the Xiaoguding Tower (Qilin Tower), and shows a Qilin flying amid clouds (Fig. 6).

The Qilin moulded brick panel picture is 184cm long and 110cm high and consists of 15 square bricks, 3 high and 5 horizontal. The bricks were made from clay, which was sculpted and then fired in a brick kiln. Without highly skilled craftsmanship and a very precise firing process, it is impossible to create such an intricate pattern with thin and uneven brick. The Jinshanling Great Wall represents the pinnacle of the Ming Dynasty Great Wall construction technology. (Fig. 7)

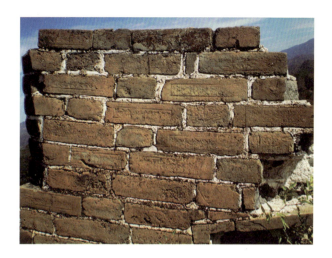

图 7
文字砖墙体 （摄影：贾海麟）
Fig. 7
Brick Wall with Characters (© Jia Hailin)

图 8
文字砖文字 "万历六年墙子路造"（摄影：贾海麟）
Fig. 8
Text on the Brick states "Constructed by Qiangzilu Troop in the 6th year of Wanli" (© Jia Hailin)

1 A *Qilin* is a mythical beast with scales, hooves and horns, and is symbolic of a wise and benevolent ruler and is said to bring good luck. (Editors' note)

图 9
全国长城保护工作会议座谈会合影（滦平县金山岭长城文物管理处档案室 .1983）
Fig. 9
Group photo of the National Great Wall Protection Working Conference
(© Archive of Jinshanling Great Wall Heritage Management Office in
Luanping County, 1983)

并确定保护维修方案和资金拨款计划。委托国家文物局文物研究所长城专家朱希元先生全面负责金山岭长城修复工程（图 9）。

滦平县政府即时批准设立"滦平县金山岭长城管理处"，作为集维修、保护与利用为一体的多功能行政机构。以"金山岭长城管理处"为主体的长城维修、保护工作随即展开。

金山岭长城经历四百多年，敌台、墙体等均受到不同程度的损坏，其病害来源主要包括雷击、狂风、雨水渗透、动物、植被侵扰及人为直接或间接破坏等因素造成（图 10）。

滦平县金山岭管理处在阻断人为伤害之后，依照《文物保护法》及河北省《文物保护修缮保护工程管理办法》，秉承"原材料、原形制、原工艺、原结构"的维修原则，在克服办公条件简陋，施工环境复杂等不利因素下，遵循"不改变文物原状"维修要求，在总结砖垛口至西梁砖垛楼 50 米长城墙体试修经验的基础上，1984 年至 1986 年历时三年时间，完成大金山楼向西至西梁砖垛楼 2050 米的墙体、14 座敌楼、战台，2 座烽火台，2 处古关隘口的修复工作，并向东清理树木杂草，加固浮砖 8 千米至望京楼（图 11）。

在金山岭长城施工过程中，罗哲文及杜仙洲、齐英涛、杨烈等长城专家、学者多次到施工现场进行技术指导。

2014 年同样在国家文物局的支持下，再次实施《金山岭 "01 沙子沟楼"至"07 号东五眼楼"长城保护维修工程》，对金山岭长城东部的敌楼、墙体进行抢险维修。本次维修在既有长城保护修缮原则下，坚持以"原址保护"与"最小干预"的抢险保护要求为指导，本着边排险边清理，先归安后局部加固处理的施工步骤，完成敌楼 7 座，墙体 700 米的抢险维修设计要求。通过施工，达到排除长城本体险情，消除长城安全隐患的目的。同时有效的保持了金山岭长城原有古朴沧桑的历史风貌，受到业界同行的认可，也被喜欢热爱长城的社会人士所接受（图 12、13）。

1983 年起至 2016 年止，金山岭长城通过国拨、社会捐助、自筹等方式，累计投入保护与维修资金 2520 万元。

1986 年金山岭长城开放伊始，在朱希元先生的主持下，滦平县金山岭长城管理处就及时组建并培养了自己的长城保护队伍，通过开办长城保护培训班、举办长城座谈会等方式，培养工作人员爱长城护长城的责任意识，强化工作人员爱岗敬业的工作素质，并应用于长城保护的日常工作当中（图 14）。

In the east and west of Jinshanling, the defensive towers and walls of the Great Wall include many inscribed Great Wall bricks. Such a high number of inscribed bricks used in one area is extremely rare. The texts on the bricks include: "Constructed by Shandong Zuoying Battalion in the 5th year of Wanli"; "Constructed by Zhenru Qibingying Battalion in the 6th year of Wanli"; "Constructed by Zhenwu Youying Battalion in the 6th year of Wanli"; "Constructed by Yansui Battalion in the 6th year of Wanli"; and "Constructed by Zhenru Qibingying Battalion in the 7th year of Wanli", etc. There are more than a dozen texts which record the regiment which constructed different sections of the Great Wall and the year in which they were built. These inscribed bricks are not only of high historical research value, but also a major wonder on the Great Wall. (Fig. 8)

With the support of Tan Lun and Zhang Juzheng, Commander Qi Jiguang reformed and reconstructed the existing twelve hundred li of the Great Wall in Ji Zhen, "following the terrain, and putting up fortresses at stra-

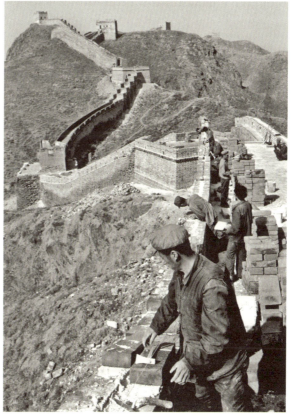

图 10
2013 年 6 月 26 日支墙敞楼前窗被雷击中（摄影：贾海麟）
Fig. 10
On June 26, 2013, the arrow window of the open-walled tower was struck by lightning (© Jia Hailin)

图 11
维修中的金山岭长城（摄影：成大林 .1984）
Fig. 11
Maintenance works at Jinshanling Great Wall (© Cheng Da-lin, 1984)

2013 年实施长城保护员机制。金山岭长城管理处在末开放的长城段落，聘请沿线有责任心，热爱长城的当地居民作为长城保护员，开展定期的长城巡查与保护工作。

管理处除不定期的对保护员进行长城知识培训外，还为聘用的每名保护员配备上岗标志、测绘工具、笔记本、周巡查登记表、生活用品等物品。同时，按照文物收入用于文物保护原则，管理处从金山岭长城景区门票收入中，分别为每位保护员每年发放 6000 元的生活补助，这些费用是长城沿线保护员年度补助费用中最高的。

依照中国世界文化遗产监测工作的总体部署。自 2006 年起，金山岭长城即开展实施世界遗产地的监测工作，稳步推进并完善"长城本体、气象、自然环境、游客量"等四位一体的监测模式。定点定位监测记录长城本体的膨胀、倾斜、沉降等自然变化。同时对雷击、大风、雨雪等恶劣天气现象进行数据采集，统计记录游客人数及周边环境、行政管理变化等对长城的影响。2008 年与当地气象局合作投资 20 万元人民币，在景区设置建成包含 6 要素的气象观测基站，使观测方式技术化，科学化。

目前更加系统全面的《金山岭长城动态监测预警系统实施方案》的评审正在进行中。这一动态监测系统的完成，对遗产本体及周边环境监测能力的提升将是质的飞越（图 15）。

金山岭长城作为 15 世纪军事智慧与匠人技艺融合的结晶，是前人留给子孙的宝贵文化遗产。而近现代的时间里，金山岭长城也是国难时长城抗战的前线，同样是新中国国歌《义勇军进行曲》的诞生地，是中央电视台每日清晨与国歌共同迎接旭日朝阳画面的外景拍摄地。

人文景观与自然环境相融合的金山岭长城，达到了"天人合一"的美的境界。春的韵律，夏的浪漫，秋的辉煌，冬的遐想，不同季节展现不同

图 12
抢险加固前的冰道沟楼 （摄影：贾海麟）
Fig. 12
Bingdaogou Tower before conservation (© Jia Hailin)

tegic points", and created a new form of chambered towers. A robust, tight and complete military defensive system with certain depth inward and outward was formed as the Jinshanling Great Wall.

The average elevation of the Jinshanling area is about 500m. The Great Wall here is magnificent and majestic, riding along the ridge of the mountain, and rising and falling between the gullies. On the outer side of the Wall, a number of particular features were built, including: beacon towers, cut cliffs, horse barrier walls, branch walls, and outskirt walls. On and attached to the Wall were built barrier walls, cannon emplacements, offensive towers, and defensive towers, and to the rear a series of command posts. These features are collectively representative of and typical of Ming Dynasty military engineering and architecture. With an open mountainous panorama, concentrated defensive towers, a stunning landscape, the grandeur of its well-preserved architecture, Jinshanling is praised as an masterpiece of the Wan Li Great Wall.[1]

In 1983, the State Administration of Cultural Heritage held the National Great Wall Protection Work Conference in Luanping County. At the meeting, the principles of maintenance of the Jinshanling Great Wall were discussed, and the protection and maintenance plan and fund allocation plan were agreed. Mr. Zhu Xi-yuan, an expert from the Chinese Academy of Cultural Heritage (CACH), was entrusted with the overall restoration of the Jinshanling Great Wall. (Fig. 9)

图 13
抢险加固后的冰道沟楼（摄影：贾海麟）
Fig. 13
Bingdaogou Tower after conservation (© Jia Hailin)

图 14
滦平县涝洼乡长城保护员座谈会（摄影：贾海麟）
Fig. 14
Symposium of Great Wall Protectors in Luanping County (© Jia Hailin)

The Luanping County Government immediately approved the establishment of the Jinshanling Great Wall Management Office of Luanping County as a multi-functional administrative organisation integrating maintenance, protection and use. The restoration work began soon after the Office was established.

Jinshanling Great Wall is more than 400 years old and during this time the defensive towers and walls have

---

1 The 'Wan Li Great Wall' is a popular name for the most famous section of the Ming Great Wall and literally means 'the Great Wall of Ten Thousand Li' (Editors' note)

图 15
日出金山（摄影：郭中兴）
Fig. 15
Sunrise in Jinshan (© Guo Zhongxing)

的长城壮美画卷，使游人陶醉其中。建设部顾问、诗人郑孝燮先生到金山岭长城参观，胜赞此地"万里长城，金山独秀"。

　　"万里长城，金山独秀"，金山岭长城每年都吸引着大批中外游客前来参观游览，游客人数呈逐年上升趋势。2014 年度，截止 12 月底，景区共接待中外游客 227592 人次。游人中有节假日正常游客、长城爱好者及考察研究人员、影视广告制作人员、专业及业余摄影爱好者等。年龄最高者为 93 岁男性，最小为足月婴儿。

　　2014 年，全年单日游客人数最高峰为五月一日，单日客流人数为 5127 人次。全年预约预订游客47261 人次（含门票、用餐、住宿、订车等）。讲解员讲解 330 人次、直接服务接待人数约为 65000 人次。实现年收入 1100 万元人民币，旅游综合收入 7130 万元人民币。带动遗产地居民直接从事长城保护或与长城有关的经营活动参与者 110 人次。

　　金山岭长城在推进长城景观产业化的同时，组织主办或承接国内外各种大型社会公益类活动。如2016 年成功举办"千名美国人登长城"，"中国卢森堡建交 45 周年庆典"等活动。每年如期举办的"长

been damaged to varying degrees by different forces, including lightning, strong winds, rainwater penetration, and direct or indirect human activities. (Fig. 10)

In addition to the prevention of the manmade damage, the Jinshanling Management Office of Luanping County abides by the Cultural Relics Protection Law and the Management Measures for the Restoration Projects of Cultural Relics in Hebei Province, and adheres to the restoration principle of 'original materials, original form, original process and original structure'. Despite poor administrative accommodation and a complicated and challenging terrain in which to carry out conservation work, Jinshanling Management Office has followed the maintenance principle of 'do not change the original condition of cultural relics'. After a trial restoration on the 50m of the Wall from Zhuanduokou to Xiliang Brick Tower, it took three years, from 1984 to 1986, to complete the restoration of 2,050m of the Wall from the west of Dajinshan Tower to the Xiliang Brick Tower, and 14 defensive towers and offensive towers, 2 beacon towers, and 2 of the ancient fortified passes. In addition, invasive vegetation was removed and loose bricks were stabilized in the eastern section over 8 km to Wangjing Tower. (Fig. 11)

During the restoration of the Jinshanling Great Wall, Luo Zhewen, Du Xianzhou, Qi Yingtao, Yang Lie and other Great Wall experts and scholars visited the site many times to provide technical guidance.

In 2014, with the support of the State Administration of Cultural Heritage, a further restoration project from Jingshanling Shazigou Tower 01 to Dongwuyan Tower 07 was carried out to rescue the defensive towers and walls in the eastern part of the Jinshanling Great Wall. This repair was guided, on the basis of previous principles, by the principles of 'in situ protection' and 'minimum intervention'. During the restoration, broken bricks from the collapsed parts were cleared away and whole bricks were replaced step by step. Consolidation was done on those parts at risk of further collapse, most of which involved simple re-bedding of displaced bricks back into their original position. The restoration covered 7 defensive towers and the 700m of the Wall, achieving the objective of the elimination of structural risks. The time-worn and old features of the original Jinshanling Great Wall were maintained, which was applauded by heritage experts and accepted by the public who treasure the Great Wall. (Fig. 12)

From 1983 to 2016, the Jinshanling Great Wall has invested a total of 25.2 million RMB in restoration and repair. These funds come from government, charitable donations and operating income.

From the opening of the Jinshanling Great Wall in 1986, under the auspices of Mr. Zhu Xiyuan, the Jinshanling Great Wall Management Office of Luanping County established and developed its own professional team. Through organizing Great Wall protection training courses and holding workshops and symposium, a sense of responsibility for protecting the Great Wall has been cultivated among the staff and their capability has been strengthened which is reflected in the daily protection of the Great Wall. (Fig. 14)

In 2013, the system of Great Wall Patrollers was set up. Jinshanling Great Wall Management Office engaged responsible local residents as Great Wall Patrollers to carry out regular inspection of sections of the Great Wall that are not yet open to the public.

In addition to training the Patrollers, the Management Office also provides them with official insignia, surveying tools, notebooks, weekly inspection registration forms, daily necessities and other items. In line with the

表 1 金山岭长城维修简表（单位：人民币元）
Table 1: Jinshanling Great Wall Restoration Record (Currency: RMB)

维修时间 Time (Year)	维修地点 Place	维修内容 Content	资金来源 Sources of funds	金额 Amount
1984 年	砖垛口至西方台试修 50 米墙体 Repaired the 50-metre wall from Zhuanduokou to Xifangtai Tower	修复 Repair	国家文物局 National Cultural Relics Bureau	10 万 100,000
1984 年 – 1986 年	砖垛口至大金山楼修复长城 2000 米，敌楼 14 座，烽火台 2 座，关隘 2 处 Repaired 2000-metres wall from Zhuanduokou to Dajinshan tower, 14 defensive towers, 2 Beacons, and 2 customs gates.	修复 Repair	国家文物局 National Cultural Relics Bureau	110 万 1.1 million
1998 年	麒麟楼至碾子沟楼沿线文字砖墙 600 米 600 metres text brick wall from the Qilin Tower to the Nianzigou Tower	抢险加固 Conservation	自 筹 Operating Income	50 万 500,000
2007 年	后川口段长城 60 米 60 metres for the Houchuankou section of the Great Wall	墙体抢险加固 Conservation of Wall	社会捐助 Charitable Donations	100 万 1 million
2009 年	砖垛楼 Brick tower	恢复砖垛楼 Great Wall Lightning Protection Project	社会捐助 Charitable Donations	40 万 400,000
2010 年	大遗址保护项目 Large Archaeological Site Conservation Project	《金山岭长城总体保护规划》编制 Compilation of Jinshanling Great Wall Overall Protection Plan	河北省文物局 Hebei Province Bureau of Cultural Relics	70 万 700,000
2010 年	后川口至沙子沟楼 260 米 260 metres from Houchuankou to Shazigou Tower	墙体维修保护 Wall maintenance protection	国家文物局 National Cultural Relics Bureau	150 万 1.5 million
2010 年	金山岭长城沿线敌楼 Defensive towers along the Jinshanling Great Wall	长城防雷项目 Great Wall Lightning Protection Project	国家文物局 National Cultural Relics Bureau	300 万 3 million
2012 年	缓冲区范围外 Off-buffer zone	文物看护用房 消防井 护坡护栏 Cultural relics care room Fire well Slope guardrail	国家发改委 National Development and Reform Commission	400 万 4 million
2013 年	西六眼楼至碾子沟楼沿线 Along West Liuyanlou Tower and Nianzigou Tower	敌楼、墙体抢险加固 Conservation of defensive towers and walls	自 筹 Operating income	50 万 500,000

续表 Continued

维修时间 Time (Year)	维修地点 Place	维修内容 Content	资金来源 Sources of funds	金额 Amount
2014 年	沙子沟楼至东五眼楼 700 米墙体，敌楼 7 座 700-metres walls from Shazigou Tower to Wuyanlou Tower, and 7 defensive towers	抢险维修加固 Conservation	国家文物局 National Cultural Relics Bureau	400 万 4 million
2016 年	对五处挡马墙病害部分进行归安处理 Carrying out restoration treatment for the five parts of the horse walls	石质墙体加固，补砌 Stone wall Conservation	自 筹 Operating income	40 万 400,000
1983 年 – 2017 年	累计碎修保护敌楼、墙体 Repair to protect defensive towers and walls	加固 Conservation	自 筹 Operating income	800 万 8 million
1983 年——2017 年累计投入保护资金 Cumulative investment protection funds from 1983—2017			2520 万 2.52 million	

principle that the revenue from cultural relics should be used for the protection of cultural relics, the Management Office pays each Patroller an annual living subsidy of 6,000 RMB from the ticket revenue of Jinshanling Great Wall Scenic Area. This is the highest annual subsidy for Patrollers along the Great Wall.

Within the framework set up by the national World Cultural Heritage monitoring system, since 2006 Jinshanling Great Wall has monitored the state of conservation of the World Heritage Site and has steadily promoted and improved the 'four-in-one' monitoring model of 'Great Wall: Fabric, Meteorology, Natural Environment, and Tourist Volume'. Fixed-point monitoring is used to record natural changes such as bulging, leaning and sinking of the Great Wall structures. At the same time, data are collected on severe weather phenomena such as lightning strikes, strong winds, rain and snow. The impact of tourists, changes in the surrounding environment, and administrative changes on the Great Wall are also recorded. In 2008, in collaboration with the local meteorological bureau, 200,000 RMB were invested to set up a meteorological observatory inside the Scenic Area.

A review of the implementation plan of the Jinshanling Great Wall Dynamic Monitoring and Early Warning System is currently in progress. The full implementation of this dynamic monitoring system will enhance the ability to monitor the condition of the site and its surrounding environment. (Fig. 15)

As the culmination of military expertise and craftsmanship in the 15th century, the Jinshanling Great Wall is a precious cultural heritage site left to us by our ancestors. In modern times, the Jinshanling Great Wall was also the front line of national resistance in the war against Japan. It is also the birthplace of the national anthem "The March of the Volunteers", and the scene of CCTV's footage of the rising sun which accompanies the national anthem every morning.

Jinshanling Great Wall, a combination of cultural landscape and natural environment, represents 'harmony between the heavenly and the human'. From the rhythm of spring, the romance of summer, the glory of autumn, the delusion of winter, different pictures of the Great Wall in different seasons intox-

表 2 2014 年度金山岭长城游客人数统计表（单位：人次）

Table 2 Statistics of the number of visitors to Jinshanling Great Wall in 2014 (unit: person)

月 份 Month	游客人数 Visitor numbers		单月合计 Monthly total
1	内宾 Domestic visitors	1294	1984
	外宾 Foreign visitors	690	
2	内宾 Domestic visitors	2435	3232
	外宾 Foreign visitors	797	
3	内宾 Domestic visitors	4583	6230
	外宾 Foreign visitors	1647	
4	内宾 Domestic visitors	21619	26606
	外宾 Foreign visitors	4987	
5	内宾 Domestic visitors	20775	24436
	外宾 Foreign visitors	3661	
6	内宾 Domestic visitors	10458	14063
	外宾 Foreign visitors	3605	
7	内宾 Domestic visitors	28500	35864
	外宾 Foreign visitors	7364	
8	内宾 Domestic visitors	35319	43388
	外宾 Foreign visitors	8069	
9	内宾 Domestic visitors	17391	22505
	外宾 Foreign visitors	5114	
10	内宾 Domestic visitors	29276	36505
	外宾 Foreign visitors	7229	
11	内宾 Domestic visitors	7748	10353
	外宾 Foreign visitors	2605	
12	内宾 Domestic visitors	1797	2426
	外宾 Foreign visitors	629	
总计 Total	227592	内宾合计 Domestic Visitors Total 181195 外宾合计 Foreign Visitors Total	46397

icate visitors. Mr. Zheng Xiaoxie, a consultant at the Ministry of Construction and also a poet, visited the Jinshanling Great Wall and praised it, saying "Jinshan is outstanding among all the Great Walls".

Jinshanling Great Wall attracts a large number of visitors from home and abroad every year, and the number of visitors is increasing year by year. In 2014, there were 227,592 visitors from home and abroad. These included regular holiday tourists, Great Wall enthusiasts and researchers, film and television crews, and professional and amateur photographers. The oldest tourist was a 93-year-old male visitor, the youngest one a new-born baby.

In 2014, the busiest single day was on May 1, when there were 5,127 visitors. A total of 47,261 visitors made bookings during the year, including tickets, meals, accommodation, and travel. Guided tours were delivered 330 times and the number of people taking guided tours was about 65,000. The annual income from entrance fees was 11 million RMB and the overall comprehensive tourism income was 71.3 million RMB. This generated employment for 110 local residents directly engaged in protection of the Great Wall or operational activities related to the Great Wall.

Jinshanling Great Wall organised large-scale charitable fundraising activities at home and abroad while promoting the local economy of the Great Wall. For example, in 2016 it held a successful 'Thousands of Americans Climbing the Great Wall' event, and ceremonies marking 'The 45th Anniversary of China-Luxembourg Diplomatic Relations'. The 'Great Wall Apricot Flower Festival', 'Great Wall Hiking Festival', 'Great Wall International Marathon' and 'Great Wall Four Seasons Landscape Photography Exhibition' are held every year to provide visitors with a variety of experiences on the Jinshanling Great Wall. At the same time, these social activities have also become important promotional activities, well recognized by the general public. (Fig. 16)

To promote the profound cultural heritage of the Great Wall and the magnificent Jinshanling Great Wall landscape, the Luanping County Government took advantage of its location in the Beijing-Tianjin region to create a Jinshanling Great Wall Culture economic circle, and meanwhile, it combined with the region's Shanrong Culture[1], Yulu Palace Culture[2] and Mandarin Hometown Culture[3] to form an unique pillar of the cultural indus-

---

1 Luanping County is the most representative area of the ethnic communities of the mountains, and the discovery of a large number of bronze daggers, horse ornaments, and frog face jars not only records the life of the mountain people and the goods they produced, but also shows the historical civilization created by the ancestors here. The Luanping County Government invested RMB 100 million to build the country's first Rongshan Cultural Theme Museum and Rongshan Cultural Theme Park to create a distinctive Rongshan cultural brand in Luanping County.

2 Luanping County is the place where the Qing Dynasty royal family had to pass by when they went from the Beijing Forbidden City to Chengde Summer Mountain Resort. There are many palaces in the county, such as the Bakshi Camp Palace, the Two-room Temporary Palace, and the Xingzhou Temporary Palace. Meanwhile, many folk stories are told about the area. The peony in the Xingzhou Palace which was transplanted from the Imperial Garden of the Forbidden City by the Emperor Kangxi still blossoms every year. Ihe cultural rout of the Royal Imperial Palace is one of the theme cultural industries for the development of tourism in Luanping County.

3 Mandarin is a modern standard Chinese with the Beijing dialect as the standard sound, and the northern dialect as the basic dialect, and the modern simplified Chinese books as the grammar standard. In 1953, the pronunciation of Jingoutun Township in Luanping County, Chengde City, Hebei Province became the main collection place for standard pronunciation of Mandarin. After the standard was established, it was promoted nationwide in 1955.

图 16
2015 年度长城马拉松（摄影：郭中兴）
Fig.16
2015 Great Wall Marathon (© Guo Zhongxing)

城杏花节""长城徒步大会""长城国际马拉松""长城四季风光摄影展"等活动，为来到金山岭长城的参观者提供不同的游览感受。同时这些社会活动也成为金山岭长城的金牌活动，受到社会各界的欢迎和好评（图 16）。

为挖掘深厚浓重的长城文化内涵，展示宏伟壮丽的金山岭长城景观。滦平县政府利用环京津的区位优势，着力打造"金山岭长城文化"经济圈，同时与县内"山戎文化"[1]"御路行宫文化"[2]"普通话之乡文化"[3]相结合，形成独有的富有历史与民族活力的滦平县支柱产业文化。

长城作为中华民族伟大力量的象征，作为人类追求和平与安宁的见证，作为民族相互融合的纽带和桥梁，作为文学艺术的宝库和建筑艺术的长廊，长城是中华民族留给世界的瑰宝，金山岭长城无愧于这一瑰宝上的明珠。

1　滦平县是山戎民族活动最具代表性的区域，大量的青铜短剑、车马饰品、蛙面蹲坐石人等山戎文物的发现，不仅记录了山戎人的生产生活，也展示了山戎先民在此地创造的历史文明。滦平县政府投资亿元人民币建成全国首家山戎文化主题博物馆和山戎文化主题公园，打造滦平县特色山戎文化品牌。

2　滦平县为清朝皇室由北京紫禁城前往承德"避暑山庄"的必经之地，县内设有巴克什营行宫、两间房行宫、兴州行宫等多处行宫，同时流传众多民间故事，兴州行宫内康熙皇帝下旨从紫禁城御花园移栽的牡丹花依旧年年开放。打造皇家御道行宫文化板块，是滦平县发展全域旅游的主题文化产业之一。

3　"普通话"是以北京语音为标准音，以北方话（官话）为基础方言，以典范的现代白话文著作作为语法规范的现代标准汉语。1953 年，河北省承德市滦平县金勾屯乡的语音成为普通话标准发音的主要采集地。

tries sector of Luanping County.

As a symbol of the great power of the Chinese nation, the Great Wall serves as a witness to the pursuit of peace and tranquility. As a bridge between national integration, a treasure house of literature and art and a gallery of architectural artistry, the Great Wall is a treasure given by the Chinese nation to the world. Jinshanling Great Wall is a pearl in this treasure.

参考文献
Bibliography

[1] 滦平县志编委会. 滦平县志 [M]. 沈阳 : 辽海出版社，1997:167.

Luanping County Editorial Board. Luanping County Book. Shenyang: Liaohai Publishing House, 1997: 167.

[2] 衣志坚，安忠和编. 金山岭长城 [M]. 沈阳 : 内蒙古文化出版社，2001:98.

Yi, Z.J., and An, Z.H.(eds). Jinshanling Great Wall. Shenyang: Inner Mongolia Culture Publishing House, 2001: 98.

[3] 贾海麟，高兴旺. 中国·滦平金山岭长城 [M]. 北京 : 华夏出版社，2010:192.

Jia, H.L., Gao, X.W(eds). China · Luanping Jinshanling Great Wall. Beijing: Huaxia Publishing House, 2010: 192.

长城保护的思考与实践——从我参与的项目说起

侯　珂

（中国文物保护基金会，中国北京）

摘　要

2016 年 9 月，中国文物保护基金会与腾讯公益慈善基金会联合发起了"保护长城　加我一个"的长城保护公益活动[1]。这是中国文化遗产保护事业进程中，规模较大、互联网技术投入较多、社会公众参与比较多的一次尝试。

以往的长城保护，是以专家和政府官员为主，主要是专业技术力量和政府行政部门的思维为主，欠缺普遍的公众参与。通过观察，我的思考是，文化遗产保护的本质应当是什么？想达到的目的是什么？

文化遗产保护的本质应当是让公众全方位、深层次地参与，让公众接触、保护、欣赏、享有，成为受益者。在这个总体思路的统领下，中国文物保护基金会和腾讯基金会在这个项目上的定位是，双方发挥各自优势开展合作，文保基金会主要推动长城本体的保护修缮，腾讯基金会则以其先进的互联网技术和科技元素赋能长城保护，让更多年轻人走近长城，点燃年轻人对文化遗产的保护热情。

一年多来，我对以往政府主导修缮长城进行了梳理，了解到其中有些不太理想的状况，而我们此次修缮长城，就要针对这些问题，尝试一些改变，解决一些问题。经过近两年的思考与实践，收获了一些经验，总结出一些优点和遗憾，谨以此文与大家分享。

关键词：长城保护　社会参与

一、"保护长城 加我一个"项目的基本情况

中国文物保护基金会创立于 1990 年，是由国家文物局主管的具有独立法人资格的全国公募性公益基金会，是我国文化遗产领域最早建立的全国性 NGO 组织，2017 年取得慈善组织资格认定，成立二十多年来，一直围绕文物保护事业开展工作。2016 年伊始，基金会新一届理事会成立，决定开展以长城为题材的公募活动。之所以选取长城，是因为较之其他不可移动文物资源，长城在国人心中更具有全民性，少受地域性特征的限制。

中国长城跨越多种地貌及多个行政区域，且多处于不发达或欠发达地区，各地政府对长城保护资金的投入与需求相比往往捉襟见肘；同时，长城保护涉及国家、地方政府、文保机构、当地居民等各方面利益，保护和管理工作十分复杂，需要多方参与，精诚合作。在此背景下，2016 年 9 月，中国文物保护基金会与腾讯公益慈善基金会合作发起了以"保护长城，加我一个"为主题的长城保护公募项目[1]，这是一次文化遗产保护与互联网科技跨界合作的尝试，主要方向是对两段长城进行保护修缮，同时开展一系列以长城文化传播、长城 IP 内容挖掘和转化的活动，旨在引导更多人，尤其是年轻人关注长城保护。

REFLECTIONS ON RESTORATION PRACTICES ON THE GREAT WALL FROM THE PROJECTS I HAVE PARTICIPATED IN

Hou Ke

China Foundation for Cultural Heritage Conservation - Beijing - China

Abstract

In September 2016, the China Foundation for Cultural Heritage Conservation (CFCHC) and Tencent© Foundation launched a public fundraising campaign to support a joint initiative named "Protect the Great Wall. Count me in!"[1]. It is one of the first attempts in the history of cultural heritage conservation in China which involves substantial internet technology input and extensive public participation, especially from urban citizens and local inhabitants along the Great Wall.

Traditionally, programmes of restoration of the Great Wall have generally been dominated by experts and government agencies, with little public or local involvement. This paper discusses some concerns identified through evaluation of the functioning and results of these programmes. It argues that cultural heritage conservation programmes should be openly accessible to the public, and should assist the public to appreciate and fully understand the benefits and processes of cultural heritage conservation. In pursuing these objectives, the CFCHC and Tencent© Foundation bring together complementary skills and expertise. The CFCHC is focused on the conservation fieldwork, while Tencent© Foundation introduces the latest internet technology to make the programme more dynamic and engaging for young people.

Over the last 2 years, through evaluating government-led projects, I have sought to identify strengths and weaknesses of conservation practices and procedures, and to identify specific aspects which can be improved. It is hoped that the experience accumulated, as summarised in this article, might be helpful in informing future approaches to heritage conservation in China.

Keywords: The Great Wall Protection, public involvement

THE "PROTECT THE GREAT WALL. COUNT ME IN!" PROJECT

Founded in 1990, the China Foundation for Cultural Heritage Conservation (CFCHC) is a national charitable foundation with independent legal status under the administration of the National Cultural Heritage Administration. It is the first national third sector organization established in the field of cultural heritage in China. It was accredited as a registered charity in 2017. For nearly 30 years since its inception, CFCHC has been working on the preservation of cultural relics. In early 2016, a new council of CFCHC was established, which decided to launch a public fundraising initiative on the theme of the Great Wall. The Great Wall was chosen because it

图1
保护长城加我一个发布会（图片来源：中国文物保护基金会）
Fig. 1
'PROTECT THE GREAT WALL. COUNT ME IN!' openning ceremony (© CFCHC)

项目实施点选定河北省的喜峰口和北京的箭扣段落，这两处，都是纳入了国家文物局"十三五"期间重点修缮计划的长城段落，地势险要、景观雄奇，具有丰富的历史文化内涵，受到的关注度高，社会影响力大。箭扣段落筹款采用线下向企业募集的方式，喜峰口修缮主要是线上筹款，通过微信支付，小额捐款，并辅以线下劝募。

公募活动自启动以来，取得了较好的社会效果，33万余人通过腾讯互联网公益平台实现保护长城的公益梦想。重要的是，筹款期间，中国文物保护基金会及时披露资金信息和项目进展情况，举办"长城之友大讲堂"，普及长城保护知识，主办长城保护工程理念与实践研讨会，利用腾讯公益平台推出动漫宣传短视频，制作H5通过微信向捐款人反馈信息，在节假日期间向所有捐款人推送致谢微信。这些新颖的方式增加了项目举办者与捐赠人的互动，达到了宣传长城文化，提高公众长城保护意识的目的，也使参与者有实实在在的获得感，成为文化遗产领域受到关注度最高的公益项目。在接下来的工程实施阶段，中国文物保护基金会积极将考古的工作方式引入施工作业中，由专业考古机构对施工清理进行指导；开工后，组织现场直播、制作记录两段长城修缮全过程的纪录片、组织公众现场观摩修缮，听取公众意见，接受监督等。这些方法手段的运用以及活动开展的目的，

belongs to the whole nation in the mind of the Chinese people and, in contrast to other cultural sites and monuments, it is not associated with just one location or region.

The Great Wall spans a host of landforms and administrative areas, mostly in underdeveloped parts of the country. The local government administrations along its course more often than not have inadequate funding for the preservation of the Great Wall. At the same time, the state administrations, local governments, cultural protection agencies, local residents and other parties are all stakeholders in the protection of the Great Wall, making its conservation and management highly complicated, and close cooperation between multiple partners is necessary. Against this backdrop, the CFCHC and Tencent Foundation came together in September 2016 to launch a public fundraising initiative for the protection of the Great Wall with the theme of "Protect the Great Wall. Count me in!". This initiative is an attempt to explore the potential for cooperation between cultural heritage protection and internet technology. The conservation programme which this fundraising initiative seeks to support is primarily focused on the restoration and preservation of two sections of the Great Wall. It also aims to carry out a host of activities to promote the culture of the Great Wall, and to develop new platform content and applications, with a view to guiding more people, especially young people, to support the preservation of the Great Wall. The sites selected under this project are the section at Xifengkou, in Hebei Province, and the Jiankou section in Beijing. Both are priority sites for restoration as part of the 13th Five-Year Plan period by the National Cultural Heritage Administration. With treacherous terrain, magnificent landscapes, and rich histories and cultures, the two sections attract great public attention and have a huge social influence. Funding for the Jiankou section project is raised from offline activities. Funding for the Xifengkou restoration project is mainly raised through small online donations via WeChat, supplemented by offline funding appeals.

Since its launch, the public fundraising appeal has generated a significant response from the public. Over 330,000 people have realised their wish to help the protection of the Great Wall through Tencent's charity platform. Throughout the fundraising campaign, the CFCHC regularly published information about the progress of the fund and its projects. We held the "Friends of the Great Wall Lecture Series" to spread awareness of the protection of the Great Wall, and hosted seminars on the principles and activities of the conservation programme for the Great Wall. Through Tencent's charity platform, a promotional animation video was launched to enhance knowledge of the Great Wall, and a HTML5 page was developed to keep donors informed, with relevant updates sent via WeChat, and thank-you WeChat messages were sent to all donors during national festivals and holidays. These novel ways helped the interaction between project organizers and donors, and achieved the purpose of promoting the culture of the Great Wall and raising awareness for the protection of the Great Wall. They also enabled participants to have a sense of tangible benefits from their contributions and this became the highest-profile charitably sponsored project in the field of cultural heritage. In subsequent phases of the project the CFCHC will actively incorporate archaeological work in the conservation programme, and professional archaeological organisations will identify the original archaeological remains of the Wall and direct the clearance of debris and site preparation prior to restoration. When the project is launched, it will provide

是从更高更广的视野，把一项保护工程做成全方位内容丰富的文化遗产公益项目，提高大众的审美情趣，激发公众的创造力。

二、基金会参与修缮长城的几点创新性尝试

箭扣和喜峰口长城修缮是第一次由基金会从头至尾参与运作的项目，在一定程度上，是由基金会操盘运作。启动以来，我们不断调研听取各方意见，努力思考，基金会操盘这个项目，应当与传统做法、与政府主导的修缮有何不同？以往的做法存在哪些亟待解决的问题？我们能否在依法合规的前提下寻找合理路径，尝试一些改变？经过近两年探索磨合，思考出了针对性的措施。一个深切的体会是，"能不能修""怎么修""由谁修""修得如何"以及摆在面前的机制体制创新问题，要比"有没有钱修"更为重要。

（一）首先要解决的是"让不让修""怎么修"的问题

在技术方案的编制上，以往是以政府部门和专家思维为主导，箭扣和喜峰口修缮方案的论证过程，

图 2
箭扣长城修缮前局部（图片来源：中国文物保护基金会）
Fig. 2
Jiankou Great Wall, before restoration (© CFCHC)

live streaming of the site, documentaries on the restoration of the two sections throughout the work, arrange on-the-spot observation of restoration for the general public, receive their opinions, and open the site to them. These methods and activities aim to turn the conservation projects into a broader public cultural heritage initiative, encompassing a rich and wide range of social and cultural perspectives, thereby encouraging the public's aesthetic appreciation and inspiring creativity.

INNOVATIVE ATTEMPTS FOR CFCHC TO PARTICIPATE IN THE RESTORATION OF THE GREAT WALL

It is the first time that CFCHC has ever been involved throughout the whole process of restoration projects. As a joint sponsor of the project, CFCHC has to be responsible for the overall implementation of Jiankou and Xifengkou restoration. Therefore we have been thinking very hard, after listening to different opinions from the wider public, to find out about the differences between this project, operated by CFCHC, and traditional government-led restoration programmes, and considered the problems that needed to be solved in previous ways of working. We have asked ourselves whether feasible solutions to some of the problems can be introduced within existing regulatory and legal frameworks. After nearly two years of exploration, we have come up with some proposed measures. We believe that the questions of whether it should be restored?, how it should be restored?, who will undertake the restoration?, what is the restoration result? - and the issues of changing the mechanism through which restoration projects are implemented - are more important than the question of the availability of funding.

Deciding what should be restored and how should it be restored

Previously, the preparation of technical solutions for restoration projects was dominated by the government departments and by expert opinion. During the discussions on restoration programmes for Jiankou and Xifengkou, government departments, with consideration of the special nature of the programme, accepted CRCHC's recommendations and included a wider range of opinions from the general public. Taking the Jiankou section as an example, CFCHC invited local Cultural Relics Departments, Great Wall restoration experts, programme designers, donor representatives, and representatives of villages surrounding these sections to visit the site several times and inspect the elements at risk in order to better inform decisions about the restoration. For the 744-metre section to be restored, the on-site consultation took more than seven hours. For each section of deterioration requiring restoration, investigators conducted serious discussions, listened to opinions and came up with specifications of work to be done. These were recorded by the design department-in-charge. This process is time-consuming, but it is also a necessary process to ensure that the restoration measures can stand up to wider public scrutiny.

In order to lay solid theoretical foundations for the restoration of the two sections, CFCHC held the "Forum on Great Wall Restoration and Rehabilitation Concepts and Practice" at Shanhai Pass in June 2017. The organizers of the forum invited Cultural Relics Departments and Great Wall protection experts,

政府部门充分考虑到项目运作的特点，接受基金会的建议，吸纳更广泛的公众的意见。以箭扣长城为例，基金会先后邀请文物部门、长城修缮专家、方案设计单位、捐资人代表、长城所在地村民代表等多次赴现场逐段查看病害险情，深化修缮措施。744 米待修缮段落，现场勘察七个多小时，勘察人员遇到每一处病害均认真讨论、听取意见、拿出措施，由设计单位记录在案。这个过程是耗时的，却也是保证修缮措施经得起推敲的必要历程。

为了给两段长城修缮打下坚实的理论基础，2017 年 6 月，基金会在山海关举办"长城保护修缮理念与实践论坛"，论坛邀请长城沿线共 13 个省市文物部门和长城保护专家、设计施工监理等单位参会，研讨了长城保护过程中具有共性的问题，例如，长城修缮如何坚持"最小干预"原则，是否应当坚持其

图 3

喜峰口长城（图片来源：中国文物保护基金会）

Fig. 3

Xifengkou Great Wall (© CFCHC)

designers, constructors and independent supervisors from 13 provinces and municipalities along the Great Wall. Participants discussed common problems in the protection of the Great Wall. These included: how to adhere to the principle of 'minimum intervention' in restoration of the Great Wall; how to uphold the significance and values of the cultural heritage site itself; how to take into account the uniqueness of the Great Wall as a cultural landscape; how to retain the authenticity of its dilapidated and ancient scenery; and how to manage the vegetation surrounding the Great Wall. On the restoration of the Jiankou and Xifengkou sections, the participants reached consensus that the emphasis should be to ensure structural stability. Targeted measures should be taken to avoid collapses in specific areas instead of undertaking wholesale restoration.

CFCHC has enabled wider participation in developing agreed solutions so that all parties can express their concerns and thoughts on the protection of the Great Wall from many perspectives. Restoration measures are fully discussed and therefore are more easily accepted by the public.

Promoting improvements in the system of restoration

The restoration plans for Jiankou and Xifengkou have been approved by the National Cultural Heritage Administration after several rounds of assessment and refinement. It is unprecedented for a third sector organisation to take charge of a Great Wall restoration project. Some issues have to be solved in advance to make alteration to traditional processes of managing restoration projects. Introducing these changes is more challenging than addressing the technical problems of restoration.

With respect to the restoration of Jiankou and Xifengkou, the government departments, the CFCHC and Tencent are each under great pressure to succeed. Because this restoration will be carried out under the spotlight of public opinion, it will be subject to public inspection and scrutiny, and even questioning. The project must be properly handled. To this end, the CFCHC set two goals: First, the two restored sections of the Great Wall should become a model and a demonstration project for the restoration of the Great Wall as a whole, and its restoration principles, techniques and methods should provide guidelines to others. Second, it should demonstrate improvements in the mechanisms and processes by which restoration projects are designed and implemented, through applying a greater flexibility in approach. In this way some problems in restoration project-management have been solved, and some weaknesses in specific aspects of the restoration processes have been corrected, so that greater pragmatism is applied to the restoration of the Great Wall while still respecting protection legislation.

The first problem with the approach to restoration projects is that decisions about the use of funds have too often been driven by financial regulations rather than the specific requirements of each restoration project. In the past, restoration of the Great Wall was state-funded. The project owner[1] (typically the local government) had to

---

1 Usually, the project owner, or Party A in contract terms, is the public institute which manages the site on behalf the government. For a restoration project, it is the owner, or Party A, who is responsible for organizing the whole process, applying for and receiving public funding, and the letting of contracts to designers and constructors, etc. (Editors's note)

图 4
箭扣现场讨论修缮（图片来源：中国文物保护基金会）
Fig. 4
Discussion on restoration at Jiankou (© CFCHC)

不可移动文物属性，同时也要兼顾长城作为人文景观的独特性，保留其历经千年的残破、古朴沧桑的景色，以及长城上的植被处理等问题。与会人员对箭扣和喜峰口长城修缮取得的共识是，重在解决结构稳定问题，有针对性地采取措施，避免出现新的坍塌，而不是完全重新修复。

　　基金会之所以推动技术方案的形成过程有更多话语权参与，在于要保障各方从多角度表达自己对长城保护的关心和思考。技术措施经过充分讨论，更易被公众认可。

　　（二）推动机制体制的突破
　　箭扣和喜峰口的修缮方案经过几番论证和完善，终获国家文物局批复，在项目运作上，社会组织参与长城修缮，是一个新生事物，没有先例可循。项目开展的前提是要解决一些机制上存在的问题，涉及对以往工作的突破，这方面的改变，要比技术问题遇到的思想碰撞更多，也更为关键。
　　箭扣和喜峰口的修缮，对于政府部门、文保基金会、腾讯这几方而言，都面临不小的压力，因为这是一次暴露在聚光灯下的修缮，必然要接受公众的检验和监督，甚至质询和问询，项目实施必须做好。为此，基金会定出两个目标：一是两段长城修缮成为全国长城保护的样板和示范工程，其修缮的理念、

report to the official organisation for budget review according to the regulations on the use of government funds. After several evaluations, the final assessed engineering cost was frequently less than the amount of funds actually required for the work. The reason is that the restoration costs determined through the official financial evaluation process is based on the standards for general construction projects (the 'general quota standard'), whereas restoration of the Great Wall involves a great many special circumstances. For instance, as the Great Wall is mostly built on cliffs, additional costs for the transportation of materials will be incurred during the restoration. These expenses are rarely or never considered under the general construction project regulations which only include transport to a standard, easily accessible site. In order to maintain their reasonable profit, construction companies usually have to increase the scope of restoration works, resulting in the excessive restoration of the Great Wall. The costs for the restoration projects at Jiankou and Xifengkou have been based on the 'objective quota standard', and the expenses actually incurred in the project have been methodically evaluated, and all are included in the total engineering costs.

A further shortcoming in traditional processes of managing restoration projects is that a strict budgetary timetable has to be enforced for the use of government funds. To complete the agreed expenditure within the financial year for which it has been allocated, work has to be carried out in the winter - a season not conducive to construction. This frequently results in mortars freezing and then thawing in the following Spring and work has to be re-done. The funding for the restoration projects at Jiankou and Xifengkou comes from social fundraising, and hence can be spent to a timetable which achieves the best conservation results. After communication and explanation with the donors, we reached consensus that the costs must be verified in a realistic manner appropriate for the restoration of the two sections. The 'objective quota' is therefore adopted to ensure normal profit margins for the construction contractor and to avoid excessive restoration. At the same time, the project schedule is arranged according to the weather conditions and the seasons, so as to ensure effective fund management and to guarantee the quality of the project.

The second problem relates to the relationship between design and construction. Some projects along the Great Wall have had great design, but the resulting construction works have left a lot to be desired. Due to the regulations concerning tendering processes for government-funded projects, the design and construction functions are normally carried out by different parties. Some practical issues encountered during construction cannot often be foreseen during the design process. If the designers do not follow the whole construction process on site, they are thus unable to provide necessary professional guidance throughout the construction. Our evaluations have identified there is frequently a lack of coordination between the different parties involved in conducting restoration projects. For the restoration work at Jiankou and Xifengkou, the tendering process expressly stipulates the adoption of 'the resident designer system', which requires the lead designers to guide the construction throughout and to offer solutions to problems and questions as they arise. This ensures that the design concepts and intentions are carried out during the construction in a complete and timely manner and that project quality is maintained through technical support. In addition, 'the resident designer system' helps those construction contractors of the Great Wall to learn more about, and raise overall standards in, conducting restoration projects.

技术和手段要成为引领，二是借助项目的灵活性实现机制上的突破，解决项目管理中的一些问题，纠正以往工作中一些不得以而为之的不理想状况，使长城修缮回归常识，尽可能体现长城保护的规律。

第一，是资金使用遵循文物保护规律。修缮费用采用客观定额标准，对工程中实际发生的费用合理评估确定，全部据实列入工程成本。以往长城修缮，资金来源于国家财政拨款，工程业主单位（地方政府）须按照财政资金的使用要求，报请官方机构进行预算评审，几番评审后，最终评定的工程造价比实际需要资金量少，原因是，财评适用的修缮取费依据是一般建设工程取费标准，而长城修缮涉及很多特殊情况，例如，长城多是建筑在山崖之上，修缮中会发生二次搬运费，这类费用在一般建设工程取费标准中是考虑较少或没有考虑的（只到地头不管山），施工单位通常用加大工程量的办法维持利润平衡，其后果是，导致了长城的过度修缮。再比如，使用财政资金须严格执行财政预算进度，为了完成财政年度内的资金支出任务，至冬天不利于施工的季节仍然在赶工，到了第二年春天，出现冻融，就必须返工，这些都是不符合文物保护规律的做法。此次箭扣和喜峰口的资金来源于社会募集，提供了一个很好的纠正机会，经过与捐资人的沟通和解释，我们达成了共识，这两段长城修缮一定要实事求是地核算费用，采用客观定额，保证施工单位的正常利润，避免过度修缮；同时，考虑天气因素合理安排工程进度，工程实施不赶工，遵循季节规律，实现科学的资金管理，保障工程质量。

第二，是采取设计驻场机制。以往长城修缮有的项目会出现方案设计得好，但是施工效果却不尽如人意。这是由于按照招投标程序的要求，设计和施工多数情况下不是同一个主体，施工中经常会发生设计图纸未考虑到的状况，而设计人员未跟随施工全过程，做不到设计指导施工。我们注意到了这个环节存在的问题，对箭扣和喜峰口的修缮，在招标过程，就明确向设计方提出设计驻场要求，要求设计骨干全过程指导施工，随叫随到，遇到问题和疑问第一时间解决，保证设计理念和意图完整、及时地贯彻到施工中，实现从技术支撑上保障工程质量。另一方面，设计驻场制也有助于推动从事长城设计施工的企业积累更多经验对保护措施进行研究。

第三，是在工程管理上，努力探索机制突破，箭扣修缮实行"双甲方制"。依据中国文物保护法律法规的规定，长城所在地的政府部门是修缮责任主体，是法定业主单位，具体实施工程招标组织等工作。在项目进程中，困绕各方的一个想法是，既然此次修缮资金是由基金会募集的，是否可以由基金会单独作为业主单位组织招标？这个问题不解决，就无法推进工作。解决办法要求我们既要依法合规，又要做一些灵活的变通，使各方均能接受。经过论证，我们

图5

喜峰口现场各方讨论修缮机制问题（图片来源：中国文物保护基金会）

Fig. 5

Discussion on management process at Xifengkou (© CFCHC)

The third aspect of the project processes which requires improvement concerns the mechanisms by which project ownership is defined. According to China's laws and regulations on cultural relics protection, the government department in charge of each section of the Great Wall is the main body in charge of restoration and is the legal owner specifically responsible for tendering processes, and so on. In the course of the project, one of the questions which has arisen is whether CFCHC can be responsible for the tendering process since it has raised funding for the restoration. Any solution to this issue must ensure that the law is complied with, while at the same time allowing flexibility which is acceptable to all parties. After much deliberation, the 'Double Party A system' was introduced for the restoration project for the Jiankou section. Under the 'Double Party A system', the roles and responsibilities normally undertaken by the owner - for example, managing the tendering and management of project implementation - are jointly undertaken by CFCHC and the local government, but the statutory supervisory duties are still undertaken by governments at all levels. The legal basis of the 'Double Party A system' is that certain roles and responsibilities can be delegated through agreement, while administrative functions such as supervision and regulation cannot be assigned. This approach not only clearly separates the powers and responsibilities for CFCHC and the local government, but also enables complementary work between the funder and the owner to be coordinated.

The administrative arrangements for the Xifengkou project are different from those for the Jiankou project. In terms of the legal relationship, the Foundation is purely the funder, while the statutory duties of the owner are still borne by the local government's Cultural Relics Department with jurisdiction over that section of the Great Wall. The Department is responsible for the tendering, construction organization and management, and so on. The CFCHC's opinions and input are sought and consulted upon as necessary. Both the 'Double Party A system' for Jiankou and Xifengkou's administrative model are the results of careful consideration and analysis by CFCHC. They solve the problem of how charitable funding can participate in the restoration of the Great Wall, and make clear the roles and responsibilities of all parties including social organizations, governments, donors, and the construction body selected through the tendering process. These are important principles and models for improving the mechanisms through which restoration of the Great Wall is conducted. We believe that they can be applied to other cases in which charitable funding organisations participate in the restoration of cultural heritage sites in the future.

The digital documentation of the restoration of the Great Wall attracts the attention of the public

As the restoration projects of the Jiankou and Xifengkou sections began, CFCHC cooperated with a professional team to make a special documentary on the implementation process. The documentary threads together the main characters involved with the history of the monument. It helps the public to learn about the stories of ordinary people involved in the restoration of the Great Wall and the technical difficulties of restoration. Through this real-life experience-based story-telling the interest of the public is stimulated more effectively, spreading the

探索出了箭扣项目工程管理的"双甲方制"。"双甲方制"就是原来由业主单位（地方政府）独自享有并承担的民事权利和责任由基金会和地方政府共同承担，比如招标组织、工程实施管理工作，但法定的政府的行政管理监督职责仍由各级政府承担。"双甲方制"的法理基础在于，民事权利和责任可以通过授权共担，而行政管理监督权力不可以让渡。这一做法，既清晰分割基金会与地方政府的权责，又实现了出资人与业主单位在工作上的互补。喜峰口的运作模式，不同于箭扣。在法律关系上，基金会是单纯的出资人，业主单位的法定职责仍由长城所在地的政府文物部门承担，具体负责招标、施工组织管理等工作，必要环节征求基金会的意见。无论是箭扣的"双甲方制"还是喜峰口的运作模式，都是基金会经过认真思考总结出的重要成果，解决了社会资本参与长城保护的运作模式问题，厘清了社会组织、政府、捐资人、中标施工方等各方的权利（力）义务责任，是我们实现长城保护修缮机制突破的重要思考和实践，相信今后可以复制运用到社会力量参与文物保护的其他案例中。

（三）伴随长城维修进行的科技与数字化的记录展示拉近公众的距离

伴随箭扣和喜峰口长城的修缮工程开工，基金会与专业团队合作，全程跟拍两段长城的维修过程，制作专题纪录片。纪录片以两段长城维修工程为重点，以参与长城维修的各种人物为主线，呈现个体与历史的交汇，让公众了解长城保护中普通人的故事，了解长城维修的技术难度，用真实的情感和讲故事的方式拉近与公众的距离，以期更好地传播文化遗产保护理念。

图 6
箭扣维修过程中，科技助力长城保护（图片来源：中国文物保护基金会）
Fig. 6
Digital documentation during restoration at Jiankou (© CFCHC)

concept of cultural heritage preservation.

For the restoration of the Jiankou section, CFCHC harnessed the technology of UAV mapping and AI for the first time, providing a new perspective and model for Great Wall restoration. In 2018, CFCHC cooperated with Intel to launch the "Tech Helps Great Wall Restoration" project. During the restoration of the Jiankou section, Intel used UAV mapping technology to inspect remotely each element of the site through high-definition image data and 3D modelling, and to make drawings, showing the current condition of the Great Wall visually. AI technology is used for analysis and virtual reconstruction of the data collected in order to provide auxiliary modelling for subsequent restoration. In addition, to make the restoration process as visually accessible as possible for the public, CFCHC also cooperated with the Peking University's School of Archaeology and Museology's Archaeological Virtual Simulation Experimental Teaching Center to carry out the recording and interpretation of the restoration of No. 152 defensive tower in the Jiankou section. Digital record and 3D modelling of the engineering implementation of No. 152 defensive tower, and the Wall on either side of it, created a visual digital restoration archive. CFCHC will now make these resources available online as a way to popularize, and raise public understanding of, the restoration of the Great Wall.

THOUGHTS

Overall, public participation in the protection of China's cultural relics is in its infancy, and it is not as prominent in the work of China's charitable sector as supporting the alleviation of poverty, or educational projects. China's approach to cultural relics protection is framed, through legislation and national policies, as being "government-led with social participation". For many years, the Cultural Relics Departments at all levels of government have played the leading role in cultural relics protection. However, China is a vast country rich in cultural relics, which cannot all be adequately protected through government action alone. All elements of society should be involved. Through multifaceted participation, each person whatever their professional background and expertise can play a great role in this. CFCHC's "Protect the Great Wall. Count me in!" initiative is an innovative attempt to enable this. Innovation, by definition, challenges and disrupts previous thinking and behaviours. The impact of new ideas on existing concepts inevitably takes time. Our experience suggests that proactive communication, the development of consensus, and aiming for the maximum common denominator for all stakeholders are the key priorities for achieving progress in growing public participation in protection of our cultural heritage.

In promoting the public protection of cultural relics and organising charitable activities, the fundamental aim is to return to the essence of cultural heritage protection. The Great Wall is the nexus that links the great plain of China with ethnic groups outside the Great Wall. In the new era, what we should do is to forge a relationship between the Great Wall and the lives of contemporary people and their feelings. The restoration of the Great Wall is the symbol of the restoration of Chinese cultural heritage. To restore the Great Wall, it is necessary

此次箭扣长城保护维修，基金会引入科技力量，首次与无人机测绘、AI 人工智能技术结合，为长城保护提供全新的视角和模式。2018 年，基金会与英特尔（Intel）合作开展了"科技助力长城保护"项目，在箭扣长城修缮过程中，英特尔采用无人机测绘技术，通过高清图像数据和 3D 建模对维修段落进行远程检查和制图，以视觉化方式呈现长城的现状。对采集到的数据，运用人工智能技术进行分析处理和虚拟重建，为修缮工作提供辅助性预判。此外，为了使修缮过程尽可能地为公众呈现直观可视化效果，基金会还与北京大学考古文博学院考古虚拟仿真实验教学中心合作开展了箭扣长城 152 号敌楼修缮记录与展示，对 152 号敌楼及两侧边墙的工程实施过程进行数字记录和三维建模，生成一套直观可视的数字化维修档案。下一步基金会将这些资源在线上为公众提供访问、使用，作为普及长城保护的一种方式，让公众了解和理解长城修缮过程。

三、一些体会

整体来讲，中国的文物保护事业，公众参与目前处于起步阶段，与扶贫救济类、助学类等公益事业相比，处于"公益边缘"地带。加之中国的文物保护事业从立法和国家政策层面的定位是"政府主导，社会参与"，多年来，各级政府文物部门是文物保护的主体。但不可忽视的是，中国是文物资源丰富大国，文物保护仅仅靠政府唱独角戏是远远不够的，社会的方方面面都应当参与进来，参与的形式是多角度的，每个人的专业背景和特殊能力，都可以找到发力的巨大空间。中国文物保护基金会此次倡导的"保护长城 加我一个"大型公益活动，是一次创新性的尝试，创新就意味着会对以往习惯和思维或多或少带来冲击和扰动，新事物对既有观念的冲击必然是一个过程，回头来看，密切沟通、推心置腹、取得共识，使利益相关者都认可、取得最大公约数是推动工作的重中之重。

倡导公众保护文物、组织开展公益活动，其根本目的还是应回到文化遗产保护的本质上来。在历史上，长城是联结关内关外、农耕文明与游牧文明的纽带，在新的时代背景下，我们更应该做的是，让长城与当代人的生活和情感发生关系。长城保护，可以说是中国文化遗产保护的缩影，修缮长城，既要尊重历史，完整地留存它的历史形态，保护其文化多样性，也要考虑将它融入当今人的生活。长城是都市人和当地人的公共空间，其意义的大小，在一定程度上，取决于它和人群、和整个社会发生关系的面有多广。长城保护中，通常有政府、有文物部门、有专家力量、甚或有旅游部门、商业开发者。我认为，真正的主体应当是公众，在记录、保护以及宣传过程中，公众所掌握的知识以及诉求的文化权利应当得到尊重。中国的长城资源历经千百年在各种自然条件的限制下能够保存下来实属不易，怎样利用高科技的手段，怎样利用方方面面的力量共同把这些珍贵资源的真正价值发挥出来，值得我们不断思考与实践。近两年来，中国文物保护基金会与各方面力量合作，在传播、动员、普及、展示方面做了一些事情，尤其是让年轻人更多地关注长城，取得了不错的收效。我们清楚地知道，文化遗产保护，一定要与人发生最多的联系，这是生命力所在。我们的工作才刚刚起步，这个领域还有许多值得我们不断思考和实践的空间，作为社会组织，我们愿意和政府、和专业力量、和方方面面的人共同把长城保护事业做得更好。

to respect history, to preserve its historical form in its entirety, to protect its cultural diversity, and to integrate it into the lives of people today. The Great Wall is a public space for people in cities and for local communities alike. Its significance depends to a certain degree on how much it relates to the population and society as a whole. Restoration of the Great Wall has traditionally primarily involved governments, Cultural Relics Departments, experts, or even tourism departments and commercial developers. The author believes that the real entity should be the public.

In the process of recording, restoration, and publicity, the knowledge of the public and their cultural rights should be respected. The task of ensuring the survival of the fabric of China's Great Wall, after thousands of years, is enormous. The issues of how to harness high-tech, and how to pool the strength of all parties to give full play to the true value of these precious resources, are well worthy of our consideration. In the past two years, CFCHC has cooperated with various parties in communicating the importance of conservation of the Great Wall and in mobilizing public participation, especially among young people, in conservation projects. Great results have been achieved. We know clearly that good cultural heritage protection depends on effective engagement with people; therein lies its vitality. Our work has just got off the ground. There are still many aspects in this field that deserve our consideration and action. As a charitable organisation, we stand ready to work with the government, professional bodies, and all parties to achieve even greater success in the restoration of the Great Wall.

参考文献
Bibliography

[1] 中国文物保护基金会 . "保护长城，加我一个" 中国文物保护基金会长城保护 2016 公募活动全面启动 [EB/OL].2016.

China Foundation for the Protection of Cultural Relics. "'Protect the Great Wall, Count me in' China Foundation for Cultural Heritage Conservation the Great Wall Conservation 2016 Opening of Joint Crowdfounding." 2016.

http://www.ccrpf.org.cn/Fund/Detail/c52779cd-c497-41c4-99ea-4c9c40cbcecb.

HADRIAN'S WALL AND THE ROMAN FORT AT GREAT CHESTERS - CONSERVATION IN PRACTICE

MIKE COLLINS

Historic England - Newcastle upon Tyne - UK

Abstract

This paper sets out the practical conservation challenges posed by Hadrian's Wall and an associated Wall fort at Great Chesters Farm, Northumberland. This looks at the challenges of funding in the context of private ownership of heritage assets, the prioritisation that must take place when dealing with limited resources, the balancing of potentially competing conservation aims, and the way that broad philosophical approaches are turned into balanced practical conservation on the ground.

Keywords: Hadrian's Wall, Great Chesters, Roman, fort, frontier, conservation, consolidation, repair.

INTRODUCTION

This paper examines the practical and philosophical approaches taken to repair of a section of Hadrian's Wall and the walls of a Roman fort at Great Chesters Farm, Northumberland. These remains consisted of:

- authentic Roman fort Walls
- Hadrian's Wall, which has been incorporated into modern field walls
- Further modern field walls, sometimes constructed from re-used Roman stone, sitting on top of the remains of Hadrian's Wall

The huge contribution to this project of the landowner, Mr W Woodman and Natural England, without whom this important work would not have taken place, is gratefully acknowledged.

HERITAGE AT RISK AT GREAT CHESTERS

Since 1999 Historic England and its predecessors have maintained a register of heritage assets of the highest significance considered to be at risk from loss or damage. The vast majority of sites on the register are in private ownership. Many of these face an uncertain future because they either have no beneficial use, are unrelated to the owners business, or because the cost of bringing the site into good repair makes this economically unviable.

The aim of this Heritage at Risk Register has been to highlight these most vulnerable heritage assets, to

哈德良长城和大切斯特罗马要塞的保护实践

麦克·考林斯

（英格兰遗产委员会，英国纽卡斯尔）

摘　要

本文展示了哈德良长城和诺桑伯兰郡大切斯特农场内的长城要塞保护实践中的挑战。本文考察在文化资产的私有产权情况下融资带来的种种挑战：在资源有限时如何确定任务的优先顺序，如何在可能产生冲突的保护目标间取得平衡，以及如何将宽泛的保护理念转化为实际的保护实践。

关键词：哈德良长城　大切斯特　罗马　要塞　边疆　保护　加固　维修

引　言

本文阐述了修复诺桑伯兰大切斯特农场内哈德良长城和罗马要塞墙体的实践和理念。这些遗址包括：

·罗马要塞墙体本体

·哈德良长城，已被砌入现代农场界墙

·其他现代农场界墙，部分重新利用了罗马时期块石，直接建造在哈德良长城遗址上

该项目获得了土地所有人 W·伍德曼先生和英格兰自然委员会 (Natural England) 的大力支持。若没有他们的支持，这一重要项目就无法开展，特此致谢。

一、大切斯特地区的濒危遗产

1999 年以来，英格兰遗产委员会及其前身一直对意义重大且面临损失或破坏风险的文化遗产进行濒危遗产登记。濒危遗产名录中大部分文化遗产属于私人所有。其中很多遗产的未来非常不确定，其中很多遗产的未来存在不确定性，原因可能有三：遗产缺乏使用效益、遗产与持有者的业务无关、对遗产进行有效修复在经济上难以承担。

建立濒危遗产名目的目的是明确那些最需要保护的文化遗产，使英格兰遗产委员会、遗产所有者、地方政府及中央政府可利用有限资源优先对其进行保护。

在濒危遗产名录的早期版本中，大切斯特农场中的哈德良长城遗址和要塞城墙的保存状况一直是关注的重点。这段哈德良长城在 19 世纪 90 年代被古物学家发掘，一直在未加保护的状态下暴露在外，而要塞遗迹的可见部分也经过同期发掘和 20 世纪 50 年代的再次发掘，同样暴露在外。虽然在 20 世纪 60 年代和 80 年代，要塞得到了部分加固，但仅限于极有限的抢救性修复。这次维修使用了水泥沙浆，本身保护方式受到争议，而遗址的长期保护问题并未得到解决。

prioritise the scarce resources (both money and staff time) that Historic England, the owners, local and central government can put in to their preservation.

From the earliest editions of the Register, the condition of the remains of Hadrian's Wall and the wall fort at Great Chesters Farm have been of great concern. The Wall here had been the subject of antiquarian excavations in the 1890's and left exposed without conservation work, whilst the visible remains of the fort were exposed during excavation at the same time and also in the 1950's. Whilst some consolidation work took place on the fort in the 1960's and 1980's, this took the form of very limited emergency repair. This was carried out using cement-based mortars, a process which itself created conservation issues, and left the longer-term conservation of the site unaddressed.

By 1999 the site was in a very poor condition, and at a tipping point where we were starting to see the loss of intact Roman fabric from both Hadrian's Wall and the fort.

FUNDING CHALLENGES

Initial estimates for the costs of a programme of consolidation work to address the threats to the remains at Great Chesters were around £250000. Even allowing for the inclusion of Great Chesters on the Heritage at Risk Register, putting together a project of this scale presented significant challenges.

As with much of the rest of Hadrian's Wall, these remains are in private ownership. In this case they are owned by a farmer, whose use of the land is focused on grazing for sheep and cattle. Although a highly responsible site owner, given the scale of cost involved and lack of direct benefit that Hadrian's Wall brings to their business, it is entirely understandable that it was not a realistic and viable proposition for the owner to fund the work. Equally, the grants available to owners of such 'at risk' monuments from Historic England were insufficient to undertake a project of this scale.

Having ruled out these two funding sources usually applied to 'at risk' monuments, further discussions of the challenges took place intermittently during the period from 1999 to 2006, and whilst a variety of alternatives were explored, no actual repair works took place and the condition of the monument continued to deteriorate slowly.

Ultimately it was the use of the monument as part of a farm that unlocked funding. As part of the system of financial support for farmers in the UK, they are eligible to apply for a scheme called 'Countryside Stewardship' funded by the European Union. This scheme provided funding for farmers with particularly important natural or heritage assets, to help them to improve their condition or repair them. Decisions about whether to offer funding through this scheme were taken by Natural England.

In the case of Great Chesters, its inclusion on the Heritage at Risk Register made it a high priority for funding both nationally and locally. This, together with the enthusiastic support of both the farmer and officers within Natural England, led to a funding offer under the Countryside Stewardship scheme for the full costs of the necessary repair works. This promise of funding, and the resultant repairs to the monument, also allowed all parties to justify allocating the staff time necessary to work up the detail of the works involved, assist the farmer

到 1999 年时，遗址状况非常糟糕，罗马时代的哈德良长城和要塞本体已经开始从我们眼前消失。

二、资金来源的挑战

为应对大切斯特农场内遗迹面临的威胁，加固工程最初预计花费 250000 镑。即使将大切斯特农场遗迹列入濒危遗产名录之中，开展如此规模的项目也带来了巨大挑战。

同哈德良长城其余大部分遗址一样，这些遗址为私人所有。这里该遗址属于一名农场主，遗址所在土地主要用于放牧牛羊。即使所有者有着高度责任感，然而修缮哈德良长城成本高昂却无法对其经营带来直接效益，因此要求所有者出资既不现实也不可行。同样地，英格兰遗产委员会为"濒危"古迹所有者的拨款额也不足以承担如此规模的项目。

排除了濒危遗产通常利用的这两项资金来源后，在 1999 年到 2006 年期间，陆续有不少人讨论如何应对此类挑战。在这期间，虽然研究过一些替代办法，但实质性的修复工作并未展开，这些古迹的状况也在缓慢恶化。

最终，古迹作为作农场的一部分成为破解资金难题的钥匙。在对英国农场主给予财政支持的政策中，他们有资格申请一个由欧盟出资的"守护乡村"项目。该项目为那些领地内拥有重要自然资源或文化遗产资源的农场主提供资金，帮助他们改善资源状况或对资源进行修复。是否通过该项目提供资金由英格兰自然委员会决定。

在大切斯特的案例中，列入濒危遗产名录使得该遗址能够优先获得国家和地方资金支持。加上农场主和英格兰自然委员会官员的大力支持，修复所需得以由"守护乡村"项目基金全额承担。在资金保证下，其后的维修使得各方得以安排必要人员制定工作细节，协助农场主进行招投标，并在实施现场为工作提供指导。

三、确定优先工作

英格兰自然委员会提供资金固然是雪中送炭，但对任何类似大切斯特这样规模的修复项目来说，经费仍然有限，因此总是需要权衡哪些工作对保护遗址重要价值是必须的，哪些工作只是锦上添花而非优先事项。

同时，也需要对修复工作的干预程度作出重要决定。要让修复更长效，就要对遗址本体进行更大干预，然而这意味着更大的资金投入，也意味着减少遗址其他部位的修缮强度，必须在两者间实现微妙的平衡。

在大切斯特，作出相关决定一是根据可动用的财政资源，二是权衡经各方同意的若干关键优先事项。

关键优先事项首先是确保罗马遗址不再进一步消失。这虽然看上去显而易见，但也意味着该项目将不可能处理遗址其它方面的重要事务。其中的一个例子是将要塞西门堵住（图 1），而理想条件下是将新生杂草和泥土清理，更好展现这个罗马晚期履行的要塞，这也是整段哈德良长城中唯一可见的罗马晚期建筑。

在此基础上，第二个关键目标是减少对遗迹的干预。这个总的理念原则的出发点是尽可能保护哈德

in tendering, and advise on the works when they got onto site.

PRIORITISATION

Despite the welcome funding from Natural England, on any project like Great Chesters financial resources are still constrained, and there are always choices to be made about what works to include as necessary for the protection of the significance of the site, and what works are desirable but not a priority.

There are also important decisions to be taken about the degree of intervention that the work will involve. This requires a careful balancing of the potential greater longevity of repairs that involve a greater degree of intervention to the fabric of the monument, against the greater cost that results, which may means doing less work elsewhere on the site.

At Great Chesters, these decisions were informed both by the financial resources available and by balancing key agreed priorities.

The key priority was to secure the historic Roman fabric from further loss. Whilst such prioritisation seems obvious, this did mean that other parts of the significance of the site were not addressed by the project. An example of this is the blocking of the west gate of the fort (Fig. 1) where ideally clearance of recent grass and soil would have taken place to allow appreciation of this late-Roman change to the fort, in the only place where this phase is visible on Hadrian's Wall.

Leading on from this, the second key aim was to minimise intervention to the monument. This general philosophical principle has at its root the desire to preserve the archaeological remains of Hadrian's Wall as authentically as possible, and also to preserve the wild upland context of the site, which is so evocative and redolent of the eventual abandonment of the Roman frontier.

Finally, at a practical level, the aim was to carry out the level of work necessary to secure the site from further loss for a period of 20 years. Any shorter period would have called into question the level of investment required, whilst a longer period (perhaps of 50 years) would have been likely to have involved a level of intervention to the monument which was undesirable for philosophical reasons, and involved a level of expense which would have used the available funding without protecting all of the site.

PARTNERSHIP AND SCARCE SKILLS

It is important to be clear that a project like this work at Great Chesters is not something that any one organisation or individual can take forward by themselves. It requires a team effort, with interested parties working in partnership, taking on board the different needs and perspectives that each has, and fitting together scarce specialist skills into a single project.

In the case of Great Chesters, the day-to-day project team consisted of:

· Conservation architect

良长城考古遗址的真实性，并且保持遗址所在山地的荒野风貌，使人们能够切身联想到最终被废弃的罗马边疆。

最后，在执行层面的目标是开展必要程度的工作，确保遗址在未来二十年期间免于继续消失的危险。期限过短会引发对修缮投入规模的质疑，而过长（如50 年）则很可能过度干预，这不仅与保护理念冲突，而且因此投入的巨大花费使得遗址整体会因资金不足而得不到保护。

Fig. 1
Late Roman blocking of the west gate of Great Chesters fort (© Historic England)
图 1
罗马晚期对大切斯特要塞西门的封堵（版权：英格兰遗产委员会）

四、合作伙伴和稀缺技艺

需要明确的是，在大切斯特开展的这项目不是任何一个组织或个人能够独自进行的。它需要整个团队努力，相关利益方共同合作，考虑各方不同的需求和角度，将各稀有特殊技能共同投入到该项目中。

大切斯特的案例中，日常的项目团队包括：
· 文物保护建筑师
· 石质文物专业修复小组
· 块石干砌工匠
· 考古学家，进行现场监督并记录
项目团队与由更广泛利益相关方组成的小组共同合作也至关重要，包括：
· 农场主 / 土地所有人——没有他们就无法开展任何工作
· 英格兰遗产委员会
· 英格兰自然委员会——出资机构
· 诺桑伯兰国家公园管理处
· 哈德良长城国家步道

五、入场通道

该项目中发挥合作伙伴关系的一个例子是车辆和修复材料进入遗址的问题。通道不得不建在在潮湿和脆弱的土地上，同时不能对周围考古遗址造成损害。最初的计划是采用可变动的道路系统，既保护地面又避免在考古遗址上形成永久道路，这似乎是一个有效方法。

· Specialist stone masonry repair team

· Dry stone wallers

· Archaeologists to supervise the work and undertake recording

It was also crucial for this group to work with a wider team of interested parties, including:

· The farmer/landowner - without whose help nothing could take place

· Historic England

· Natural England - the funding body

· The Northumberland National Park Authority

· The Hadrian's Wall Path National Trail

ACCESS

One example of partnership working from this project was the issue of access for vehicles and materials to the repair site. Access had to be created across wet and vulnerable ground, without causing harm to the surrounding archaeological remains. The initial plan was to use a system of flexible trackway, which was seen as a good way of protecting the ground and avoiding creating new permanent roads across the archaeology.

Significant doubts about the effectiveness of this solution were expressed by the farmer, given his experience of the ground conditions on his land, and he was proved to be correct - the trackway tended to be pushed apart and into the ground, and did not stand up to the repeated use required for the conservation works. Rapid discussions then took place, and a temporary stone access road was constructed across the site, which did prove to be sustainable. This was constructed on a membrane, to allow its removal without damage to the underlying archaeology after completion of the project.

RECORDING

The Great Chesters project was fortunate in having access to a drawn record of all of the visible remains of Hadrian's Wall carried out in the 1980's and 1990's (Fig. 2). Although technology has moved on, and today we would probably use laser scanning or structure-from-motion approaches, this provided a record of the remains before any conservation work, and a base to record these works as they progressed.

CONSOLIDATION WORKS AND ISSUES

In practical terms, the sequence of repair for the remains of Hadrian's Wall was:

· Removal of the modern dry stone field wall down to intact Roman remains under archaeological supervision (Fig. 3)

农场主根据对自己土地地表状况的了解，对这一方法的有效性提出了强烈质疑。他的质疑证明是正确的——这种道路会在压力作用下产生位移并嵌入土壤，无法在整个施工过程中经受反复使用。经过迅速讨论，在整个遗址施工现场修建了临时的石铺通道，并最终证明是可持续使用的。这条通道铺在一层薄膜上，在项目完工后可以移除，不会对下面的考古遗址造成损害。

六、记　录

大切斯特项目有幸可以利用1980年和1990年对哈德良长城可见遗址的测绘图记录（图2）。虽然技术已更新，现今我们可能会使用激光扫描或运动恢复结构的方法，但老技术为我们提供了修复工作开展前的遗址状况记录，也是工程开展过程记录的基础。

七、加固工程和问题

在操作上，哈德良长城墙体的修复步骤是：

·在考古学家监督下由上至下移除现代农场干石墙，直到原始罗马遗迹处（图3）

·使用石灰砂浆将上层松动的罗马块石归安，只在必要时添加块石以支撑上部原始罗马结构（图4）

·对上层哈德良长城进行考古绘图记录

·在需要修建防止牲畜跨越的农场界墙的部分，在哈德良长城墙体上部加

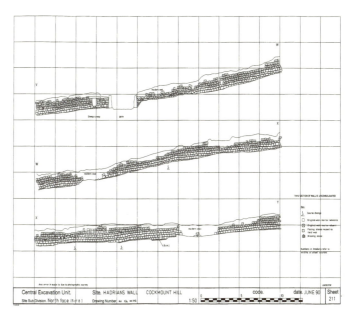

Fig. 2
Drawn record of a section of Hadrian's Wall at Great Chesters used in the project (© Historic England)
图2
该项目的哈德良长城大切斯特区段的测绘图记录（版权：英格兰遗产委员会）

Fig. 3
Hadrian's Wall remains after removal of modern field wall (© Historic England)
图3
移除现代农场石墙后，露出的哈德良长城（版权：英格兰遗产委员会）

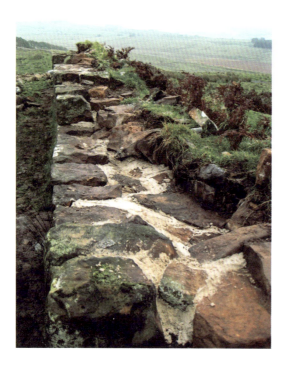

Fig. 4
Re-bedded Roman stonework of the top of Hadrian's
Wall (© Historic England)
图 4
加固归安的哈德良长城上层块石（版权：英格兰遗产委
员会）

· Use of lime mortar to re-bed the upper loose layers of Roman stonework, with additional stone only added if necessary to support intact Roman work above (Fig. 4)

· Archaeological recording in plan of the upper level of Hadrian's Wall

· Where necessary to create an effective stock-proof field boundary, a dry stone field wall was then constructed on top. This wall aimed to reuse the stone from the original boundary, which was built from recycled Roman stone. This kept the historical material on site, as part of the story of Great Chesters, but used a style of construction which allowed it to be differentiated from authentic Roman work (Fig 5), particularly alongside the recording work detailed above

On the fort at Great Chesters, the works were slightly simpler because there was more unencumbered Roman masonry present. Again, the minimal intervention approach was taken, largely involving the re-bedding of loose Roman material, although one area near the west gate had structural issues requiring a small area of rebuilding. This latter work was undertaken using the pre-work recording to ensure that the original Roman construction was faithfully reproduced. In some areas additional material had to be added in where necessary to support masonry above, again in a style which differentiates it from the surrounding Roman work (Fig 6.)

CONCLUSIONS TEN YEARS ON

The aims of the project at Great Chesters were successfully fulfilled: nearly a decade on from the first works the repairs have halted decay and secured the Roman remains from further loss. This has also been done in a way which preserves the wild upland landscape of this part of the Wall. The repairs are well on course to exceed their original twenty year design life.

Thinking more widely, collaborative partnership working has allowed this major project to be funded in a creative way in difficult financial circumstances, and helped create a legacy of good empathetic relationships between heritage professionals and the farmer which can only be a good thing for all concerned.

建干石垒砌的墙体。这道墙体力求使用罗马界墙的原始石料，这些石料原本是回收利用的罗马石料。这样得以在原址保留存历史材料，作为大切斯特故事的一部分，但是采用与罗马建筑原工艺有所区别的建筑方式（图5），尤其在上文提到的详细记录区域。

大切斯特要塞处的工程稍微简单一些，因为此处现存的罗马石砌建筑受到的叠压较小。同样，坚持最少干涉原则，大部分工作是将松动的罗马建筑材料归安固定，但是靠近西门的一处有结构性问题，需要重建其中的一小片区域。工程实施前对这片区域进行记录确保随后真实再现原始的罗马构造。一些区域中不得不用额外材料补砌为上方墙体结构提供必需的支撑，同样地采取与周围罗马建筑明显区分的方式进行修复（图6）。

八、十年后的结论

大切斯特修缮项目的目标得以成功实现：从修复工程起至今近十年，罗马遗迹进一步损坏的趋势得到遏制，保证其未受进一步损坏。工程实施也保留了所在区域的天然高地景观。修复的效果也有望超过最初的20年设计年限。

从更大范围的考虑，此合作模式使得这个大型项目在财政困难的状况下创造性地获得了资金支持，同时帮助创立并延续了文化遗产专家和农场主之间互谅互信的良好关系，惠及各方。

Fig. 5
Use of dry stone walling on top of intact remains of Hadrian's Wall (© Historic England)
图 5
在哈德良长城完整原始遗迹上部补砌的干垒石墙（版权: 英格兰遗产委员会）

Fig. 6
Minimal intervention repair on the fort at Great Chesters, with supporting masonry differentiated from original Roman work (© Historic England)
图 6
大切斯特要塞的最小干预修复，加固用的砌体与原始的罗马墙体区分（版权: 英格兰遗产委员会）

一个社会组织在中国长城保护中的角色

张　俊

（长城小站，中国北京）

摘　要

以长城小站为案例，介绍了民间组织在中国长城保护中开展的实验与作用，包括：充分动员社会各界力量；培养与拓展愿意关注、体验、参与、深度介入长城保护的人群；并为各级人群更多参与长城保护构筑成长阶梯等；同时讨论了民间组织得以发展的中国社会变迁背景。

关键词：民间组织　社会力量　长城保护

一、宏观概览

在深入分析中国社会组织在中国长城保护中的角色与作用之前，我们需要先通过一些数据了解中国社会及长城现状。

依据相关统计数据，截至 2016 年底，中国人口规模在 138,271 万人[1]，全国共有社会组织[1]70.2 万个[2]。其中文物保护类社会组织不到 1,000 家，而其中长城保护方向的社会组织不到 30 家。

根据国家文物局公布的第三次全国不可移动文物普查成果，截至 2011 年，全国共登记不可移动文物 766722 多处[3]。依据国家文物局在 2016 年年底发布的《中国长城保护报告》，依据长城资源调查的最新统计结果，各类长城资源遗存总数 43721 处（座 / 段），其中墙体 10051 段，壕堑 / 界壕 1764 段，单体建筑 29510 座，关、堡 2211 座，其他遗存 185 处。墙壕遗存总长度 21196.18 千米[4]。

在中国，全国文物系统从业人员 14 万[5]，涉及长城区域内与长城保护相关从业人员保守估计干部在 5000~7000 人左右。为解决长城保护中人力资源不足的问题，另行聘用长城保护员约 5000 人。

二、案例选取

在中国长城领域，不同形式的社会组织，依据它的成立背景与宗旨，以及日常运作的行为，大体可以区分为政府主导和民间主导两种模式。

政府主导模式里包含 1）承担某种重大社会 / 半政府使命的：如中国文物保护基金会长城保护专项基金、中国长城学会等；或者 2）公共服务提供者：如北京义工联合会文物巡检大队；

民间主导模式中包含 1）以个人为中心，基于名人或者行业领袖，如威廉·林赛先生的国际长城之友；2）以目标为中心，基于能力、兴趣、特长，如学术型 NGO、摄影团体等。

1　中国社会组织分为：社会团体、基金会、民办非企业单位三种形式。

THE ROLE OF A THIRD-SECTOR ORGANISATION IN GREAT WALL CONSERVATION

ZHANG JUN

The Great Wall Station–Beijing –China

Abstract

This paper introduces the role of third sector organisations through the innovative projects carried out by the Great Wall Station. These initiatives aim to engage all sectors of society and to train and expand the number of people who are willing to learn about, experience, participate in and deeply engage with the conservation of the Great Wall. It seeks to build a growth ladder by which people throughout society can climb higher and higher in the conservation process. This paper also discusses the background of Chinese social change that stimulates the development of third sector organisations.

Keywords: Third sector organisations; social power; Great Wall conservation

GENERALIZED OVERVIEW

Before delving into the role and function of Chinese third sector organisations in the conservation of the Great Wall of China, we need to first understand the current social and organisational context in which they operate.

At the end of 2016, China's population was 1.383 billion[1] and there were 2,702 registered third sector organisations[1] nationwide[2]. However, fewer than 1,000 of these organisations are devoted to heritage conservation, and fewer than 30 of them specialise in the field of Great Wall conservation.

According to the results of the third national survey of immovable cultural relics (sites, buildings and monuments) released by the State Administration of Cultural Heritage (SACH), as of 2011, there were 766,722 registered immovable cultural relics in China[3]. According to the "Report for the Conservation of the Great Wall of China" issued by SACH at the end of 2016, the latest statistics indicate that the total number of surviving ele-

---

1 Many translations use the term 'non-governmental organisation' ('NGO'). However 'NGO' has a narrower meaning in English than the of types of organisation discussed in this paper. The term 'third sector' includes all those organisations which are neither public or government bodies nor private commercial organisations. There are three broad classifications of third sector organisations that are formally registered with civil affair departments which undertake public benefit activities in China collectively known as 'social organisations'. These are: 'social groups' which are not-for-profit organsiations above a certain level of membership; 'foundations' are not-for-profit organisations funded by private and corporate donations; and 'private not-for-profit organisations' which are smaller scale than 'social groups'. In addition there are a number of non-governmental bodies engaged in public benefit activities, but which have a close relationship with government. (Editors' note).

图1

2017 年 5 月长城小站志愿者在河北青边口长城清理垃圾、植树（版权：长城小站）

Fig. 1

Volunteers at Qingbiankou, Hebei, for garbage collection and tree planting, May 2017 (© Great Wall Station)

本文研究分析的长城小站，属于民间主导、以目标为中心类型的民间组织。

民间组织长城小站成立于 1999 年 5 月 8 日，初期是由长城爱好者与长城志愿者自发组建并运营的公益性网站，网址为 www.thegreatwall.com.cn。长城小站宣称其自身以"热爱长城、热爱生活"的宗旨，通过网络和影像的力量来促进长城知识与文化的整理、传播、分享，促进长城的保护。二十年来，这家纯民间自发组建的 NGO，保持了不断创新发展的趋势，在长城保护领域不断有新的成绩与贡献，从而得到社会各界认可 [6]。

2016 年 11 月，在中国国家文物局发布的《中国长城保护报告》，提及"长城小站"等长城保护志愿者组织蓬勃发展，成为社会参与长城保护的生力军 [4]。2017 年 12 月，长城小站获选为中国文物保护基金会第九届"薪火相传——寻找中国文物故事杰出传播者""讲好中国文物故事杰出团队" [7]。2018 年 3 月，长城小站获选为北京市慈善义工联合会第六届"京津冀最美慈善义工十大榜样团体" [8]。

由于其自发的纯民间属性，并以长城保护为核心目标，组织行为选择非常独立，因此适合作为考察对象进行分析。

三、对社会力量的认识

与很多中国纯民间的文物保护组织类似，参与长城小站各项活动成员的组成，一眼看上去会感觉非

ments is 43,721 (blocks/sections/components), including 10,051 sections of walls and 1,764 sections of trenches/boundary trenches. There are 29,510 individual structures, 2,211 passes and fortresses, and 185 other remains. The total length of surviving Wall remains is 21,196 km[4].

In China, there are 140,000 practitioners within the national conservation system[5], of whom approximately 5,000 to 7,000 are involved in Great Wall conservation within the Great Wall area. This is insufficient to meet the conservation needs of the Great Wall, and to address this problem about 5,000 citizens were recruited as Great Wall Patrollers.

CASE SELECTION

Two broad categories of third sector organization are involved in conservation of the Great Wall of China: government-led and non-government-led.

The government-led model includes undertaking major social/semi-government missions such as: the establishment the Great Wall Conservation Fund provided by the China Foundation for Cultural Heritage Conservation (CFCHC) and Tencent Corporation, the foundation of the China Great Wall Society, etc.; or establishing bodies to deliver public contracts, such as the Beijing Volunteer Association Inspection Brigade for Cultural Heritage.

The non-government-led model includes those organisations founded and led by famous or prominent individuals, such as William Lindesay's International Friends of the Great Wall; and those other organisations which are goal-oriented and which are based on the abilities, interests, and expertise of groups of individuals, such as academic groups, photography groups, etc.

The Great Wall Station, which is studied and analysed in this paper, is defined as a non-government-led, goal-oriented third sector organisation.

The Great Wall Station was established on 8 May, 1999. It was originally a website for promoting participation in voluntary activities, spontaneously established and operated by volunteers and enthusiasts for the Great Wall. The website address is www.thegreatwall.com.cn. The aim of the Great Wall Station is to promote "Love for the Great Wall and affection for Life". It takes advantage of the power of the internet and of images to facilitate the consolidation, dissemination, and sharing of knowledge of the Great Wall and its culture so as to enhance the conservation of the Great Wall. For two decades, this independent body has pursued a course of continuous innovation and development, and its achievements and contributions in the field of Great Wall conservation have been recognised by all sectors of society[6].

In November 2016, the "Report for the Conservation of Great Wall of China" issued by the State Administration of Cultural Heritage, acknowledged that Great Wall volunteer conservation organisations such as The Great Wall Station flourished and had become a new force for community engagement[4]. In December 2017, the Great Wall Station was selected as the "Outstanding Team for Communicating Chinese Cultural Heritage Stories"[7] at the "9th Generation to Generation Search for the Outstanding Communicator of the Story of Chinese Cultural Heritage" organized by

常芜杂，但又充满活力。

目前中国社会在民间组织管理工作上，伴随社会政治和经济的发展，一直在进行改革和调整，已经有了不少进步，但法律层面的限制仍然较多。因此，长城小站的很多活动和工作，是以项目制的方式进行开展的，完全以兴趣和目标为导向。因此参加活动的成员会来自于社会各界——不同的职业、不同的背景、不同的阶层，但在具体工作中，都能在围绕如何保护长城这个人类共同的遗产问题面前，进行平等协作。

举更具体一些例子。比如哈德良长城边，最著名的足球队要属纽卡斯尔联队了。虽然每场足球赛，上场球员数量只有 11 人加 3 名替补，但是每次球赛，球队圣詹姆斯公园球场能销售的门票有 5 万张。但是除了到现场去观看比赛的 5 万球迷，经营者会通过电视直播比赛。整个纽卡斯尔及附近地区，有数百万球迷通过观看电视观看球队比赛。这样，市场容量从 5 万增加到了数百万，球队和球迷之间的感情也被维护住了。

纽卡斯尔联队的比赛，其实是在英超这个框架下举行的。英超的球迷更多，在英国，就超过 2000 万。在全球，球迷总数约有 20 亿。足球市场人群呈现金字塔形分布，越往塔尖，参与度越深，忠诚度越高。

同样的分析方法，可以用来分析在长城保护领域上的人员组成和社会各界力量分析。

前文所及，在中国，全国有长城保护员五千人左右，长城区域内文物干部也有 5000~7000 左右，但并非全职做长城。再往外扩，相关的人群就是长城志愿者群体，全国乐观估计，也许能够填满纽卡斯尔联队的圣詹姆斯公园球场。全国文物从业人员及文物相关社会力量人员总数预计在数十万级别，不一定能超过纽卡斯尔球迷总数。加上中国目前 13 亿人口基数，也构成了一个金字塔。和足球市场的金字塔比较起来，这个金字塔虽然基座很大，但本体又瘦又小。

基于如上对社会力量分布的分析，长城小站的管理团队认为：

1. 目前在长城保护领域，中国参与进来的各级社会力量总体存在巨大的不足，每一份愿意参与的力量都是弥足珍贵的；

2. 但中国人口基数庞大，意味着有巨大潜力；

3. 因此，需要开展如下工作：一是想办法巩固和扩大各层的人群，使这个金字塔能变"胖"起来；与此同时构建各层之间的上升通道，使这个金字塔变"高"起来 [9]。

因此长城小站在以下几个主要方向上开展了工作：

1. 公众哺育，尽可能地拓展公众对长城关注，吸引对长城感兴趣的人群。

2. 直接对保护行动的参与，包括：

1）阻击长城破坏行为，并为举报者提供方法指引；

2）支持长城保护相关者（政府、一线保护员、长城乡民）行动。

3. 构筑成长阶梯，包括：

1）开展长城志愿行动实践；

2）为非业内人士学习与开展长城研究创造便利条件；

3）支持其他长城保护组织、第三方组织；

4）构筑人人参与通道。

CFCHC. In March 2018, The Great Wall Station was selected as the 6th annual "Beijing-Tianjin-Hebei Best Charity Volunteer Model Group" of the Beijing Charity Volunteer Association[8].

Due to its spontaneous creation and non-governmental nature, and its core objective of protecting the Great Wall through independent activities, the Great Wall Station is worth exploring as a case study.

MOBILISING THE POWER OF SOCIETY

As with many other third sector organisations involved in heritage conservation in China, the members of the Great Wall Station who take part in various activities are a diverse, dynamic and powerful force.

As part of the political and economic development of society, China has carried out reforms and adjustments in the management of third sector organisations. A considerable amount of progress has been made, but there are still several restrictions at the legal level. Therefore, many of the activities of The Great Wall Station are carried out in a project based manner and are driven by enthusiasm and objectives. The members participating in events come from all sectors of society and represent diverse professions, different backgrounds and different levels of status. However, when it comes to specific projects, they can all work together through their shared objective of protecting the Great Wall as part of the common heritage of mankind.

As another example of the potential power of social force, the most famous football team along Hadrian's Wall is Newcastle United. Although there are only 11 players and 3 substitutes in a game, each time they play at St James' Park there are 50,000 fans who go to watch the game; in addition, it is also broadcast to millions more who watch it on television. In this way, the participating audience has increased from 50,000 to millions, and the relationship between the team and the fans has been expanded and strengthened.

Newcastle United's games are broadcast under the framework of the Premier League to a UK national audience of many millions, and then in turn across the world to the global audience of football fans. The total audience can be represented as a pyramid: the closer to the top, the deeper the level of participation and greater the loyalty of the people.

The same method can be used to analyse the composition of personnel involved in Great Wall conservation. At the top of the pyramid of those who engage in conservation of the Great Wall are the are 5,000 Great Wall Patrollers across the Great Wall regions. Next are about 5,000 to 7,000 cultural heritage professionals involved in working on the Great Wall, although not all of them are engaged full-time in work related to the Great Wall. Then we have the Great Wall volunteer groups, who may number enough to fill St James' Park. The total number of heritage conservation staff together with related social workers in China is estimated in the hundreds of thousands, perhaps the same as the total number of Newcastle fans worldwide. However, were we to add China's total 1.3 billion population to the base of our Great Wall conservation pyramid, it would have a very wide base indeed.

The management team of The Great Wall Station believes that:

· At present, in the field of Great Wall conservation, huge gaps exist between each level at which the

图 2
人群分布金字塔（版权：长城小站）
Fig. 2
Social Group Analysis (© Great Wall Station)

四、公众哺育开展

公众哺育的目标是，通过丰富多彩的活动，让公众能感受到长城的丰富多彩，找到能和个体兴趣产生共鸣的点。简而言之，就是用各种手段让民众对长城产生更多兴趣，带来更多热爱。因此在长城小站在其成立的二十年里，一直不断地组织各种公共活动。

例如：十余年里，该组织策划实施或协助举办了40余场影展，举办了上百场各类讲座、文化沙龙。

例如：其成员组织、协助、参与出版了长城主题的出版物十余种，用图书期刊为媒体进行长城文化传播。在早期互联网时代，该组织通过其网站制作大量科普专题。在移动互联网高速发展起来之后，该组织通过以微信公众号等形式积极进行新媒体文化传播，其原创内容在圈内好誉度甚高。这些工作基本都是由志愿者来实践完成的。

大量的工作出发点，是在保证学术正确性的基础上，让长城的内容变的有趣好玩，让人们对长城能既敬重、又亲爱喜欢。

这些努力里，有一个重要的工作方向，就是如何在教育领域里主动传播长城知识与文化。

在中国，教育是一件非常严肃的事情，人们希望通过良好的教育使孩子获得未来良好的发展机会。在课堂上获得的知识其关注度相对来说会比较高，如能越早培养孩子们对长城及中国文化的兴趣，未来的效果会越好！

general public participate. Every individual who is willing to participate will be valued;

· China's large population base implies that there is huge potential for engagement;

· Therefore we must find ways to consolidate and expand the number of people at all levels of the pyramid, and facilitate channels leading upwards to make the pyramid taller [9].

Therefore, The Great Wall Station is focusing on the following:

· Developing educational initiatives to expand public understanding of the Great Wall and stimulate public interest in it.

· Promoting participation in conservation activity, by providing methodological guidelines to assist people in reporting destruction of the Great Wall, and supporting the activities of stakeholders (government, front-line protectors, and local residents around the Great Wall area) in the conservation of the Great Wall.

· Constructing a ladder for the growth of engagement by:

-Promoting voluntary action in support of the Great Wall;

-Facilitating the participation of non-professionals in learning and in research about the Great Wall;

-Supporting other Great Wall conservation organisations, and third-party organisations; and

-Creating a channel for everyone to participate.

DEVELOPING EDUCATIONAL INITIATIVES

The objective of public education is to enable the public to experience the richness of the Great Wall through a variety of activities. In short, it is to generate more public interest in the Great Wall and thereby generate more enthusiasm for it. Therefore, over the past two decades since its establishment The Great Wall Station has held various public events. For instance, it has planned or assisted in organising more than 40 photographic shows and has held hundreds of lectures and cultural seminars. Its members have organised, assisted, and contributed to more than ten publications on the theme of the Great Wall, including books and periodicals to promote cultural understanding. During the early days of the internet, the organisation promoted a large number of popular science topics through its website. With the rapid development of the mobile internet, the organisation has actively facilitated dissemination of new media culture in the form of the WeChat public account, and the original content it produced was highly praised within the heritage sector. All of these tasks were largely done by volunteers. The intention of most of this work is to make the content about the Great Wall more interesting and fun while ensuring academic correctness, so that people can respect and appreciate the Great Wall.

A core strategic objective of the organisation is to spread knowledge of the Great Wall and its culture through education. In China, education is a very serious matter. People hope that through a good education, their children will have better career opportunities. Children pay most attention to what they are taught at school. Therefore, it is important to cultivate children's interest about the Great Wall and Chinese culture at an early stage to have a sustained impact on their knowledge and attitudes. In order to maximise the effectiveness of

　　为充分利用好进入学校讲课的机会，长城小站组织了专门课程编写团队，针对不同年龄段儿童的学习和认知能力、潜在兴趣点等，进行深入分析，设计了分级的长城课程。另组建了志愿者讲师团，对志愿者讲师也开展有针对性的课程培训，保障教学目标能顺利实施。

　　例如，针对小学一年级和二年级（K1&K2）阶段，课程设计内容主要是长城美学欣赏与长城纸工。

　　K1、K2阶段的孩子刚刚入学不久，没有复杂的历史地理知识背景，因此在课程设计上主要以兴趣培养为主。成形的课程内容主要分为两个部分，前一部分是对长城的美学欣赏，在和孩子们进行一些互动交流好后，讲师一边播放精心选择过的由专业摄影师拍摄的精彩长城图片，一边朗诵如诗歌般有韵律的说明文字，让孩子们在惊叹之余，欣赏到长城之美，欣赏到文字之美，然后通过一个视频向孩子们传达长城保护理念。后半部分，设计了一个简单的长城纸工，在游戏过程中，让孩子们体验长城建筑、守城士兵和构建地形之间的关系。

　　针对小学三年级和四年级（K3&K4）阶段，课程设计内容为一堂综合课程。如果学校愿意的话，可以继续选择前往长城进行体验并在长城上开展相关游戏。

　　进入K3、K4阶段的孩子，其学习能力已经进一步增强，有一定的知识储备和问题分析探讨能力。在此基础上展开的综合课程，从历史和地理两个维度向同学展示丰富的长城建筑类型及其背后的思想与故事，并联系讨论生活中的长城现象，让孩子们将现实与历史产生关联。课程最后落足于长城保护，探讨每个人能为长城做些什么。

图3

K5 & K6 阶段长城公益课堂（摄影：张　曼）

Fig. 3

A Class at Grade K5 & K6 on the Great Wall (© Zhang Man)

teaching about the Great Wall in schools, The Great Wall Station has arranged for a special 'course design team' to analyse the learning and cognitive abilities and the potential interests of children of different ages, and the team then designed a modular course about the Great Wall. Another group of volunteer lecturers was set up to train school teachers to ensure the smooth roll-out of these courses.

The content designed for the lessons targeted at students of the first and second grades of primary school (K1 & K2) was mainly about aesthetic appreciation of the literature and artwork about the Great Wall. Children in the K1 and K2 stages have just started school and do not have any detailed historical and geographical background knowledge. Therefore, the curriculum design mainly focuses on stimulating their interest. The course content is divided into two parts. The first part is about aesthetic appreciation of the Great Wall. After initially engaging with the children, the teacher will play a film of carefully selected photos of the Great Wall shot by professional photographers while reading some explanatory poetic captions. This allows the children to marvel at the beauty of the Great Wall and appreciate the beauty of Chinese characters at the same time. This is followed by an explanation of the concept of conservation of the Great Wall through a video. In the second part, a simple Great Wall paper-cutting coursebook has been designed to allow children to experience the relationship between the architecture, the conservators and the topography of the Great Wall through play.

The lessons designed for students of the third and fourth grades of primary school (K3 & K4) are intended to provide a more comprehensive course. If the school agrees, the children can continue to experience in situ and play games related to the Great Wall. Children who enter the K3 and K4 stages have already developed their learning abilities in problem analysis and research and have established a certain amount of background knowledge. The course introduces students to the various features of the Great Wall, and how it was designed, from the perspective of history and geography. Through describing and discussing the physical fabric of the Great Wall the children are able to connect the monument with history. The course ends by discussing the conservation of the Great Wall and explores what individuals can do to help protect it.

By the fifth and sixth grades (K5 & K6) of primary school, the children have acquired strong learning abilities. Therefore, their curriculum was designed to expand further the perspectives of the students. The teachers guide the children to examine the Great Wall, and its complex cultural and historical origins, from various angles and to consider its role in the development of Chinese civilization. In this process, the children's capabilities are further developed; the teachers set homework to publish their own classroom blackboard newspaper and they guide students on how they can explore the subject further on their own after class.

In 2016, The Great Wall Station provided courses for schoolchildren within the Beijing area and began to spread knowledge about the Great Wall and its culture and conservation in primary and secondary schools. By January 2018, more than 50 courses had been conducted in more than 30 schools. According to the plan published at its annual meeting, The Great Wall Station will further enhance and broaden the course content, and will expand the volunteer lecturer group.

针对小学五年级和六年级（K5&K6）阶段，孩子们的能力已经很强。因此课程设计则进一步地拓展同学们的视角，教师引领孩子从各个角度审视长城及其两侧的文明，重新认识人类发展。在这个过程中，会引入很多能力培养，并在课后由学校老师协助，开展诸如手抄报等作业，引导孩子们课后开展进一步的自学。

2016 年长城小站在北京市范围内开展长城公益课堂，在北京市中小学校内课堂开始传播长城文化与保护知识，截止 2018 年 1 月，已在三十余所学校开展 50 多次各类课程。据该组织在其年会上发表的工作计划，长城小站将进一步加强与拓宽课程的教学内容，在适当的时候，进一步拓展志愿者讲师团的规模。

五、直接保护参与

（一）阻击长城破坏行为，从难到易

由于长城庞大的体量，带来的长城周边环境的复杂性，长城的管理，一直存在很多难点。志愿者在长城沿线经常会遇到一些当下正在发生的长城破坏行为。在阻止这些破坏行为的过程中，会涉及到长城的管理体系、地方利益格局及法律条文的执行与解释等诸多问题。对于民间组织，并没有执法权，遇到长城破坏行为，采取多种手段进行制止。

第一，通过长城小站广泛的网络联系，迅速反映长城破坏行为。2006 年 9 月 15 日，长城小站的志愿者洪峰等前往北京市延庆县四海冶口考察长城。四海冶口是明长城宣府东路最大的一处关隘，俗称北口子。《延庆州志·边防》称四海冶"边外宝山寺、天乞力等处尽为敌人驻巢"。就是说，明代嘉靖年间，四海冶边墙外就有大量蒙古人驻扎。志愿者沿城墙痕迹找到北口子小城遗址时，发现城墙遗址被挖开。志愿者当时并不知道这是否是有组织有计划的清理，还是私自开挖，总体感觉挖掘现场非常混乱。由于当时已近正午，现场空无一人，在拍摄现场照片后离开。志愿者回京后就在小站论坛上把图片上传，询问是否有人了解这一开挖行为是否得到有关部门批准。这一信息被延庆文物部门的站友范学新老师看到后，立刻将信息转给了延庆文委执法队。执法队立刻前往该地点检查，发现情况属实，为附近村民私自在四海冶口（也称北口子）小城遗址开挖取石，破坏行为得以制止和纠正。

第二，运用法律法规武器，与长城破坏行为作斗争。2007 年 5 月 2 日中午，长城小站的一队徒步考察山西长城的志愿者，在通过山西大同与内蒙古丰镇交界处国道 208 公路时，发现穿有"大同公路"反光背心的工人正在公路旁的明代土长城上施工，工人在土长城上开挖地基并砌起一道像北京八达岭长城一样制式垛口墙，同时工人从长城另一侧挖沟取土筛沙，当做建筑材料。志愿者立刻上前和施工工人了解情况，并询问施工是否得到批准。同时指出在长城上取土肯定是违法了新颁布的《长城保护条例》[10] 行为，要求立刻停止取土，同行志愿者开始拍照并录像取证。几分钟后，施工现场负责人赶到，表明他们是公路养护段的，要在这里建一个类长城垛口的矮墙表明进入山西界。在和该负责人确认了该施工并没有向当地的文物部门进行申报后，志愿者和他讲解新颁布的《长城保护条例》，表明现在的施工是违法行为，如果继续下去，需要承担相应的法律责任。现场负责人态度不错，认识到问题的严重性，当时让工人暂停施工。志愿者同时开始和北京联系，并通过长城专家成大林老师和国家文物局值班室汇报

PROMOTING PARTICIPATION IN CONSERVATION ACTIVITY

Preventing the destruction of the Great Wall

There are many challenges in the management of the Great Wall because of its enormous scale and the complexity of the topography through which it runs. Volunteers often encounter examples of damage to the Great Wall. The process of preventing destruction involves the management system of the Great Wall, the mediation of local interests, and the implementation and interpretation of legal provisions and regulations. Since third sector organisations lack legal enforcement powers, they need to adopt different measures to prevent the destruction of the Great Wall.

The first means is to report any damage as soon as possible through the organisation's extensive network of connections to official bodies. On 15 September, 2006, Hong Feng, a volunteer of The Great Wall Station, went to the Great Wall in Sihaiyekou, Yanqing County, Beijing, for a site patrol. Sihaiyekou is the largest fortified pass in the East Lu under Xuanfu[1] in the Ming Great Wall, commonly known as Beikouzi. The Frontier Defence chapter in the Yanqing State Annuals said that "the area outside Sihaiye, the Baoshan Temple, Tianqili and other places were occupied by the invaders". That is to say, during the Jiajing period of the Ming Dynasty, a large number of Mongolians were stationed outside the Sihaiye frontier line.

When the volunteers followed the line of the Great Wall to the site of Beikouzi, they found that the ruins of the city wall had been removed. The volunteers did not know whether this was officially organised and planned or a private excavation. The overall impression was that the excavation site was a complete mess. Since it was near noon at the time of the visit, the site was empty and the volunteers left after taking photos. Soon after returning to Beijing, they uploaded the pictures on the forum of The Great Wall Station and asked if anyone knew whether the excavation had been approved by the relevant government authorities. The information was seen by Fan Xuexin, of the Yanqing Cultural Heritage Department, and was immediately passed to the Yanqing Cultural Committee Law Enforcement Team. The law enforcement team went to the site to check and found that the local villagers had privately excavated the stone from the ruins, and their destructive behaviour was stopped.

The second mechanism is to use laws and regulations to fight against the destruction of the Great Wall. At noon on 2 May 2007, a team of Great Wall Station volunteers visited the Great Wall in Shanxi Province on foot. When passing National Highway 208 at the junction of Datong, Shanxi and Fengzhen, Inner Mongolia, they found that workers, wearing Datong Highway labeled reflective vests, were carrying out construction work on the Ming Dynasty Great Wall. The workers had dug the earthen foundation of the Wall and built a standard battlement like the Badaling Great Wall in Beijing, while others were digging the ditch on the other side of the Great Wall and sieving the sand for building material. The volunteers approached the construction workers to investigate and asked if the construction was approved. At the same time, they pointed out that removing the earth from the vicinity of the Great Wall is a violation of the newly promulgated Great Wall Conservation Regulations[10] and they instructed the workers to stop digging imme-

---

1 Also called *Xuanfu Zhen*, one of the nine Zhens along the Ming Dynasty Great Wall (Editors' note)

了现场情况。志愿者坚持到现场负责人彻底下令停工，并将施工人员与车辆撤离现场，并原地守候一个小时，确认无人员返回施工后，离开现场。依据后面了解的情况，5 月 3 日，大同和新荣区文物部门组成了联合调查队，前往调查，并对相关单位进行了行政处分，已经砌到长城上的矮墙被拆除，长城上被挖开的土坑被回填。

第三，通过国家文物局设立文物违法举报电话及时反映情况。在 2015 年 8 月 14 日，中国国家文物局为应对复杂的文物破坏情况，成立了文物违法举报中心 [11]，这个举报中心，也负责接受长城破坏情况的举报。2016 年 9 月 28 日，宁夏长城保护志愿者李世翔在前往宁夏灵武市考察白土岗烽火台时发现在烽火台旁停着挖掘机与重载车辆正在施工作业。李世翔立刻打电话给有经验的长城小站站友询问该如何处理，站友立刻让李世翔给举报中心打电话，并指导了应该如何取证。当日上午宁夏文物局即安排工作

图 4

人人能为长城做的五件事（版权：长城小站）

Fig. 4

5 things that you can do for the Great Wall (© Great Wall Station)

diately, while other volunteers began to take photos and videos as evidence. A few minutes later, the person in charge of the construction site arrived, indicating that they were responsible for maintenance of the road and were planning to build a small section of wall in the shape of the Great Wall battlement to indicate the crossing into Shanxi. After confirming that the work did not have permission, the volunteers explained the newly promulgated Great Wall Protection Regulation, stating that the construction in progress was illegal. The site manager recognised the severity of the problem and construction work was suspended. The volunteers contacted Beijing and reported the situation through the Great Wall expert Cheng Dalin and the SACH duty-room. The volunteers stayed at the site until the site manager had ceased all construction and had removed men and vehicles from the site. The volunteers waited for another hour in the field to ensure that no one returned to the site. On 3 May the cultural heritage department of Datong and Xinrong District formed a joint investigation team, carried out an investigation, and administrative sanctions were taken against the relevant units. The small-scale model wall that had been built was demolished and the excavated pit was filled in.

Thirdly, a cultural relics hotline has been set up by SACH to enable incidents to be reported quickly. On 14 August 2015, SACH established the Cultural Relics Reporting Centre for illegal activities[11] in response to the widespread problem of the destruction of cultural heritage. This reporting centre is also covers the Great Wall. On 28 September 2016, Li Shixiang, a volunteer of the Great Wall Station from Ningxia, visited the Baitugang beacon tower in Lingwu City, Ningxia Autonomous Region, and found excavators and heavy loading vehicles next to the beacon tower in the process of construction. Li Shixiang immediately called the experienced people of The Great Wall Station to seek advice on what to do. They advised Li Shixiang to contact the Reporting Centre through the hotline and provided him with instructions on how to record evidence of what was happening. On the morning of the same day, the Cultural Relics Bureau of Ningxia AR arranged for a group to go to the site. After confirming that the site from which earth was being removed was within the Great Wall Conservation Area, the group notified the Land and Resources Department and the township government and reported the case to the local police station. On the same day, they found the person responsible for the damage, took appropriate action against him and then implemented measures to restore the original appearance of the Great Wall Conservation Area.

The establishment of the Cultural Heritage Reporting Centre under SACH is a fast-track channel for preventing destruction of cultural heritage in accordance with the Great Wall Protection Regulation.

Based on its practical experience of preventing destruction of the Great Wall for two decades, The Great Wall Station uses the hotline as a key tool in its conservation activities. It gives ordinary volunteers the opportunity, when they discover damage, of becoming a hero of cultural heritage conservation, by knowing what to do and who to approach for help. The Great Wall Station listed using this hotline as one of the "five things that everyone can do for the Great Wall". It hopes that everyone will know about it and make use of it and so become a guardian of the Great Wall and of cultural heritage conservation.

In order to apply legal protection of cultural heritage effectively, particularly in the remote locations in which the Great Wall is situated, the accurate recording of time, place and of evidence of illegal activities is vital to ensure prompt and effective action to halt and prevent further destruction. Therefore, in addition to promoting the hotline, The

组前往现场核实，工作组在现场核实确认为在长城保护区域内非法取土后，即向国土资源部门、乡政府通报情况，向属地派出所报案。当日找到相关责任人，完成调查后做出相关处理，并恢复了长城保护区域原貌。国家文物局违法举报中心的设立，是在《长城保护条例》之后，国家有关部门提供的一条阻止文物破坏的快速通道。基于十多年在阻止长城破坏过程中的实践体验，长城小站对这条新通道特别重视。因为这条通道通达以后，普通人面对长城破坏时，只要打电话进行举报，就有了成为文物保护英雄的可能，而不是束手无策，不知道找谁去好。长城小站把这条通道列到了他们发起的"人人能为长城做的五件事"中，希望所有的人都能知道和使用这条通道。当每个人都知道如何使用这个方法后，大家就都成为了长城及文物保护的守卫军。

在实际实践中，对文物破坏的举报，还是有一定的技术要求。因为举报是一个法律行动的前提，而长城大多在偏远荒芜的地区，因此只有具备清晰的时间、地点、事件线索的法律举报，才能协助相关人员迅速锁定案发现场，阻止破坏。在这一方面，长城小站除了广为宣传举报中心这条举报通道外，也积极提供对处在长城破坏现场的志愿者进行心理支持和举证指导，帮助他们进行成功举报。

在多年的实践过程中，长城小站志愿者体会到，尽快、充分地利用好各种法律工具，能倍增保护的力量。

（二）支持长城保护相关者行动

在长城保护的格局内，对于直接与长城保护的相关者，民间力量可以提供多方面多层次的支持。

对政府核心部门工作的支持主要会以智库的形式出现，不在本文中进行详细讨论。

在长城保护体系中，处于第一线位置的是约 5000 名长城保护员。这些长城保护员分布在长城沿线的村落之中，由乡村政府统一安排。其成员大部分是本地区年龄较大的农民[1]。目前长城保护员的补贴，由地方财政安排支持。各地经济条件不一，所以补贴程度也不一致。在大多数地区，长城保护员的收入极低，约在 100~200 人民币／月左右。如果长城保护员正常巡视长城的话，工作量非常大，对于上了年纪的保护员来说，也是一个负担

如何让长城保护员完成好自身职责，长城小站进行了一定的探索工作。一方面，长城小站前往实地考察寻找优秀的长城保护员代表。对于确认的长城保护员优秀个人事迹，小站进一步安排志愿者，深入采访、拍摄录像，对公众宣传和讲述他们的故事。

对于优秀的长城保护员，长城小站还会让他们加入自己的社群，成为更多人的朋友，使他们在长城保护员的岗位上，虽然没有足够的收入，但是能感受到社会的尊敬，在必要时，还能得到众人的帮助及精神上的鼓励。

长城小站还在制定长城保护员的培训方案，以便能提升长城保护员工作能力和生活生产能力。

在长城保护的格局内，有另一个未引起重视的利益相关者：长城乡民。

在长城边长大的长城乡民，长城是他们小时候的玩具，是他们家用来堆放杂物的空间，他们也这段长城的修建者——他们祖先故事的传承者。如果他们身边的长城彻底消失，那么关于这段墙及当年修墙祖先的故事也就会逐渐不再有人提起。

---

1 在中国农村，青壮年大多会选择前往城市打工以获取更多收入。

Great Wall Station also provides psychological support, and guidance on the gathering of evidence, to volunteers who witness destruction along the Great Wall so as to help them report incidents successfully.

After years of experience, The Great Wall Station volunteers realise that using various legal mechanisms properly and quickly can have an important impact on conservation.

Supporting the actions of the Great Wall Patrollers

In the overall system of conservation of the Great Wall, the non-governmental sector can provide multi-aspect and multi-level support for those people most directly engaged in day-to-day conservation. Non-governmental sector support for the work of government departments mainly appears in the form of contributing to policy-making think tanks and is not discussed in detail in this article.

There are about 5,000 Great Wall Patrollers in the front line of conservation of the Great Wall. They are spread out among the villages along the Great Wall and are organised through the village and township councils. Most of the Patrollers are elderly local farmers[1]. At present, the stipends of the Great Wall Patrollers are provided through local financial arrangements. Economic conditions vary from village to village, so the level of stipend also varies. In most areas, the income of a Great Wall Protector is extremely low, about 100-200 RMB/month. The workload is very heavy if the Great Wall Patrollers regularly inspect the Great Wall, and it is also a physical burden for the mainly elderly Patrollers.

The Great Wall Station has carried out a number of trials on how to help the Great Wall Patrollers fulfill their duties. It conducted field visits to find outstanding representatives of Great Wall Patrollers, and it arranged for volunteers to conduct in-depth interviews with them and to film videos to promote their stories to the public. The Great Wall Station also helps the excellent Great Wall Patrollers to join their own on-line communities and become friends of more people, so that they can feel the respect of society, and even though they earn very little as Great Wall Patrollers they can obtain the spiritual support of the public. The Great Wall Station is also developing a training programme for the Great Wall Patrollers to improve their skills and quality of life.

In the overall system of conservation of the Great Wall, another stakeholder group that lacks recognition comprises the village communities along the Great Wall. The villagers who grew up along the Great Wall considered it as their childhood playground, and extra space to store their odds and ends. They also represent the original builders of the Great Wall and are the inheritors of the stories of their ancestors. If the Great Wall in their neighbourhood disappears completely, then the stories and memories of the ancestors who constructed it will gradually vanish from people's lives.

Volunteers have found that the villagers along the Great Wall can have a significant impact on its conservation. The removal and inappropriate re-use of the stone and brick is an important reason behind the disappearance of the Great Wall.

One example is that of the Great Wall of Wulonggou, located in Laiyuan County, Hebei Province, which was originally well preserved because of a legend that houses built of old bricks are inauspicious. One day in

---

1 In rural China, most young adults choose to work in big cities for higher income.

在长城边深入的过程中，长城小站志愿者发现长城边的乡民是长城保护至关重要的一个环节。发生在长城边对长城建筑材料的小蚕食、不合理利用，是长城消失的重要原因。

一个案例是，位于河北省涞源县的乌龙沟长城原本保存的特别完好，因为村里有用老砖盖房不吉利的传说。2004年有一天，长城小站的志愿者孙文静再次来到乌龙沟长城时，忽然发现有大量被新推倒的长城垛墙。她非常震惊，到村里打听垛墙倒塌的缘由。后来终于了解到，是因为最近村里来人收蝎子，一个蝎子几分钱到一两毛钱。长城垛墙的石头缝里有蝎子，孩子们就上长城把垛墙推倒了捉蝎子卖钱。后来在长城沿线，志愿者发现在长城上捉蝎子这种情况很多地方都发生过。

如何解决这个问题？经过讨论，分析了破坏长城的主体是孩子们，而孩子们主要集中在当地的中学上课，于是在2004年，长城小站志愿者发起长城沿线长城宣传保护活动，首站目标就是乌龙沟当地的中学。通过和学校联络，志愿者得以成行，为孩子们带去礼物的同时，长城小站志愿者送上了一堂长城文化及保护知识课程。了解了长城伟大及破坏行为的严重性后，孩子们纷纷表态，不再上长城去捉蝎子。

2005年，该活动正式确立为"家住长城边"项目，在实践中逐渐转型，致力于通过长城沿线学校助学来进行长城与文化的保护宣传工作。目前长城小站在长城沿线维护有20余所小学。

经过10多年努力，目前长城小站的志愿者已经在长城沿线已经帮助了超过20所学校。"家住长城边"的项目愿景是期望在未来能帮助到更多的学校，最终在长城两边，构建起保护长城的珍珠链[12]。

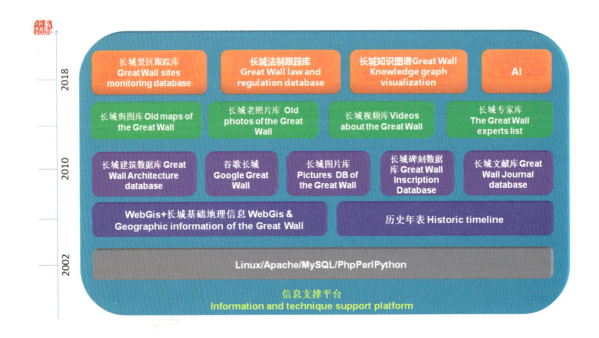

图 5

长城小站开发的开放长城数据库系统（版权：长城小站）

Fig. 5

Open information platform developed by the Great Wall Station (© Great Wall Station)

2004, when Sun Wenjing, a Great Wall Station volunteer, visited the site, she found large sections of the walls that had recently fallen down. She was very shocked and went to the village to find out why the Wall had collapsed. Eventually she learned that it was because there were scorpions in the stone cracks of the battlement, and the children pushed down the Wall to catch the scorpions for money. Subsequently other volunteers found that catching scorpions happened in many places along the Great Wall.

After further investigation, it was confirmed that it was children who were responsible for this destruction, and that most of them were middle school students. In 2004, The Great Wall Station volunteers launched a programme along the Great Wall to address the problem. The first stop was the middle school at Wulonggou. Through established contacts with local schools, the volunteers were able to visit and bring gifts to the schoolchildren. At the same time, the volunteers presented lectures on conservation of the Great Wall. After understanding the severe consequences of their destructive behaviour, the children declared that they would never catch scorpions again on the Great Wall.

In 2005 a project called "Living along the Great Wall" was officially established. It gradually transformed into a project which promoted the culture and conservation of Great Wall through engagement with the schools along the Great Wall. The Great Wall Station now maintains relationships with more than 20 primary schools along the Great Wall. The vision of the project "Living along the Great Wall" is to help more schools in the future, and ultimately to construct a conservation string of pearls to protect the Great Wall and the cultural heritage of its surrounding areas[12].

BUILDING A LADDER FOR GROWTH OF ENGAGEMENT

An open Great Wall database system

Another important objective is to build a ladder by which all sections of society can develop their understanding and involvement in the Great Wall. The more profoundly that participants are engaged, the greater their sense of ownership will be. But generating deeper involvement requires more effort, such as ensuring the spread of a more comprehensive understanding of the history and architecture of the Great Wall. This means that participants need to engage in more in-depth learning.

In order to facilitate volunteer participation in the conservation of the Great Wall, it is necessary to remove the barriers to participation. Based on its long-term practical experience, the Great Wall Station provides a variety of public services to help people learn more. One of these is the building of an open and free Great Wall database system.

The main problem for independent researchers and protectors who wish to engage deeply in the conservation of the Great Wall is the lack of information and channels for amateurs to obtain basic information. This means that people need to spend more time and money in order to get started or to improve their knowledge. The Great Wall has a long history of more than 2,000 years and the data from its 20,000-kilometre line are quite scattered.

Volunteers of The Great Wall Station are equipped with inter-disciplinary understanding, so they can bring together different aspects of knowledge. Once the prototype for the structure of the system was established, the internal

六、成长阶梯构筑

（一）开放的长城数据库系统

另一个重要的设计是构筑各阶人员向上成长的阶梯。参与者越深入，就越有成就感。但是要深入参与，就意味着需要更多的付出，比如要对长城的历史和建筑知识有更全面的掌握，这意味着参与者需要深入学习，并跨越越来越陡的学习曲线。

为了帮助志愿者更方便地更快捷的参与长城保护，避免无关因素的干扰或者阻挠。长城小站基于其多年实践经验，提供多种公共服务，帮助人们深入长城领域。

长城小站的一项实践是系统构筑公开的免费的长城数据库系统。

对于民间的研究者和保护者，要深度参与长城保护，首要面临的问题是资料的匮乏，甚至连了解查询基本信息的渠道都非常缺乏。因此要入门或者提升自身水平，都必须付出更多的时间、金钱。而历经2000多年历史的长城知识浩如烟海，2万多公里沿线长城数据也非常散乱。民间进行长城研究和保护面临各种问题。

长城小站的志愿者具有跨行业的特点，因此能有机会汇聚各种智慧。在小站形成雏形后，小站内部技术团队便自发地讨论、规划小站的数据库系统，通过志愿者们的努力，持续地构建系统架构、丰富与完善数据内容。

在设计中，底层提供时间和空间两个坐标系，使得任何具体点段的长城，都能被方便定位。在这个基础上，进一步建立基础要素库，然后向上构建专题数据库。

通过网友的努力，长城小站系统建设有中国长城建筑数据库（保存有全国4万余处长城建筑数据）、中国长城（铭刻）碑刻数据库、中国长城文献数据库、视频数据库、谷歌长城、历代年表、长城专家库等系列数据库、工具集等。

这项工具还在持续进行下去，新的专题数据库已经在进一步的设计及数据准备之中。

这些公开、免费的数据库系统，为民间长城研究提供了基础支持，打破非业务因素导致的成本，大大降低了参与各项长城工作的准入门槛，使智力得以汇聚、公共成本得以降低。

（二）开放的公共平台

为了能让更多人体验长城保护工作，长城小站设计从浅到深多种程度的志愿活动，便于公众依据自身时间、能力、兴趣进行选择和参与，例如：

· 随手公益——组织调查或者捐赠图书给长城边的学校

· 家住长城边——前往学校进行助学和宣教

· 长城志愿者讲师团——以授课方式进入中小学

· 新技术保护长城团队——使用各种新技术为长城研究与保护助力

同时，长城小站一方面积极支持其他长城友邻组织的发展，为他们出谋划策；一方面鼓励、协助其他领域的组织、机构通过其平台来帮助到长城和它身边的人们。

technical team discussed and designed the database. Through the efforts of volunteers, the system framework has been steadily developed and the content has been enriched and improved. In the design, the base layer provides two coordinated systems of time and space, so that any specific point on the Great Wall can be readily located. The inventory of the monument's basic elements is then further developed, and thus the thematic database is built up.

Through the efforts of the internet users, The Great Wall Station has established an Architectural Database for the Great Wall of China (containing more than 40,000 elements): the Great Wall Inscribed Tablets Database, the Great Wall China Literature Database, a Video Database, a Google Great Wall database, the Great Wall Chronology database, the Great Wall expert database, and other databases and toolkits. This system is still under development, and the new thematic database is already in the process of further design and data preparation. These open and free database systems provide basic support for the study of the Great Wall, reducing the practical barriers and costs to participation in Great Wall studies. This promotes the contribution of wider knowledge and expertise and thereby reduces the burden on state investment in this field.

Open public platform

To enable more people to participate in the conservation of the Great Wall, The Great Wall Station has designed a range of volunteer activities, so that the public can choose to participate according to their own schedule, abilities and interest. Examples include:

· Charitable activities: organising surveys or donating books to schools along the Great Wall

· Living along the Great Wall— visiting schools to assist in and to promote education about the Great Wall

· The Great Wall Volunteer Lecturers Group - going into primary and secondary schools to deliver lectures

· The Great Wall Protection New Technology Team - using a variety of new technologies to assist in Great Wall research and conservation

At the same time, The Great Wall Station actively supports the development of other Great Wall friendship organisations. It provides advice and encourages and assists organisations and institutions in other fields to support the Great Wall and the people who are involved in its conservation.

Everyone can make a contribution to the Great Wall

Based on preliminary work, The Great Wall Station found that the practical conservation of the Great Wall involves several components. In terms of motivating public participation, we can identify five elements on which activities should be focused so as to enhance the conservation of the Great Wall:

· The public perceptions, knowledge and cultural appreciation of the Great Wall

· Environmental protection around the Great Wall

· General protection for the Great Wall and its associated components

· The mobilisation of Great Wall protection resources

· Mechanisms for handling emergencies

（三）、人人能为长城贡献

在这些工作的基础上，长城小站进一步分析，长城保护其实涉及到多个方面。在发动公众力量广泛参与的角度上，可以找到五个方向为长城保护出力：

1. 长城公众形象、知识、文化的传播；

2. 长城周边环境营造保护；

3. 长城建筑及附属物的一般性保护；

4. 长城的保护力量动员；

5. 长城突发性事件处理机制。

这么多角度可以参与，往往却无人参与的原因，往往是因为民众没意识到要做些什么、不知道该做些什么或该怎么具体做。如果能有一些善意的提醒，往往能成为智慧与行动的开始。

这个发现成为长城小站内部的一个大讨论，并且伴随了很多探索性实验。在经过五年的集体讨论和实践经验总结，长城小站从这五个方向上各自遴选出具有强烈代表性、且又极易操作的五种行为，构筑起面向更广泛的公众推荐的"人人能为长城做的五件事"

1. 与朋友分享你的长城照片和体验；

2. 带走垃圾，维护长城的清洁；

3. 劝阻在长城上刻画的行为，维持长城原有风貌；

4. 给孩子们捐一本书—帮助长城边的乡村，即在帮助长城；

5. 如果你发现疑似破坏长城的行为，请拍照、录像并立即报告给文物执法机构或民间长城保护组织。

2016 年 1 月，长城小站与 34 家单位、媒体、机构共同发起倡议"人人能为长城做的五件事"，一起为保护长城添砖加瓦 [13]。

结　语

中国长城体量庞大，分布偏远。目前在整个长城保护领域，国家和社会能提供的力量都偏于薄弱，因而在保护的实践中，需要更多的社会力量广泛参与。长城小站基于保护力量所呈现的瘦金字塔形现实分析，提出多层、多维度动员与发挥社会力量体验及深度参与长城保护的理论、方法、模式，并积极进行了实践及经验总结，为更多社会力量参与长城保护实践提供了有益的探索和尝试。

The reason why people do not participate in the conservation of the Great Wall, even though there are various opportunities available, is often because they do not realise what they can do or how to do it. If we can help with this, then they will act. When we discovered that this was the main reason for a lack of participation, there was considerable debate about how to address it within The Great Wall Station. After five years of collective discussions and experimenting with ideas, The Great Wall Station identified five activities which are most widely beneficial and also easy to implement, and created the initiative "Five things that everyone can do for the Great Wall". This encourages the wider public to:

· Share photos and experiences of the Great Wall with your friends

· Take away litter and maintain the cleanliness of the Great Wall

· Deter people from carving inscriptions and images on the Great Wall to help maintain its original features

· Donate a book for schoolchildren in the villages around the Great Wall,

· Take a photo, make a video and immediately report any suspected damage to the cultural heritage

enforcement agency or your local voluntary Great Wall conservation organisation.

In January 2016, The Great Wall Station along with 34 organizations, media and institutions jointly launched the initiative to help us all protect the Great Wall together[13].

CONCLUSION

The Great Wall of China is a monument which spans a huge and largely remote geographical area. At present the effectiveness of both state and public conservation across the whole area of the Great Wall is weak, so it is essential to strengthen it through mobilising public engagement. The Great Wall Station proposes that multi-layer and multi-dimensional theories, methods and models of mobilising and developing the strength of public experience and participation in the conservation of the Great Wall, should be fully utilized, and that conservation best practice and innovative methods are deployed to further harness social power in practical protection.

参考文献
Bibliography

[1] 国家统计局 . 国家统计数据 [EB/OL].

National Bureau of Statistics. National data. http://data.stats.gov.cn/index.htm.2017 年

[2] 民政部 .2016 年社会服务发展统计公报 [EB/OL].(2017-08-03)[2017-08-03].

Ministry of Civil Affairs of the People's Republic of China. Statistical Report on the Development of Social Services 2016. August 3, 2017. August 3, 2017.

http://www.mca.gov.cn/article/sj/tjgb/201708/20170800005382.shtml.

[3] 记者杨雪梅 . 全国不可移动文物 "家底" 766722 处 [N]. 人民日版 2011-12-30.

Yang, X.M. "The 766,722 sites of the National immovable cultural relics 'inventory'." December 30, 2011.

[4] 国家文物局 . 中国长城保护报告（全文版）[EB/OL].(2016-11-30)[2016-11-30]. http://www.sach.gov.cn/art/2016/11/30/art_1946_135711.html.

State Administration of Cultural Heritage. Report on the Protection of the Great Wall of China (full text). Nov 30, 2016. Nov 30, 2016.

[5] 刘曙光，柴晓明 . 文物工作研究——聚焦 2015[M]. 北京：文物出版社，2017：249.

Liu, S.G., and Chai, X.M. Research on Cultural relics work: Focus 2015. Beijing: Cultural Relics Press, 2017: 249.

[6] 杨国庆 . 中国古城墙（第一卷）[M]. 南京：江苏人民出版社，2017：93.

Yang, G.Q. Ancient City Wall of China (Vol.1). Nanjing: Jiangsu People's Publishing. 2017: 93.

[7] 国家文物局 . 第九届 "薪火相传——寻找中国文物故事杰出传播者" 揭晓 [EB/OL].(2017-12-18) [2017-12-18]. http://www.sach.gov.cn/art/2017/12/18/art_722_145894.html.

State Administration of Cultural Heritage. "The Ninth 'Generation to Generation-Seeking for The Outstanding Communicator of the Chinese Cultural Heritage Story' was announced." December 18, 2017. December 18, 2017.

[8] 人民网 . 京津冀 "最美慈善义工" 揭晓 [EB/OL].(2018-04-02)[2018-04-02].

People's Network. "Beijing-Tianjin-Hebei 'most Beautiful Charity Volunteer' announced." April 2, 2018. April 2, 2018. http://bj.people.com.cn/n2/2018/0402/c82840-31414681.html.

[9] 中国文物保护基金会秘书处 . 社会力量参与文物保护论坛文集 [M]. 北京：文物出版社，2017：135.

Secretariat of the China Foundation for Cultural Heritage Conservation. Proceedings of the Forum on the participation of Social Forces in the Protection of Cultural relics. Beijing: Cultural Relics Press, 2017:135.

[10] 长城保护条例 (国务院令第 476 号)[EB/OL].(2006-09-20).

Regulations on the Protection of the Great Wall (decree No. 476 of the State Council). Sep 20, 2006. http://www.gov.cn/zhengce/2006-10/23/content_2602458.htm.

[11] 国家文物局文物违法举报中心挂牌运行 [EB/OL].(2015-08-17)[2015-08-17].

"The Cultural relics violation reporting Center of the State Administration of Cultural Heritage is listed for operation." August 17, 2015. August 17, 2015.

http://www.sach.gov.cn/art/2015/8/17/art_722_123782.html.

[12] 程长进，张俊 . 呵护长城，民间志愿者在行动 [J]. 世界遗产，2013(5).

Cheng, C.J., and Zhang, J. "Protect the Great Wall, non-governmental volunteers in action." World Heritage, 2013(5).

[13] 郭晓蓉 . 保护长城 从五件小事做起 [N]. 中国文物报，2016-01-19(2).

Guo, X.R. "The protection of the Great Wall begins with five small things." China Cultural Relics News, January 19, 2016(2).

Chapter Three
Survey, Research and Monitoring

山西北齐长城（摄影：于 冰）

The Northern Qi Great Wall in Shanxi (© Yu Bing)

第三章
长城调查研究和监测

博得瓦德要塞（版权：Roger Clegg）
Birdoswald Roman Fort (© Roger Clegg)

HADRIAN'S WALL SURVEY AND EXCAVATION

TONY WILMOTT

Historic England - Portsmouth - UK

Abstract

This paper outlines some of the different survey techniques which have been deployed on Hadrian's Wall in recent years. These techniques have revealed the extent of the Hadrian's Wall historic landscape, and serve as a valuable tool to inform policy on protection and research. The paper also examines some case studies of excavation and the various justifications and contexts for such work. Many of the survey methods are of recent origin, and before they became available excavation was the principal means for exploring the monument. Excavation continues to be the means by which information on time-depth and complexity is recovered.

Keywords: Hadrian's Wall, excavation, Survey, air photography, lidar, mapping.

The study of Hadrian's Wall has a long ancestry, with important contributions being published as early as the 17th century[1]. Scientific study of the Wall, however, began in the 19th century. The earliest survey of Hadrian's Wall was commissioned by the Duke of Northumberland in 1852[2] and the map which resulted was re-published in many works on the Wall for the rest of the century. In 1964 a specialist map of the Wall was prepared by the Ordnance Survey[3]. Though this was useful both academically and for visitors to the Wall it could not be considered a tool for management. The two first iterations of the Management Plan for the Hadrian's Wall World Heritage Site[4][5] recognised that accurate mapping was key to understanding and conserving a cultural landscape like that in which Hadrian's Wall is set and recommended the production of a comprehensive, up-to-date and accurate record of the Wall and its setting zone. To this end, the Hadrian's Wall National Mapping Programme (NMP) was established in 2002[6]. The UK is fortunate in having access to a huge archive of aerial photography dating from the 1920s to the present day. The NMP used the entire archive of photographs of Hadrian's Wall and its landscape setting to create accurate mapping of the monument. Over 27,000 photographs were examined and an archive of digital mapping and text records were produced. New flying was also carried out as part of the programme. Naturally, the photography revealed archaeological landscape traces from all periods from prehistory to the present, and all of these were mapped. New records were made for 2,748 sites, and a further 806 records were enhanced. A good example combining the enhancement of existing knowledge with new information gained by more recent flying was at White Moss, Cumbria, where a number of known Roman camps were revealed in more detail, with the addition of three further superimposed camps (Fig. 1). Importantly these photographs revealed lines of pits (or possibly ovens) which indicate the internal arrangement of the camps

哈德良长城调查及发掘

托尼·维尔莫特

（英格兰遗产委员会，英国朴茨茅斯）

摘　要

本文总结了近年来应用于哈德良长城的若干不同调查技术。这些技术展现了哈德良长城历史景观的范围，并作为一个有价值的工具，为保护和研究政策提供信息。本文还介绍了几个考古发掘的案例，并探讨开展发掘工作的原由和背景。许多调查方法近年才得到应用，在此之前，发掘仍是认识遗迹的主要方式。如今，发掘仍然是获取时间—地层深度和复杂性信息的有效手段。

关键词：哈德良长城　发掘　调查　航空摄影　激光雷达　测绘

哈德良场长城的研究历史悠久，早在 17 世纪就有重要研究成果得到发表[1]。然而，对哈德良长城的科学研究则是从 19 世纪开始的。1852 年，最早对哈德良长城的调查由诺森伯兰公爵委托[2]，调查绘制的地图在 19 世纪后半叶有关哈德良长城的很多著作中多次发表。1964 年，英国国家测绘局（Ordnance Survey）[3] 绘制了哈德良长城专业地图。这份地图尽管无论是对学术还是对哈德良长城参观者而言都十分实用，但却无法成为管理工具。在最早的两版《哈德良长城世界遗产地管理规划》[4][5] 中，都明确哈德良长城作为文化景观的性质，指出准确测绘是认识和保护哈德良长城这类文化景观的关键，建议对哈德良长城及其周围区域进行全面，最新和准确的记录。为此，哈德良长城国家测绘项目（Hadrian's Wall National Mapping Programme，简称 NMP）于 2002 年立项[6]。幸运的是，英国保存有自 1920 年以来海量航拍照片档案。哈德良长城国家测绘项目利用了所有涉及哈德良长城及景观环境的航拍照片来对遗迹进行精准的测绘。共分析了 27000 余张航拍照片，由此制作了数字测绘和文本记录档案。作为项目的内容之一，还实施了新的航拍。这些航拍照片揭示了从史前到现在所有阶段的考古景观迹象，并进行了完整全面测绘。档案记录增加了 2748 处新景观，另有 806 份记录得到进一步完善。有一个例子可以很好展示如何将最新航拍信息与已知信息的完善相结合。在坎布里亚郡的怀特莫斯（White Moss），一些已知罗马营地的信息被细化，另外还发现了三处相互叠加的营地（图 1）。重要的是，这些照片中发现了一排排坑洞（或炉灶），揭示出营地的内部布局，而这一方面向来鲜为人知[7]。国家测绘项目的最终成果形成一整套图表记录，将罗马边界准确地定位于更广阔的景观环境和时间背景框架中。此项目不仅为认识和管理遗迹提供了宝贵的工具，其成果也被应用于哈德良长城考古遗迹分布图的绘制，为研究人员、游客和感兴趣的大众提供信息。

即便在测绘项目完结后，英格兰遗产委员会随之继续开展了一个密集的考古航拍项目。该项目拍摄的新影像可以同之前拍摄的照片进行对比，从而评估现如今的保护状况和随着时间变化遗迹发生的改变。这也帮助评估古迹的状况和识别潜在的损害或威胁。这些影像还作为图片材料被用于学术成果，普通出

- an aspect about which little is known[7]. The end result of the NMP was a cartographic record which placed the Roman frontier firmly into its broader landscape and chronological context. Not only did the NMP produce a valuable tool for the understanding and management of the monument, it was also used to produce an accurate archaeological map of the wall to inform researchers, visitors and the interested public.

Even after the completion of the mapping project, Historic England has continued an intensive programme of archaeological flying. The new images which this produces can be compared with older photographs in order to assess the present-day state of preservation, and changes to the monuments through time. This aids in assessing the condition of the monuments and in identifying potential threats and damage. The photography is also used as illustrative material in a variety of contexts including academic and general publications, websites and guidebooks.

A relatively recent important innovation has been the use of airborne laser scanning or lidar. This technique has been successful in the discovery of new camps and other features within the Wall landscape and has also enhanced knowledge of the landscape of known sites, particularly at Birdoswald where the Roman fort, Wall and Vallum can be seen within a landscape of later, medieval, plough furrows (Fig. 2). A new method of using aerial data, is 'structure from motion' - a photogrammetric method which allows the production of accurate 3D data which can be used in a variety of ways. At Birdoswald it has been used to produce a 3D model which is now on

Fig. 1

The cropmark traces of the White Moss/Moss Side camps with lines of pits (NMR NY4560/10 (12761/05) 15-AUG-1995 © Crown Copyright: NMR), with a plan of the multiple phases of camp - lines of tents marked by the double lines of pits visible as cropmarks

图 1

农作物生长（cropmarks）反映出来的怀特莫斯／莫斯塞德营地柱洞边界，和不同时期营地平面图——可见由双排柱洞反映出来的营帐排列格局（皇家版权：NMR NY4560/10(12761/05)15-AUG-1995)

版物，网站和旅游指南等。

机载激光扫描，又称激光雷达(airborne laser scanning or lidar) 则是最近的另一项重要的创新。该技术成功地发现了新的营地和哈德良长城的其他特征，同时还增强了对已知遗址景观的了解。尤其在博得瓦德（Birdoswald）[1]，我们可以看到罗马要塞，城墙和南部壕沟的遗迹处于中世纪耕地景观之中（图2）。此外，还有一种新的使用航拍数据的方法叫做"运动恢复结构（structure from motion）"。这种摄影测量方法能够生成准确的 3D 数据并以多种方式应用。该方法在博得瓦德被用于制作 3D 模型，正在英格兰遗产信托的新展览上展出。

地球物理调查（Geophysical survey）应用电阻率、磁力测定和最近的探地雷

Fig. 2
Lidar survey of the fort at Birdoswald, showing the fort, Wall and Vallum beneath a landscape of medieval ridge-and-furrow ploughing (© Newcastle University)
图 2
对博得瓦德要塞的激光雷达调查，展示出中世纪垄沟犁田景观下的要塞、长城和南部壕沟遗迹（版权：纽卡斯尔大学）

达等各种技术，是一项历史悠久的遥感手段。在过去的三十年中，这些技术被广泛地应用于区域内的遗迹上。其中大部分研究目标是了解要塞外围的平民聚落(vici)，已故艾伦·比金斯(Alan Biggins)和大卫·泰勒(David Taylor)的研究特别突出。在玛丽波特镇开展的调查(图3)也许是若干此类调查中最壮观的一个。它展现出远比之前所想象的要大得多的聚落范围，并体现其形态的复杂性 [8]。这些技术一直不断地在提高测绘信息的质量，并使更多信息被发现和记录。因此，很有必要时常使用最新的设备对这些地区再次展开调查。

除了这些较新的方法，有着悠久的英格兰传统的土方分析调查也依然沿用至今。对促进哈德良长城景观的理解上，该方法依然有着重要贡献，尤其是针对边境体系中一些较少得到研究和理解的方面，如哈德良长城北部壕沟的形态变化过程 [9]。

这些调查展现了哈德良长城景观的复杂性，以及古代聚落的空间范围。他们成为认识和管理遗迹的尤为重要的工具。然而，当考古发掘对这些调查成果进行检验时，我们也清楚地意识到它们并未展示出全部的考古特征。

考古发掘所揭示的信息毫无疑问远远复杂于调查技术所能了解的，因为它揭示了地层的时间深度，随着时间和历史阶段的变化情况。考古发掘可以提供大量证据来确定罗马边境地区的的年代和生活状况，这些证据包括器物证据物和古环境证据。如今，有越来越多的科学方法可以用来对发掘出的物料进行分析，包括放射性碳定年法，树轮年代学，孢粉学和 DNA 等。

1　古罗马要塞，周边有保存最完整的一段哈德良长城墙体——译者注。

display within English Heritage's new exhibition.

Geophysical survey, in the shape of resistivity, magnetometry and, more recently, ground-penetrating radar is a long-established method of remote sensing. During the last three decades these techniques have been extensively deployed on sites across the zone. Much of this work, particularly by the late Alan Biggins and David Taylor, has been aimed toward an understanding of the extra mural vici of forts. The survey carried out at Maryport (Fig. 3) is perhaps the most spectacular of a number of such surveys that have demonstrated the extent of these settlements, much larger than previously imagined, and shown their morphological complexity[8]. These techniques are constantly improving and allowing more to be seen and recorded, it is therefore useful from time to time to resurvey areas using the latest equipment.

In addition to these more recent methods, the long British tradition of analytical earthwork survey continues. This still has a major contribution to make to the understanding of the Wall landscape, in particular with respect to some of the less studied and less understood aspects of the frontier complex, such as the morphology of the Wall ditch[9].

These surveys have revealed the complexity of the Hadrian's Wall landscape, and the spatial extent of the ancient settlements, and they are a crucially important tool for the understanding and management of sites. Despite this, when survey results are tested by excavation it becomes clear that they do not show all archaeological features.

The story revealed by excavation is inevitably more complex than that shown by survey techniques, as this reveals stratigraphic time depth, changes through time and phasing. It produces a myriad of evidence for dating and for life on the frontier in the form of artefactual and palaeoenvironmental evidence. Excavated material is now capable of analysis through an increasing range of scientific methods, from radiocarbon dating and dendrochronology to palynology and DNA, among many others.

For most of the period during which Hadrian's Wall has been actively researched, the principal, indeed the only method, was excavation. There is an extraordinarily long history of research through excavation on the Wall, beginning in the 1840s, much of it under the aegis of John Clayton of Chesters. Many of these works were undertaken simply to clear the remains, and it was not until the 1890s that scientific excavation began, with the work of Francis Haverfield, R. C. Bosanquet and J. P. Gibson[10]. During the 20th and 21st centuries hundreds of excavations have taken place. During the 1920s and 30s, these were aimed at establishing the archaeological relationships between the different visible elements of the frontier complex and these works still provide a basic framework for our understanding of the sequence. In the 1920s the first excavations designed to work out the chronology of fort buildings were undertaken. Excavation at Corbridge continued from the pre-war years until 1973.

There have been, and still are, a number of drivers for excavation work today. One of the most important is in response to development. The increasing pace of development in the 1960s and 1970s, and the consequent threat to archaeological monuments and remains, led to 'rescue' excavations being undertaken by several bod-

在对哈德良长城的研究最活跃的那段时间里，绝大多数时候使用的主要的、实际上也唯一的方法就是发掘。通过发掘哈德良长城来进行研究的做法由来已久，最早始于19世纪40年代，而大多数的发掘工作都是在切斯特的约翰·克莱顿（John Clayton）支持下开展的。这些工作中，有很多仅仅只是对遗迹进行清理。真正科学发掘则是自19世纪90年代才开始，由弗朗西斯·哈弗菲尔德（Francis Haverfield），R.C.博赞基特（R. C. Bosanquet）和J.P.吉布森（J. P. Gibson）主持[10]。到了20世纪至21世纪期间，已经开展了数百次发掘。20世纪20至30年代间进行的发掘，主要目的是在不同可见罗马边界遗迹之间建立考古学关系，这些工作至今仍作为考古学序列的基本框架。20世纪20年代的第一轮科学发掘，旨在建立要塞建筑的年代序列。科布里奇（Corbridge）[1]的发掘从战前一直持续进行到1973年。

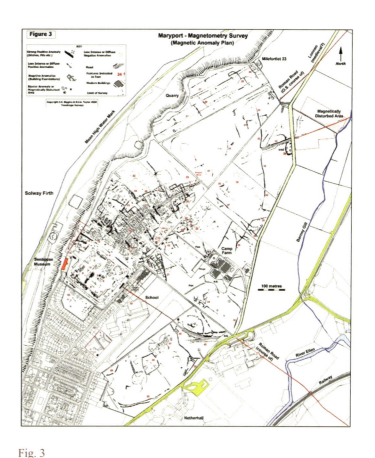

Fig. 3
Magnetometer survey of the Roman fort and extra-mural settlement at Maryport (© Timescape Archaeological Surveys)
图 3
对玛丽波特镇的罗马要塞和外围聚落的磁力测定调查（版权：Timescape Archaeological Surveys）

　　一直以来，包括现在，开展考古发掘的原由有若干。其中最重要的因素之一是配合基本建设开发。20世纪60和70年代建设开发日益加速，对考古遗迹造成威胁，促使若干机构开始进行"抢救性"发掘。这其中就包括英格兰遗产信托及其前身在卡莱尔（Carlisle）和哈德良边疆遗址穿过的大部分农村地区[11]进行的发掘，纽卡斯尔大学在科布里奇[12]和沃尔森德（Wallsend）[13]进行的发掘。在20世纪70年代中期创设了许多考古单位，而这些机构便承担了抢救工作。自1992年起，考古工作成为规划程序中一个实质性的考量因素，以尽可能减少建设开发影响。在有些地方，对考古资源的干预或破坏是不可避免的。例如，有些南—北走向大型基础设施建设项目横穿哈德良长城，以及在纽卡斯尔和卡莱尔城市建成区内的建设项目，这种情况下提前进行发掘和记录十分必要。发掘所需的费用现在由开发商承担，无论项目性质是公共还是私人。纵贯南北的基础设施项目包括纽卡斯尔西绕城公路工程项目[14]，卡莱尔西绕城公路工程，以及如西北乙烯管道等大型管线项目[15]。

1　古罗马城镇Corstopitum上演变至今的城镇，古罗马时是为哈德良长城驻军提供后勤保障的城镇——译者注。

ies, including English Heritage and its predecessors in Carlisle and in much of the rural area through which the frontier runs[11], and by Newcastle University at Corbridge[12] and Wallsend[13]. During the mid-1970s a number of archaeological units were set up and these bodies undertook rescue work. Since 1992 archaeology has been a material consideration in the planning process and where possible the impact is mitigated. Where interference with, or destruction of the archaeological resource cannot be avoided, for example when the Wall lies in the path of major north-south infrastructure projects, and in the case of development within the urban areas of Newcastle and Carlisle, excavation and recording must take place. This work is now undertaken at the cost of the developers, be they public or private concerns. Examples of north-south infrastructure include the Newcastle western by-pass[14], the Carlisle bypass and also major pipelines such as the North West Ethylene pipeline[15].

These works often produce considerable research dividends, in fact every new excavation on the Wall line produces new evidence and insights. A good example of this comes from work in the urban area of Newcastle since 2000, which has revealed a hitherto unknown component of the Hadrian's Wall system; obstacles positioned on the berm between the curtain wall and the wall ditch[16]. This discovery has re-opened the long discussion of the primary purpose of the frontier; whether it was a control system, or designed for military/defensive purposes[17].

It is not only through development that archaeology is threatened, but also through agricultural and natural processes. Thus at Birdoswald a severe landslip caused by excessive rainfall combined with undercutting of the cliff by the river threatened the archaeology of the fort's cremation cemetery. A long strip of land along the cliff edge was totally excavated, removing and recording the archaeological material under medium to long-term threat[18]. This was the first extensive excavation of a Roman cemetery at a Wall fort. At Black Carts, the regular movement of cattle was eroding the Vallum and the activities of rabbits threatened to undermine some of the earthwork elements of the site. Excavation provided insights into the pre-Roman landscape, buried and preserved beneath the mounds of the Vallum[19]. This work was an example of excavation informing decisions on future management. This was also true of a project which undertook evaluation trenching on 12 milecastles which were on land under active cultivation, in order to examine whether active plough damage was taking place, and if so, to mitigate this by entering into agreement with the landowner[20].

Work towards the provision of facilities for visitors can also be a driver for excavation. This was true at Birdoswald where, in 1999, the 18th-century farmbuildings and courtyards were transformed into a residential visitor centre. The farm itself was built into the corner of the Roman fort, reusing its stonework and the buildings overly very shallowly buried vestiges of Roman buildings. Major excavations were conducted, funded by the developer, in this case Cumbria County Council, which allowed us to understand a quarter of the fort plan that had been sealed with concrete for a couple of centuries (Fig. 4)[21]. The results of these excavations and other research work on the site are now interpreted within the new facilities. The process of excavation is in itself a draw to visitor, and large scale, long running research excavations have taken place under public funding which have been open to visitors resulting in the creation of excellent archaeological visitor and educational resources, particularly

Fig. 4
The foundations of Roman buildings excavated beneath the concrete farmyard at the Roman fort of Birdoswald (© Historic England)
图 4
在博得瓦德罗马要塞，从混凝土农院下发掘出的罗马时期建筑基址（版权：英格兰遗产委员会）

  这些工程往往会带来大量新的研究发现。事实上，对哈德良长城沿线每次新的发掘都会带来新的证据和见解。自 2000 年起在纽卡斯尔市区开展的考古就是一个很好的例子，发现了哈德良长城防御体系中一个前所未闻的构成，即设置在城墙与北部壕沟间的狭道之上的障碍物[16]。学界对修建边界墙的主要目的的探讨由来已久，而这一发现再次引发了热议：它究竟是一个管控系统，还是出于军事 / 防御目的而建[17]。

  除了建设开发，农业活动和自然过程也会给考古遗迹带来威胁。在博得瓦德，强降雨导致的一处重大山体滑坡，加之河流对悬崖的掏蚀，都威胁着该要塞的火葬墓地考古遗址。因此，沿悬崖边缘的一块狭长区域进行了全面的发掘，全面揭露并记录受到中期和长期威胁的地层[18]。这种对长城要塞的罗马墓地的大范围发掘，在历史上尚属首次。在黑车（Blach Carts) 区域，牧牛的常规活动正侵蚀着南部壕沟，而兔子的活动给遗址土木防御工事的部分要素带来了破坏的威胁。相关发掘工作使人们对古罗马征服之前的景观有了新认识。这些遗迹叠压在南部壕沟的两侧堆土之下，保存下来[19]。这项考古工作成为范例，

at Birdoswald, South Shields and Wallsend. The excavations conducted by the Vindolanda Trust over more than 40 years, and continuing, have created a major visitor attraction and a very important museum. The remarkable conditions of archaeological survival on the site have resulted in recovery of a huge volume of organic artefacts, including a major archive of ink writing tablets, which has revolutionised thinking on the day - to - day running of the Roman Army. The Trust's funding model relies largely on income from the huge number of visitors who are fascinated to watch excavation in progress.

Excavation is also carried out simply for research purposes. From 2011 - 15, commissioned by the Senhouse Museum Trust, Newcastle University carried out research excavations in order to enhance understanding of the archaeological context of the museum's existing collections - particularly that of the many Roman altars found in pits in 1870, and presumed to be ritual deposits. Re-excavation showed that the altars had been buried as part of packing around timber posts - a very different context than previously assumed. This demonstrates also that reviewing old evidence - in both excavation and survey - in the light of new evidence and ideas is a very valuable process.

体现发掘如何对未来的管理决策提供信息。在另一案例中也是如此，对 12 个位于农业地带的里堡进行了探沟评估，从而确认频繁犁耕是否导致破坏；如果确实导致遗址破坏，将与土地所有者签署协议以减少此类破坏 [20]。

开展发掘工作的又一原由是为了给游客提供设施。在博得瓦德便是如此。1999 年，将 18 世纪的农舍和庭院改建为可提供住宿的游客中心。这座农场当时建在罗马要塞的一角，利用了罗马要塞的石料，建于埋藏较浅的罗马建筑基址之上。主要发掘工作都是由开发商实施并出资的，该项目开发商是坎布里亚郡议会。这些工作让我们能够了解被混凝土封存了几个世纪的要塞四分之一的布局（图 4）[21]。在新建的游客中心，这些发掘成果和其他对遗迹进行的研究成果进行了展示。发掘过程本身就是吸引游客的一项重要内容，而这项由公共资助的大规模的、长期的研究性发掘一直以来对游客开放，创造了极佳的考古参观和教育资源。该成果在博得瓦德，南希尔兹和沃尔森德尤为显著。由文多兰达信托（Vindolanda Trust）主持的发掘工作已超过 40 年并仍在继续，由此形成一处大型旅游景区和一座重要的博物馆。遗址绝佳的环境使考古遗物保存良好，出土了大量有机文物，其中就包括大量墨书木简档案，使我们对罗马军队的日常运营管理有了革命性认知。文多兰达信托的资金来源主要来自游客收入，大量游客向往亲眼见到发掘过程。

也有一些发掘工作仅仅是以研究为目的。从 2011 至 2015 年，纽卡斯尔大学受到森豪斯罗马博物馆信托（Senhouse Museum Trust）的委托进行研究发掘，以增进对现有馆藏文物考古背景的了解，特别是了解那些 1870 年在很多坑洞中发现的大量罗马祭坛石，之前人们认为这些祭坛石是因祭祀目的埋于地于。再次发掘的结果表明，这些埋藏的祭坛石是用作木柱周围的填充物的。这同之前的假设可谓大相径庭。同时这也表明，把发掘和调查获得的旧证据与新证据和观点进行重新比较分析是非常有价值的做法。

参考文献
Bibliography

[1] Birley, E. Research on Hadrian's Wall. Kendal: 1961.

E. 伯利 . 哈德良长城的研究 [M]. 肯德尔 :1961.

[2] MacLauchlan, H. Memoir written during a survey of Hadrian's Wall. London: 1852.

H. 麦克劳科伦 . 写于哈德良长城考察期间的回忆录 [M]. 伦敦 :1852.

[3] Ordnance. Survey Map of Hadrian's Wall. London: 1964.

英国地形测量局 . 哈德良长城地图 [Z]. 伦敦 :1964.

[4] English Heritage. Hadrian's Wall World Heritage Site: Management Plan 1996. London: 1996.

英格兰遗产信托 . 哈德良长城世界遗产地 : 管理规划 1996[R]. 伦敦 :1996.

[5] English Heritage. Hadrian's Wall World Heritage Site: Management Plan 2002-2007. London: 2002.

英格兰遗产信托 . 哈德良长城世界遗产地 : 管理规划 2002-2007[R]. 伦敦 :2002.

[6] Oakey, M. "Hadrian's Wall World Heritage Site National Mapping Programme Project: Summary

Report." English Heritage Research Dept. Report Series 73, Swindon: 2009.

M. 奥基. 哈德良长城世界遗产地国家测绘项目：摘　要报告 [M]. 英格兰遗产信托研究部报告系列丛书 73，斯文顿 :2009.

[7] Small, F. "Hadrian's Wall NMP Project, Brampton to Birdoswald: National Mapping Project Report." English Heritage Research Dept. Report Series 69, Swindon: 2008.

F. 斯莫尔. 哈德良长城 NMP 项目，从布兰普顿到博得瓦德：国家测绘项目报告 [R]. 英格兰遗产信托研究部报告系列丛书 69, 斯文顿 :2008.

[8] Biggins, J.A., and Taylor, D.J.A. "The Roman fort and Vicus at Maryport: geophysical survey, 2000-2004." In Romans on the Solway: Essays in honour of Richard Bellhouse, edited by Wilson and Caruana. Carlisle: 2004.

J.A. 比金斯，D.J.A. 泰勒. 玛丽波特镇的罗马要塞和平民聚落：地球物理调查、2000-2004[C]. 威尔逊，卡鲁阿纳编. 索尔威的罗马人：纪念理查德·贝尔豪斯的散文. 卡莱尔 :2004.

[9] Welfare, H. "Causeways, at Milecastles, across the Ditch of Hadrian's Wall." Archaeologia Aeliana, 2000, 5(28): 13-25.

H. 维尔法. 跨越哈德良长城壕沟的里堡堤道 [J].Archaeologia Aeliana， 2000,5(28):13-25.

[10] Breeze, D.J. J. Collingwood Bruce's Handbook to the Roman Wall, (14th edn). Newcastle: 2006.

D.J. 布雷兹. 科灵伍德·布鲁斯的罗马长城指南 (第 14 版)[M]. 纽卡斯尔 :2006.

[11] Wilmott, T. "Introduction: English Heritage research on Hadrian's Wall, 1976-2000." In Hadrian's Wall: Archaeological Research by English Heritage 1976-2000, edited by T. Wilmott. Swindon: 2009: 1-7.

T. 威尔莫特."引言：英格兰遗产信托对哈德良长城的研究,1976-2000"[J].T. 威尔莫特编, 哈德良长城：英格兰遗产信托的考古研究 1976-2000. 斯文顿 :2009:1-7.

[12] Hanson, W.S., Daniels, C.M., Dore, J.N., and Gillam, J.P. "The Agricolan supply base at Red House, Corbridge." Archaeologia Aeliana, 1979, 5(7): 1-98.

W.S. 汉森，C.M. 丹尼斯，J.N. 多尔，J.P. 吉拉姆. 科布里奇红屋阿格里佐拉的补给基地 [J]. Archaeologia Aeliana，1979，5(7):1-98.

[13] Rushworth, A., and Croom A. Segedunum: Excavations by Charles Daniels in the Roman fort at Wallsend (1975-84). Oxford: 2006.

A. 鲁什沃斯，A. 克鲁姆. 塞格杜努姆：查尔斯·丹尼尔斯在沃尔森德对罗马要塞的发掘 (1975-84)[M]. 牛津 :2006.

[14] Bidwell, P.T., and Watson, M. "Excavations on Hadrian's Wall at Denton, Newcastle upon Tyne." Archaeologia Aeliana, 1996, 5(24): 1-56.

P.T. 比德韦尔，M. 沃森. 在泰恩河畔纽卡斯尔丹顿地区对哈德良长城进行的发掘 [J]. Archaeologia Aeliana.1996,5(24):1-56.

[15] Drury, D. "Crossing Hadrian's Wall: the 1991 excavation." in Transect through Time; the archaeological landscape of the Shell North Western Ethylene Pipieline, edited by J. Lambert. Lancaster:

Lancaster Imprints,1996(1): 84-86.

D. 德鲁里. 穿过哈德良长城：1991 年的发掘 [J].J. 兰伯特编，时间的断面：壳牌化工的西北乙烯管道的考古景观. 兰卡斯特：兰卡斯特出版社 ,1996(1):84-86.

[16] McKelvey, J., and Bidwell, P. "Excavations and watching briefs along the berm of Hadrian's Wall at Throckley, Newcastle upon Tyne in 2001-2002." Arbeia Journal, 2005(8): 29-52.

J. 麦凯尔维，P. 比德韦尔 .2001-2002 年间对泰恩河畔纽卡斯尔索克里地区哈德良长城的狭道沿线进行的发掘和考察简报 [J]. 阿伯亚期刊，2005(8):29-52.

[17] Bidwell, P.T. "The system of obstacles on Hadrian's Wall; their extent, date and purpose." Arbeia Journal, 2005, (8): 53-76.

P.T. 比德韦尔 . 哈德良长城上的障碍物体系：其范围、日期及目的 [J]. 阿伯亚期刊，2005(8): 53-76.

[18] Wilmott, T. "The cemetery of the Hadrian's Wall fort at Birdoswald." Carlisle: forthcoming.

T. 威尔莫特 . 哈德良长城博得瓦德要塞的火葬墓地 [J]. 卡莱尔：即将发表 .

[19] Wilmott, T., and Bennet, J. "The linear elements of the Hadrian's Wall complex: four investigations 1983–2000." in Hadrian's Wall: Archaeological Research by English Heritage 1976-2000, edited by T. Wilmott. Swindon: 2009:72-136.

T. 威尔莫特，J. 贝内特 . 哈德良长城的线性元素：1983-2000 年的四次调查 [J]. T. 威尔莫特编 , 哈德良长城：1976-2000 英格兰遗产信托的考古研究 . 斯文顿 :2009:73-136.

[20] Wilmott, T. "The Hadrian's Wall Milecastles Project: 1999-2000". in Hadrian's Wall: Archaeological Research by English Heritage 1976-2000, edited by T. Wilmott. Swindon: 2009: 137- 202.

T. 威尔莫特 . 哈德良长城里堡项目：1999-2000[J].T. 威尔莫特编 . 哈德良长城：1976-2000 英格兰遗产信托的考古研究 . 斯文顿 :2009:137-202.

[21] Wilmott, T., Cool, H., and Evans, J. "Excavations at the Hadrian's Wall fort of Birdoswald (Banna), Cumbria: 1996–2000." in Hadrian's Wall: Archaeological Research by English Heritage 1976-2000, edited by T. Wilmott. Swindon: 2009: 203-395.

T. 威尔莫特，H. 库尔，J. 埃文斯 . 对哈德良长城坎布里亚郡博得瓦德 (班纳) 罗马要塞的发掘：1996-2000[J].T. 威尔莫特编 . 哈德良长城：1976-2000 英格兰遗产信托的考古研究 . 斯文顿：2009: 203-395.

中国最古老的长城——楚长城调查、发掘与保护

李一丕

（河南省文物考古研究院，中国郑州）

摘　要

依据中国古代信史记载，公元前 656 年楚长城就已出现在历史舞台上，是中国最早出现在历史舞台上的一条长城。2008 年 10 月以来，我们对楚长城做了持续性的调查、发掘等深入研究工作。依据调查情况看，目前经过确认的楚长城主要分布在中国中东部，河南省西南部的南阳盆地北部边缘和东部边缘上，长 300 余千米。依据对楚长城遗址的发掘情况看，楚长城人工建筑，特别是人工修筑的墙体时代明确、结构清楚、建造有序、筑法考究。楚长城遗址里出土的遗物少量时代可以达到中国古代的春秋中期；大部分集中在春秋晚期至战国早期；部分处于战国中期。关于楚长城遗址的保护，我们不能只关注长城本体的保护，还要加强对楚长城周边独特的环境、风貌及采石场等的保护。

关键词：楚长城　调查　发掘　保护

楚长城在中国素有"长城之父"的美誉。文献中记载的楚长城名"方城"。依据中国古代信史记载，公元前 656 年楚长城就已出现在了历史舞台上[1]。在中国长城史中，楚长城是最早出现在历史舞台上的一条长城。此外，依据近十年来楚长城资源调查、发掘等情况看，楚长城遗址里出土的遗物的时代也是比较早的。本文首先概述性介绍了 2008 年以来楚长城资源调查和发掘情况，最后还介绍了笔者在楚长城研究过程中关于楚长城保护的一些思索。不当之处，祈请学界专家批评指正。

一、楚长城的调查情况

长城资源调查中的楚长城调查项目实地调查开始于 2008 年 10 月，2011 年 7 月通过中国国家文物局验收。此后，我们又做了一些持续性、深入的研究工作。

依据调查情况可知，楚长城大体分布于中国的中东部，位于中国第二阶梯地形和第三阶梯地形即山岗之地与平原的交接地带（图 1）。在行政区划上，楚长城的分布区域属中国河南省西南部（图 2）。该区域在地理上又以河南省南阳市的名字命名为南阳盆地。依据文献记载，楚长城主要分布在南阳盆地西部、北部、东部边缘地带及信阳地区。目前，经过调查确认的楚长城北起自伏牛山主峰尧山，循伏牛山支脉向东，大体沿今天平顶山鲁山县与南阳南召县交界处、平顶山叶县与南阳方城县交界处，向东蜿蜒至平顶山舞钢市石漫滩水库东端大坝处折转向南，然后沿驻马店泌阳县东部的五峰山、塔山、白云山、铜山一线绵延，向南直达桐柏山主峰太白顶。这条楚长城分布线大体分布于南阳盆地的北部和东部边缘上。目前，经调查确认的楚长城分布线仅是文献中记载的楚长城的一段，长约 300 余千米。

THE SURVEY, EXCAVATION AND PROTECTION OF THE CHU GREAT WALL, THE OLDEST SECTION OF THE GREAT WALL

Li Yipi

Henan Provincial Institute of Cultural Heritage and Archaeology - Zhengzhou - China

Abstract

According to Chinese historical records, the Chu Great Wall dates from as early as 656 BC and is the oldest section of the Great Wall. Since October 2008, we have conducted continuous survey, excavation, and other in-depth studies of the Chu Great Wall. Survey and archaeological evidence have confirmed that the Chu Great Wall spans central and eastern China, running along the north and east borders of the Nanyang Basin in southwest Henan Province for over 300km. As seen from excavation, the man-made remains of the Chu Great Wall, especially those of the Wall itself, can be clearly identified in terms of their date, structures, stratifications, and the specific techniques of their construction. A few artefacts unearthed from the sites of the Chu Great Wall can be dated to the middle Spring and Autumn period; most of the artefacts date to between the late Spring and Autumn period and the early Warring States period; and some of the artefacts date to the middle Warring States period. In terms of Chu Great Wall protection, the priority is to protect the Great Wall itself and to enhance the protection of its unique setting and surrounding features, including quarries and other elements.

Keywords: the Chu Great Wall, survey, excavation, protection

Known as the "Father of the Great Wall", the Chu Great Wall is called the "Square City" in historical records. According to authenticated Chinese historical records, the Chu Great Wall existed as early as 656 BC[1], and is the oldest known section of the Great Wall. In addition, as seen from survey and excavation in the last decade, the relics unearthed on the sites of the Chu Great Wall date back to very early times. This paper first outlines the survey and excavation of the Chu Great Wall undertaken since 2008 and presents ideas

图1

楚长城在中国的位置

Fig. 1

Location of the Chu Great Wall in China

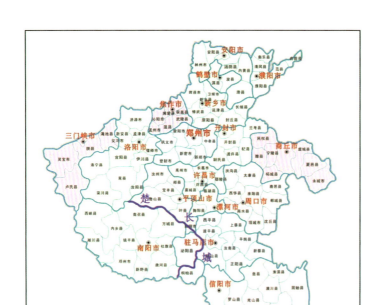

图 2
楚长城在河南省的位置
Fig.2
Location of the Chu Great Wall in Henan Province

无论国度，不同时期的长城，首先都是要有一条绵延较长距离的分布线的，这是所有长城的共性。已故中国长城界的泰斗罗哲文先生就认为长城是要有一条线的，这条分布线是不封闭的，与城市的城墙无论方形、圆形或其他形状都要交圈封闭的情况是不一样的[2]。如前文所述，楚长城亦不例外，也是有一条绵延较长距离分布线的，但这条分布线又是十分复杂的。

楚长城分布线的复杂性，首先表现在其构成是十分复杂的。依据调查情况，楚长城分布线是由人工修筑的绵延较长距离的墙体、关隘、城址、烽火台、兵营遗址、古代道路以及自然山险、自然河流等多种元素构成的有机统一的防御线。其次，楚长城分布线上的防御形式也是比较复杂的。不同地段楚长城的防御形式和防御特点是不一样的。整体地势海拔高度在 330 米以下的地段，由于地势较低，可以凭借的自然天险比较少，从而大规模修筑绵延较长距离的人工墙体，加强人工防御设施的修筑；整体地势海拔高度在 330 ~ 400 米之间的地段，楚长城的防御形式表现为人工修筑绵延较长距离的墙体防御和利用自然山险防御相结合的防御形式。具体而言，在两山之间的垭口处，修筑人工墙体进行防御，在山顶上，依靠自然山险进行防御；越过山顶，到了山体另一侧垭口处，仍然修筑人工墙体进行防御，而到了更远处山顶上，依然依靠自然山险进行防御……这种防御形式直观上给我们的印象是一段人工墙体、一段自然山险、一段人工墙体、一段自然山险……人工墙体和自然山险间次衔接，有机统一在一起，构成一条严密的防御线。整体地势海拔高度在 400 米以上的地段，楚长城的防御形式表现为以自然山险防御为主，关隘、城址扼守山间通道为辅的防御形式。此外，楚长城的分布线也不是一条孤立存在的防御线。依据调查情况看，在楚长城分布线内侧，往往分布有关城和军事重镇。这些关城、军事重镇在军事力量和后勤补给上对前方的楚长城分布线起到支撑和侧应的作用。如果没有这些内侧关城、军事重镇的支撑和策应，那么前方楚长城分布线的防御就失去了生生不息的活力来源，是不能持久的。调查中还发现在楚长城分布线外侧近处，即南阳盆地北沿和东沿外侧近处，自西向东，再向南，有多组城址环绕分布。更远处，亦有许多城址环绕分布在楚长城分布线外围远处。这些城址既是楚长城分布线外围向外进攻的前沿哨所和基地，又是楚长城分布线外围的防御屏障，同时还构成了楚长城分布线外围的防御纵深。如果没有这些防御屏障和防御纵深，那么楚长城分布线就直接暴露在敌人面前，利于敌人的打击和摧毁，不利于楚长城的防御。

about Chu Great Wall protection arising from my studies. Criticisms of this paper from academia are welcome.

THE CHU GREAT WALL SURVEY

The Chu Great Wall survey, as part of the national Great Wall Resource Survey began in October 2008, and its results were evaluated and accepted by the State Administration of Cultural Heritage in July 2011. Since then, we have conducted further in-depth studies.

The survey confirmed that the Chu Great Wall roughly spans central and eastern China, and runs through a region where low hills and plains join (Fig. 1). Administratively, the Chu Great Wall is situated in southwest Henan Province (Fig. 2), in an area named Nanyang Basin, after Nanyang City, Henan Province. Historical records indicate that the Chu Great Wall primarily followed the west, north and east borders of the Nanyang Basin and Xinyang region. The remains of Chu Great Wall that are identified as the result of survey begins to the north of Yaoshan Mountain, the highest peak of the Funiu Mountains, extends east along the branch ranges of the Funiu Mountains and roughly along the border between Lushan County of Pingdingshan and Nanzhao County of Nanyang and the border between Yexian County of Pingdingshan and Fangcheng County of Nanyang to the dam at the east end of the Shimantan Reservoir in Wugang City of Pingdingshan. It then turns southward along the Wufeng Mountain, the Tashan Mountain, the Baiyun Mountain and the Tongshan Mountain in the east of Biyang County of Zhumadian to the Taibai Peak, the highest peak of the Tongbai Mountain. The 300-plus km of the Chu Great Wall identified in the survey is only part of what is described in historical records.

The late Great Wall scholar Mr. Luo Zhewen believed that, unlike city walls enclosing areas in square, round or other shapes, what can be included in the Great Wall system must at least include a line of continuous barriers[2]. The Chu Great Wall is justified by an extended long linear and complex system.

The complexity of the route of the Chu Great Wall is shown in part by the variety of its components. The extended linear system of the Chu Great Wall is an organically integrated defence line consisting of extensive lengths of man-made walls, fortified passes, fortresses, beacon towers, barracks, and ancient roads, as well as natural precipices, rivers and other elements. Different sections of the Chu Great Wall also have different defensive features. Since areas with an altitude of less than 330m have few natural barriers, long stretches of man-made walls and defences were heavily built there. In areas with an altitude of between 330-400m, the Chu Great Wall's form of defence is a combination of man-made long walls and natural precipices. Essentially, where there was a mountain pass a man-made defensive wall was built, while on the top of a mountain, the natural precipice was used for defence. Man-made walls and natural precipices tend to alternate and are organically integrated to form a tight defensive line. In areas with an altitude above 400m, the Chu Great Wall's form of defence is dominated by natural precipices, supplemented by fortified passes and fortresses used to defend roads between mountains. The Chu Great Wall's system is not a single line of defence. As seen from the survey, to the rear or interior side of the Chu Great Wall are frontier fortresses and major fortresses, in which soldiers who manned the Wall

二、楚长城的发掘情况

如前文所述，楚长城分布线是由人工修筑的绵延较长距离的墙体、关隘、城址、烽火台、兵营遗址、古代道路以及自然山险、自然河流等多种元素构成的有机统一的防御线。为了做好有关楚长城的科学、深入的研究，自 2008 年以来，经中国国家文物局批准，我们对构成楚长城的人工墙体、关隘的关墙、构成要塞的城址、烽火台、兵营遗址及古代道路等均做过不同程度的考古发掘工作。下面以构成楚长城的人工墙体和烽火台的发掘为例，简要介绍有关情况如下：

（一）楚长城人工墙体的发掘

经中国国家文物局批准，2009 年 6 ～ 9 月，我们曾对河南省平顶山舞钢市平岭楚长城西段的人工墙体进行了科学考古发掘。

舞钢市平岭楚长城遗址位于舞钢市区以西，正介于平岭西山和马头崖山之间（图 3）。该段人工墙

图 3
舞钢市平岭楚长城分布环境（东—西）（摄影：李一丕）
Fig. 3
Setting (east-west) of the Pingling Chu Great Wall in Wugang City (© Li Yipi)

were garrisoned and which provided military and logistical support along the Chu Great Wall. Without these, the Chu Great Wall's defence could not have stood long. Similarly, survey showed that near the exterior side of the Chu Great Wall, towards the north and east borders of the Nanyang Basin, there are many groups of forts and fortresses that extend east and then south. In other places, there are fortified towns spreading more deeply into the exterior. These towns were both offensive outposts and defensive barriers extending into the exterior beyond the Chu Great Wall. Without these outer defences the route of the Chu Great Wall would have been exposed to advances of the enemy, who could have easily attempted to attack and destroy the Wall.

EXCAVATION OF THE CHU GREAT WALL

To improve the accuracy and detail of our archaeological understanding of the Chu Great Wall, since 2008 we have carried out both large-scale and smaller archaeological excavations, investigating the Chu Great Wall's complex defensive system, including the man-made walls, walls of the fortified passes, fortress sites, beacon towers and barracks, as well as ancient roads. The next section outlines the excavations of the Wall and the beacon towers.

Excavation of the walls of the Chu Great Wall

After approval by SACH, we excavated the Wall of the west section of the Pingling Chu Great Wall in Wugang City, Pingdingshan, Henan Province, between June and September 2009.

The site is located to the west of the urban area of Wugang City and between Pinglingxi Mountain and Matouya Mountain (Fig. 3). The above-ground stones of the Wall are tumbled and appear like a ridge (Fig. 4). The Wall extends down from a point halfway up the east slope of Pinglingxi Mountain, then east to the area north of Matouya Mountain, and finally south, to halfway up the north slope of Matouya Mountain.

The 2009 excavation was on the east slope of Pinglingxi Mountain, on a site sloping downwards from west to east. The base layers of the Great Wall vary with topography. In the higher, western part of the excavation area, an east-west stone wall was built on the south and north sides of the slightly levelled surface of the moun-

图 4

舞钢市平岭楚长城发掘前原貌（东—西）（摄影：李一丕）

Fig. 4

The Pingling Chu Great Wall in Wugang City, before excavation (east-west) (© Li Yipi)

1	石砌墙体 Stone wall
2	石砌墙体 Stone wall
3	黄色土块层 Layer of yellow soil
4	红色土块层 Layer of red soil
5	木炭层 Layer of charcoal sticks
6	自然山体 Natural base

图 5
舞钢平岭西段楚长城人工墙体发掘现场（摄影：李一丕）
Fig. 5
Excavation of the wall of the west section of the Pingling Chu Great Wall in Wugang (© Li Yipi)

体地表石块已凌乱，呈垄状（图4），自平岭西山东坡半山腰处沿山坡而下，向东延伸至马头崖山以北，折转向南，沿马头崖山北坡而上，至半山腰处而止。

　　此次发掘的区域位于平岭西山的东坡上，地势西高东低。依据地势，不同地段的长城墙体底基的处理是不一样的。发掘区西部地势较高处，是将自然山体稍加修整后，直接在修整后的地面上南、北两侧各修建一条东西向平行分布的石砌墙体。北侧石砌墙体上下都比较规整，宽约 2.25 ~ 2.35 米，残高约 1.15 米。南侧石砌墙体下部比较规整，上部的石块已凌乱。南侧石砌墙体下部宽约 1.85 米，残高约 74 厘米。 南、北两道石砌墙体之间宽约 4.9 米。南、北两道石砌墙体之间，底部堆积有粗细不同的炭化的木棍。炭化的木棍层厚 10 厘米左右。炭化木棍的摆放痕迹清晰可见，南北向放置。炭化的木棍层上被红色土层叠压。红色土层可分两层。下层红土多呈块状，较硬，颜色较鲜亮。上层红土则黏性大，颜色较深，软硬均匀。在南、北两道石砌墙体之间，偏北侧的红土堆积较厚，偏南侧较薄。红色土层之上，由北向南

图 6
舞钢平岭西段楚长城人工墙体底部堆积的炭化木棍层（摄影：李一丕）
Fig. 6
Layer of charcoal sticks piled up under the wall of the west section of the Pingling Chu Great Wall in Wugang (© Li Yipi)

tain. The Wall is formed of two outer stone walls with a soil and timber core. Both the upper and lower parts of the north outer stone wall are largely intact and are 2.25-2.35m wide with a surviving height of about 1.15m. The lower part of the south outer stone wall is also generally intact although the stones on its upper part are tumbled. The lower part of the south stone wall has a width of 1.85m and a surviving height of around 74cm. The stone walls are about 4.9m apart. The core of the wall is formed of a layer, roughly 10cm thick, of charred wooden sticks of varying thickness which lie under two layers of red soil. The red soil in the lower layer appears largely as clods and is rather hard and bright coloured. The red soil in the upper layer, however, is sticky, half hard and rather dark in colour. The red soil is thicker against the northern outer wall and, on top of it, piled north-south, are several layers of soil clods in different shades of yellow. Between the south and north stone walls is the main wall; the south and north stone walls act as retaining walls, literally encasing the main wall from both sides. Outside each of the stone facing walls are small sloping projections at the base. These are steeper on the north wall than the south. These are built at the base of walls to reinforce the base layer below the stone walls (Figs. 5 and 6).

The base layers of the Great Wall in the central-west of the excavation area have soil foundation trenches. After a trench was dug, two stone walls were built along its southern and northern edges and the space between (the core) was filled with soil on the same pattern as described above. In some areas, the sloping projections were built at the outside foot of the two stone walls over the foundation trenches.

The base layers of the Great Wall in the east of the excavation area are slightly different from those in the west. In the east of the excavation area, east-west outer stone walls were directly built onto the levelled ground. The north outer stone wall is fairly visible, having a width of about 2m, and a surviving height of about 85cm. The south outer stone wall has collapsed. In the east of the excavation area, a layer of stones, 40 to 85cm thick, was piled up between the south and north stone walls at the base of the core. In this stone layer are charcoal sticks of varying thickness and length (Fig. 7). The thickest have a diameter of 5-6cm and the thinnest 1-2cm. Some sticks are only about 6cm long and some are about 1m long; traces of sawing or chopping can be seen clearly on some of the cross-sections. On top of the stone layer is a red soil layer, on which several layers of yellow soil clods in different shades of yellow are piled in a sloping fashion. The small sloping projections outside and at the foot of the north stone wall are distinctly noticeable. Similar projections survive in some sections of the south outer stone wall, but others may have been damaged.

We know from excavation that the Wall in this section was built by both piling and ramming. The rammed parts have layers 3-7cm thick; while some appear to have been built of rammed round stones as the bottoms of the recesses left after ramming are round, with a diameter of about 23cm.

The wall of the western section of the Pingling Chu Great Wall in Wugang City has a surviving width of about 16.1m and a surviving height of about 1.1m. It is known from the survey and excavation that the widths of the walls of different sections of the Chu Great Wall vary. They are normally about 15-20m. On the plains, the walls are rather wide, and sections up to around 40m wide have been identified to date. Parts of the Chu Great Wall here are much less than a metre high; other parts still survive to a height of over 2m.

图 7
舞钢平岭西段楚长城人工墙体底部石块层里掺杂的炭化木棍（摄影：李一丕）
Fig. 7
Charcoal sticks mixed in the stone layer under the wall of the west section of the Pingling Chu Great Wall in Wugang (© Li Yipi)

倾斜堆积几层颜色深浅不一的黄色土块层。南、北两道石砌墙体之间为主墙体；南、北两道石砌墙体相当于在主墙体两侧包砌的石墙；南、北两道石砌墙体的外侧根部各修筑有小型护坡。北侧护坡稍陡，南侧护坡稍缓。这种护坡较小，修建在墙基的根部，起加固石砌墙体底基的作用（图 5、6）。

发掘区中部偏西处的长城墙体底基则是挖建有生土或活土基槽。基槽挖建成后，再在基槽内南、北两侧，贴基槽壁修建两道石砌墙体。两道石砌墙体之间的堆积情况与发掘区西部的情况相同。局部在基槽之上，两道石砌墙体外侧，亦修建有小型护坡。

发掘区东部长城墙体底基与西部稍有不同。发掘区东部的底基亦是在修整过的地面上直接修建南、北两道东西向平行分布的石砌墙体。北侧石砌墙体比较明显，宽约 2 米，残高约 85 厘米。南侧石砌墙体已倒塌，石块已凌乱。在发掘区东部，大体界于南、北两道石砌墙体之间的位置，先堆积厚约 40～85 厘米的石块层。石块层自上至下都掺杂有粗细、长短不同的炭化木棍。炭化的木棍粗者，直径 5～6 厘米；细者，直径 1～2 厘米。部分仅长约 6 厘米，部分长约 1 米。部分炭化木棍的横截面上，锯砍的茬痕清晰可见（图 7）。石块层之上，堆积红土层。红色土层之上，亦由北向南倾斜堆积几层颜色深浅不一的黄色土块层。北侧石砌墙体外侧根部的小型护坡比较明显，而南侧部分地段存在同样的护坡，部分地段的护坡可能已遭破坏。

通过发掘可知，该段人工墙体的筑法以堆筑为主，局部夯筑。夯筑的部位，局部比较考究，夯层厚约 3～7 厘米；局部则可能是用不带棱角的圆形石头夯筑而成，夯窝底部稍圆，直径约 23 厘米。

舞钢市平岭西段楚长城人工墙体残宽约 16.1 米，残高约 1.1 米。依据调查和发掘情况可知，不同地段的楚长城人工墙体的宽度是不一样的。一般宽度约 15～20 米。平原地段，墙体则较宽。目前所见平原地段墙体最宽者可达 40 米左右。楚长城人工墙体的残高，低者仅有几十厘米，高者可达 2 米以上。

依据舞钢市平岭西段楚长城人工墙体的发掘情况看，有两个方面是非常值得我们格外关注的。

其一，舞钢市平岭西段楚长城人工墙体的底基处理是非常科学和考究的。该段墙体修建在平岭西山东坡上，地势西高东低。由于山坡坡度和墙体自身重量的原因，墙体东端和地平面接触的受力点受力最重。山坡坡度越陡，受力点受力越重。由于作用力和反作用力的原因，受力越重，在山坡上修建的楚长城墙体越容易变形崩塌。因此，该段墙体在修建的时候，首先在地势最低的最东端底部堆积一层厚约 40～85 厘米的石块层，人为地将东端地势抬高，将山坡坡度变缓，从而缓冲了受力的力度，保证墙体的牢固性。此外，由于山坡地势西高东低，西端墙体受力最小，东端受力最大，在挤压过程中，中部墙体最容易变

Two specific aspects of the west section of the Pingling Chu Great Wall in Wugang City are worth noting. First, the base layers of the Wall are specifically and meticulously engineered. The Wall was built on the east slope of the Pinglingxi Mountain. Due to the gradient of the slope and the weight of the wall, the point where the east end of the wall meets the ground bears the greatest stress. The steeper the slope, the greater the stress at this point and the walls will be prone to deformation and collapse. To counter this, when the Wall was under construction, a layer of stones, 40-85cm thick, was piled under the (lowest) east end so as to artificially raise this end and make the mountain slope gentler. This relieved the stress and made the wall firm. In the west, where the mountain slope is higher, the wall bears the least stress, so the middle part of the wall, being squeezed between the two, is most prone to deformation. Therefore, the base layers of the middle part of the wall were built particularly carefully and were provided with foundation trenches.

Second, the layer of charcoal sticks piled under the wall is a particularly interesting phenomenon. The charcoal sticks were piled on the levelled mountain slope in advance. In addition the charcoal sticks are concentrated under the wall-core, showing that they were deliberately placed under the wall. The survey showed that charcoal sticks are extensively piled under dozens of kilometres of walls comprising the Chu Great Wall. This is a rare feature in the history of ancient Chinese city walls and architecture.

The piling of charcoal sticks under the walls of the Chu Great Wall may be associated with the unique route of the Chu Great Wall, and with the regional climate. The Chu Great Wall extends along the watershed between the Huaihe River basin and the Hanshui Basin in the Nanyang Basin. Of all the Great Wall sections, the Chu Great Wall is the only one in or to the south of the Huaihe River basin. The Qinling Mountains-Huaihe River line is the famous climatic dividing-line between northern and southern China, and it marks the change between China's subtropical and temperate zones, and the humid and sub-humid climates. The Qinling Mountains-Huaihe River line is also on the 800mm annual isohyet. Annual precipitation in the region to the south of the line is greater than 800 mm, and that in the region north of the line is less than 800mm. North of the line, the rainy seasons are concentrated and short, primarily falling in July to August. South of the line, the rainy seasons are much longer. Because of this environment, the foundations of the Chu Great Wall had to be much more moisture-proof and dehumidifying than other sections of the Great Wall. Charcoal is a known desiccant and can be used as a moisture-proof layer. Archaeological excavations of large tombs from the Easter Zhou dynasty also found piling of stones or charcoal used as a moisture-proof layer and a desiccant. Some researchers have suggested that charred bamboo is piled under the foundations of some sutra libraries and grotto temples, and believe that charred bamboo greatly helped preserve these sites. So the piling of charcoal under the wall-cores appears to be necessitated by the unique route of the Chu Great Wall and by the regional climates. Carbon-14 dating and species analysis of the charcoal has now been initiated to understand in more detail the time and environment of the Chu Great Wall.

Excavation of the beacon towers of the Chu Great Wall

Quite a number of beacon towers were also found during the Chu Great Wall survey, and a few were archaeo-

形，所以中部墙体底基处理最考究——挖建有基槽。

其二，舞钢市平岭西段楚长城人工墙体的底部堆积有炭化木棍层的现象是一种非常特殊的现象。炭化的木棍堆积在事先经过修整的山坡坡面之上。此外，炭化的木棍集中分布于主墙体（内、外两侧的石砌墙体之间）底部。这表明墙体底部堆积炭化木棍的现象是有意为之。调查中，发现楚长城人工墙体底部皆堆积有炭化的木棍。在几十公里的墙体底部皆堆积炭化木棍的现象，在中国古代城池史和建筑史上是不多见的。

楚长城人工墙体的底部堆积炭化木棍层的现象可能是和楚长城独特的分布位置及独特的区域气候有关。目前，已经认定的楚长城分布线主要位于南阳盆地北部和东部边缘上，基本上沿分水岭绵延，即整体上位于南阳盆地盆沿外围的淮河流域和盆地之内的汉水流域的分界线上。目前中国国家文物局已公布的具有长城的省、自治区或直辖市一共15个。在15个省份的长城中，楚长城是唯一一个位于淮河流域偏南或以南区域的长城。秦岭—淮河一线是中国比较著名的一条南北气候分界线。这条分界线既是中国亚热带和温带的分界线，又是湿润和半湿润气候的分界线。秦岭—淮河一线还是800毫米年等降水量线的界限。该线以南年降水量大于800毫米，以北年降水量小于800毫米。该线以北雨季集中而短促，主要在7、8月份，以南雨季要长得多。区域内大的环境气候决定了楚长城在修建过程中，人工建筑地基防潮、除湿的要求要明显高于中国境内的其他长城。众所周知，木炭的一个十分重要的功效就是可以起到防潮、除湿的干燥剂作用。从中国考古发掘情况看，一些东周时代的大型墓葬存在积石积炭的现象。这些墓葬就是利用木炭来起到防潮和除湿的干燥作用的。一些研究者还发现在一些藏经楼、石窟庵的地基下堆积有竹炭，并认为这些藏经楼和石窟庵之所以能保存千年之久，就是因为在建筑物地基下堆积的竹炭起了重要的干燥作用，这亦是一种例证。今后我们将对楚长城人工墙体之下堆积的木炭进行碳十四测年分析和树种分析，进而从科技角度探讨楚长城的修建年代和楚长城附近树种分布情况。

总之，在中国长城中，楚长城分布位置及分布区域内气候的独特性，正好和楚长城人工墙体底基下堆积炭化木棍这种案例的唯一性，是契合在一起的。这说明了楚长城人工墙体底基下堆积木炭的现象很可能是与其分布位置及区域内气候的特殊性有关的。

（二）楚长城烽火台的发掘

在楚长城资源调查中，还调查发现了一批烽火台，并对个别烽火台进行了考古发掘。调查发现的这批烽火台就名字而言多叫望火楼，后因语音厄变或称之为望花楼、万花楼、看花楼、看河楼、玩火炉、王和楼，亦有名叫烽火台、狼烟洞等的。楚长城沿线及楚长城之外和之内皆有烽火台分布。这些烽火台大多仅残留有土台一座。土台外表近似圆形覆锅状，少数则呈上小底大的圆形覆斗状。多数土台中间堆积大量红烧土。红烧土里边多钻探出有木炭。从断面上可以看出，部分土台为堆筑，部分土台则为夯筑。个别土台地表发现有较多的筒瓦、板瓦。

据研究，中国汉代河西地区的烽火台（烽燧）主要建筑物是一个墩台。墩台一般呈方锥体，上有小屋一间，称为望楼。墩台旁边有坞院等建筑。以此为参照，此次调查的楚长城烽火台中，个别烽火台土台附近即残留有坞院痕迹。坞院院墙与土台相连。部分烽火台土台的断面上显示土台顶部挖建有半地穴式房子。

logically excavated. Most of these beacon towers are called Wanghuolou[1], which was later mispronounced as Wanghualou, Wanhualou, Kanhualou, Kanhelou, Wanhuolu or Wanghelou. Some beacon towers are also called Fenghuotai, Langyandong and other terms. Beacon towers are distributed along and near both sides of the Chu Great Wall. In most places only the earthen platforms of these beacon towers survive. Most of these look like overturned round pots, and a few of them appear like an overturned rice box. Most of the platforms have considerable amounts of red scorched earth piled in the middle. Charcoal was frequently embedded in the red scorched earth. The sections showed that some of the platforms were built by piling, and some were built by ramming. Many pan tiles and semi-circular tiles were found on the surfaces of a small number of the earthen platforms.

According to studies, a beacon tower in the Hexi (western Yellow River) area from the Han dynasty was a mound, normally square or conical, with a shelter, called a watchtower, on the top. Beside the mound there are auxiliary facilities such as a courtyard. With this as a reference, traces of courtyards were found in the survey near the earthen platforms of a few beacon towers on the Chu Great Wall. The walls of the courtyards adjoin the earthen platforms. On some beacon towers the section of the platform shows that a semi-underground dwelling existed on the top of the earthen platform.

After approval by SACH, we excavated the Wanghuolou Beacon Tower to the south of Mijiahe Village, Silidian Township, Fangcheng County, Nanyang, between March and June 2011. It is known from the excavation that the main building of the Wanghuolou Beacon Tower is a square rammed-earth platform constructed on levelled ground. After the earthen platform was built, a largely square semi-underground dwelling with round corners was dug into its top. This is about 4.1m long from east to west, about 3.85m wide from north to south, and 0.57 to 1.1m deep. The doorway is at the southeast corner. The angle between the doorway and the direction of the house is 187°. The sub-surface walls are coated with a layer of a baked mixture of mud and straw about 0.5 to 0.8cm thick. Slightly north of the middle point of the east sub-surface wall, there are three kitchen ranges, which, are oriented north-south and abut on the east wall. The exterior of the chimney of Z1 and Z2 (Z represents a kitchen range) on the south side is covered by a complete curved tile. A fragment of a pottery three-legged cauldron was found in Z1. Around the dwelling there are 20 postholes, which have a diameter of about 10 to 40cm (Fig. 8).

The opening of the semi-underground dwelling is under the surface soil layer. The man-made earthen platform supporting the dwelling was not excavated. However, a number of three-legged earthenware cauldrons, long-necked pottery jars (Fig. 9), basins, earthenware rice steamers, iron tanged bronze arrowheads (Fig. 10) and many pan tiles and semi-circular tiles were unearthed from inside the dwelling. Typical utensils discovered date no later than the middle Warring States period, demonstrating that the dwelling was still in use as late as this. The earliest date indicated is the same as that of the Chu Great Wall.

Building materials excavated include pan tiles, semi-circular tiles, and clay bricks. A mud-and-straw mixture was also found, part of which had impressions of bamboo or wooden sticks. Some charcoal was found inside the dwelling.

---

1 Literally means 'watch fire tower' (Editors' note)

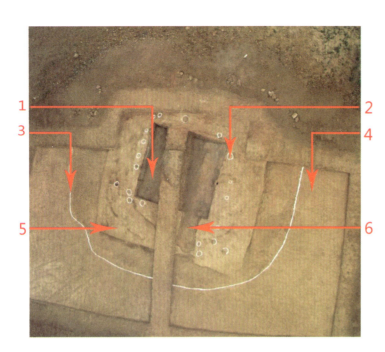

1	房屋基址 Dwelling area
2	柱洞 Posthole
3	修整边线 Readjusted outline
4	探方 Excavation unit
5	夯土台 Rammed earthen platform
6	门道 Doorway

图 8
方城县四里店乡米家河村南望火楼烽火台发掘现场（摄影：祝贺）
Fig. 8
Excavation of the Wanghuolou Beacon Tower to the south of Mijiahe Village, Silidian Township, Fangcheng County (© Zhu He)

经中国国家文物局批准，2011 年 3 ～ 6 月，我们曾对南阳方城县四里店乡米家河村南望火楼烽火台进行了考古发掘。通过发掘可知，该望火楼烽火台的主体建筑为一土台。该土台呈方形，夯筑而成。土台修建之前，先将地面修整平整。土台修建之后，在顶部挖建一个圆角近方形的半地穴式房子。该房子东西长约 4.1 米，南北宽约 3.85 米，深 0.57 ～ 1.1 米。门道位于东南角，凸出于房子之外。以门道为准，房子方向为 187°。地穴壁上涂抹一层厚约 0.5 ～ 0.8 厘米的草拌泥，并经过烘烤。紧贴地穴的东壁中部偏北处，有三个灶南北并列分布。其中南侧的 Z1、Z2（Z 代表灶）的烟囱外围被一块完整的板瓦包裹。在 Z1 内，发现陶鬲残片一块。房子周围有柱洞20 个。柱洞直径粗者约 40 厘米，细者约 10 厘米（图 8）。

图 9
方城县四里店乡米家河村南望火楼烽火台发掘出土的陶罐（摄影：王蔚波）
Fig. 9
Pottery jar unearthed from the Wanghuolou Beacon Tower south of Mijiahe Village, Silidian Township, Fangcheng County (© Wang Weibo)

该半地穴式房子开口于表土层下。房子所在的人工土台未解剖，但房内填土出有陶鬲、高领罐（图 9）、盆、甑、铁铤铜镞（图 10）及较多的筒瓦和板瓦等。房内出土的典型器物的时代皆不晚于战国中期。这表明至少在战国中期时，该房子仍然在使用。其年代下限与楚长城

According to studies of beacon towers in the Hexi area from the Han dynasty, the main building of this beacon tower would have been one in which soldiers were stationed to keep watch and to receive military messages sent from neighbouring beacon towers.

The survey showed that beacon towers are often distributed on both sides of a fortified pass to communicate with each other from afar. Beacon towers are also used to communicate between fortified passes or between fortified passes and fortresses. The elevations of the beacon towers of the Chu Great Wall vary with topography. One tower is only 157m above sea level; some are 250 to 300m above sea level, and others are more than 400 m above sea level. The intervals between beacon towers also vary as dictated by the topography. For example, the intervals between the beacon towers in Biyang County, Zhumadian, can be up to 4km apart; while near fortified passes or fortresses, the intervals are less than 2.5km. The intervals between the beacon towers in Silidian Township, Fangcheng County, Nanyang, are between 2 and 2.5km.

Since 2008, we have carried out archaeological excavations, of varying scale, of the Chu Great Wall: on the Wall itself, the walls of fortified passes, and fortresses, beacon towers and barracks, as well as on the ancient roads. A few artefacts unearthed from the sites of the Chu Great Wall can be dated to as early as the middle Spring and Autumn period; most of the artefacts date to between the late Spring and Autumn period and the early Warring States period; and some of the artefacts date to the middle Warring States period. The number of artefacts dating to a specific period may very possibly indicate the initiation of the construction of the Chu Great Wall, its intensive construction and continuous improvement.

图 10
方城县四里店乡米家河村南望火楼烽火台发掘出土的铁铤铜镞（摄影：王蔚波）
Fig. 10
Iron tanged bronze arrowhead unearthed from the Wanghuolou Beacon Tower to the south of Mijiahe Village, Silidian Township, Fangcheng County (© Wang Weibo)

的时代下限一致。

该房子内发掘出土的建筑材料有筒瓦、板瓦、土坯等。此外，房子内还发掘出土有草拌泥。部分草拌泥上有木棍等建筑材料的印痕，部分草拌泥上则有竹片或木条的印痕。房内填土内还见有少量木炭。

依据中国汉代河西地区烽火台研究情况看，南阳方城县四里店乡米家河村南望火楼烽火台的主体建筑应是有专门士兵戍守，起警戒、瞭望作用，专门捕捉相邻烽火台传递的军事信息的一个建筑，是一个完整烽火台的重要组成部分。

综合调查的情况看，烽火台往往分布在关隘的左右两侧，遥相呼应。此外，烽火台也往往用来联结关隘与关隘或关隘与城址的。楚长城烽火台分布位置的海拔高度因地形、地势而不同。有烽火台分布位置海拔高度仅 157 米。部分烽火台分布位置海拔高度多在 250 ～ 300 米之间。烽火台分布位置海拔高度亦有可达 400 米以上者。烽火台与烽火台之间的距离亦根据需要而不同，如驻马店泌阳县境内的烽火台与烽火台之间的距离可达 4 千米，当接近关隘、城址的时候烽火台与烽火台之间的距离缩小至 2.5 千米以下。南阳方城县四里店乡的烽火台，相邻两者间的距离为 2 ～ 2.5 千米。

此外，如前文所述，自 2008 年以来，经中国国家文物局批准，我们对构成楚长城的人工墙体、关隘的关墙、构成要塞的城址、烽火台、兵营遗址及古代道路等均做过不同程度的考古发掘工作。从发掘出土遗物看，楚长城遗址内所出遗物有少量时代可以达到中国古代的春秋时代中期；大部分遗物的时代集中在春秋晚期至战国早期；部分遗物的时代处于战国中期。出土遗物在数量上和不同历史时段的对应关系，很可能为我们勾勒了楚长城从萌芽，到集中大规模修筑，再到不断完善的历史过程。

三、楚长城的保护情况

长城作为世界文化遗产，在国际上有一些通行的保护性的公约、理念，在中国国内，中国政府及国家文物局也制定、公布了一些科学、可行的法律、法规、条例和技术规范。在此，笔者仅想结合自己在长城研究过程中的一些体会，谈一下个人对长城，特别是早期长城保护的一些思索。

其一，要注重长城周边特殊环境的保护。

笔者认为任何一个建筑，尤其是长城，都必须和所选择的地理环境紧密结合在一起的。因为只有和环境紧密地结合在一起，长城的修建行为才是科学的，长城的功用才能得到充分的发挥。这个长城在使用过程中才具有灵性。如果一个长城和周围环境结合不好，那么它的功用，特别是军事功用是发挥不出来的。

研究长城和周围环境结合的特点，对于研究长城修建规律、修建原则及功用，进而揭示某个长城的性质是具有十分重要的意义的。以楚长城为例，楚长城人工墙体基本均是沿丘岗、山体，或山间垭口外侧悬崖边缘部位修建的，军事防御方向很明确，军事实用性很强（图 11）。这即是楚长城与周围环境结合的特点和规律。但大体同样处于东周时代的河南省北部的赵南长城及北方的燕、赵（北长城）、秦等长城则完全不同。依据军事需要，这些长城本来应该沿山体修建的，却修在了山谷处；本来应该修在山谷处的，却修在了山体上。在同一座山体上，亦是一会儿沿山体外侧绵延，一会儿沿山体中间绵延，一会儿沿山体内侧绵延，没有固定的防御方向。这亦是这类长城和环境结合的特点和规律。从长城和环

PROTECTION OF THE CHU GREAT WALL

The Great Wall, a Cultural World Heritage Site, is protected by international conventions and by Chinese laws, regulations and technical specifications formulated and issued by the Chinese government and the National Cultural Heritage Administration of China. Here I present my personal ideas about the protection of the Great Wall, especially the early Walls, developed from my studies of the Chu Great Wall.

First, attention must be paid to the protection of the special setting of the Great Wall. I believe that any building, and the Great Wall in particular, must be understood within its landscape context. The construction of the Great Wall was integrated with its environment and this allowed it to function fully. If a section of the Great Wall was not properly integrated with its setting, its functions, especially its military function, could not be fulfilled.

Studying the ways in which the Great Wall relates to its setting is very important for understanding the rules and principles governing the construction of the Great Wall and its functions, and for identifying the nature of a specific section of the Great Wall. The walls of the Chu Great Wall, for example, were largely built along the ridges of hills, mountains or at the mouth of valleys with precipices towards the outside, which shows clear military defensive orientation. (Fig. 11). However, the Zhaonan (Southern Zhao) Great Wall in north Henan, the Great Walls of Yan, Zhao (Zhaobei) and Qin in northern China, which were also largely built during the same Eastern Zhou dynasty, are totally different. Some of these sections of the Great Wall were built in the bottom of valleys serving no clear military function. On the same mountain, some sections run along the outer side of the mountain, some along the ridge of the mountain, and some along the inner side of the mountain, with no fixed direction of defence. These sections of the Great Wall, with their different relationships to their landscape, appear to differ with the Chu Great Wall in their style, type, use, and even their functions.

When protecting the Great Wall, we should protect both the fabric of the Great Wall itself and the ways in which different sections of the Great Wall integrate with the landscape. When we understand how different sections of the Great Wall integrate with their settings, we can under-

图 11

叶县辛店与方城县杨楼交界处楚长城墙体及分布环境（南－北）（摄影：李一丕）

Fig. 11

The Chu Great Wall on the border between Xindian of Yexian County and Yanglou of Fangcheng County and its setting (north-south) (© Li Yipi)

图 12
叶县跑马岭北侧楚长城人工墙体内侧取土采石迹象（东－西）（摄影：李一丕）
Fig. 12
Traces of quarrying near the inner side of the Chu Great Wall on the north side of the Paomaling Mountain in Yexian County (east-west) (© Li Yipi)

境结合的特点和规律看，这些长城和楚长城应该是两种不同风格、不同类型、不同功用，甚至是不同性质的长城。

因此，我们在保护长城的时候，不能只关注长城本体，一定要把不同类型长城和周围环境结合的不同特点和规律保护起来。理解了不同长城和周边环境结合的不同特点和规律，也就从一个角度理解了我们为什么要保护长城，特别是早期长城的周边环境和风貌。

其二，加强对楚长城修筑过程中所留存的采石场等第一现场、原始迹象的保护。

楚长城的人工墙体多为土石结合构筑而成，内、外两侧为石砌墙体，中间填充纯土或土掺碎石。这些土石建筑材料多为就地取材。这就必然在楚长城人工墙体附近留存有取土和采石形成的第一现场或原始迹象。楚长城修筑过程中所形成的取土和采石第一现场或原始迹象是我们研究楚长城不可或缺的一部分，但在楚长城保护中极易被忽视。

在平顶山叶县保安镇闯王寨山西、五里坡东，跑马岭山北侧和东侧的楚长城人工墙体修建在山体悬崖边缘上。修建之前，先将山体靠崖边的地带挖掉，将地面修整平整。然后再在平整过的地面上，就地取材，利用事先挖掉的山体土石修筑墙体。至今在跑马岭山北侧（图 12）和东侧（图 13）的楚长城人工墙体内侧，山体断面上，还残留有修建楚长城人工墙体开挖土石的痕迹。

stand from one perspective why and how we should protect the Great Wall, especially the settings of the earlier sections of the Great Wall.

Second, protection of the quarries and other related features left from the construction of the Chu Great Wall should be enhanced. Most of the walls of the Chu Great Wall were built using earth and stones. The retaining walls are stone with a core of earth or earth mixed with crushed stones. Most of these building materials were obtained from local sources. As a result, it is anticipated that evidence of quarries of various kinds will be found near the Chu Great Wall through further investigation. These are essential for studies of the Chu Great Wall but can be very easily ignored in Chu Great Wall protection.

The walls of the Chu Great Wall located to the west of the Chuangwangzhai Mountain in Baoan Town, Yexian County, Pingdingshan, east of the Wulipo Mountain, and on the north and east sides of the Paomaling Mountain, were built on the edges of the precipices of the mountain. Before construction, the ground near the edges of the mountain were removed, and the ground was levelled. Then Walls were then built on the levelled ground using the earth and stones that had been cut out. Traces of quarrying left after the construction of the walls of the Chu Great Wall can still be seen near the interior side of the Chu Great Wall on the north (Fig. 12) and east (Fig. 13) sides of the Paomaling Mountain.

Exposed rocks near the inner side of the Wall on the north and east sides of the Paomaling Mountain and on parts of the mountain show traces of quarrying. These rocks are the same as those used to build the Wall. Scattered pieces of rock of different sizes on the surrounding mountain slopes are also the same as the stones used to build the Chu Great Wall which are rather smooth and regular; they appear to have been quarried and then processed. This place may have been a quarry for the construction of the Chu Great Wall. This evidence indicates the sources of the building materials and the way in which the walls of the Chu Great Wall were built, and it is crucial evidence in the study of the Chu Great Wall. Protection of the Chu Great Wall can all too easily focus on the fabric of the Great Wall itself and ignore sections of the mountains and quarries which also contain very important information.

图13
叶县跑马岭东侧楚长城人工墙体附近取土采石迹象（北—南）（摄影：李一丕）
Fig. 13
Traces of quarrying near the inner side the Chu Great Wall on the east side of the Paomaling Mountain in Yexian County (north-south) (© Li Yipi)

此外，在跑马岭山北侧和东侧的楚长城人工墙体内侧，山体断面上，裸露的岩石有被开采的痕迹。这些石料与楚长城人工墙体上的石材一致。周围山坡上，裸露于地表之上的岩石呈块状或大或小散落在山体杂草之中，亦与楚长城人工墙体上的石材材质一致。这些石块剖面相对平整、规则，也似开采、加工后遗留下的石料。这里很可能是楚长城修建过程中就地取材的一个采石场。

在跑马岭山北侧和东侧的楚长城人工墙体内侧，山体断面呈现的楚长城修筑过程中开挖山体的迹象及山体断面和山坡上的采石场，揭示了楚长城人工墙体的修筑方法及材料来源，是研究楚长城不可或缺的重要的一个方面。楚长城保护中，很容易只关注长城本体，而忽视了对这样包含着十分重要信息的山体断面和采石场的保护。

结　语

楚长城在中国素有"长城之父"的美誉，是中国早期长城的代表。从楚长城调查情况看，不同地段楚长城具有不同的防御形式和防御特点，这与后世长城人工墙体绵延较长距离的情况是不一样的，同时也说明了在楚长城的防御线构筑过程中，较多地利用了山形地势等自然因素。楚长城代表了中国长城肇始期的原始类型、原始特点和原始风貌，必然有其古朴的一面。同时受当时冷兵器时代，战争武器、形态和方式的影响，楚长城在构筑上较多地受自然山形地势的影响也是必然的。它既有一般长城的共性，又有其独特的一面。它既有一般长城所共有的分布线和防御体系，又具有浓厚的军事色彩、很强的军事实用性。

实地调查和科学考古发掘是我们研究和保护长城的基础。长城的演变是有一个逐渐完善和成熟的过程的。我们不能拿着晚期长城，甚至是现代复建的"晚期"长城的规模、气势，以及晚期长城才具有的防御设施去苛求早期长城，这显然是不科学的。有些防御设施虽然早、晚时期的长城都有，但它们的形制也是早已发生了变化的。我们要以实地调查和科学考古发掘的材料事实为据，尊重长城的演变规律，去分析、研究和保护长城。

不同历史时段的长城，不同地域和气候环境下的长城，不同材质的长城，面临的长城保护问题是不一样的。在长城的保护问题上，我们要尽量扩大思考问题的角度，要让尽量多的学科参与到长城的保护当中。我们既要把不同长城共性的一面保护下来，又要把不同长城各自的个性和特色的一面保护下来。

关于楚长城遗址的保护，我们不能只能关注长城本体的保护，还要加强对楚长城周边独特的环境、风貌及采石场等包含着重大信息，同时又极易被忽视的方面的关注和保护。

CONCLUSION

Known as the "Father of the Great Wall", the Chu Great Wall is the earliest constructed section of the Great Wall. As seen from the Chu Great Wall survey, different sections of the Chu Great Wall have different forms and defensive characteristics, differing from the later, longer Great Walls, and showing that mountain topographies and other natural elements were more often used to form the defence line of the Chu Great Wall. The Chu Great Wall, which represents the form, characteristics and features of the earliest period of the Great Wall, is inevitably comparatively simple and unsophisticated. It was influenced by the natural mountain landscape and the weaponry and form of war in that era. It has features that are both common to and distinctive from other sections of the Great Wall, with a common linear course and comprehensive yet very distinguished military functions.

Field investigations and scientific archaeological excavation are the basis of studies on the Great Wall and on its protection. The construction of the Great Wall was gradually improved. The early sections of the Great Wall are less impressive in scale and complexity than later ones. Though some types of defensive features can be found in both the early and the late sections of the Great Wall, their forms differ. We should study and protect the Great Wall based on materials and facts found from field investigations and scientific archaeological excavation and by respecting the evolution of the Great Wall.

The protection of sections of the Great Wall built in different periods, located in different regions or climatic environments, or built using different materials, raises different issues. Great Wall protection should involve considerations from as many perspectives as possible and should involve as many disciplines as possible. We should protect both the common and unique characteristics of different sections of the Great Wall, and as well as the Great Wall itself we should enhance protection of its setting and surrounding features, including the quarries and other elements that contain very important information that can easily be ignored.

参考文献
Bibliography

[1] 杨伯峻 . 春秋左传注 [M]. 北京：中华书局出版社，2000:291.

Yang, B.J. Annotated Commentary of Zuo. Beijing: Zhonghua Book Company, 2000:291.

[2] 罗哲文 . 访南召楚长城三首（并序）[M]. 中国文物报，2002-08-30.

Luo, Z.W. Three Poems and Their Preface: Visiting the Nanzhao Chu Great Wall. China Cultural Relics News, August 30, 2002.

HADRIAN'S WALL:CURRENT RESEARCH AND FUTURE DIRECTIONS

ROB COLLINS

Newcastle University - Newcastle upon Tyne - UK

Abstract

A brief overview of the research history of Hadrian's Wall is provided, highlighting the longevity of research and its dependence on archaeological data. Current research is not restricted to universities and academics, with projects directed by a number of individuals and organisations across the World Heritage Site. Despite the extent and depth of research, there are still a number of unanswered research questions, highlighted in the Hadrian's Wall research framework and being taken forward by scholars and professionals. A recently initiated project, WallCAP, is highlighted as combining research, management, and community agendas.

Keywords: Hadrian's Wall, historiography, research framework, research questions.

INTRODUCTION

Hadrian's Wall has a long research tradition spanning centuries. Given the sheer volume of data available, understanding and mastering Hadrian's Wall as a researcher can be as daunting as it is rewarding[1]. The Wall is also inextricably linked to the Roman army, each topic contributing to further development of the other. In addition, the Wall has never been studied in a vacuum - interpretation has always been framed by contemporary culture. As a result, our understanding of the Wall, as well as the priority of research has shifted over time. The following paper provides a brief synopsis of past and present research of the Wall.

HISTORICL RESEARCH OF THE WALL

The remains of Hadrian's Wall have been the focus of study for centuries, attested in the writings of the earliest antiquarians of the 17th century[2]. These early researchers of the 'Roman Wall' typically engaged either in chorographic descriptions of places, locations and ruins, or in the gathering and description of a collection, such as inscribed stones. The main academic debate across the decades of the 17th-19th centuries was identifying the Roman emperor that had the Wall built; the two primary candidates were Hadrian and Septimius Severus. Ultimately, it was the discovery of inscribed stones and knowledge of their context that proved beyond a doubt that Hadrian was the instigator of the Wall. However, a key turning point in Wall studies was the popularisation of the monument by John Colling-

哈德良长城：当前研究及未来方向

罗伯·柯林斯

（纽卡斯尔大学，英国纽卡斯尔）

摘　要

本文简要回顾哈德良长城的研究史，强调其悠久传统以及仰赖考古数据的特性。当前研究不局限在大学和学术圈，遍及整个世界遗产地的多家机构及个人也主导不少研究项目。尽管研究已有一定广度与深度，仍有不少研究问题有待探究。这些问题将成为哈德良长城研究框架的重点，各方学者及专业人士亦将深入探索。新近启动的 WallCAP 项目将响应研究、管理及社区三方面的需求。

关键词：哈德良长城　历史编纂学　研究框架　研究问题

绪　论

哈德良长城研究的传统绵延了几个世纪。对研究者而言，庞大的数据量使得认识和精通哈德良长城成为既艰苦又富有成就感的任务[1]。哈德良长城研究与古罗马军队研究也密不可分，对其中之一的研究势必推进另一方面的研究。此外，长城研究从来不是在真空中进行的，当代文化始终在重构对长城的阐释。因此，我们对长城的理解以及重点研究的对象始终在变化。下面，笔者将对长城过往及当前研究作简要梳理。

一、历史上的长城研究

几个世纪来，哈德良长城的遗存始终是研究的焦点，它们出现在最早的 17 世纪古物研究者的著作中[2]。这些"罗马长城"研究先驱的兴趣集中在对地点、位置及遗址的方志学描述，或者对收藏品的收集和描述，比如刻字砖。横贯 17 到 19 世纪，学界争论集中在长城由哪位罗马皇帝下令建造，并提出两位可能的人选：哈德良皇帝与塞维鲁皇帝。最终，几处刻字砖的发现以及围绕刻字砖展开的研究确定了哈德良皇帝是长城的建造者。19 世纪下半叶，长城研究迎来重要转折点。约翰·克林伍德·布鲁斯（John Collingwood Bruce）促成了长城研究的大众化（图 1）。布鲁斯撰写论文、著述，举办讲座以及组织参观，并得到当时古物收藏家的积极支持，使长城走入大众视线，反过来又激发了更深入的研究，其中一个重要方式就是组织十年一次的"哈德良长城朝圣之旅"（Hadrian's Wall Pilgrimage）[3]。19 世纪到 20 世纪早期的学者主要目标是厘清长城在英格兰北部的行经路线及建筑结构，包括塔楼、里堡、要塞，以及诸如南部壕堑（Vallum）及北部壕沟（ditch）等辅助设施[4]。

随着考古学前辈们发现了越来越多的墙体，随着人们越来越认识到古罗马时期文字记载的不足，考古调查之于长城研究的重要地位越发突出。不少研究问题也随之产生。塔楼与里堡变成了发

wood Bruce through the second half of the 19th century. Bruce's papers, books, lectures, and guided visits, supported by active antiquarian investigators, brought the Wall to the attention of a wider audience, in turn stimulating further research, not least through the establishment of the decennial Hadrian's Wall Pilgrimage[3]. These 19th and early 20th century scholars set about clarifying the course of the Wall across northern England and its composition of turrets, milecastles, and forts, supported by the ditch and Vallum[4].

As more of the Wall was revealed by early archaeologists and the dearth of written evidence from ancient Roman writers was accepted, it became clear that archaeological investigation was essential to understand the monument. Research questions were posed. Turrets and milecastles became a focus of excavation to understand further the building sequence of the Wall and its purpose. Forts provided vital evidence for the lifestyles of Roman soldiers posted to the Wall. Coins, ceramics, and other artefacts were identified and analysed to provide information for dating[5][6]. Data were consolidated by specialists, with epigraphers and ancient historians cataloguing inscriptions and sculpture to identify individuals of centuries past and the gods they worshipped[7][8]. The benefit of these undertakings could be seen in the parallel development of Roman archaeology in Germany and the international sharing of knowledge along with comparison of data was fundamental to the emergence of Roman frontier studies, a tradition that was formalised with the establishment of the International Congress of Roman Frontier Studies in 1949. The most recent period of research can be said to have crystalized in 1976, with the publication of a synthesis of the then current research in Hadrian's Wall[9]. Subsequently, archaeological investigation has further benefitted from the inclusion of scientific analyses, which have examined macro-botanical fossils and zoo archaeological remains, for example[10].

The accumulation and cataloguing of new knowledge through the later 19th and 20th centuries provided a stimulus to the emergence of more focused research in the early 21st century, set against the background of more comprehensive knowledge of the history and archaeology of the monument. Excavation has continued to play a vi-

Fig. 1
John Collingwood Bruce, who pioneered research into Hadrian's Wall in the 19th century (Public domain)
图1
约翰·克林伍德·布鲁斯，19世纪哈德良长城研究的先驱（公开资料）

掘重点，意在了解长城的修建顺序及建造目的。要塞则为了解驻守哈德良长城的古罗马士兵的生活方式提供了关键证据。研究和分析钱币、瓷器及其他器物为断代提供信息[5][6]。专家们整合各类数据，碑铭研究者与古代史学家对铭文与雕像进行编目登记，确定数千年前的人物身份及其祭拜的神祇[7][8]。这些研究成果也促进了同期的德国古罗马考古研究。在国际范围内共享成果与比较研究促进了古罗马边界研究的兴起，1949 年国际古罗马边界研究大会成立，将这一传统以组织形式确立下来。近期的研究成果可以说集中体现于 1976 年出版的《哈德良长城》[9]，该书汇总了当时的各方面研究成果。之后，考古研究进一步受益于科学分析手段的应用，比如大型植物化石与古代动物遗骸检测[10]。

19 世纪末到 20 世纪这些新知识的积累与编目登记为长城研究提供了综合全面的历史与考古学背景知识。以此为基础，进入 21 世纪的研究则更加集中于各类专题。在新数据的产生方面，考古发掘继续扮演关键角色，人们借此得以了解长城早期历史[11]、新特征[12]以及后来的使用情况[13]。自 2000 年以来，不少详细的研究陆续出版，巧妙地运用了数十年来无数专家学者收集的数据。每一项研究都让我们对哈德良长城有了更细致入微的了解。受篇幅限制无法详细列举，在此仅举几例，包括哈德良长城规划[14]、从砌石方法描述哈德良长城的建造过程[15]、对塔楼及里堡的评估[16]以及古罗马边界最后时期[17]。

二、近期研究

考古调查与发掘是产生新数据的重要手段。值得一提的是，过去 20 年间不断有诸如障碍坡台（berm obstacles）之类的新结构出现[12]（图 2）。可以预见，新发现也将促进对长城的新认知。

Fig. 2
Recent research has revealed new features, including these traces of obstacles alongside the Wall at Shields Road, Byker (© Tyne & Wear Archives and Museums)
图 2
近期研究发现了新的结构，包括位于拜克区（Byker）希尔兹路的这些长城沿线障碍物的痕迹（版权：泰恩·威尔地区档案及博物馆）

tal role in the production of new data, shedding light on the Wall's early history[11], new features[12] and its later occupation[13]. Since 2000, a number of detailed studies have been published that have made excellent use of data collected by numerous scholars over previous decades, each contributing to a more detailed and nuanced understanding of Hadrian's Wall. Space precludes a full list, but examples include the planning of Hadrian's Wall[14], the building of Hadrian's Wall from a masonry perspective[15], assessment of the turrets and milecastles[16], and the final years of the Roman frontier[17].

RECENT RESEARCH

Survey and excavation are pivotal in the generation of new data. Significantly, new features such as the berm obstacles have been discovered in the past 20 years[11] and it is expected that further discoveries will stimulate new interpretations.

Research along the Wall has traditionally been undertaken by academics employed by universities, notably Newcastle and Durham universities. The Iron Age & Roman Heritages project led by Richard Hingley (Durham) seeks to position public popular understanding of Hadrian's Wall relative to the rest of Iron Age and Roman Britain. Excavations at Birdoswald and Maryport led by Ian Haynes (Newcastle) and Tony Wilmott (Historic England) have provided insight into burial practice, the use of religious space and reuse of ritual materials.

However, a considerable amount of research is initiated outside of academia. Excavations have been undertaken for many decades now at Vindolanda (Vindolanda Trust) and South Shields Roman fort (Tyne & Wear Archives and Museums). The latter have also hosted the successful WallQuest project that investigated the bathhouse at Wallsend fort and extramural areas of Benwell fort, both in Tyneside. A partnership of museum organisations across the entire World Heritage Site was responsible for the multi-venue exhibition Hadrian's Cavalry, which included a large public event experimenting with Roman cavalry manoeuvres with historic reenactors. The largest contributors of new data, however, are the commercial archaeological units that undertake investigation in advance of development.

Collaboration across organisations has been vital to the conduct of research in recent years, pooling expertise and resource to tackle larger challenges. This model has worked well for Hadrian's Wall due to the number of stakeholders invested in the World Heritage Site.

HADRIAN'S WALL RESEARCH FRAMEWORK

The establishment of the Hadrian's Wall Pilgrimage essentially laid a groundwork for regular updates and reinterpretation of the monument, seen in the tradition of the publication of The Handbook of the Roman Wall[18] and the Pilgrimage Handbook[3][19][20]. These works are supplemented by a number of publications, the best of which uphold scholarly insight and interpretation in a form that is accessible to an interested public[21]. Further-

过去，长城沿线研究都由大学内的学者主导，纽卡斯尔大学与杜伦大学是两支主力。杜伦大学理查德·兴利（Richard Hingley）主持的"铁器时代与罗马遗址"项目（Iron Age & Roman Heritages）旨在将公众对哈德良长城的认知置于更宏观的铁器时代及英国罗马时期的背景关系中。博得瓦德（Birdoswald）与玛丽波特（Maryport）要塞的发掘由伊恩·海因斯（Ian Haynes，纽卡斯尔大学）与托尼·威尔莫特（Tony Wilmott，英格兰遗产委员会）共同主持，主要研究丧葬习俗、宗教空间的利用与祭祀用品再利用方面等内容。

不过，还有相当一部分研究是由非学界人士发起的。对文多兰达要塞（文多兰达信托基金主持）及南希尔兹（South Shields，泰恩·威尔地区档案及博物馆主持）罗马要塞的发掘已经进行数十年。泰恩·威尔地区档案及博物馆还成功组织了"长城探秘"项目（WallQuest），主要在泰恩赛德（Tyneside）发掘沃尔森罗马要塞（Wallsend fort）的罗马浴场，以及发掘在长城以外地区的本维尔要塞（Benwell fort）。长城沿线各大博物馆联手，在多个场馆举办了"哈德良的骑兵"展览（Hadrian's Cavalry），其中包括一项大型公开演出活动，历史重现罗马骑兵演习。不过，新数据最大来源还是商业考古机构在配合建设开发项目之前开展的考古调查。

近年来，跨机构合作开展研究意义重大，有助于统筹人才与资源，以应对更为复杂的挑战。这一模式能在哈德良长城产生良好效果，要归功于哈德良长城世界遗产地若干利害相关者的倾力投入。

三、哈德良长城研究框架

"哈德良长城朝圣之旅"活动的确立本质上为长城研究定期更新和不断阐释奠定基础，体现于不断再版《古罗马长城手册（The Handbook of the Roman Wall）》[18] 及《朝圣手册（Pilgrimage Handbook）》[3] [19][20] 的传统。作为这两部手册的补充，还有其他若干出版物，其中的佳作既包含专家学者的真知灼见，又以道不远人的姿态向公众进行阐释[21]。此外，长城研究界每年举行两次北部边界研讨会（Northern Frontier Seminar），还参与每两年举行一次的古罗马考古学大会（Roman Archaeology Conference），每三年举行一次国际古罗马边界研究大会（International Congress of Roman Frontier Studies），通过这些平台发布研究信息、探讨信息阐释。

2009 年，经过与研究界人士的广泛探讨与合作，在英格兰遗产委员会资助下，正式的哈德良长城研究框架得以发布[22]。框架以两卷形式出版，卷一介绍了现存考古遗址遗物、研究资源及遗址阐释；卷二指出了与长城相关的认识空白与研究问题，并提出针对这些问题制定的研究实施计划。

在操作中，该研究框架对长城相关管理部门十分有用，尤其是政府咨询机构及规划部门，可以助其在开发／建设之前提供最优考古学工作指导。此外，研究框架对现有考古学资源与认知进行评估，为今后的研究提供基础和参照。该研究框架将定期进行修订和更新。

四、有待研究的主题

尽管对于长城的研究历史悠久，成果颇丰，在有些方面我们仍然不甚了解，甚至一无所知。不少类

more, the Wall's research community meets twice per year to disseminate research and debate interpretation through the Northern Frontier Seminar, as well as participating in the Roman Archaeology Conference every two years and the International Congress of Roman Frontier Studies every three years.

An official research framework for Hadrian's Wall, funded by Historic England, was published in 2009[22], birthed from wide consultation and collaboration with the research community. The framework was published in two volumes. The first volume provided an overview of the existing archaeological remains and resource as well as interpretations of those remains. The second volume provided an agenda of identified gaps in knowledge and research problems related to the Wall with a strategy for implementing work to address these concerns.

In practice, the research framework has been useful for curatorial bodies, particularly those advising governmental and planning authorities, to guide best archaeological practice in advance of development/construction. Furthermore, the assessment of current archaeological resource and interpretation has established a baseline for reference in future research. It is expected that the research framework will be reviewed and updated in a fairly regular cycle.

THEMES REQUIRING FURTHER RESEARCH

Despite the very rich research history and considerable data relating to the monument, there are still many aspects that are imperfectly understood or completely unknown in regards to Hadrian's Wall. Many such themes are explicitly identified in the research framework, though a few are noted here for the benefit of the reader unfamiliar with Hadrian's Wall.

Dating is of paramount interest. While archaeological investigation has established a general sequence of building and occupation along the Wall and coins and ceramics have provided the basis of a chronology for these sequences, there is still considerable room for improving the resolution of existing dating evidence. Certain years are difficult to date with any precision; for example, lacking a stratigraphic sequence, it can be difficult to determine exactly when in the 3rd century a deposit was formed. Dating evidence is also sparse for some features of the Wall complex that relate to its construction and development. For example, the replacement of the turf Wall with a stone curtain has been argued to have occurred in the later Hadrianic period (c130-138) or later in the 2nd century (c160-190). Detailed analysis of artefacts in combination with the latest scientific techniques and calibrations are likely to yield improved archaeological chronologies.

Given the importance of museums and interpretation to popular reception and understanding of the Wall[23], it is also significant that we enhance our understanding of the architecture and visual impact of the monument. This is particularly challenging as the archaeological survival of buildings and structures rarely extends more than two metres in height. Furthermore, the similarity of ground plans of structures such as turrets, milecastles and fort buildings, coupled with the regularised spacing of such installations has created an impression of uniformity of structure and appearance along the Wall's length. Yet art historical evidence of towers from Trajan's

似的主题已经在"研究框架"一节中进行了明确阐述。考虑到有些读者对哈德良长城不熟悉，特此列举一二。

断代是首要问题。考古调查已经为长城沿线的建造与居住使用确定了基本时序；钱币与瓷器的出土也为确定时序提供参考，然而在提高断代准确性方面仍有相当大的进步空间。某些年份要精确测定相当困难。比如说，如果缺少地层顺序，就很难确定某一公元 3 世纪堆积的确切形成年代。同样缺少断代证据的还有长城本体上标志其建造和演变某些特征。例如，草被长城被石砌长城所替代究竟于哈德良执政晚期（约 130 ～ 138 年）还是 2 世纪末（约 160 ～ 190 年）。对出土文物进行细致分析，结合最新科技进行校正，或将提供更精确的考古学断代结果。

考虑到博物馆与文物阐释对推广长城相关知识的重要性[23]。提高对长城建筑及其视觉效果的认识也非常重要。考虑到长城遗址上现存的建筑高度很少超过 2 米，这一挑战任务极为艰巨。此外，长城沿线的塔楼、里堡、要塞的平面布局几乎相同，加之这些设施之间的距离也很有规律，这种相似的地面建筑布局使人以为长城的建筑在外观和格局上具有统一性。然而，罗马图拉真纪功柱（Trajan's Column，年代比哈德良长城早约 10 ～ 15 年）的艺术史证据表明塔楼至少有三种建筑形态，外观迥异；因此，哈德良长城上半部的建筑形态变化很可能较已知的更为丰富（图 3）。

长城及其驻军与其周边腹地和更广阔的边疆地带究竟有什么样的关系，目前仍无法确定。历来考古发掘主要仍限于长城建筑本体，因此塔楼及里堡之外可能有哪些遗存也是未知数。过去二十年，发现的古罗马农村聚落数量不断增加[24]。有理论认为，公元 2 世纪长城的建造可能驱离了城址附近的农民。然而，驻城部队、本地居民以及周围景观的长期关系仍不甚清晰。这些问题因为在农村聚落中缺少古罗马

Fig. 3

Possible interpretations of the original design of the turrets along Hadrian's Wall, derived from depictions of towers on Trajan's Column (© Newcastle University)

图 3

哈德良长城塔楼原始设计的多种复原阐释，源于图拉真柱上所描绘的塔楼（版权：纽卡斯尔大学）

Column (built approximately 10-15 years before Hadrian's Wall) indicates there were at least three different types of tower-structures, with markedly different appearance; the built upper-elements of Hadrian's Wall may therefore have been more variable than is currently believed.

The relationship of the Wall and its military communities to the immediate hinterlands of the monument and the broader frontier zone is also uncertain. Excavations have largely remained on or within the walls of installations, such that it is uncertain what may exist immediately adjacent to the turrets and milecastles. The past 20 years have seen an increase in the amount of rural settlements dated to the Roman period[24] and an argument has been forwarded that the construction of the Wall may have resulted in the clearance of farmers proximal to the monument in the 2nd century AD. What is uncertain, however, is the long-term relationship between the Wall garrisons, local peoples and the physical landscape. The dearth of Roman artefacts from many rural settlements and lack of skeletal remains (for stable isotope and ancient DNA analysis) presents challenges to the researcher, but there is also significant potential in archaeo-environmental studies to address some of these questions. Indeed, there is considerable scope for greater understanding of the supply and sustainability of the Wall.

Sustainability not only pertains to the Roman occupation and use of the monument. The Wall continues to be an important monument in northern England, but its historical value has to be balanced against its location in a working landscape. Through its post-Roman history, the Wall has been subject to episodes of robbing and destruction, resulting in the incomplete and ruinous monument we see today, and the monument also faces a range of threats to its continued preservation. Threats range from wear-and-tear as a result of the volume of visitors, to long-term agricultural use of fields and pastures adjacent to and lying across the monument, to landslip and erosion related to climate change. These concerns are the focus of a new project hosted by Newcastle University and funded by the Heritage Lottery Fund, the Hadrian's Wall Community Archaeology Project (WallCAP).

WallCAP will investigate and, where possible, arrest threats to the monument and its attendant features while also investigating the source geology of the Wall and where its building fabric ended up. The project incorporates digital tools and solutions to bring together community volunteers with archaeological research resources and methods to benefit the heritage of the Wall and the communities found along its length. In that regard, it is an amalgamation of a traditional research project, heritage management endeavour, and community engagement. It is anticipated that as results from fieldwork are disseminated, new research questions and possibilities will emerge.

时期器物及骸骨证据（用于进行稳定同位素和古代 DNA 分析）而使研究人员面临阻碍，不过环境考古学与研究也极有可能回答这些问题。另外，长城供给体系与持续利用研究仍有相当大的空间。

所谓持续利用，不仅限于古罗马时期对长城的使用。在英格兰北部，长城始终是一处重要的标志性建筑。在衡量其历史价值的同时，也要将其置于不断变化的景观环境之中。自古罗马时期以降，长城不断遭到劫掠与破坏，沦为今日我们所见之残垣断壁，而且其持续保存仍继续面临各种威胁。这些威胁包括大量游客来访造成的损坏，长城两侧和横跨长城沿线土地长期的耕作和畜牧，及气候变化造成的山土滑坡和侵蚀。这些威胁因素正是"哈德良长城社区考古项目（WallCAP）"所关注的重点。这一新研究项目由纽卡斯尔大学发起，并受到英国文化遗产彩票基金会的资助。

WallCAP 将调查长城及其辅助建筑的相关威胁因素，并在可能的情况下进行抑制，同时调查长城建筑材料的地质来源及建筑材料目标散落的最终去向。该项目应用数字技术，集聚社区志愿者与考古学研究资源和方法，使长城这一遗产及沿线社区获益。就这一点而言，新项目集传统研究、遗产管理与社区参与于一身，田野考古获得的结果进行分析后，预计可产生新的研究问题与成果。

参考文献
Bibliography

[1] Collins, R., and Symonds, M.F.A. "Approaching the Wall." In Breaking Down Boundaries: Hadrian's Wall in the 21st Century, edited by R. Collins and M.F.A.Symonds. JRA Suppl.Ser.93， Portsmouth (RI): 2013: 9-16.

R. 柯林斯，M.F.A. 西蒙兹 . 审视长城 [J]. R. 柯林斯 , M.F.A. 西蒙兹编 . 打破边界 :21 世纪的哈德良长城 [M]. 古罗马考古期刊补充卷 93 期 , 罗得岛朴茨茅斯 :2013:9-16.

[2] Hingley, R. Hadrian's Wall: A Life. Oxford: 2012.

R. 兴利 . 哈德良长城：一段生命历程 [M]. 牛津 :2012.

[3] Bidwell, P.T. Hadrian's Wall 1989-1999. Kendal: 1999.

P.T. 比德维尔 . 哈德良长城 1989-1999[M]. 肯达尔 :1999.

[4] Breeze, D.J. Hadrian's Wall: A History of Archaeological Thought. Kendal: 2014.

D.J. 布里兹 . 哈德良长城：见证考古思想演变 [M]. 肯达尔 :2014.

[5] Allason-Jones, L., and Miket, R. The Catalogue of Small Finds from South Shields Roman Fort. Newcastle: 1984.

L. 阿勒森 - 琼斯，R. 米凯特 . 南希尔兹罗马要塞出土小型文物编目 [M]. 纽卡斯尔 :1984.

[6] Gillam, J.P. Types of Roman Coarse Pottery Vessels in Northern Britain. Newcastle: 1969.

J.P. 吉拉姆 . 英国北部古罗马粗陶器皿的几种类型 [M]. 纽卡斯尔 :1969.

[7]Collingwood, R.G., and Wright, R.P. RIB: The Roman Inscriptions of Britain, Volume 1, Inscriptions on Stone. Oxford: 1965.

R.G. 科林伍德，R.P. 莱特 . 英国的罗马铭文：第一卷 石刻铭文 [M]. 牛津 :1965.

[8] Salway, P. The Frontier People of Roman Britain. Cambridge: 1965.

P. 萨尔韦 . 罗马时期不列颠的边境居民 [M]. 剑桥 :1965.

[9] Breeze, D.J., and Dobson, B. Hadrian's Wall. London: 1976.

D.J. 布里兹，B. 多布森 . 哈德良长城 [M]. 伦敦 :1976.

[10] Huntley, J., and Stallibrass, S(eds). "Plant and Vertebrate Remains from Archaeological sites in Northern England." Architectural and Archaeological Society of Durham and Northumberland Research Report 4, 2005.

J. 亨特利，S. 斯塔里布拉斯编 . 英格兰北部考古遗址出土的植物与脊椎动物遗骸 [R]. 杜伦郡与诺森伯兰郡农业与考古协会 4 号研究报告，2005.

[11] Hodgson, N. The Roman Fort at Wallsend (Segedunum): Excavations in 1997-98. Newcastle： 2003.

N. 霍奇森 . 沃森德（赛格杜努姆）罗马要塞：1997 年 -1998 年间的考古发掘 [M]. 纽卡斯尔 : 2003.

[12] Bidwell, P.T. "The system of obstacles on Hadrian's Wall: their extent, date, and purpose." Arbeia

Journal, 2005(8): 53-75.

P.T. 比德维尔 . 哈德良长城上的障碍体系：范围、年代与目的 [J]. 阿尔比亚杂志，2005(8): 53-75.

[13] Wilmott, T. Birdoswald, Excavations of a Roman fort on Hadrian's Wall and its successor settlements: 1987-92. London: 1997.

T. 威尔莫特 . 博得瓦德要塞，哈德良长城一处罗马要塞及后续聚落的发掘：1987-1992 年 [M]. 伦敦：1997.

[14] Poulter, J. "Surveying Roman Military Landscapes across Northern Britain." BAR British Series 492, 2009.

J. 普尔特 . 对北不列颠罗马时期军事景观的考察 [J].BAR 英国卷 492 期，2009.

[15] Hill, P.R. "The Construction of Hadrian's Wall." BAR British Series 375, 2004.

P.R. 希尔 . 哈德良长城的修筑 [J].BAR 英国卷 375 期 ,2004.

[16] Symonds, M.F.A. Protecting the Roman Empire: fortlets, frontiers, and the quest for post-conquest security. Cambridge: 2017.

M.F.A. 西蒙兹 . 保卫罗马帝国：要塞、边界及后征服时代如何安邦定国 [M]. 剑桥 :2017.

[17] Collins, R. Hadrian's Wall and the end of empire: the Roman frontier in the 4th and 5th centuries. New York: 2012.

R. 柯林斯 . 帝国末期的哈德良长城：4 世纪至 5 世纪的罗马边界 [M]. 纽约 :2012.

[18] Breeze, D.J(ed). The Handbook of the Roman Wall (14th Edn). Newcastle: 2006.

D.J. 布里兹编 . 古罗马长城手册（第 14 版）[M]. 纽卡斯尔 :2006.

[19] Hodgson, N. Hadrian's Wall 1999-2009, Kendal: 2009.

N. 霍奇森 . 哈德良长城 1999-2009[M]. 肯达尔 :2009.

[20] Collins, R., and Symonds, M.F.A. Hadrian's Wall 2009-1999. Kendal: 2019.

R. 柯林斯，M.F.A. 西蒙兹 . 哈德良长城 2009-1999[M]. 肯达尔 :2019.

[21] Hodgson, N. Hadrian's Wall: Archaeology and History at the limit of Rome's Empire. Ramsbury: 2017.

N. 霍奇森 . 哈德良长城：罗马帝国边疆的考古与历史 [M]. 拉姆斯伯里 :2017.

[22] Symonds, M.F.A., and Mason, D. Frontiers of Knowledge: A Research Framework for Hadrian's Wall. Durham: 2009.

M.F.A. 西蒙兹，D. 梅森 . 知识的前沿：哈德良长城研究框架 [M]. 杜伦 :2009.

[23] Adkins, G., and Mills, N. Hadrian's Wall Interpretation Framework: Overview and Summary. Hexham: 2011. httphttp://hadrianswallcountry.co.uk/sites/default/files/1.%20%20HWIF_Overview%20and%20summary.pdf.

G. 阿德金斯，N. 米尔斯 . 哈德良长城阐释框架：总览与概述 [EB/OL]. 海克萨姆 :2011. 地址：http://hadrianswallcountry.co.uk/sites/default/files/1.%20%20HWIF_Overview%20and%20summary.pdf.

[24] Hodgson, N. et al. The Iron Age on the Northumberland Coastal Plain. Newcastle upon Tyne: 2012.

N. 霍奇森等 . 铁器时代的诺森伯兰沿海平原 [M]. 纽卡斯尔 :2012.

MONITORING: LEARNING AS WE GO

DAVID BROUGH

Newcastle University - Newcastle upon Tyne, UK

JOHN SCOTT

Hadrian's Wall World Heritage Site Partnership Board - Carlisle - UK

Abstract

'What gets measured, gets managed' is a widely quoted management mantra, and for good reason. This is demonstrated by outlining two different aspects of monitoring a World Heritage Site. The first is the condition and conservation of the monument, covering physical condition, potential threats, and management activity. The second aspect focuses on understanding the value of the monument to visitors, communities and society more broadly. The paper concludes by reflecting on the specific situation at Hadrian's Wall and the future opportunities for effective monitoring.

Keywords: World Heritage Site, monitoring, reporting, management, conservation, protection, values

Monitoring often finds its way to the back of a project plan, something that is done at the end of a defined piece of work to say how far specific objectives have been achieved, particularly as part of a report to external funders. It is often then filed to bring a project to a close, or it is used to make the case for continuation. Yet, if we turn monitoring around and bring it to the front of our management processes, monitoring from the start of a work plan, it can enable the effectiveness of management to be continuously assessed and decision-making to be continuously and better informed. The collection and analysis of data thus becomes central to a positive cycle of understanding, improving and monitoring.

In order to maximise the value of monitoring we need to establish a clear understanding of why we are doing it and what it is intended to achieve. This provides the basis for identifying what aspects of the management of heritage we should monitor and, in turn, what specific information should be collected. There is often a temptation to collect everything that is easy to count in the hope that it will tell us something useful, and thereby to overlook some less quantitative or less accessible data which may be equally beneficial to management decisions.

In the context of World Heritage Sites it is helpful to explore two principal thematic areas of management activity: those related to the conservation and protection of the physical fabric of the monument, and those relating to optimising the social, communal, educational and economic values of the World Heritage Site. These two thematic areas inevitably overlap, particularly in visitor management.

监测：在实践中学习

大卫·布劳夫
（纽卡斯尔大学，英国纽卡斯尔）
约翰·斯科特
（哈德良长城世界遗产合作委员会，英国卡莱尔）

摘　要

"只有能被测量的东西，才能被管理"能成为管理领域广泛采纳的准则，是有其原因的。本文通过介绍一处世界遗产地监测的两个不同方面，证明这一信条。第一个方面是遗迹的保存状况，包括物理状况、潜在威胁和管理活动。第二个方面侧重于面向访客，社区和整个社会提高对遗产价值的认知。本文最后回顾哈德良长城特有的状况以及在未来进行有效监测的机会。

关键词：世界遗产地　监测　报告　管理　保存　保护　价值

监测常常在项目计划的最后出现，有时是一项工作的最后步骤，用来说明一个特定工作目标的完成情况，尤其在对外部资助人的报告中作为独立的部分出现。它常常在项目结束时进行，或者用于项目的延续。但是，如果我们换个角度思考监测，将其作为管理过程的起点，即工作计划开始时进行监测，将有助于确保管理的有效性得到持续评估，确保决策得到持续和准确信息支撑。数据收集和分析也因此成为理解－改进－监测这一良性循环的关键。

为了将监测的价值最大化，我们需要明确认识为什么要监测以及监测要达到什么目标。这是确定世界遗产地管理需要监测内容的基础，也是确定需要采集哪些特定信息的基础。我们常常倾向于收集所有容易量化的数据，并指望这些数据总能给我们提供某些有用的信息。这样容易忽视一些不易量化和较难获得的数据，而这些数据可能对做出管理决策同样有益。

在世界遗产地语境下，将管理工作分为两大专题领域十分有帮助，一个领域涉及遗产本体的保存和保护，另一个领域涉及充分发挥世界遗产地的社会，群体，教育和经济价值。不可避免地，两个专题领域有所交叉，特别是在访客管理方面。

一、监测物理状况

可能对遗址本体保存状况带来负面影响的因素大体可以分为两类，一类是人类活动因素，另一类是自然力量因素。

对遗址物理状况产生最显著威胁的人类活动是游客影响。与很多知名的世界遗产地一样，哈德良长城受到的影响不仅来源于游客数量，还来源于游客行为。虽然尽可能吸引更多的游客可提高旅游经济效

MONITORING PHYSICAL CONDITION

Factors which may impact adversely upon the physical condition of the monument can be broadly divided into those which are the result of human activities and those which are driven by natural forces.

The most significant human activity which can threaten the fabric of the monument is the impact of visitors. As with many popular World Heritage Sites, Hadrian's Wall is impacted not only by visitor numbers, but by visitor behaviour. Whilst seeking to attract as many visitors as possible, so as to grow the visitor economy, if numbers are concentrated at peak times or at particular access points the risks of degradation to the monument are heightened. High numbers of visitors in autumn and winter - when the ground is wet - causes much more damage to earthworks and to shallow archaeological deposits than in dryer seasons. Thus, visitor numbers need to be monitored not only at several points across the monument but also throughout the year. The figures for the various attractions along the Wall are available but there is less information about those visiting the spaces in between. Simple 'people-counters' have been used on gates along the National Trail but the number and distribution of these has not been extensive enough to be of maximum value. Of equal significance to the actual numbers is visitor behaviour. How people move around a visitor attraction, and where they stop and congregate, can pose risks to the monument by concentrating points of erosion. These very detailed movements should also be monitored and understood, so that they can be mitigated by appropriate management actions.

The other area of human activity affecting the condition of Hadrian's Wall is that of land-use: within the formally designated area of the World Heritage Site, across the larger Buffer Zone and throughout the wider landscape setting of the monument. This swathe of land, running from the North Sea to the Irish Sea, is home to a sizeable population. In the rural areas, arable farming, livestock grazing and forestry are actively pursued every day of the year. These activities not only help to sustain local economies but are also integral to maintaining the landscape values and character of the setting of the monument. However, some practices in each of these industries - such as deep ploughing and the feeding of stock - can, if not adequately managed, erode these values and damage the monument itself. In the urban sections of Hadrian's Wall a wider range of commercial activities pose a variety of threats to the archaeological remains, and transport and other infrastructure requirements can be equally destructive.

In both rural and urban areas, new development and redevelopment can pose similar threats, demanding a professional archaeological response. We have to accept that the Wall has to be managed within its contemporary communities, in harmony with a constantly evolving social environment and many different interests. Effective monitoring therefore requires access to information from a wide range of sources which, at first sight, may seem to be quite external to the direct management of the monument.

Natural forces which can impact on the condition of the monument also require regular monitoring. A number of species of burrowing animal, including badgers and rabbits, can disturb or destroy archaeological deposits. Vegetation, particularly trees and bracken, can also have adverse impacts on fragile archaeological remains. Changing cli-

益，但是一旦人流量在某些高峰时段出现聚集，或在某些游览点出现聚集，遗址受损风险也随之上升。与干燥季节相比，秋冬时节地面潮湿，游客数量过多会对地表土遗址和埋藏较浅的考古堆积造成更多损害。因此，游客数量监测不仅需要设置在整个哈德良长城的不同地点，还需要在全年各个季节进行。长城沿线多处游览点的监测数据现已可采集，但是游览点间的旅游人数还缺乏信息。哈德良长城国家步道沿线的入口处目前都采用简单的"数人头"方法收集数据，但是游客数量和分布情况还不详细，无法达到研究价值最大化。与游客数量同样重要的是游客行为。人们在游览点内如何移动，在哪里停留和聚集，在那反复踩踏的地点会造成集中破坏从而对遗址造成威胁。这些细节的活动也应该进行监测并研读，这样才能够通过合理的管理措施来减轻影响。

另一个影响哈德良长城保存状况的人类活动是土地利用：在正式列入世界遗产地的范围内，以及其缓冲区和遗址周围更广的景观范围内的土地利用。这一带状土地从北海延伸至爱尔兰海，是众多人口的家园。在乡村地区，耕种、放牧和造林活动每天都在进行着。这些活动不仅维持了本地经济发展，而且也是保留遗址周边景观价值和特色所不可或缺的。但是，这些农牧业活动中——例如深耕和饲养牲畜——如果未得到有效管理，有可能会对遗址本体造成损害而影响其价值。在哈德良长城所处的城市地区，大量商业活动对考古遗址带来了不同形式的威胁，同时交通和其他的基础设施建设需求也同样具有破坏性。

在乡村和城市地区，新的开发建设和改造项目都会带来同样的威胁，也需要专业考古人员采取措施。我们不得不接受这样一个现实，即长城必须在它现有的社区环境中进行管理，与持续变化的社会环境和多方利益群体和谐共存。因此有效的监测需要有广泛的信息来源，尽管很多信息乍看之下似乎与直接的遗址管理并不相干。

自然因素也会影响到遗址的保存状况，因此需要定期监测。多个穴居物种，如獾，野兔等，会扰动或损毁考古地层。植被，尤其是树木和蕨类，也会对脆弱的考古遗迹产生消极影响。气候条件的改变和更多极端天气的出现会加速植被生长或损毁遗址表面生长的保护性草皮。并且在某些地点，河流与海洋持续冲刷侵蚀，可能直接冲走考古遗存。

可应用一系列的方法和工具监测遗址物理保存状况。最重要的方法是借助各类人员的参与来进行日常观察，包括遗产地专业管理人员和志愿者，游客和当地社区。国家步道沿线的监测最为密集，来自当地社区的一队志愿者经过接受培训专门对受损或侵蚀的关键迹象进行观察，并且获得授权，在必要的情况下立即采取补救措施。该授权以"通用登录古迹许可"方式 (Generic Consent scheme) 提供，该方式由英格兰遗产委员会首先在哈德良长城创立，现今被其他英国国家步道以及历史古迹所采用。

特定区段的监测是定期进行的，监测方法包括航拍和定点拍照，电子调查和实地考察。这些监测方法通常是在编制保护计划的过程中实施的，尤其针对那些对公众开放的遗产地。而反过来当通过这些监测方法确定了某些特定因素存在潜在风险后，又将其用于定期监测的要求。

特定区段全面监测的案例是国家步道的重要节点的定点拍照体系（图1、2、3、4）。该体系始于1996年并在之后扩展到70个重点节点。现在这些节点每年进行三次拍照，每年秋季由工作人员沿国家步道徒步进行全线校核，检查各节点的现场情况并完成记录。该套监测数据库目前是全部英国世界遗产地中最完整的监测数据，使人们可以对国家步道保存状况的长期变化趋势（进而哈德良长城考古遗迹的保护状况）进行分析和评估。使用这些信息，管理方能更好地规划遗迹状况的未来风险管理并调动必要

Fig. 1

The archaeological remains of Milecastle 38 exposed to elemental and visitor erosion, April 2004. The National Trail runs directly upwards through the milecastle in the foreground, and then alongside the line of the Wall which is visible to the right of the wood (© Alan Whitworth)

图1

2004 年 4 月，受自然和访客侵蚀的 38 号里堡考古遗迹。国家步道径直穿过前景中的里堡，直接向上延伸，之后与树林右侧的墙体伴行（摄影：Alan Whitworth）

Fig. 2

Milecastle 38 in August 2014 with the protective grass covering restored (© Alan Whitworth)

图2

2014 年 8 月，38 号里堡被修复后的草皮保护覆盖（摄影：Alan Whitworth）

matic conditions and greater extremes in weather can accelerate vegetative growth or destroy the protective grasses which overlie the monument, and in some locations constant fluvial and marine erosion can simply wash away archaeological remains.

A number of methodologies and tools are used to monitor the physical condition of the monument. The most significant of these is simple day-to-day observation by a wide range of people, including professional site staff and volunteers, visitors and local communities. Such monitoring is most intensive along the National Trail where a team of dedicated volunteers from local communities are trained to look for key indicators of damage or erosion and who are authorised, where practicable, to undertake immediate remedial actions. This authorisation is provided through the Generic Consent scheme first established by Historic England for Hadrian's Wall and now adopted by other National Trails and historic monuments across the UK.

Section-specific monitoring is undertaken periodically and can include aerial and fixed-point photography, electronic and field surveys. These are often conducted as part of the process of developing conservation plans, particularly for sites which are open to the public, which in turn will set out the requirement for regular monitoring of particular elements that have been identified as potentially at risk.

The most comprehensive example of section-specific monitoring is the system of fixed-point photography at critical points along the National Trail (Figs 1, 2, 3, 4). This system was initiated in 1996 and has since been expanded to cover 70 points which are now photographed three times a year; each autumn this recording is complemented by staff walk-

Fig. 3
Milecastle 37 in 1991 showing accumulated damage from vistors' footsteps over many years (© David McGlade)
图 3
1991 年的 37 号里堡，显现出多年来访客踩踏带来的累积破坏（摄影：David McGlade）

的资源进行保护。

　　另一个监测遗址的工具是英格兰遗产委员会的濒危遗产名录[1]。清单列出所有受威胁的遗产地，以及相应的风险严重程度和紧急程度等级。名录的公布基于地方政府和英格兰遗产委员会工作人员对遗产地的认识。哈德良长城世界遗产地列入濒危遗产名录的遗址点数量和等级成为评估遗产地总体状况的有效指标，并能够长期追踪遗产地状况变化。

二、监测价值

　　监测遗址的物理状况虽然对保护和保存遗址非常重要，但是社会对遗址价值如何评价可能更有意义，是确保遗产保护目标实现的重要因素。简单而言，如果社会中的个人或团体不珍视他们自己的文化遗产，那么他们对遗产保护就会漠不关心。

ing the whole Trail to check its condition. The resulting database, the most complete set of monitoring data for any World Heritage Site in the UK, enables long-term trends in the condition of the Trail (and thus the conservation of the underlying archaeology) to be identified and understood. Using this information, the future management of risks to the fabric of the monument can be planned for and the necessary resources allocated.

A further tool for monitoring the condition of the monument is Historic England's Heritage at Risk Register[1] which identifies all the designated heritage sites which are 'at risk' and which grades the level of that risk in terms of severity and urgency. The Register is based on the combined knowledge of local authority and Historic England staff throughout England. The number and grading of sites across the World Heritage Site that are considered to be at risk provides a valuable summary of the overall condition of the monument and enables changes in its condition to be tracked over time.

MONITORING VALUE

Although monitoring of the physical condition of the monument is vital to its conservation and protection, the degree to which it is valued by society is perhaps of even greater significance in securing those objectives. Put simply, if individuals and groups within society do not value their heritage they will have no interest in its preservation.

Value is most readily identified in monetary terms, either directly to household income or to the local or national economy. Identifying the economic value of the monument can promote popular support for its protection and can also provide the necessary justification for continued public investment in its management. The economic value most directly attributable to Hadrian's Wall is that of tourism. The highest value tourism comes from overseas visitors and from those who need overnight accommodation. That value is increased by the length of stay within the region and by the amount of money that each visitor spends each day.

These elements need to be monitored and understood as fully as possible, although the number of variables means that it is doubtful that they can ever be calculated entirely accurately. Nevertheless, this monitoring is indicative in terms of the magnitude of the economic value of tourism. A number of methods are used to obtain the data to establish economic value: these include a range of interviews, surveys and questionnaires, either onsite or through accommodation- and hospitality-providers. If the methodologies are applied consistently this provides an indication of comparative performance over time. The data is fed into the STEAM analysis methodology[2] which is used by many destinations across the UK to assess the economic impact of tourism; this also enables comparisons to be made between the economic performance of different destinations.

Understanding of the economic value of visitors is incomplete without understanding who visitors are and what their differing spending behaviours and motivations are. Audience segmentation is therefore widely undertaken by many visitor attractions and destinations across the UK and along Hadrian's Wall. It is used to inform a range of aspects of visitor management, including marketing, the provision of information, the design and specification of visitor interpretation, facilities and accessibility, pricing, opening times, and transport infrastructure.

Other factors which contribute towards individuals' and society's valuation of Hadrian's Wall are less easy

Fig. 4

Milecastle 37 in 2010 showing restored grass covering after a decade of conservation measures and visitor management (© David McGlade)

图 4

2010 年的 37 号里堡，显示出十年的保护措施和游客管理后，草皮覆盖得到修复（摄影：David McGlade）

　　价值最方便的方式是通过货币来体现，不管是直接的家庭收入还是地方或国家经济都是如此。衡量遗产的经济价值有助于争取公众对遗迹保护的支持，也为公共资金持续投入遗产管理提供合理的理由。哈德良长城的直接经济价值是旅游业。旅游产业中价值最高的是海外游客以及需要留宿的游客。这一价值随着游客在区域内停留的时间和每位游客每天支出的费用增加而增加。

　　这些因素需要尽可能全面地进行监测和解读，虽然受到变量限制意味着完全准确的计算不大可能。即使如此，在研究旅游业经济价值方面，这种监测仍具有指导意义。获得数据时采取了一系列的方法来确定经济价值：包括在现场和食宿服务场所的一系列的访谈、调查和问卷。如果持续采用这些方法，假以时日，将能够提供相对的业绩指标。收集到的数据可以使用 STEAM 分析方法 [2]。全英国很多旅游景区使用该方法来评估旅游业带来的经济效益，这样不同景点还可以相互比较其经济业绩。

to quantify, but are, nevertheless, of significance. Each relates to the various ways in which different sections of society engage with or benefit from the monument.

The most obvious way in which many local communities recognise the value of the World Heritage Site is through the participation of school children in educational initiatives across Hadrian's Wall. Although the long-term value of this participation cannot be ascertained, levels of participation and educational outcomes are monitored. At another level, the academic benefits of the monument, although less widely acknowledged, can be monitored through quantifying the number of university research projects and the size of their budgets. Other communal values, such as the amenity and aesthetic values of the monument, can be monitored by measuring attendance and participation in arts and other associated events. Although not strictly quantifiable, these provide indications of the value that communities place upon the Wall.

The exact degree to which individuals, communities, and society as a whole values Hadrian's Wall is probably unquantifiable. Seeking to quantify it through monitoring, albeit incomplete or inadequate, is still a valid endeavour. It raises our understanding - in local communities and in government - of why the site is valued and how it benefits society. This, in turn, enables those who manage the World Heritage Site to maintain those key values and to enhance the level and extent of the benefits they bring.

ISSUES AND CONCLUSIONS

Despite the many and varied management benefits of monitoring the monument, there are significant practical limitations on the scope and extent to which it can be conducted.

As Humphrey Welfare describes in his paper in this volume, there are a large number of organisations involved in different aspects of managing Hadrian's Wall. Furthermore, these organisations vary in their governance and status, from branches of national government departments, to private charitable trusts and informal local groupings. The objectives of these different bodies and how they are each funded, and hence their respective internal reporting obligations, are equally varied. As a consequence, each is required to gather differing management and performance data, or broadly similar data but to do so in differing details and formats, to meet their particular reporting requirements. This means that it becomes extremely difficult to gather and collate consistent monitoring data across the entirety of Hadrian's Wall, although this remains an aspiration amongst all partner organisations.

At a more mundane level, all organisations involved in the management of the World Heritage Site are faced with the challenges of fulfilling their management obligations within the constraints of finite human and financial resources. Managers in this situation will naturally focus their resources on fulfilling their primary roles of conservation and protection of the monument, maximising use of the heritage resource and the different societal benefits that it offers. As a result, monitoring and the collation and reporting of data are frequently relegated to the status of an add-on to those primary functions and objectives of management.

In this context, even in those rare situations where heritage management bodies are less constrained in their resources,

不去理解游客身份和他们不同的花费行为和动机，就无法全面理解游客带来的经济价值。因此英国很多旅游景点以及哈德良长城沿线都采用游客细分调查方法。采用这种方法可以为游客管理提供多个方面的指导，包括市场营销，信息供应，游客阐释的设计和规程，游客设施和通达条件，定价方案，开放时间和交通基础设施等。

其他有助于提升个人和社会对哈德良长城价值认同程度的因素不太容易量化衡量，但是仍然非常重要。每个因素都与不同的社会群体参与或从遗址中受益的方式有关。

很多促进当地社区认识世界遗产地价值的途径中，最显著的方式是组织哈德良长城沿线的学校儿童参与长城教育活动，即使这种活动的长期价值无法量化，但是可以监测参与程度和教育成果。还有一个没有得到广泛认可的方面，就是学术研究从遗址中受益，这可以通过大学的研究项目数量和项目预算来进行量化。其他公共价值，如遗产周边的设施改善和美育功能能够通过测量艺术活动和其他相关活动的参与人数得到监测。虽然无法严格量化，这些记录显示了长城为社区带来的价值。

个人、社区乃至社会在整体上对哈德良长城价值认知的程度可能无法量化。但通过监测使其量化的努力，即使不够完整或不够充分，仍然是有意义的。它有助于地方社区和政府理解为什么该遗产地能受到珍视，它又如何造福社会。反过来，这种理解使得世界遗产地管理机构能够关注这些方面，从而进一步增强和扩大遗址带来的收益。

三、问题和结论

虽然监测遗址有多种多样的管理益处，但是从实际操作上，监测的范围和程度有很大的局限。

正如汉佛瑞·维尔法在本书文章中描述的，哈德良长城管理工作的方方面面涉及到大量机构的参与。不仅如此，这些机构的管理体制和法律地位也各不相同，既有国家政府部门的分支机构，也有私人慈善信托机构和非正式的地方群体。不同机构的目标以及资金来源各不相同，因此他们各自的内部报告义务也有区别。造成的结果是，不同机构需要收集不同的管理和业绩数据，或是收集大体类似的数据但是采用不同的细节和格式来满足他们各自的报告要求。这就意味着在哈德良长城全线所有区域收集和整理统一的监测数据异常困难，即使这是所有合作机构的共同愿望。

在日常层面，所有参与哈德良世界遗产地的管理机构都面临着在有限人员和资金情况下履行管理义务的挑战。这种情况下，管理者自然而然地将资源集中在保存和保护遗址这一主要职责方面，最大限度地使用遗产资源及可提供的社会效益。结果造成监测和数据收集、整理与报告工作被频繁降级到那些首要职能和管理目标之外的附加地位。

在这样的大环境中，即使在少数情况下遗产管理机构资源并不那么短缺，监测产生的人员和资金花费也必须与它能带来的管理效益成比例。监测若要有价值则必须既要保证监测数据的准确，又要能够长期持续重复。这就要求做出规划并保证在未来得到相应资源支持。信息收集得越详细，监测的规模和范围越大，相应资源分配就越困难。因此也可以理解，在决定监测范围时，一直以来的倾向是只收集小范围内最重要的数据，仅为实现遗产地管理主要目标的关键决策依据。

作为跨国罗马帝国边界世界遗产地的一部分的地位，如何确定适合哈德良长城的监测变得更加复杂。

the human and financial costs of monitoring must be proportional to the management benefits it brings. For monitoring to be of value it must be both accurate and able to be consistently replicated over time. This demands some planning and the allocation of resources into the future. The greater the detail of information collected or the greater scope and extent of monitoring, the more difficult it will be to make an appropriate allocation. Understandably therefore, in determining what should be monitored the tendency has been to restrict this to the gathering of a narrow range of data that is most critical to informing decision-making in realising the primary objectives of managing the site.

Further complexities in the determination of appropriate monitoring for Hadrian's Wall arise from its status as part of the serial transnational Frontiers of the Roman Empire World Heritage Site, as described by Sebastian Sommer in this volume. The three components of the World Heritage Site operate in different regulatory, organisational, geographical and environmental contexts, and each faces differing management challenges. Their reporting requirements, and therefore the management data that they each require are varied. They are however obliged to report jointly to UNESCO through the six-yearly Periodic Reporting process[3]. Fortunately the format of the Periodic Report is largely based on qualitative self-assessment rather than quantitative statistical reporting, and so it does not demand an absolute consistency in the monitoring data that each component part must gather.

Management collaborations and exchanges between the three component parts of the Frontiers of the Roman Empire World Heritage Site are contributing to the thinking about how Hadrian's Wall should be monitored. The comparison of different practices, particularly in relation to the use of mobile-phones and other new technologies in monitoring (and thus influencing) visitor behaviours, is opening up new possibilities.

In 2006 a number of UK World Heritage Sites attempted to design a common set of key performance indicators[4]. It was quickly realised that each Site was unique and any one-size-fits-all approach would be impracticable and meaningless. Since then, Hadrian's Wall, like other UK World Heritage Sites, has continued to base its monitoring practices on its own specific needs and the particular context in which it is managed.

塞巴斯蒂安·索默在本书的文章中介绍了罗马帝国边疆跨国遗产的情况。三处世界遗产地在不同的法律、机构、地理和环境条件中运营，每一处都面临着不同的管理挑战。它们不同的报告要求，也导致需要的管理数据各不相同。但是它们仍然有责任联合向联合国教科文组织提交六年一轮的定期报告[3]。所幸定期报告的格式大部分是基于定性的自我评估而非量化的数据报告，因此对三处世界遗产地收集的监测数据不要求绝对的统一。

罗马帝国边疆世界遗产地的三个组成部分的管理合作和交流也促使我们考虑哈德良长城应如何监测。通过比较不同的做法，尤其利用手机和其他新科技监测（借此影响）游客行为的相关技术打开了新的可能性。

2006 年，若干英国世界遗产地试图设计一套共用的关键业绩指标[4]。很快，他们意识到每一个遗产地都是独一无二的，任何一刀切的方式都不切实际且毫无意义。自此之后，哈德良长城，与其他英国的世界遗产地一样，继续基于其本身的具体需求和其管理的特定背景决定其监测实践。

参考文献
Bibliography

[1] Historic England. Heritage at Risk Register 2018., London: Historic England, 2018. April 18, 2019.

英格兰遗产委员会 .2018 濒危文化遗产名录 . 伦敦 : 英格兰遗产委员会，2018.2019-04-18.

https://historicengland.org.uk/images-books/publications/har-2018-registers/.

[2] Global Tourism Solutions (UK) Ltd. Scarborough Tourism Economic Assessment Model. Penrith：2019. April 18, 2019.

全球旅游业解决方案（英国）有限责任公司 . 史卡保罗旅游经济评估模型 [EB/OL].2019. 2019-04-18.

http://www.globaltourismsolutions.co.uk/steam-model.

[3] UNESCO. Periodic Reporting. 2019. April 18, 2019.

联合国教科文组织 . 定期报告 [EB/OL].2019. 2019-04-18.

http://whc.unesco.org/en/periodicreporting/.

[4] Bedu, I. et al. Tool kit for World Heritage Site Monitoring Indicators. London: ICOMOS-UK, 2007, unpublished.

I. 别杜等 . 世界遗产地监测指标工具箱 [Z]. 伦敦 : 国际古迹遗址理事会 - 英国，2007，未发表 .

中国长城监测：理念、实践与展望

张依萌

（中国文化遗产研究院，中国北京）

摘　要

21 世纪初，中国逐步建立了世界遗产监测体系。莫高窟和长城在 20 世纪 80 年代开展的早期监测工作形成了中国世界遗产监测重视科技手段应用的传统。

长城全长 21196.18 千米，行经 15 省级行政区的 404 县区市，规模庞大、本体与环境复杂、社会关注度高的特点，决定了其监测工作应当因地制宜、统筹协调，以制度作为保证，加强社会参与。

遵循这些原则，长城监测工作稳步推进，保护立法不断完善，执法督察效果显著。依托长城资源保护管理信息系统建设和长城保护员制度，包括雷达差分干涉测量（DinSAR）、无人机巡查和辅助人工巡查的"长城监测巡查系统"应用程序得以在不同尺度的长城监测工作中进行实验，并鼓励公众参与。

"监测"并不等于"技术监测"，而是一种管理手段，以风险预防为目的。长城保护紧迫性与监测研究长期性与之间的矛盾，是监测工作面临的根本挑战。转变观念，发挥人的潜力，从整体上统筹管理、控制监测成本，加强宣传和舆论引导，从而建立以问题和风险为导向、以社会力量为支撑的监测体系与管理机制，是长城监测应当坚持的工作方向。

关键词：中国长城　世界遗产　监测　理念　实践

一、中国世界遗产监测概况

（一）起源与传统

1987 年，中国长城、敦煌莫高窟等 6 处重要文化遗产列入世界遗产名录。彼时国际上还没有"世界遗产监测"的概念。但中国对这些遗产地开展的保护工作，有很多已经属于监测的范畴。

敦煌莫高窟是我国最早通过监测仪器设备采集数据，对文化遗产环境监测工作的文化遗产之一。从 20 世纪 50 年代开始，莫高窟就在国家的支持之下进行多次的现状与病害调查，积累了丰富、完整的资料，为监测工作的开展奠定了坚实的基础。80 年代，敦煌研究院即与美国盖蒂保护研究所和日本东京国立文化财研究所开展国际合作，引进先进设备开展石窟本体与环境的科学监测[1]。

同一时期，地质矿产部曾对北京市[2]、宁夏回族自治区[3] 的明长城进行过区域性的航空遥感调查，用以掌握长城长度、分布与保存状况变化。这些工作为长城的大尺度监测积累了经验，同时出现了中国世界遗产监测的一个趋势，即注重科技手段的运用。

（二）中国世界遗产监测体系的建立

1994 年，世界遗产监测成为世界遗产保护工作的一项制度[4]。21 世纪初，我国正式引入了文化遗

MONITORING THE GREAT WALL:PRINCIPLES, PRACTICE AND OUTLOOK

Zhang Yimeng

Chinese Academy of Cultural Heritage–Beijing –China

Abstract

At the beginning of the 21st century, China established its own World Heritage monitoring system. The early practices at the Mogao Grottoes and in sections of the Great Wall in the 1980s established a technology-focused tradition in monitoring World Heritage Sites in China.

Stretching for 21,196 km, the Great Wall crosses 404 counties, cities and districts in 15 provinces, autonomous regions and direct municipalites. Its size, complexity and high social value requires monitoring work to be tailored to local conditions, to be coordinated as a whole, supported through robust systems, and available to the public.

Following these principles, monitoring of the Great Wall has been steadily advanced and regulation has continuously improved, and the effects of law enforcement and supervision have been remarkable. Through the platforms of the Great Wall Resource Information System and Great Wall Patroller System, technologies such as Differential Interferometric Synthetic Aperture Radar (SInSAR), unmanned aerial vehicle (UAV) survey, and a mobile app, "Wandering Great Wall (the Great Wall Monitoring and Patrol System)" (GRMS), have been tested for different levels of Great Wall monitoring. In applying these systems and technologies, public participation has also been encouraged.

'Monitoring' does not simply mean 'technical monitoring' or the collection of data; it is a broader management process, aimed at risk prevention. The competing demands between urgent monitoring of elements at risk of deterioration and more general longer-term monitoring of the monument as a whole is a fundamental challenge in monitoring the Great Wall.

Key aims for monitoring of the Great Wall are to establish a monitoring system and management mechanisms focused on addressing problems and risks and supported by the public. This requires changing perceptions of monitoring, giving full play to human potential, establishing overall management systems, controlling costs, strengthening the promotion of understanding, and guiding public opinion.

Keywords: the Great Wall, Monitoring, Principles, Word Heritage Site

WORLD CULTURAL HERITAGE MONITORING IN CHINA

Origin and evolution

In 1987, six major cultural heritage sites, including the Great Wall of China and the Mogao Grottoes in

产监测的概念，并将其作为一项独立的工作。

制度层面，在 1982 年颁布、2002 年修订的《中华人民共和国文物保护法》框架下，自 2006 年开始，一系列世界遗产监测相关法律法规相继出台。

2006 年 11 月 4 日和 12 月 8 日，国家文物局先后颁布了《中国世界文化遗产保护管理办法》和《中国世界遗产监测巡视管理办法》，成为中国世界遗产监测工作的指导文件；次年 11 月出台《世界文化遗产监测规程（征求意见稿）》。

根据《国家文物博物馆事业发展"十二五"规划》要求，"十二五"期间（2006–2010）中国的世界遗产监测工作有四大任务：一是构建法规体系；二是完善工作机制；三是加强能力建设；四是建立信息系统。

各遗产地在"十一五"期间国家制定的世界遗产监测各项法律规范的基础之上，陆续出台遗产地的监测管理办法，世界遗产监测的国家 – 遗产地两级法规体系逐步形成。

在机构建设层面，2001 年，武夷山率先建立了专业的世界遗产监测中心，对大气、噪声、水文、气象及动植物资源等开展监测，并采用卫星遥感技术对遗产地的人文环境进行了动态监控。2011 年 6 月，中国文化遗产研究院成立中国世界文化遗产监测中心，成为全国性的世界遗产监测的专门管理和研究机构。截止到 2014 年，全国各世界遗产地开展了不同程度的遗产监测工作。有 8 处世界遗产地成立了专门的监测机构，其中就包括长城世界遗产地嘉峪关的"嘉峪关世界文化遗产监测中心"。中国的世界遗产监测工作取得了一系列进展，国家 – 省 – 遗产地三级监测管理体系逐步得到建立和成熟。

（三）监测实践

2012 年，中国文化遗产研究院世界遗产中心联合专业地理信息测绘机构研发完成了"中国世界遗产监测预警总平台"和部署在各遗产地的"通用平台"。一些遗产地也自主研发了适用于本遗产地的监测系统。在充分调研中国各世界遗产地实际需求的基础上，中心编制了《中国世界遗产监测预警总平台监测指标体系》。总平台正式上线，各遗产地开始按照通用标准定期采集和上报监测数据，迄今已累计采集数据达 20TB，中国的世界遗产地管理工作有了全局把握和统筹管理的可能。

操作层面，根据国家文物局的相关要求，中心先后选取了苏州园林等 12 个遗产地开展监测试点工作，在此基础上，逐步扩展到全部世界遗产地。同样自 2012 年起，中国世界文化遗产监测中心每年组织一次由全国各世界遗产地管理人员参加的年会，并形成监测年报。截至 2017 年，全国 117 家世界遗产管理机构中，有 51 处世界遗产地建立了监测机构 [5]。

联合国教科文组织也针对武当山古建筑群、三孔、拉萨布达拉宫历史建筑群等遗产进行了多次反应性监测 [6]，提出了改进管理工作的合理建议。

二、长城监测理念与实践

（一）长城的特点

2006 年，国家文物局启动了为期十年的"长城保护工程" [7] 项目，旨在全面加强长城保护管理工作。2006–2010 年，作为该项目的先导工作，国家文物局与国家测绘局联合开展了全国长城资源调查工作，

Dunhuang, were inscribed on the World Heritage List, when the concept of 'World Heritage Monitoring' had not yet been established. However, many of China's activities in protecting these heritage sites at that time would today be described as monitoring.

The Mogao Grottoes was one of the first cultural heritage sites in China to collect environmental monitoring data through technical instruments and equipment. Many surveys on the condition and threats to the site had been carried out since the 1950s with the support of the state, and had accumulated abundant and comprehensive data. This laid a solid foundation for future monitoring of the Mogao Grottoes. In the 1980s, the Dunhuang Academy, in cooperation with the Getty Institute and the Tokyo National Research Institute for Cultural Properties, introduced advanced equipment to monitor the fabric and environment of the Mogao Grottoes[1].

In the same era, two regional remote sensing investigation projects on the Great Wall in Beijing[2] and Ningxia Province[3], were initiated and conducted by the Ministry of Geology and Mineral Resources to identify the length, distribution and conservation status of the Great Wall. Experience of large-scale monitoring of the Great Wall was steadily accumulated, and the use of scientific and technological means laid a distinctive foundation for China's World Heritage monitoring.

Establishment of China's world heritage monitoring system

In 1994, World Heritage monitoring was first suggested in a UNESCO document[4], and it was officially adopted by China at the beginning of 21st century. A series of national regulations related to the monitoring of World Heritage have been issued since 2006 under the framework of "Law of the People's Republic of China on the Protection of Cultural Relics" promulgated in 1982. (The latest amendment was made in 2002.)

On 4th November and 8th December 2006, the State Administration of Cultural Heritage (SACH) published "Measures for the Protection and Management of China's World Cultural Heritage" and "Measures for the Monitoring and Inspection of China's World Heritage", which were followed by "Specifications for the Monitoring of World Cultural Heritage (draft for comments)" released in November 2007. These have become the guiding documents for monitoring China's World Heritage.

In "The 12th Five-Year Plan for the Development of National Cultural Heritage and Museums", four objectives were identified for the monitoring of World Heritage between 2006-2010: the establishment of a legal system; the improvement of working mechanisms; capacity-building; and the construction of information systems. Based on national regulations on World Heritage monitoring introduced since 2006, relevant management documents have been successively issued by many World Heritage Sites (WHS) in China. A two-level regulatory system for World Heritage monitoring has been gradually established.

At the management level, in 2001, Wuyi Mountain took the lead in establishing a professional World Heritage Monitoring Centre to monitor the site's atmosphere, noise, hydrology, meteorology, fauna and flora, and to dynamically monitor the human environment of the heritage site based on the application of satellite remote-sensing technology.

A decade later, the World Cultural Heritage Monitoring Centre of China (WCHCC) was established within

对中国境内的历代长城遗存进行了全面、系统的调查，并于 2012 年对调查结果进行了认定工作，并公布了权威的长城长度与分布范围等数据，第一次摸清了长城的家底，也使长城成为中国第一个完成了全面系统调查的线性文化遗产。

长城资源认定数据显示，中国长城分布于黑龙江、吉林、辽宁、北京、天津、河北、山西、内蒙古、山东、河南、陕西、宁夏、甘肃、青海、新疆等 15 个省（自治区、直辖市）的 404 个县域，包括墙体、壕堑、单体建筑、关堡及相关遗存共计 43721 处，总长度 21196.18 千米 [8]（图 1）。

作为大型"线性文化遗产"（Lineal or Serial Cultural Heritages）[9]，长城的主要特点有二：

一是规模庞大，构成复杂。长城是世界上规模最大的文化遗产。无论是本体构成，还是遗产地自然与人文环境，其复杂程度均首屈一指。

长城的建筑时代跨越 2500 年，材质包括夯土、石砌、包砖等不同类型，各地、各时代建筑工艺不同，保存状况迥异。

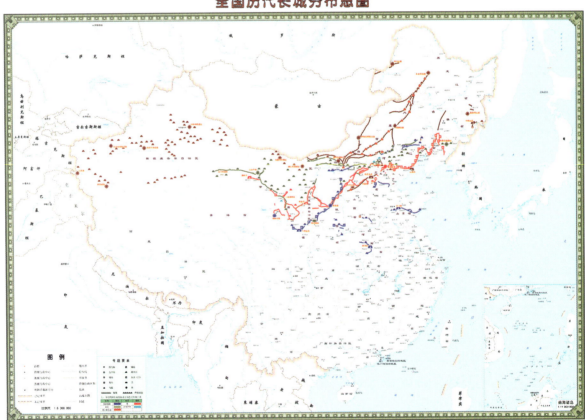

图 1
全国历代长城分布图（版权：国家文物局）
Fig. 1
Distribution map of the Great Wall of China of all ages (© NCHA)

the Chinese Academy of Cultural Heritage as a national special management and research institution for World Heritage monitoring. By the end of 2014, varying levels of heritage monitoring programmes had been carried out for WHSs in China. Monitoring centres were established in eight WHSs including the Jiayuguan Great Wall site. A three-level monitoring and management system of state-, provincial-, and heritage site- levels has gradually been established and has matured.

Monitoring practices

In 2012, the WCHCC and a professional survey institution jointly developed the "China World Heritage Monitoring and Warning General Platform" at the headquarters of CACH, and the 'Common terminal system' to be deployed at heritage sites. Several independent monitoring systems compatible to the general system had also been designed and used by specific heritage sites. On the basis of full investigation of the actual needs of various WHS in China, the Indicators System of the General Platform for World Heritage Monitoring and Early Warning in China was compiled. Once the general platform was officially launched, data from all WHSs has been collected and reported to consistent formats and standards. The platform now has 20Tb of data and has made the overall understanding and management of China's WHS monitoring possible.

At the operational level, WCHCC selected 12 WHSs to carry out pilot projects according to the requirements of NCHA. After the success of the pilots, work was gradually expanded to all the WHSs. An annual conference was established in 2012, attended by the managers of all WHSs throughout the country, and it published an annual monitoring report. By the end of 2017, 51 subordinate specialised monitoring institutions out of 117 World Cultural Heritage administrations had been established in China[5].

UNESCO's World Heritage Centre has also carried out a number of reactive monitoring reports on the Ancient Building Complex in the Wudang Mountains, the Temple and Cemetery of Confucius and the Kong Family Mansion in Qufu, the Historic Ensemble of the Potala Palace, Lhasa, and other heritage sites[6], and reasonable suggestions for improving management were put forward.

PRINCIPLES AND PRACTICES OF MONITORING THE GREAT WALL

The characteristics of the Great Wall

In 2006, the SACH launched the 10-year "Great Wall Conservation Programme"[7] which aimed to comprehensively strengthen the Great Wall's protection and management. Between 2006-2010, as a forerunner of the project, a comprehensive and systematic survey of the remains of the Great Wall from successive dynasties in China, called "the Great Wall Resource Survey", was carried out under the framework of collaboration between NCHA and the State Administration of Surveying Mapping and Geoinformation (incorporated into the Ministry of National Resource in 2019). The latest authoritative data, including the exact overall length and extent then identified, was released in 2012, which made the Great Wall China's first large-scale cultural heritage site to be

长城从东部沿海湿润地区，延伸至西北干旱区，行经山地、丘陵、平原、盆地、深林、草原、戈壁、沙漠；长城穿越城镇、乡村、无人区，人口密度从大于 1600 人 / 千米 ^{2}，到小于 1 人 / 千米 ^{2} 不等；沿线 404 个县域中，有的县属于经济发达地区，另外一些则属于经济欠发达地区，其中国家级贫困县达到 111 个 [10]。

二是长城具有超高的社会影响力。20 世纪 30 年代，著名的"长城抗战"爆发，长城极大地激发了中国人民坚持抗战的决心，并逐渐演变成为中华民族的象征。毛泽东的诗句"不到长城非好汉"，邓小平、习仲勋同志提出"爱我中华，修我长城"的口号等，都不断强化了这种象征意义，并且扩大了它的世界影响。有数据显示，1954-2005 年，仅八达岭长城一处，就曾接待过 392 位国家元首 [11]。在民间，公众对长城的关注度极高，并且参与长城保护管理的意愿和程度也很高。中国世界文化遗产监测中心的 2017 年舆情监测数据显示，全网关于世界遗产的相关新闻报道超过 44 万次，其中长城以 68874 次位列第二 [12]（图 2）。

（二）长城监测原则与实践

针对上述特点，长城的监测工作与其他遗产地相比，也有其自身的特殊需求。经过多年的监测实践总结，我们确立了最基本的长城监测原则，即"因地制宜、统筹协调、制度保证、社会参与"，并用这些原则指导新的实践。

1. 因地制宜

长城本体与环境的地域差异很大，因此，长城的监测工作需要有针对性地进行。具体来讲，就是监测主体、内容、指标和方案等，都要根据各地的实际来确定。

监测主体方面。目前，参与中国长城监测的人员，主要由专业文物管理人员、长城保护员和民间志愿者组成。

据统计，从事长城管理的文物干部，数量约为 5000 人左右 [13]。他们中的大多数人并不是专职长城管理人员，因此相较于 21000 千米的长城而言，并不足以支撑整个监测工作。作为专业管理人员的补充，长城沿线各地政府或基层文物部门聘请了约 5000 名长城保护员 [14] 进行定期的日常巡查，并向文物部门报告情况。长城保护员的构成，以长城沿线居民为主，其中绝大多数并不具备文物专业素养，整体素质偏低。而关于民间志愿者的情况，目前尚无准确的统计数据。但根据国家文物局文物违法案件举报中心的统计，自 2010 年以来，社会举报长城违法案件数量呈逐年上升趋势，而举报大多来自行业外的志愿者，因此，这也是一支不可忽视的力量。

对于一般隐患的发现和处理，专业文物干部和长城保护员已经能够胜任。但一些特殊的长城病害或针对长城的特定行为所形成的风险，则需要更加专业的人员来识别。比如长城保护维修工程项目的实施，多少会造成长城本体的改变。这种改变是否是积极的，工程理念是否科学，施工过程中是否达到设计要求等等，需要进行跟踪监测，而这个层级的监测工作，应当由驻场设计师或监理人员来完成。

监测内容和指标方面。长城面临诸多风险因素，而这些因素的分布是极不平衡的。比如降水对长城的影响：在西部地区，一些长城点段位于沙漠戈壁中，年均降水量少于 100 毫米。对这些地区洪水发生频率虽然不高，但破坏危险却很大；对于不同材质的长城来说，同样规模的降水，造成的影响也不同，如夯土

integrally and systematically investigated. The Great Wall of China is distributed across 404 counties of 15 provinces, autonomous regions, municipalities directly under the Central Government including Heilongjiang, Jilin, Liaoning, Beijing, Tianjin, Hebei, Shanxi, Inner Mongolia, Shandong, Henan, Shaanxi, Ningxia, Gansu, Qinghai and Xinjiang. It is 21,196 km long with 43,721 surviving sections of walls, trenches, towers, passes, fortresses and related relics[8]. (Fig. 1)

As a large-scale "Linear Cultural Heritage site"[9], the main characteristics of the Great Wall are as follows:

The Great Wall is the largest cultural heritage site in the world, and its composition is also extremely complicated. Having been constructed throughout more than 2500 years of the Chinese empire, from materials varying from rammed earth, to stone, and brick, the contruction techniques used in each age varied, just as the conservation status of different sections also varies considerably.

The Great Wall extends from humid areas, along the eastern coast, to arid regions in the northwest, through mountains, hills, plains, basins, deep forests, grasslands and deserts, and it travels through towns, villages and depopulated zones, with population densities ranging from more than 1600 people/km2 to less than 1 person/km2. Some of the 404 counties along the Wall have advanced economies while others have developing economies, among which 111 were state-poverty counties, though this number is rapidly decreasing[10].

The Great Wall also has important historical, social and political significance. In the 1930s, the famous 'Great Wall campaign' broke out between China and Japan. The Great Wall greatly inspired the Chinese people's determination to persist in the anti-Japanese War, and it gradually evolved into a symbol of the Chinese nation. From Mao Zedong's poem "One who failed to reach the Great Wall is not a hero," to the slogan "Love China and build the Great Wall," put forward in 1984 by Deng Xiaoping and Xi Zhongxun, the symbolic role and the geopolitical significance of the Great Wall have been constantly reinforced. Data shows that the Badaling section of the Great Wall alone has received 392 national leaders from all over the world[11]. The public also pay great attention to the Great Wall, and their willingness and desire to participate in its protection and management are extraordinarily high. According to public opinion monitoring data, 68,874 out of over 440,000 postings related to WHSs in China in 2016 related to the Great Wall which took 15.6% of the postings about all of the 40 Cultural World Heritage Sites and made it the second most topical WHS of the year[12]. (Fig. 2)

Principles and practices of monitoring the Great Wall

In view of the above characteristics, monitoring the Great Wall has its own special needs compared with other WHS. After years of practice, basic principles for monitoring the Great Wall have been established. All monitoring needs to be appropriate to local conditions, coordinated as an integrated system; based on a reliable and functional system, and involving social participation.

Suiting local conditions

The Great Wall's fabric and environment varies in different sections and regions. Therefore, site-specific relevance in monitoring operations is crucial. Specifically, the aspects which are monitored, the data that are col-

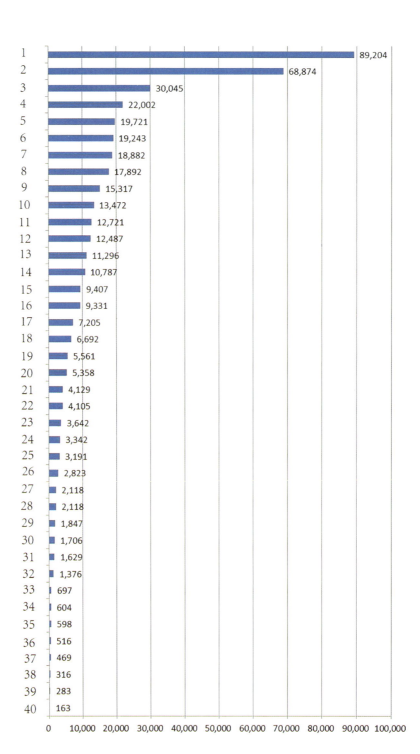

图 2

2016 年全国各项世界文化遗产新闻报道数量

Fig. 2

Statistics of each WHS media coverage 2016

1 明清故宫
Imperial Palaces of the Ming and Qing Dynasties in Beijing and Shenyang

2 长城
Great Wall

3 黄山
Mount Huangshan

4 武夷山
Mount Wuyi

5 丽江古城
Old Town of Lijiang

6 杭州西湖文化景区
West Lake Cultural Landscape of Hangzhou

7 鼓浪屿：历史国际社区
Kulangsu,a Historic International Settlement

8 泰山
Mount Taishan

9 明清皇帝陵寝
Imperial Tombs of the Ming and Qing Dynasties

10 秦始皇陵及兵马俑
Mausoleum of the First Qin Emperor

11 五台山
Mount Wutai

12 丝绸之路：长安－天山廊道的路网
Silk Roads: the Routes Network of Chang'an–Tianshan Corridor

13 莫高窟
Mogao Caves

14 福建土楼
Fujian Tulou

15 北京皇家园林－颐和园
Summer Palace,an Imperial Garden in Beijing

16 庐山国家公园
Lushan National Park

17 大运河
The Grand Canal

18 平遥古城
Ancient City of Ping Yao

19 北京皇家祭坛－天坛
Temple of Heaven: an Imperial Sacrificial Altar in Beijing

20 武当山古建筑群
Ancient Building Complex in the Wudang Mountains

21 曲阜孔庙、孔林和孔府
Temple and Cemetery of Confucius and the Kong Family Mansion in Qufu

22 布达拉宫古建筑群
Historic Ensemble of the Potala Palace, Lhasa

23 周口店北京人遗址
Peking Man Site at Zhoukoudian

24 龙门石窟
Longmen Grottoes

25 承德避暑山庄及其周围寺庙
Mountain Resort and its Outlying Temples, Chengde

26 青城山－都江堰
Mount Qingcheng and the Dujiangyan Irrigation System

27 大足石刻
Dazu Rock Carvings

28 红河哈尼梯田文化景观
Cultural Landscape of Honghe Hani Rice Terraces

29 峨眉山－乐山大佛
Mount Emei Scenic Area, including Leshan Giant Buddha Scenic Area

30 云冈石窟
Yungang Grottoes

31 左江花山岩画文化景观
Zuojiang Huashan Rock Art Cultural Landscape

32 高句丽王城、王陵及墓葬
Capital Cities and Tombs of the Ancient Koguryo Kingdom

33 登封"天地之中"历史建筑群
Historic Monuments of Dengfeng in "The Centre of Heaven and Earth"

34 殷墟
Yin Xu

35 苏州古典园林
Classical Gardens of Suzhou

36 元上都遗址
Site of Xanadu

37 土司遗址
Tusi Sites

38 皖南古村落－西递宏村
Ancient Villages in Southern Anhui – Xidi and Hongcun

39 澳门历史城区
Historic center of Macao

40 开平碉楼与村落
Kaiping Diaolou and Villages

长城受水的影响可能就比石砌长城要大。究竟降水达到多少毫米的时候会对长城的结构稳定性形成影响，就需要在积累了足够多的数据之后进行量化分析。预警指标不明确，是目前长城监测工作的一个短板。

监测方案方面。我们以长城保护员的巡查周期为例。由于各地长城的交通条件和保存条件差异明显，我们无法对全国长城保护员的巡查周期进行统一规定。交通便利、生产建设活动频繁、长城安全隐患较大的地区，巡查周期就应当尽量短；而一些崇山峻岭、沙漠戈壁中的长城段落，沿线人迹罕至，本体状态相对稳定，同时又很难到达，在确定巡查周期时，就要考虑巡查条件和成本问题。

2. 统筹协调

长城资源调查范围覆盖东经 30.5°–75.2°，北纬 32.5°–50.3°，高程海拔 0-3400 米，地域面积超过 4 万平方公里。调查范围之广、数据量之大，前所未有。"长城资源调查"项目采用多种技术手段采集了超过 5TB 的长城数据[15]。对如此大规模的文化遗产开展监测工作，既要总体把握情况，又要注重细节，做到宏观与微观相结合，人与技术相结合。

受国家文物局委托，中国文化遗产研究院和国家基础地理信息中心基于长城资源调查成果，建立了长城资源信息数据库，设计与构建了可实现多条件查询、实时更新、实时监测的"长城资源保护管理信息系统"。

"长城资源保护管理信息系统"分为数据管理、数据应用和公众服务三个子系统。数据管理系统主要对长城资源数据进行存储、更新；数据应用系统（http://www.greatwallheritage.com）主要面向专业管理和研究人员，需要申请账号登录，用于长城保护管理业务，包括的填报、审核、查询、复杂统计、地图定位、地图制作与浏览等；公众服务子系统即面向社会开放的"中国长城遗产"网站（http://www.greatwallheritage.cn），已于 2016 年 12 月 1 日正式上线。

目前信息系统的数据包括各时期长城资源调查数据，长城认定数据和长城保护管理业务数据，包括长城保护规划、长城保护工程、涉及长城保护范围的建设工程等项目数据，以及长城日常养护、"四有"工作、执法巡查、案件督查及相关法律文件、长城资源利用（旅游、宣传教育等）等，实现了各类数据之间的交互查询和检索（图 3）。

"长城资源保护管理信息系统"提供了精确的长城地图，对于长城的统一管理，尤其是对位于行政区边界的长城管辖权的明确具有重要作用。为长城的全线监测提供了数据和技术支撑，使之成为可能。以此为基础，我们尝试通过多种手段，对长城开展不同尺度的监测工作，以评估各种技术在不同环境条件下的长城监测效果。

2016 年，国家文物局督察司曾在陕西省府谷县[17]、甘肃省敦煌市和嘉峪关市、张家口市崇礼区[18]等地进行了长城无人机巡查，通过多时段的航片对比，发现了长城资源调查工作结束之后，建设活动导致的一些长城破坏现象（图 4）[1]。但这属于事后发现，长城已经遭受了破坏。为探索无人机技术在长城监测中的应用前景，2017 年，国家文物局委托中国文化遗产研究院进行长城无人机监测试点工作。同年开始，中国文化遗产研究院委托中国科学院遥感与数字地球研究所对河北省张家口市崇礼区和宁夏回族自治区青铜峡市境内的长城开展了可以监测到长城的毫米级形变的雷达差分干涉测量（DinSAR，后文简称雷达干涉）试点工作，对两个县域内长城的结构稳定性及其影响因素进行宏观的评估，发现了监测区

1　图片已经过脱密处理，并获得了作者使用授权。

lected, the indicators which are assessed, and the methods which are deployed, should all be determined according to the actual situation of each particular site or section.

Currently, personnel involved in monitoring the Great Wall are mainly publicly employed professional cultural heritage management staff, civilian Great Wall Patrollers, and volunteers. There are about 5,000 professional cultural heritage staff engaged in the management of the Great Wall[13], most of whom do not work full-time on the Great Wall. The number of staff employed to work on the Great Wall is apparently insufficient to manage all 21,000 km of the Great Wall as well as to support its monitoring.

As a supplement to professional managers, over 5,000 Great Wall Patrollers were engaged from local residents by governments or by local cultural heritage departments along the Great Wall[14] to conduct regular inspections and report Great Wall incidents to the departments. Most Great Wall Patrollers have not been professionally trained. There is no accurate statistical data on the number and work of non-governmental volunteers. However, NCHA's Cultural Relics Report Centre hotline data shows that the number of reports (mostly from volunteers from the general public) about illegal actions on the Great Wall has been increasing year by year since 2010, making this contribution indispensible.

General threats to the monument can be identified by these employees and by Patrollers. However, the identification of some particular risks arising from specific activities along the Great Wall relies on more professional teams. For example, conservation and restoration projects will, to a greater or lesser extent, alter the Great Wall's original form. Whether this change is positive, or the engineering and design concepts are scientifically-based, or the construction process meets the design requirements, or not, etc., are issues that need to be monitored by professionals such as the resident designers or independent supervisors of restoration projects.

The Great Wall faces multiple risks which vary dramatically across its different sections. Taking the impact of precipitation as an example, some parts of the Great Wall are located in desert areas with an average annual precipitation of less than 100mm where flooding is infrequent but potentially very damaging. The impact of the same level of precipitation for sections of the Great Wall made of different materials would, however, be very different; for example, the impact of water intrusion on the rammed-earth walls would be greater than that on the stone walls.

Quantitative analysis is needed after accumulating enough data to determine the degree of influence of precipitation on the structural stability of each section of the Great Wall. The early warning indicators are still not adequately defined, which is a crucial weakness in monitoring the Great Wall.

In reality, we cannot uniformly stipulate an appropriate inspection cycle for the Great Wall Patrollers because the levels of risk to the Great Wall in different sections vary considerably. In areas which are readily accessible and where there are frequent construction projects, the inspection cycle should be as short as possible, while in less accessible places, such as mountainous areas, deserts or depopulated zones where the condition of the Great Wall is currently relatively stable, the costs of inspection need to be carefully calculated.

Coordinating monitoring as a whole

The Great Wall remains cover an area of more than 40,000 km² within 30.5°to 75.2°E, 32.5°to 50.3°N, and

图 3

升级后的长城资源保护管理信息系统 – 应用子系统主页面 [16]

Fig. 3

The Home page of the Great Wall Resource Information System

内若干处结构不稳定或形变较明显的长城段落 [19]。影像这些长城点段结构稳定性的因素包括洪水、降雨等自然因素，也包括道路建设、开矿等人类活动，各影响因素与具体的长城点段一一对应（图 5）[1]。在 2018 年国家文物局开展的汛期长城险情评估工作中，这一监测结果得到了印证 [20]。

无论雷达干涉，还是无人机巡查，其监测结果都需要现场验证。这项工作，可以结合长城保护员的巡查工作来完成。为了便利长城保护员的日常工作，提高长城巡查数据的采集效率、准确度和进行数据分析，中国文化遗产研究院与国信司南（北京）地理信息技术有限公司合作研发了"长城监测巡查系统"应用程序（后文简称巡查 app）。该程序与"长城资源保护管理信息系统"基于相同技术，并使用同一数据库，集成了长城资源认定数据和基于天地图的长城分布图，可下载到手机端，对长城点段、保护员巡查路线等进行定位，上传照片、巡查记录，并与旧照片进行对比。目前，该程序的安卓与 IOS 版本均已上线。

巡查 app 作为人工巡查的辅助手段，致力于发挥人在长城监测工作中的潜力。目前，对于落砖、裂缝发育等比较轻微的长城变化，通过肉眼观察来识别，仍然是最有效、成本最低的方式。我们在河北省迁西县、张家口市崇礼区、滦平县金山岭长城景区，以及宁夏回族自治区青铜峡市聘用了一些长城保护员，请他们试用巡查 app 采集长城监测信息，目前已积累了两年的数据。一方面可以在一个相对小的区域内，对各长城点段的主要风险因素进行识别和风险高低的对比。通过观察，我们已经发现在迁西县榆木岭长城大岭寨口北山 01 号敌台（认定编号 130227352101170055，俗称羊圈楼）附近人类活动频率明显比周边其他长城点段要高，敌台本体变化也更明显，下一步，我们将与当地文物管理机构取得联系，

---

1 图片已经过脱密处理，并获得了作者使用授权。

between 0-3400m above sea level. The scope of its survey and the amount of data generated are unprecedented. During the GWRS, various technical means were applied and more than 5Tb of Great Wall data were collected[15]. To monitor such a large-scale cultural heritage site, we should not only assess the overall situation, but also consider section specific details, so as to integrate macro and micro data, and combine human observation with technological monitoring.

As authorised by NCHA, CACH, together with the Geo-Compass Information Technology Co. Ltd (GCITC), has established the Great Wall Resource Information Database, and developed the Great Wall Resource Information System. These have enabled multi-condition interrogation and real-time updates, and they combine three subsystems of Data management (DM), application (DA) and public service (PS).

DM mainly stores and updates Great Wall resource data, while DA (http://www.greatwallheritage.com) enables data rewriting, reporting and auditing, searching, advanced statistical analysis, coordinate positioning, cartography and browsing, etc., for management and research. A personal identification access application is open to professional institutes and scholars. PS (http://www.greatwallheritage.cn) is a website available for the general public, which went online on 1st December 2016.

At present, the System contains data from the results of the GWRS and archives of the Great Wall management systems, including planning, conservation and restoration projects, and construction projects including those in the buffer zone of the Great Wall sites, and routine maintenance. It also contains data on the archives of the legal prerequisites for Chinese cultural heritage sites known as the 'Four haves'. Legislation and law en-

(a) 变化前 Before　　　　　　　(b) 变化后 After

图 4

无人机巡查监测所见长城沿线地物变化情况

Fig. 4

Ground feature changes along the Great Wall observed by UAV inspection

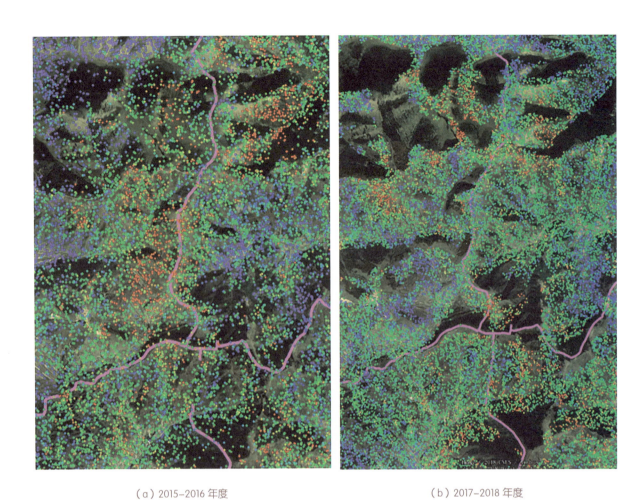

（a）2015–2016 年度　　　　　　　　　　　（b）2017–2018 年度

图 5
通过雷达干涉监测发现的结构不稳定长城点段[20]
Fig. 5
Structural instability of the Great Wall in 2015-2016 discovered by DInSAR (The red areas are in danger)

并建议他们重点关注这座敌台，采取相应保护措施。另一方面，崇礼区和青铜峡市的雷达干涉、无人机巡查监测结果也得到了部分验证。

3. 社会参与

社会的高关注度，决定了长城监测必须是一个开放性的工作。我们尽可能地坚持开放原则，并引导社会力量参与长城的长期监测。

例如，2012 年 6 月，长城资源认定工作完成，国家文物局在北京居庸关长城脚下举行了新闻发布会，通过中央电视台将长城长度、分布情况等最新数据第一时间即向社会公布。

"长城资源保护管理信息系统"和"巡查app"也都建立了面向专业人士和社会公众的两个版本。"长城资源保护管理信息系统 – 公众服务子系统（中国长城遗产网）"将经过脱密处理的长城资源详细数据全部公布于众；巡查 app 设计了普通游客登录页面。游客版操作更简单，任何使用 app 的人都可以上传

forcement, inspection and supervision and use (in respect of tourism, promotion and education, etc.), are also included. Interactive interrogation and retrieval of all data mentioned above is also enabled through the system (Fig. 3).

The Great Wall Resources Information System (GWRIS) provides an accurate map of the Great Wall. This plays an important role in inter-administrative management, especially in clarifying jurisdiction of the Great Wall along administrative boundaries. Data and technical support have made it possible to carry out monitoring work on different scales by various means, in order to evaluate the effectiveness of these methods under different environmental conditions.

In 2016, a UAV survey project was conducted by the Supervisory Department of NCHA in Fugu County of Shaanxi Province[17], Dunhuang and Jiayuguan of Gansu Province, and Chongli District of Zhangjiakou City, Hebei province[18]. By comparing aerial photographs over different years, damage to the Great Wall caused by construction activities was discovered (fig. 4). This damage had, however, already happened. In order to explore the potential application of UAV technology in WHS monitoring, in 2017 NCHA commissioned CACH to carry out a pilot UAV monitoring programme on the Great Wall. In cooperation with the Institute of Remote Sensing and Digital Earth, Chinese Academy of Sciences (RADI), the Small Baseline Subsets Approach (SBSA) of Differential Interferometric Synthetic Aperture Radar (DInSAR) was applied to detect millimetre-scale degradation of the Great Wall in Chongli District of Zhangjiakou City, Hebei Province, and Qingtongxia City, Ningxia Autonomous Region, to evaluate the structural stability of the Great Wall. It also assessed the factors influencing stability, including natural factors such as flood and rainfall, as well as human activities such as road construction and mining, which corresponded to specific sections of the Great Wall in the two counties. Several unstable structures or obvious problems were found[19] (Fig. 5). The result above has been confirmed by field inspection on flood-season risk assessment of the Great Wall conducted by NCHA in 2018[20].

To facilitate the work of the Great Wall Patrollers, and to improve the efficiency, accuracy and amount of data they collect, CACH and GCITC collaborated to develop the smartphone application "Wandering Great Wall" (Great Wall Monitoring and Patrolling System, abbreviated as WGW hereafter). Sharing the same technology and the same database, WGW integrates data from the Great Wall resource survey and identification, and the Great Wall distribution map based on the national map site "Tianditu", which can locate the coordinates of sections of the Great Wall, as well as the inspection routes of the Patrollers. Photos and patrolling records in text form can be uploaded for multiphase image/text contrast. Both Android and IOS versions of the app are currently online.

As a supplementary method of on-site inspection, WGW is devoted to maximising the use of human resources in monitoring the Great Wall. For identifying changes such as fallen bricks and the development of structural cracks, on-site inspection is still the most effective and low-cost method of monitoring. We have engaged some Great Wall Patrollers in Qianxi County, Chongli District, Jinshanling Great Wall Scenic Spot of Luanping County, and Qingtongxia City, to collect data on the Great Wall through WGW as an experiment. This has enabled the main risk factors of each Great Wall section to be identified and compared within a relatively small area.

长城照片，上报长城破坏等（图6）。

　　中国文化遗产研究院、北京市文物局等专业机构与民间组织"长城小站"建立了密切的联系，与他们共同开展长城保护宣传教育活动，并请他们协助监督北京市、山西省等地的长城保护工作。在他们的支持下，一系列长城违法案件被及时发现和上报，并得到了妥善处理。

　　中国国内还有一批热情的民间志愿者，多年来自发地进行长城老照片收集、定位和复拍，他们收集的老照片，拍摄年代最早可以上溯至19世纪末。通过他们的工作，我们能够了解到100年间长城的变化情况，专业人员依靠这些材料，得以对一些长城点段保存状况、保护维修理念变化进行总结和评估。

　　此外，国家文物局2017年度长城执法专项督察工作还将社会力量参与长城保护情况作为考核项目之一，具体指标包括各地长城管理机构是否与当地相关社会组织建立联系、是否建立社会举报热线等。

三、长城监测的挑战与展望

　　长城的破坏几乎每天都在发生，目前我们的管理力量与水平却远远不足以对长城全线进行实时有效的监控。我们认为，长城保护的紧迫性与长城监测研究的长期性之间的矛盾，在短期内不可能彻底解决。

图6

"长城漫步" app 手机端页面（中国文化遗产研究院国信司南 提供）

Fig. 6

Layouts of the "Wandering Great Wall" app (© CACH & Geo-Compass)

Through observation of the WGW data accumulated over two years, we have found that the frequency of human activities near Dalingzhaikou Beishan tower No. 01 in Qianxi County (coded 130227352101170055, commonly known as Sheepfold Tower) is much higher than that of other sections of the Great Wall around it, and the deformation of the tower itself is obvious. We contacted the local authority and recommended that they take suitable protective measures for this tower. It has also enabled the results of DInSAR and UAV inspection in Chongli District and Qingtongxia City to be partially verified by WGW.

Social participation

Due to the high level of public interest in and concern for the Great Wall, the monitoring of the Great Wall must be openly presented to the public. We have endeavoured to embrace this and facilitate public access to ongoing monitoring information concerning the Great Wall.

As an example of this, in June 2012, as soon as the identification of Great Wall Resources was completed, a press conference was held by SACH at the foot of the Great Wall in Juyongguan, Beijing, to release the latest data on the length and distribution of the Great Wall to the public through CCTV.

The GWRIS and WGW then together established two versions of the survey data, one for professionals and one for the public. GWRIS-PS released all declassified data from the Great Wall survey, while WGW designed a tourist edition which is easier to operate. Anyone who uses WGW can upload photos of the Great Wall and report damage to the authorities through it (Fig. 6).

Professional institutions, such as CACH and the Beijing Municipal Administration of Cultural Heritage, have established close contacts with third-sector organisations such as the "Great Wall Station" (GWS); they have have jointly carried out promotional and education activities for the protection of the Great Wall, and have invited people to assist in supervising the management of the Great Wall. With public support, a series of cases of damage to the Great Wall were reported and handled properly and promptly.

There is also a group of enthusiastic local history volunteers in China who have spontaneously collected, identified and reproduced old photographs of the Great Wall dating back to late 19th century. Their work has greatly benefited professionals in understanding the changes in the past century, and can help to indicate and evaluate progress in the development of conservation of the Great Wall over this period.

In addition, the official supervision for Law Enforcement of the Great Wall also takes public involvement as one of its assessment criteria. Specific indicators included the channels and types of engagement between local authorities and the public.

CHALLENGES AND OUTLOOK

Destruction of elements of the Great Wall is ongoing, and our current management capacity is far from being enough to monitor the whole line of the Great Wall in real time and effectively. We believe that the competing priorities of monitoring sections currently at risk and of more general long-term monitoring of

但如果我们能够把握几个关键性挑战，采取"小步快走"的方式积极加以应对，相信这对矛盾在可预见的未来，可以得到缓解。具体说来，有如下几个方面：

（一）走出概念误区，明确监测目的

根据英汉词典的解释，"监测"（monitoring）有"监听、监视、监控、追踪、检查"等含义[21]。牛津美国辞典对"monitor"的解释是"保持监视，对工作进行记录、测试或者控制"[22]。其目的在于"系统持续收集并分析一段时间内工作进程信息，鉴别优缺点，为负责这项工作的人提供充分信息，使他们能够在恰当时间做出恰当决定以提高质量"[23]。总而言之，世界遗产监测，就是通过周期性的相关数据采集，对世界遗产破坏风险进行管控。基于以上认识，以"四有"工作、文物保护员日常巡护和文物部门定期文物执法巡查为代表的传统文物保护管理工作均可以视为监测工作的组成部分。

这样看来，中文似乎没有一个专门的词汇与"monitoring"相对应。我们现在使用的"监测"一词的含义，倾向于利用科学仪器或科技手段来监控和检测。

前面提到，中国世界遗产监测出现一个注重技术应用的趋势。这一趋势，再加翻译的不准确，导致形成一种误解，即"监测"就是"技术监测"。当谈到"监测"时，往往侧重于建设信息系统和使用各种仪器设备。相比之下，监测作为一种管理手段的本质则倾向于被忽略。尽管国家文物局和中国世界文化遗产中心的相关监测文件明确监测含义的广泛性，但在包括长城在内的中国世界遗产监测工作中仍普遍存在这一问题。

由此导致监测工作被当作单纯的数据采集手段。就长城而言，各地采集了海量的监测数据，但这些数据是否是监测所需要的，目前并没有权威的标准和判断。目的性的模糊，又致使针对这些长城监测数据进行的有效分析也非常少。这样一来，监测工作也就失去了意义。因此，走出概念误区，是中国长城监测需要解决的首要问题。只有正确理解了监测的含义，才能明确监测的目的，保证监测工作的有效。国家文物局连续两年举办了长城保护管理培训班，向基层长城管理者传播科学的长城保护理念，包括长城监测的正确认识。目前，长城沿线97个设区市的长城管理机构负责人已经完成了轮训，接下来，培训对象将扩展到县级长城管理机构和长城保护员，从而逐步扭转各地"为监测而监测"的工作局面。随着国内外文物工作交流日益密切，将继续推动长城监测工作的改善。

（二）更加协调的管理，更加均衡的工作

根据《中华人民共和国文物保护法》的相关规定，中国的文物保护制度遵循"属地管理"的原则，即遗产地所在行政区（主要是县级行政区）对遗产地行使管辖权。

2016年国家文物局长城文物行政执法专项督察数据显示，长城沿线共有485个各类机构，包括地方政府、文物局、文物管理所、文化馆、博物馆等不同性质的机构对长城行使管理权[14]。一方面，长城过于庞大，建立统一管理机构的条件目前还不成熟，因此各地的长城管理状况各异，监测数据的采集也没有统一标准。各地监测资源不均衡，监测能力与水平参差不齐。另一方面，在当代中国，很多长城段落成为行政区的边界，这样一来，就造成了长城的管辖权的模糊，甚至冲突，进而形成数据壁垒。一些长城点段多头管理，另一些则无人问津，同时各地监测数据又不能共享。这对长城的监测工作而言，是

the Great Wall cannot be resolved in the short term, but may be alleviated in the foreseeable future if we can grasp several key challenges and take a 'small step and quick walk' approach to positively address issues such as:

Clarifying the meaning and purpose of monitoring

'Monitoring' is defined as "surveillance, supervision, controlling, tracking and checking"[21]. The Oxford American Dictionary interprets the verb 'monitor' as "to keep watch over, to record or test or control the working of"[22]. Monitoring is "the systematic and continuous collecting and analysing of information about the progress of a piece of work over time, to identify strengths and weaknesses and to provide the people responsible for the work with sufficient information to make the right decisions at the right time in order to improve its quality"[23]. In short, World Heritage Monitoring is to control the risk of damage to World Heritage Sites through periodic data collection. Based on this understanding, the traditional Chinese methods of protection management such as the 'Four Haves', routine patrolling, and the supervision of law enforcement, can be regarded as integral parts of monitoring.

It seems, however, that there is no Chinese word corresponding to Western meanings of 'monitoring'. The use of the term 'monitoring' in China is now associated with detecting and gauging the condition of the monument through scientific instruments or technological methods.

The trend of China's World Heritage monitoring, as mentioned above, has been towards the application of technical means. This trend, coupled with inaccurate translation, has encouraged the perception that 'monitoring' is equal to 'technical measurement'. When 'monitoring' is discussed, the focus tends to center on information systems, instruments and equipment, while the nature of monitoring as a tool of management tends to be neglected. This is despite clear guidance from NCHA and WCHCC on the broader definition of monitoring. These issues are at the heart of many of the current problems of monitoring the Great Wall.

Due to this, monitoring is often regarded as primarily a process of data acquisition. As far as the Great Wall is concerned, a considerable amount of monitoring data has been collected with no authoritative standard to judge whether this data is useful or not. What is lacking is clarity of purpose in collecting this data and general co-ordination in its collation and analysis, which reduces the value of monitoring overall. Therefore, addressing these issues and promoting more holistic approaches should be given top priority in improving the monitoring of the Great Wall. Only through correctly understanding its purpose can monitoring be clearly defined and its effectiveness be improved.

The good news is that for two consecutive years, NCHA has held training courses on the protection and management of the Great Wall to disseminate scientific ideas on the protection of the Great Wall - including the correct understanding of monitoring - to front-line cultural heritage managers. Trainees from 97 municipalities along the Great Wall have now completed the cycle of training, which will now be extended to county-level officials and Great Wall Patrollers, thus gradually changing the 'monitoring for monitoring's sake' attitude across the country. It is now antic-

一个极大的障碍。

不仅如此，这些问题的解决，还有赖国家层面加强顶层设计，不仅加强各级文物系统的统筹协调，还要加强与文物系统之外规划、土地、环境、旅游、财政等政府部门的协调，加强与社会力量、当地社区和公众的协调，理顺管理机制，加强统筹，优化配置资源，也应当为各地长城管理机构之间的沟通协调创造条件。

（三）监测成本控制

长城的庞大体量，以及中国世界遗产监测的"唯技术"倾向，都极易导致长城监测成本高昂。以下仅据两例加以测算说明：

中国文化遗产研究院与中科院遥感所合作开展的雷达干涉监测试点工作覆盖了两个县域，采用开源中分辨率 SAR 卫星（Sentinel-1）数据，进行了为期一年、尺度为 250×200 平方公里的监测工作，成本为十余万元人民币，相当于甘肃省 2017 年城镇非私营单位从业人员平均工资（63374 元 / 年）的 2 到 3 倍左右，或该省当年最低工资标准（1320–1470 元 / 月）的 6 至 7 倍[24]。若采用高分辨率卫星数据，再加上数据处理、管理等费用，则成本将达到百万级。而这一成本所覆盖的监测范围仅占长城的 0.5%。

总而言之，在长城全线开展高技术含量的监测工作，并不现实。我们仍然需要立足现有经济、技术和制度条件，探索更加经济有效的，具有普遍适用性的长城监测方法。

（四）更有效的宣传和舆论引导

长城受到社会关注程度高，长城的社会参与程度也很高，决定了社会舆情监测的重要性。公众参与程度越高，来自公众的监督甚至是批评也会越多。这一方面对于及时发现长城保护、维修和管理中存在的问题，但另一方面也可能会对长城管理带来压力，特别在公众不知情或不理解长城保护复杂性的情况下。因此长城保护管理相关机构应当重视沟通工作，向公众解释长城保护管理的各项规定及相关考虑。提高公众沟通的有效性，提高公众对长城保护管理的理解，有助于促进社会力量为长城保护管理做出更多积极贡献。

综上所述，经过 30 年的实践，中国长城监测工作取得了不俗的成绩，但也存在亟待解决的突出问题。总体而言，长城监测的关键是观念和制度，也就是人的因素，而不是技术。

当前的长城监测实践，除长城保护员的日常巡查和简单记录能够覆盖绝大多数长城点段之外，多数项目集中在几个很小的区域内进行，并且大都具有研究性质，或处于实验阶段，无论是数据还是经验的积累，都远远不够。然而从另一个角度来看，人工巡查监测是最容易推广的一种监测方法，并且存在巨大的发展潜力。我们的最终目的是能够绘制长城的整体动态风险地图，从而建立以问题和风险为导向、以社会力量为支撑的监测体系与管理机制，最终实现长城的预防性保护。技术手段的应用是这一系列操作的最末端，而理念的修正、制度的建立，工作的贯彻，甚至于技术的研发和操作，无不是由人来完成。发挥人的潜力，使技术服务于人，才是符合中国国情和长城实际的世界遗产监测发展之路。

ipated that increasingly frequent exchanges between cultural heritage managers in China and those in the rest of the world will further inform our thinking about how we can continue to improve the management and coordination of monitoring the Great Wall.

More coordinated monitoring management and activities

According to the "Law of the People's Republic of China on the Protection of Cultural Heritage", China's cultural heritage management system follows the principle of 'localised management'. That is, the authorities of the administrative region where the heritage site is located (mainly at the county level) exercise jurisdiction over cultural heritage sites.

The report of the "Special Supervision for Law Enforcement of the Great Wall 2016" showed that there are 485 heritage institutions along the Great Wall which are responsible for its management, including local governments, functional departments, institutes, museums, and other institutions of different types[14]. The conditions for establishing a unified management over the Great Wall are, however, not yet mature. Resources, capacities and capabilities for monitoring are uneven in different areas. In addition, in contemporary China many sections of the Great Wall have become the boundaries between administrative regions, where the jurisdiction over the Great Wall is blurred and conflicts occasionally happen, thus creating incompatibilities in data. Some sections of the Great Wall are managed by multiple institutions, while the management of others is neglected. And, of course, coordination is needed, not only within the heritage sector between different levels, but beyond, with other sectors such as planning, land management, environment, tourism, finance, etc., and with the third sector, local communities and the general public.

To solve these problems, top-level leadership - including overall planning, optimising resource allocation, and integrating management mechanisms - is needed to coordinate all endeavours.

Cost Control

The huge size of the Great Wall and the tendency towards 'technicalism' are likely to lead to a high cost of monitoring the Great Wall. The following two examples are given to illustrate this point:

The SBSA programme was deployed in two counties using open source medium-resolution SAR satellite (Sentinel-1) data and covering a scale of 250 by 200 km. It lasted for a year and cost over 100,000 RMB, which is about two to three times of the average wage of urban non-private employees (63,374 RMB per year), or eight to nine times of the minimum wage level (1,470 RMB per month) in Gansu Province in 2017[24]. The cost of using this high-resolution satellite data would reach millions of RMB, when the expenses of data processing and management are factored in. However, this programme only covered two counties - approximately 0.5% of the Great Wall.

In summary, carrying out high-tech monitoring work along the whole line of the Great Wall is currently financially unrealistic. More economical, effective and universally applicable monitoring methods for the Great Wall, based on current circumstances, are still to be explored.

More effective communication and the direction of public opinion

The public prominence of the Great Wall, and the greater level of public involvement in its conservation, as discussed elsewhere in this publication, emphasises the importance of understanding public perceptions and attitudes towards it. With greater public involvement comes greater public scrutiny, and even criticism of its management. This can beneficial, for example in identifying malpractice in the maintenance, restoration and management of the Great Wall. It can, however, also be detrimental to management of the Great Wall, particularly when it is ill-informed or based on lack of understanding of the complexity of managing the World Heritage Site. It is therefore incumbent on all those concerned with its management that they explain to the public how the Great Wall is managed and why it is managed in this way. Improvement of the effectiveness of these public communications, and therefore of public understanding of its management, would also contribute to enabling the general public to make more positive contributions to its monitoring and conservation.

In summary, after 30 years of initiatives, great achievements in monitoring the Great Wall of China have been made, but there are also outstanding problems to be solved. In essence, the keys to the effective monitoring of the Great Wall are primarily human factors, namely in understanding its principles and management functions, rather than its technological dimensions.

Among contemporary practices in monitoring the Great Wall, most of the new initiatives have been deployed in a few small areas, except for the daily patrols and simple observations of the Great Wall Patrollers, which cover most of the sections of the Great Wall. Most of those projects are of a research nature or are in their experimental stages, and have not yet produced sufficient data for analysis and assessment. However, from another point of view, on-site inspection is the easiest monitoring method to promote, and has great potential for further development. Our goal is to map the overall dynamic risks to the Great Wall, so as to establish a system and management mechanism which is focused upon identified dangers and risks and which is supported by the public, to achieve effective protection of the Great Wall. The application of technology should be the end stage of this process, and improving understanding of the principles of monitoring, the establishment of systems, the implementation of initiatives, and even the development and application of technology are each dependent on human initiative. By bringing human potential fully into play and making technology serve human beings, the monitoring and overall management of the Great Wall and of all China's World Heritage Sites can be enhanced through closer alignment with their specific requirements and characteristics, and within the wider context of present-day China.

参考文献
Bibliography

[1] 樊锦诗 . 基于世界文化遗产价值的世界文化遗产地的管理与监测——以敦煌莫高窟为例 [J]. 敦煌研究 ,2008(6):1-5+114.

Fan, J.S. "Management and Monitoring of World Cultural Heritage Sites Based on World Cultural Heritage Value: A Case Study of Dunhuang Mogao Grottoes." Dunhuang Research, 2008(6):1-5+114.

[2] 曾朝铭，顾巍 . 北京地区长城航空遥感调查 [J]. 文物，1987(7):60-67.

Zeng, C.M, and Gu, W. "Aerial Remote Sensing Survey of the Great Wall in Beijing." Cultural Relics, 1987(7): 60-67.

[3] 黎风，顾巍，曹灿霞 . 宁夏长城航空遥感调查研究 [J]. 国土资源遥感，1994(3):11-16.

Li, F., Gu, W., and Cao, C.X. "Aerial Remote Sensing Investigation and Research of the Great Wall in Ningxia." Land and Resources Remote Sensing, 1994(3): 11-16.

[4] 联合国教科文组织世界遗产委员会 . 实施保护世界自然与文化遗产公约的操作指南（1994 年修订版）[EB/OL]. 1994 年 12 月 12-17 日 .

UNESCO World Heritage Committee. Revision of the Operational Guidelines for the implementation of the World Heritage Convention.December 12-17, 1994.

http://whc.unesco.org/en/documents/?action=list&searchDocuments=Operational+Guideline&maxrows=106

[5] 中国文化遗产研究院 . 我国世界遗产保护管理现状及趋势分析——中国世界文化遗产 2017 年度总报告 [R]. 中国文化遗产，2018(6)：4-28.

CACH "World Cultural Heritage 2017 Annual Report: Analysis on the Status and Trend of World Cultural Heritage Protection and Management in China." China Cultural Heritage, 2018(6): 4-28.

[6] 王毅，赵云 . 建立中国的世界文化遗产反应性监测机制刍议 [J]. 中国文物科学研究，2016(2): 43-45.

Wang, Y., and Zhao, Y. "On Establishment of China's World Cultural Heritage Responsive Monitoring Mechanism." Chinese Research on Cultural Heritage Science, 2016(2): 43-45.

[7] 国家文物局 . 长城保护工程（2005-2014）总体工作方案 [R].2005 年 11 月 .

SACH. General Work Programme of Great Wall Conservation Project (2005-2014). In Handbook of Great Wall Resources Survey. Beijing: 2010:8-13.

[8] 国家文物局 . 长城资源认定资料手册 [R]. 内部资料 . 北京：2012：15.

SACH. "Handbook on the Identification of the Great Wall Resources". Beijing: 2012:

[9] 单霁翔 . 大型线性文化遗产保护初论：突破与压力 [J]. 南方文物，2006(3):02-05.

Shan, J.X. "Preliminary Discussion on the Protection of Large-scale Linear or Serial Cultural Heritages:

Breakthrough and Pressure." Relics from South, 2006(3): 2-5.

[10] 国务院扶贫开发领导小组办公室网站 [EB/OL].2012-3-19.

The State Council Leading Group Office of Poverty Allevation and Development. 2012. http://www.cpad. gov.cn/publicfiles/business/htmlfiles/FPB/fpyw/201203/175445.html.

[11] 八达岭长城文化艺术协会.关于对半个世纪八达岭长城接待国家元首、政府首脑情况的调研. 中国长城学会编，万里长城暨中国长城学会优秀文集 [C]. 北京：2005：129-134.

Badaling Great Wall Culture and Art Association. A survey on the reception of heads of state and government by the Badaling Great Wall for half a century was conducted. In The Great Wall and Excellent Collection of Works of the China Great Wall Society, edited by CGWS. Beijing: 2005: 129-134.

[12] 中国文化遗产研究院.我国世界遗产保护管理现状及趋势分析——中国世界文化遗产 2017 年度 总报告 [J]. 中国文化遗产，2018(6): 4-28.

CACH. "World Cultural Heritage 2017 Annual Report: Analysis on the Status and Trend of World Cultural Heritage Protection and Management in China." China Cultural Heritage, 2019(6): 4-28.

[13] 国家文物局.长城资源保护管理信息系统 [EB/OL].2016.

SACH. Great Wall Resource Protection Management Information System. 2016.

http://www.greatwallheritage.com.

[14] 中国文化遗产研究院."2017 年度长城执法专项督察"项目研究报告 [R]. 北京：2018:125.

CACH. Research Report on "Special Supervision of Administrative Law Enforcement on the Great Wall 2017". Beijing: 2018: 125.

[15] 于冰、许礼林、张依萌.空间信息技术在长城资源调查中的应用进展 [J]. 中国文物科学研究， 2015(1): 67-73.

Yu, B., Xu, L.L., and Zhang, Y.M. "Progress in the Application of Spatial Information Technology in the Investigation of Great Wall Resources." Chinese Research on Cultural Heritage Science, 2015(1): 67-73.

[16] 图片来源：国家文物局"长城资源保护管理信息系统".

Image source: NCAH. Great Wall Resource Information System.

http://www.greatwallheritage.com.

[17] 航天天绘科技有限公司.国家文物局陕西省府谷县明长城无人机＋卫星遥感监测试点项目总结 报告 [R].2016: 28-34.

Hangtian Tianhui Technology Co. Ltd. NCHA, Report on Pilot Project of Ming Great Wall UAV+Satellite Remote Sensing Monitoring in Fugu County, Shaanxi Province. Beijing: 2016: 28-34.

[18] 中国文化遗产研究院，国信司南（北京）地理信息技术有限公司.长城无人机监测及数据处理 项目 - 结项报告 [R]. 北京：2018.

CACH, Geo-Compass. The Great Wall UAV Surveillance and Data Processing Project. Beijing: 2018.

[19] 陈富龙.明长城监测试点县域雷达遥感监测项目工作报告 [R]. 中国科学院遥感与数字地球研究 所，2018 年 7 月.

Chen, F.L. Report on the radar remote sensing monitoring pilot project of Ming Great Wall. RADI, Beijing: 2018.

[20] 张依萌，刘文艳，许慧君 ."重大文化遗产地综合保护与利用研究——以长城为例" 研究报告 [R]. 中国文化遗产研究院，北京：2018 年 7 月 .

Zhang, Y.M., Liu, W.Y., Xu, H.J., and Li, D.W. Research Report on "Comprehensive Protection and Utilization of Major Cultural Heritage Sites - Taking the Great Wall as an Example". CACH, Beijing: 2018.

[21] 新英汉词典编写组 . 新英汉词典 [M]. 上海：上海人民出版社 .1976:950.

New English-Chinese Dictionary Writing Group. New English-Chinese Dictionary. Shanghai: Shanghai People's Publishing House, 1976:950.

[22] 牛津大学 . 牛津美国辞典 [M]. 牛津：牛津大学出版社，1980:576.

Oxford University. Oxford American Dictionary. Oxford: Oxford University Press, 1980:576.

[23]Gosling L. and Edwards M. Toolkits - A Practical Guide to Assessment Monitoring, Review and Evaluation (apud Abbot K. and Guijt I., 1998). In Monitoring World Heritage. Vicenza: Save the Children Fund, 1995:115.

L. 高斯林，M. 爱德华兹 . 工具包 - 评估监测、评论和评定的实用指南 (二次参考 K. 阿博特，I. 盖特 1998)[M]. 监测世界遗产 . 维琴察：救助儿童基金会，1995:115.

[24] 甘肃省统计局 .2018 甘肃发展年鉴 [EB/OL].

Gansu Province Bureau of Statistics . Gansu Development Yearbook 2018.

http://www.gstj.gov.cn/tjnj/2018/indexch.htm.

Chapter Four
Tourist Management and Social Engagement

内蒙古秦长城（摄影：于 冰）
Qin Great Wall in Inner Mogolia (© Yu Bing)

第四章
长城游客管理和社会参与

豪塞斯特兹峭壁（版权：Roger Clegg）
Houseteads Crags (© Roger Clegg)

HADRIAN'S WALL - TOURISM, ACCESS AND ITS CONSEQUENCES: MANAGING THE HADRIAN'S WALL PATH NATIONAL TRAIL

Paget Lazzari, Mike Collins

Northumberland National Park Authority - Hexham - UK and Historic England - Newcastle upon Tyne –UK

Abstract

This paper explores the creation and management of the Hadrian's Wall Path National Trail. Now a key part of public access and enjoyment of the Wall, the paper explores how initial concerns about the impact of the Trail were overcome during its initial planning and the key principles that inform its management. The paper goes on to look at practical decision-making on the Trail, measures taken to help the efficiency and prioritisation of management works, and the vitally important role that volunteers play in this.

Keywords: Hadrian's Wall, Path, Trail, access, conservation.

INTRODUCTION - THE HADRIAN'S WALL PATH NATIONAL TRAIL

The Hadrian's Wall Path National Trail ('the Trail') runs for 134km across the north of England, following where possible the line of the Roman frontier. The majority of its route is on land that is privately owned, but where the public has the right to follow a path. Its creation has given improved access to the public interested in the archaeology of the Wall, as well as to those wanting to enjoy the countryside more generally. The Trail was created with both these audiences in mind, one of a family of 16 National Trails, which together are thought to represent the best walking that England and Wales have to offer, alongside over 190,000km of publically accessible paths (Rights of Way).

CREATION OF THE TRAIL

The process that led to the creation of the Trail took more than half a century to develop and it needs to be seen in the context of the development of countryside access in the UK more generally. Although the creation of long-distance footpaths had been suggested from the early 1930s, it wasn't until the government's National Parks Committee Report of 1947 that the idea of a network of such paths started to be promoted.

On Hadrian's Wall this idea of a path along the Wall gradually began to be developed. From the 1960s onwards, archaeologists and others interested in conservation were also becoming increasingly concerned about the impact on the remains of the Roman frontier of the large numbers of visitors to the Wall. The creation of a path along the Wall gradually began to be seen as a potential way to address some of these concerns, particularly

哈德良长城的旅游、通道及其后续效应：如何管理哈德良长城国家步道

帕吉特·拉扎里

（诺桑伯兰国家公园管理局，英国赫克瑟姆）

麦克·考林斯

（英格兰遗产委员会，英国纽卡斯尔）

摘　要

本文介绍哈德良长城国家步道的创设与管理。今天的步道已成为大众走近长城，欣赏长城的重要方式。本文讨论的则是步道创立之初的规划阶段如何解决建设步道可能影响长城的种种顾虑，同时探讨影响其管理的几项关键原则。文章进而讨论步道的实际决策过程、改善管理效率和管理任务分级的相应措施以及志愿者在此过程中扮演的关键角色。

关键词：哈德良长城　小道　步道　通行　遗产保护

绪论：哈德良长城国家步道

哈德良长城国家步道（the Hadrian's Wall Path National Trail，简称"步道"）全长 134 公里，横穿英格兰北部，只要条件许可其路线紧随哈德良长城罗马边界。路线途经土地大部分为私人所有，不过行人有道路通行权。步道的修建使对长城考古感兴趣的公众能更好地走近长城，而那些仅仅想欣赏田园风光的公众也从中获益。步道在当初设计时就考虑到这两方面的需求，成为 16 条国家步道之一。在总长达 190000 公里的公众有权通行（路权）的小道（path）路网中，国家步道（National Trail）被认为是在英格兰与威尔士地区远足的最佳代表。

一、步道的产生

创设步道的筹备过程长达半个多世纪，与英国乡村通行设施发展的大背景息息相关。早在 20 世纪 30 年代初，便已有人提出要创设长距离步行通道，然而直到政府发布《1947 年国家公园委员会报告》，此类小道网络的理念才正式得到推广。

在哈德良长城，沿线建设小道的想法逐渐开始萌芽。20 世纪 60 年代开始，考古学家与其他关心遗产保护的热心人士越来越担心大量访客来到长城会影响罗马边界遗址。沿长城修建小道渐渐被视为可以消除此类顾虑的潜在方式，特别是这种形式可以引导游客观赏更大范围内的长城，而不是只集中参观长城中部少数几处重要遗址。

through the spreading of visitors along more of the Wall and away from just the key sites of its central sector.

Archaeological concerns

Despite this, as the idea of a path along the Wall developed slowly in the 1980s, many archaeologists remained concerned about its potential impact. These concerns centered not only on the direct impact of visitors attracted by the idea of being able to walk the Wall from end to end, but also on the impact on the setting of the Wall from the need to create more hard surfaced paths to deal with erosion, particularly in the wild upland landscape of the central sector within Northumberland National Park. It became clear that for any path on Hadrian's Wall to be accepted these concerns would need to be addressed in the planning and implementation.

Approach to the management of the Trail

When the Countryside Commission (an independent body reporting to Government) was tasked in the late 1980s with creating a National Trail along the Wall, the details of their proposals were developed in consultation with both archaeologists and access experts. This included taking into account the archaeological sensitivity of the land and the ability of particular areas to stand up to heavy wear from visitors in the choice of route. It also led to the development of three guiding principles which would be applied to the Trail:

- The most appropriate surface for the path would be a grass sward. This would best protect the archaeology of the Wall and its setting, and provide the best experience to walkers. It was only where this surface could not be sustained that the Trail would consider a hard path surface to protect the archaeological remains;
- There would be a policy of pre-emptive management and maintenance. This would mean investing time and money in routine intensive grassland management, rather than in creation of hard-surfaced paths, to help sustain the grass surface that protects the underlying archaeology and its setting;
- All sections of the Trail would be managed and maintained to the highest standards.

The Countryside Commission set out this approach in its 1993 submission to the UK government asking formally for permission to create the Trail. This document also highlighted the other potential benefits that the project would bring:

- The creation of the Trail would allow the path which ran on top of Hadrian's Wall itself to be diverted to less sensitive ground alongside it;

Historically, in several locations in the central sector of the Wall existing visitor numbers were leading to erosion of the archaeological remains. Where the grass sward could not be sustained, the Trail would allow access to funds to install carefully-designed hard surfaces to address these issues (Figs. 1 & 2).

With the reassurances that this approach provided, the government was able to give permission for the Hadrian's Wall Trail, reassured that the archaeological community was broadly in support. Since the opening of the Trail in 2003 there have been periods of concern about its condition and the consequent impact on underlying archaeology. However, thanks to a great deal of hard work by Trail staff and continued financial support through Natural England (the

（一）考古方面的顾虑

尽管如此，当长城小道建设的概念在 20 世纪 80 年代缓慢发展时，仍有不少考古学家对其潜在影响深感忧虑。他们不仅担心开放长城全线步行通道，会吸引大量游客，这将带来直接影响；而且担心对长城周边环境的影响，因为需要铺设更为坚硬的路面以防范磨损，尤其是在诺桑伯兰国家公园腹地的原始山地景观之中。很显然，无论长城小道的建设方案如何，要想使其得到认可都必须在规划与实施环节解决上述问题。

（二）步道的管理措施

20 世纪 80 年代末，乡村管理委员会（隶属于中央政府的独立机构）受命进行哈德良长城国家步道的创设工作。征询考古学家及路政专家的意见后，委员会形成了一系列方案。在路线选择上，方案考虑了土地在考古学方面的敏感性，以及某些特殊区域承受因人流造成严重损耗的能力。这些意见最终形成三条指导性原则，后来应用于步道的实施：

- 步道表面以草皮覆盖为最佳，因为草皮可最大程度保护长城的考古价值及其周围环境，同时为徒步者提供最优体验。只有当草皮表面不可维持时，步道才可考虑铺设硬质路面，以保护考古遗迹。
- 步道管理和维护采取预防性保护策略：即将时间和资金投入日常草地的精心管理，而不是投入铺设硬质路面上，目的是通过维护草皮表面来保护下方的考古遗迹和周围环境。
- 步道各段都将按最高标准进行管理和维护。

乡村管理委员会将此原则纳入哈德良长城步道设计方案，并于 1993 年向英国政府提交文件，申请正式批准步道的创设。这份文件同时强调了创设步道会带来的其他潜在效益：

- 创设步道可将那些原本建于墙体上的小道改线，引导至墙体旁边不太脆弱的地带。

历史上，既有客流量已经对长城中段的若干处遗迹造成侵蚀。对于草皮不可维持的路段，允许申请拨款对步道铺设特殊设计的硬质路面（图 1、2）。

确认这措施的有效性后，并确认这些措施得到考古界人士广泛支持后，中央政府批准了哈德良长城步道建设。自 2003 年步道开放以来，人们曾几度担心步道状态及其对下方考古遗址产生的影响。不过，感谢步道管理局工作人员的巨大努力，感谢英格兰自然委员会（中央政府在自然环境保护和开放的顾问机构）提供的持续资金支持，避免了步道对考古遗址产生重大破坏，扩大长城考古遗迹的开放度也继续产生巨大的公共效益。

二、步道的当前运行

步道目前由两名全职维护巡查员及一名兼职步道官员管理，三人全部属于诺桑伯兰国家公园管理局。管理成本由以下两个渠道承担：中央政府拨款（通过英格兰自然委员会），以及各个相关高速公路管理部门（负责管理辖区范围内无障碍通道网络）提供的现金与物资资助。各高速公路管理部门、诺桑伯兰国家公园、英格兰自然委员会和英格兰遗产委员会组成伙伴关系，监督步道管理人员工作。目前的运营

Fig. 1
The Trail route at Cuddy's Crags (Northumberland) in 1991, showing the erosion of archaeological remains south of Hadrian's Wall (© Northumberland National Park Authority)
图 1
1991 年卡迪峭壁（诺森伯兰郡）的国家步道路线，显示出哈德良长城南部考古遗迹受到的侵蚀（版权：诺森伯兰国家公园管理局）

government's advisor on natural environment and access), significant damage to the archaeology of the Wall has been avoided and the great public benefits of increased access to this archaeology have continued to be realized.

CURRENT OPERATION OF THE TRAIL

The Trail is now managed by two full-time maintenance rangers and a part-time Trail Officer, all based within the Northumberland National Park Authority. The costs of this management are met through a combination of central government funding (via Natural England), as well as money and in-kind support from each of the Highways Authorities (those responsible for the network of accessible paths in their area). The work of the Trail staff is overseen by a Partnership involving each of the Highways Authorities, the Northumberland National Park, Natural England and Historic England. Current costs are in the region of £150,000 per year.

Case study - King Arthur's Well

Although the principle of the Trail having a grass surface wherever possible remains the case, there will always be places where this cannot be sustained. Indeed, this may increasingly be the case given current predictions for wetter weather patterns on Hadrian's Wall as a consequence of climate change.

One area where this proved to be the case was King Arthur's Well in the central sector of Hadrian's Wall.

Fig. 2
Cuddy's Crags in 2003, after creation of a path surface designed to prevent erosion (© Northumberland National Park Authority)
图 2
2003 年的卡迪峭壁，修建了为防止侵蚀而特别设计的路面后（版权：诺森伯兰国家公园管理局）

成本控制在年均 15 万英镑左右[1]。

（一）案例——亚瑟王井 (King Arthur's Well)

尽最大可能铺设草皮路面是步道建设的主要原则，然而总有草皮无法维持的情况出现。事实上，根据现有预测，由于气候变暖，哈德良长城区域气候条件将更为潮湿多雨，致使草皮更加难以为继。

哈德良长城中段的亚瑟王井便是一个例子。步道开放后数年间，路面积水加之极陡的斜坡，在墙体南侧的考古遗址区域逐渐形成一片严重侵蚀区域。多次尝试对其进行草皮修复，却以失败告终。最终，我们认为要保护考古遗迹，只有铺设硬质路面。

决策制定后，重中之重便是路面设计要最大限度减小对遗迹周边环境和景观的影响，并最大限度减少对所要保护的考古遗迹的干预。在设计过程中特别关注上述几项关键点，同时借鉴了诺森伯兰国家公园工作人员以往在哈德良长城及其他工作中的丰富经验。

在小道选线确定后，在考古专业人士的监督下在现场开挖了一条浅基槽作为小道基础（图 3）。小道路面采用本地圆型卵石铺设。此项工程的目的是修建易于行走的步道，自然而然地吸引徒步者沿此步道行走，同时与天然基岩融为一体，避免被误解为长城或其他古罗马遗迹。由于新道路要在

---

1 约合人民币 130 万元——译者注

Here, in the years after the opening of the Trail, a combination of wet ground and a very steep slope led to the gradual creation of an area of significant erosion into the archaeology to the south of the Wall. After strenuous efforts to repair this using the intensive grassland management used elsewhere on the Trail failed, it was concluded that only the creation of a hard-surfaced path could protect the archaeology.

This decision having been taken, the priority was to design a path in a way that minimized its impact on the setting of the monument and landscape and involved minimum intervention into the archaeology it was meant to protect. The approach taken focused on these key outcomes and built on the extensive experience of staff from the Northumberland National Park in this kind of work both on Hadrian's Wall and elsewhere.

After a route for the path had been agreed on site, a shallow tray was excavated under archaeological supervision to contain the path (Fig. 3).The path surface was constructed using local stone boulders. The aim of this work was to create a surface that was easy to walk on and along a route that walkers on the Trail would naturally gravitate to, but at the same time to blend with the natural stone bedrock and to avoid being mistaken for the Wall or other Roman remains. Because the natural process through which a new path gradually softens visually take time, the initial result will often look quite stark before blending into the landscape.

At King Arthur's Well, nearly 10 years after completion, the path has been outstandingly successful. Not only has the main aim of protection of the archaeology been achieved, but the path design has allowed it to balance all of the potentially competing visual aims. Perhaps the greatest accolade for the path is the lack of comments noting its presence in the landscape, because most visitors assume that it has always been there (Fig. 4).

Fig.3

King Arthur's Well: Excavation of 'tray' to hold stone surface of path (© Northumberland National Park Authority)

图 3

亚瑟王井：挖掘"基槽"以固定步道的块石路面（版权：诺森伯兰国家公园管理局）

视觉上实现柔化需要一定的自然过程，这一过程历时较长，因此新道路在融入周围景观前往往观感比较突兀。（图4）

（二）"通用"（generic）登录古迹许可

为保护哈德良长城遗迹，开展任何工程都需要特别许可——登录古迹许可（scheduled monument consent, 缩写为SMC）。这一规定适用于所有活动，无论它是否破坏古迹，还是为步道管理意在保护古迹免受破坏，都必须申请许可。

步道管理的基本原则之一即是采取预防性措施，其目的在于抢在长城遗迹被破坏之前防止问题进一步恶化。理论上，SMC许可申请过程要求在任何工程开展前进行，而预防性工作要求一定的灵活性，两者之间存在一定的矛盾。

步道谋划者通过采取"通用"许可的方式来解决这一矛盾。其中包括一份文件，预先许可步道日常管理需要进行的各项工程。该文件详细规定了工程规程，确保工程开展过程中不对古迹造成破坏，同时规定了需要考古人员监督的工程种类。该许可涵盖哈德良长城所有登录古迹，涵盖步道工作人员需要开展的所有维护工程，无论何时何地发现任何问题，都得以依许可规定采取及时措施，从而为预防性政策提供制度保障。

对步道管理而言，这是一项重要的创新。管理人员可以自主决策，进行实地维护和管理工作，而无需反复申请SMC。只要遵循许可指导文件中规定的方法，他们的行为就是合法的。同时，通过创新探索了不同管理方式，尤其是草地管理方面。目前，该方式已在许多其他古迹和区域推广。

（三）调查、监测与志愿者

维持步道保持良好状态、明确管理工作轻重缓急的关键工作之一就是调查和监测步道状态。在这方面，步道管理

Fig.4
Completed path: King Arthur's Well (© Northumberland National Park Authority)
图4
完工后的步道：亚瑟王井（版权：诺森伯兰国家公园管理局）

The 'generic' scheduled monument consent

The protection given to the remains of Hadrian's Wall means that those carrying out work require special permission, called scheduled monument consent (or SMC). This applies whether or not the works are harmful or, in the case of the management of the Trail, whether they are specifically designed to prevent damage to the monument.

One of the general principles of Trail management is to undertake work on a preemptive basis. The aim is to stop problems getting any worse before they cause damage to the archaeology of the Wall. The SMC process, in requiring permission prior to any works taking place, in theory works against the flexibility required for preemptive work.

Those involved in the Trail have addressed this through the development of a 'generic' consent. This consists of a document which gives prior consent for routine management works on the Trail. It provides specifications for these works, ensuring that they are approached in a way that avoids harmful impact on the monument and identifies which types of work require archaeological supervision. The SMC permission granted applies to all of the monuments along Hadrian's Wall and whatever maintenance work Trail staff need to do, wherever and whenever any problems occur, thus supporting the responsive approach required.

This has been an important initiative for the management of the Trail. It enables staff to make decisions and undertake maintenance and management works in the field without having to come back and apply for SMC, knowing that provided they follow the approach in the guidance document they are within the law. It also provides a useful reminder of the available management options that can be tried, particularly in grassland management, and is an initiative that has now been taken up on many other monuments and areas.

Surveying, monitoring and volunteers

One of the keys to keeping the Trail in good condition and prioritizing management works lies in surveying and monitoring its condition. In this area of work, the Trail relies on a variety of data sources:

· Fixed point photography undertaken three times a year;

· A yearly survey along the whole length of the Trail;

· Data collected electronically by the Trail staff on the issues that they come across;

· Data collected by volunteers who patrol individual sections of the Trail and report back.

This last group is particularly important. Volunteers provide data on the condition of the Trail and carry out basic management works on 'their' sections, but many of them also assist with larger maintenance tasks, clearing trees and scrub and generally helping the full-time staff (Fig. 5). They are a vital part of Trail management and their engagement with Hadrian's Wall through the Trail is a great example of the kind of public participation, ownership and discovery of heritage that we want to grow in the future.

Fig. 5

National Trail volunteer taking part in the clearance of scrub, to allow walkers to spread out across a wider area and reduce their impact (© Northumberland National Park Authority)

图 5

国家步道志愿者参与清除灌木，拓宽游客可以徒步的区域以减少行走带来的影响（版权：诺森伯兰国家公园管理局）

采取多方面的数据来源：

    ·每年三次的定点拍照；

    ·步道全线的年度调查；

    ·步道员工发现问题时采集的电子数据；

    ·步道各段志愿者在巡查时采集并上报的数据。

    最后一条尤为关键。志愿者提供了步道状况的数据，在各自负责的路段开展基本的管理工作，不少人也协助更大型的维护任务，清除树木和灌木，协助全职人员的工作（图5）。他们是步道管理重要的组成部分，他们通过步道参与哈德良长城保护管理，是公众参与、培养公众主人翁意识以及传播遗产价值的突出典范，我们希望在今后进一步推广。

从国际遗产保护文件看文化遗产的责任

张朝枝　卓少冰　高　俊

（中山大学旅游学院，中国广州）

[澳]西拉里·德克劳斯

（悉尼科技大学，澳大利亚悉尼）

摘　要

本文旨在阐释国际遗产保护主要相关文件所涉及的文化遗产责任。通过对 1931 年以来 24 份国际遗产保护文件的内容分析，我们发现文化遗产保护主体涉及缔约国、国际组织、旅游业及相关组织、遗产监测组织、遗产社区和个人。随着时间的推移，遗产责任的主体、对象和内容都有了很大的扩展，这可以归因于多样化的实际挑战以及不断强化的遗产保护意识。本研究将有助于遗产管理的利益相关者更好地理解遗产责任的内涵、并促进遗产可持续旅游的发展。

关键词：遗产责任　可持续旅游　文化遗产保护　内容分析　演变

绪　论

遗产意味着责任[1][2]。"遗产"概念本身意味着特定的群体或社区有责任继承和延续遗产[3][2]。尽管"遗产责任"缺乏学术研究[4]，但这一概念在各种国际公约、宪章和条约中都被加以强调。例如，早在 1964 年，《威尼斯宪章》的序言中就指出："人民越来越认识到人类各种价值的统一性，从而把古代的纪念物看作共同的遗产。大家承认，为子孙后代而妥善地保护它们是我们共同的责任。我们必须一点不走样地把它们的全部信息传下去。"[5] 同样，根据《保护世界文化和自然遗产公约》的要求，"整个国际社会有责任通过提供集体性援助来参与保护具有突出的普遍价值的文化和自然遗产；这种援助尽管不能代替有关国家采取的行动，但将成为它的有效补充"[6]。

遗产旅游已成为旅游业增长最快的分支产业之一，遗产保护与旅游发展之间关系日益密切[7]。与遗产有关的责任问题也引起了旅游学者的极大兴趣。事实上，从更广泛的角度来看，在过去几十年全球化发展的背景下，旅游研究界已经进入了一个伦理关注阶段，并将伦理问题的关注作为的一种新的研究范式[8]。与这种范式转变相关的研究工作包括：正义旅游转向[9]、批判旅游转向[10]、希望旅游转向[11]、道德转向[12] 等。这一系列研究要求旅游业以提高质量为中心，以更加和谐、可持续和公平的方式发展。在负责任旅游的背景下，利益相关方对旅游可持续发展的责任问题，引起了广泛的讨论[13]。尽管如此，目前的研究主要集中在旅游企业的社会责任方面[14][15][16]，而在旅游业利益相关者群体中，关于遗产本身责任问题鲜有探讨[4][17]。尽管旅游业利益相关者对于他们有责任促进遗产保护和遗产旅游可持续发展已经形成共识[18][19][20]，但考虑到遗产在旅游业发展中扮演了越来越重要的角色，同时遗产保护也面临

CULTURAL HERITAGE RESPONSIBILITIES: A REVIEW OF INTERNATIONAL HERITAGE CONSERVATION DOCUMENTS

Zhang Chaozhi, Zhuo Shaobing, Gao Jun

Sun Yat-Sen University - Guangzhou - China

Hilary Du Cros

University of Technology Sydney - Sydney - Australia

Abstract

The purpose of this paper is to clarify what kind of cultural heritage responsibilities the relevant international heritage conservation documents ascribe, and to whom. Through a content analysis of 24 international heritage conservation documents since 1931, this research finds that those responsible for cultural heritage protection include State Parties, international organisations, the tourism industry and related organisations, heritage monitoring bodies, the heritage management community, and other individuals. The parties involved, and the types and scope of heritage responsibilities have expanded significantly over time. This can be attributed to increasing and changing practical challenges as well as greater social awareness about heritage conservation. The research will enable stakeholders involved in heritage management to understand better the meaning of heritage responsibilities, and to promote sustainable heritage tourism development.

Keywords: Heritage responsibility, sustainable tourism, cultural heritage conservation, content analysis, evolution

INTRODUCTION

Heritage means responsibility[1][2]. Indeed, the concept of heritage, often connected to a particular group or community, denotes a certain obligation or responsibility for its inheritance[3][2]. Responsibility for heritage has been emphasized in various international conventions, charters, and treaties, but has received little attention from academic researchers[4]. As early as 1964, the Venice Charter stated in its preamble, "People are becoming more and more conscious of the unity of human values and regard ancient monuments as a common heritage. The common responsibility to safeguard them for future generations is recognised. It is our duty to hand them on in the full richness of their authenticity"[5]. Similarly, the UNESCO Convention Concerning the Protection of the World Cultural and Natural Heritage states "… it is incumbent on the international community as a whole to participate in the protection of the cultural and natural heritage of outstanding universal value, by the granting of

如（在前南斯拉夫、伊拉克、阿富汗、哥伦比亚等国爆发的）武装冲突等诸多威胁 [21]、旅游带来的负面影响 [22]、新产生的民族冲突以及遗产旅游中的责任问题 [23]，（遗产责任）仍然是一个需要探讨的问题。

为此，本研究试图从责任的角度来研究遗产和遗产旅游，力求通过澄清主要国际遗产保护文件所讨论的文化遗产责任的主体、对象和内容来填补这一空白。

一、研究方法

作者在联合国教科文组织（UNESCO）、国际古迹遗址理事会（ICOMOS）和国际文化财产保护与修复研究中心（ICCROM）的网站上搜索并下载了 1931 年签署的《关于历史性纪念物修复的雅典宪章》（Conservation of Artistic and Historic Monuments）[1]，即所谓《雅典宪章》以来的相关文件。这三个组织在世界范围内，对遗产保护具有广泛的影响，其实践和文件都得到了高度认可。作为本文的分析对象，我们共获得 24 份具有广泛国际影响并明确涉及遗产责任问题的文件（表 1）。这些文件根据功能和性质的不同，主要分为三类，即条约（公约）、不具约束力的政策性文件（如建议、声明、宪章）和其他指南（手册）。

表 1：作为本文研究对象的文化遗产保护相关文件一览表
Table 1. Heritage conservation documents adopted for analysis

序号 NO.	文件名称 Title	发布者 Organisation	发布时间 Issuing year
1	《关于历史性纪念物修复的雅典宪章》 （雅典宪章） The Athens Charter for the Restoration of Historic Monuments (The Athens Charter)	第一届历史纪念物建筑师及技师国际会议 Athens Conference	1931
2	《关于发生武装冲突情况下保护文化财产的公约》 （海牙公约） Protocol to the Convention for the Protection of Cultural Property in the Event of Armed Conflict (The Hague Convention)	联合国教科文组织 UNESCO	1954
3	《关于保护景观和遗址的风貌与特性的建议》 Recommendation Concerning the Safeguarding of Beauty and Character of Landscapes and Sites	联合国教科文组织 UNESCO	1962
4	《保护文物建筑及历史地段的国际宪章》 （威尼斯宪章） International Charter for the Conservation and Restoration of Monuments and Sites (Venice Charter)	国际古迹遗址理事会 ICOMOS	1964

---

1 雅典会议（1931 年）反映了世界各地专家对遗产保护需求的不断扩展（growing）的认识，并介绍了国际遗产的概念，是遗产保护理念发展演变（evoluton）的重要里程碑。

(http://www.icomos.org/en/about-icomos/mission-and-vision/history).

续表 1 Continued

序号 NO.	文件名称 Title	发布者 Organisation	发布时间 Issuing year
5	《关于保护受到公共或私人工程危害的文化财产的建议》 （1968 年建议）* Recommendation Concerning the Preservation of Cultural Property Endangered by Public or Private Works	联合国教科文组织 UNESCO	1968
6	《保护世界文化和自然遗产公约》 （世界遗产公约）* Convention Concerning the Protection of the World Cultural and Natural Heritage	联合国教科文组织 UNESCO	1972
7	《关于在国家一级保护文化和自然遗产的建议》 （1972 年建议）* Recommendation Concerning the Protection, at National Level, of the Cultural and Natural Heritage	联合国教科文组织 UNESCO	1972
8	《关于历史地区的保护及其当代作用的建议》 （内罗毕建议）. Recommendation Concerning the Safeguarding and Contemporary Role of Historic Areas (The Nairobi Recommendation)	联合国教科文组织 UNESCO	1976
9	历史园林 （佛罗伦萨宪章） Historic Gardens (The Florence Charter)	国际古迹遗址理事会 ICOMOS	1981
10	《保护历史城镇与城区宪章》 （华盛顿宪章） Charter for the Conservation of Historic Towns and Urban Areas (Washington Charter)	国际古迹遗址理事会 ICOMOS	1987
11	《考古遗产保护与管理宪章》 （考古遗产宪章）* Charter for the Protection and Management of the Archaeological Heritage	国际古迹遗址理事会 ICOMOS	1990
12	《世界文化遗产地管理指南》 （管理指南）* Management Guidelines for World Cultural Heritage Sites	国际文化财产保护及修复研究中心 ICCROM	1993
13	《奈良真实性文件》 （奈良文件）* The Nara Document on Authenticity	国际古迹遗址理事会 ICOMOS	1994
14	《国际文化旅游宪章》 （文旅宪章）* International Cultural Tourism Charter	国际古迹遗址理事会 ICOMOS	1999
15	《关于发生武装冲突时保护文化财产公约第二议定书》 Second Protocol to the Hague Convention of 1954 for the Protection of Cultural Property in the Event of Armed Conflict	联合国教科文组织 UNESCO	1999
16	《关于乡土建筑遗产的宪章》 （乡土遗产宪章）* Charter on the Built Vernacular Heritage	国际古迹遗址理事会 ICOMOS	1999

续表 1 Continued

序号 NO.	文件名称 Title	发布者 Organisation	发布时间 Issuing year
17	《关于保护具有文化意义地点的宪章》 （巴拉宪章） Charter for the Conservation of Places of Cultural Significance	国际古迹遗址理事会澳大利亚委员会 Australia ICOMOS	1999
18	《水下文化遗产保护公约》 （水下遗产公约） Convention on the Protection of the Underwater Heritage	联合国教科文组织 UNESCO	2001
19	《世界遗产地旅游管理：世界遗产地管理者实用手册》 （实用手册）* Managing Tourism at World Heritage Sites: a Practical Manual for World Heritage Site Managers	联合国教科文组织 UNESCO	2002
20	《关于蓄意破坏文化遗产问题的宣言》 （2003 年宣言）* Declaration concerning the Intentional Destruction of Cultural Heritage	联合国教科文组织 UNESCO	2003
21	《保存数字遗产宪章》 Charter on the Preservation of Digital Heritage	联合国教科文组织 UNESCO	2003
22	《保护非物质文化遗产公约》 Convention for the Safeguarding of the Intangible Cultural Heritage	联合国教科文组织 UNESCO	2003
23	《文化遗产地阐释与展示宪章》 （文化遗产地宪章）* The ICOMOS Charter for the Interpretation and Preservation of Cultural Heritage Sites	国际古迹遗址理事会 ICOMOS	2008
24	实施《保护世界文化和自然遗产公约》的操作指南 （操作指南）* Operational Guidelines for the Implementation of the World Heritage Convention	联合国教科文组织 UNESCO	2013

注：从技术角度讲，《关于保护具有文化意义地点的宪章》不能被视为国际遗产保护文件，因为它是由国际古迹遗址理事会澳大利亚委员会（一个国家遗产组织）发布的。尽管如此，考虑到其广泛的国际影响，我们也将其纳入了分析。

Technically speaking, the Charter for the Conservation of Places of Cultural Significance cannot be counted as an international heritage conservation document as it was issued by Australia ICOMOS, a national heritage organisation. Nonetheless, given its wide international influence, it was included in the analysis.

* 简称为译者为后文行文方便增加。

Abbreviation used by translator for convenience of writing.

　　为了揭示这些文件所涉及的文化遗产责任类型，我们在进行内容分析时，用三个主要问题对其加以引导：（1）哪些主体应履行这些责任？（2）他们的具体职责是什么？（3）随着时间的推移，主体及其职责是如何演变的？内容分析可以是分类计算词频的纯定量分析，也可以是侧重归纳推理和解释的定性分析[24][25]。考虑到本文的研究目的（本质上是探索性的）以及数据样本量较少，本研究采用了纯定性的内容分析。首先，我们通过仔细研读所有文件，以掌握其主要内容。同时，有关责任问题的内容，特别是包含"某种责任（responsibility）/某些责任（responsibilities）""对……负责""职责/特殊角色"和"职能"等术语和短语的文本进行标记；其次，仔细阅读标记的文本，以确定主体及其相应的责任，

collective assistance which, although not taking the place of action by the State concerned, will serve as an efficient complement thereto"[6].

Given the increasingly close relationship between heritage conservation and tourism development, reflected in the fact that heritage tourism has become one of the fastest growing sub-sectors of tourism[7], responsibility issues relating to heritage are also of great interest to tourism scholars. Indeed, in a wider perspective, over the past few decades, in the context of greater globalisation, the academic sphere of tourism has entered an ethical platform and delineated ethical concerns as part of a new paradigm[8]. Research efforts relating to this paradigm shift have included those related to just tourism [9], critical tourism[10], hopeful tourism[11], moral turn[12], and so on. This body of literature calls for more harmonious, sustainable and equitable forms of tourism with a focus on quality. Against such a background, the responsibilities of stakeholders for sustainable tourism development have attracted widespread debate, particularly within the context of responsible tourism[13]. Nonetheless, extant studies are mainly focused on tourism businesses with regard to corporate social responsibility[14][15][16], whereas research on responsibility issues pertaining to heritage itself among tourism stakeholders remains undeveloped[4] [17], despite a consensus among tourism stakeholders that they have a responsibility for both heritage protection and sustainable heritage tourism development[18][19][20]. This is problematic, given the increasingly important role of heritage in tourism development, and the threats facing heritage conservation, such as armed conflicts (e.g. in the former Yugoslavia, in Iraq, Afghanistan, Colombia, and so on)[21], the negative impacts of tourism[22], and emerging conflicts over ethical and responsibility issues in heritage tourism[23].

This study seeks to fill this gap by clarifying what kind of cultural heritage responsibilities the most relevant international heritage conservation documents ascribe, and to whom. It is intended to contribute to heritage studies as well as to heritage tourism studies from a responsibility perspective.

METHODOLOGY

For the purposes of the current study, the authors searched the websites of UNESCO, ICOMOS, and the International Center for the Study of the Preservation and Restoration of Cultural Property (ICCROM) to download relevant documents since 1931 when Conservation of Artistic and Historic Monuments1, the so-called Athens Charter, was issued. These three organisations have considerable influence on heritage protection worldwide and are well-recognized in practice as well as in the literature. In total, 24 documents, which have been internationally influential and which make clear reference to responsibility issues, were obtained for analysis (Table 1). These documents largely fall into three categories, based on their respective function and character, namely:

---

1 The Athens Conference (1931) represented a major step in the evolution of ideas on heritage, as it reflected the growing consciousness of the need for heritage conservation among specialists worldwide, and introduced the concept of international heritage (http://www.icomos.org/en/about-icomos/mission-and-vision/history).

以回答上述两个问题。第三，为了揭示遗产责任的演变（问题三），我们在分析中采用了历时性的视角。具体来说，一方面，按照时间顺序对责任的主体、对象和内容进行审视；另一方面，也按照时间顺序对每个文件的一般内容进行审视，以全面了解遗产责任随着时间推移而发生的变化。

二、研究发现

（一）遗产责任的主体和内容

经过分析，我们将遗产责任主体分为六类（表2），其各自的责任内容见表3。本文将遗产责任主体定义为负责使用和保护文化资产的团体、组织或个人。

表 2. 遗产责任主体分类
Table 2. Categories of the 'subject' of heritage responsibility

文化遗产 Heritage 保护文件类别 Conservation Documents \ 主体类别 Agents	政府及其职能部门 State Parties and their Institutions	国际组织 International Organisations	旅游业和国家旅游管理机构（国家旅游部门）Tourism Industry and National Tourism Offices (NTOs)	遗产监测机构 Heritage-Monitoring Organisations	遗产地社区 Host Communities	其他个人 Other Individuals
1964/ 威尼斯宪章 Venice Charter	★					
1968/ 关于保护受到公共或私人工程危害的文化财产的建议 UNESCO Recommendation	★					
1972/ 关于在国家一级保护文化和自然遗产的建议 UNESCO Recommendation	★					
1972/ 世界遗产公约 UNESCO Convention	★	★				
1976/ 内罗毕建议 Nairobi Recommendation	★					★

续表 2 Continued

主体类别 Agents / 文化遗产 保护文件类别 Heritage Conservation Documents	政府及其职能部门 State Parties and their Institutions	国际组织 International Organisations	旅游业和国家旅游管理机构（国家旅游部门）Tourism Industry and National Tourism Offices (NTOs)	遗产监测机构 Heritage-Monitoring Organisations	遗产地社区 Host Communities	其他个人 Other Individuals
1990/ 考古遗产保护与管理宪章 ICOMOS Charter	★					★
1993/ 世界文化遗产地管理指南 Management Guidelines	★	★	★	★		
1994/ 奈良文件 Nara Document					★	
1999a/ 国际文化旅游宪章 International Cultural Tourism Charter	★	★	★	★	★	★
2001/ 水下文化遗产保护公约 UNESCO Convention	★	★				★
2002/ 实用手册 Managing Tourism at World Heritage Sites: a Practical Manual for World Heritage Site Managers (Practical Manual)	★	★	★	★		★
2003/ 保存数字遗产宪章 UNESCO Charter	★	★		★		
2008/ 文化遗产阐释与展示宪章 Cultural Heritage Site Charter	★	★		★	★	★
2013/ 操作指南 UNESCO Guidelines	★	★	★	★	★	★

表 3. 文化遗产责任主要类型一览表

Table 3. Summary of the main types of heritage responsibility

主体 Subjects	遗产责任类型 Types of Heritage Responsibility
政府及其职能部门 State Parties and their Institutions	1. 制定政策与规划："通过一项旨在使文化和自然遗产在社会生活中起一定作用并把遗产保护纳入全面规划计划的总政策"(1972 世界遗产公约 第 5 条 (a)) 2. 建立机构："建立一个或几个负责文化和自然遗产的保护、保存和展出的机构"(1972 世界遗产公约 第 5 条 (b)) 3. 采取"适当的法律、科学、技术、行政和财政措施"(1972 世界遗产公约 第 5 条 (d)) 4. 研究／教育和信息（information）项目：发展科学和技术研究；促进建立和发展……国家或地区培训中心 (1972 世界遗产公约 第 5 条 (c/e))；努力增强该国人民对……文化和自然遗产的赞赏和尊重 (1972 世界遗产公约 第 27 条 (1)) 5. 国际援助与合作：尊重其他缔约国、开展合作、提供援助 (1972 世界遗产公约 第 6 条) 6. 履行世界遗产委员会的职责：递交（文化遗产和自然遗产的）财产的清单。(1972 世界遗产公约 第 11 条)，定期向世界遗产基金纳款 (1972 世界遗产公约 第 16 条)，为遗产保护募捐 (1972 世界遗产公约 第 18 条) 递交（遗产相关的）活动报告 (1972 世界遗产公约 第 29 条) 1. Development of policy and planning programs: "to adopt a general policy⋯and to integrate the protection of that heritage into comprehensive planning programs" (1972 Convention: Article 5(a)) 2. Establishment of services: to set up one or more service(s) for the protection, conservation, and presentation of the cultural and natural heritage (1972 Convention: Article 5(b)) 3. Taking "the appropriate legal, scientific, technical, administrative and financial measures" (1972 Convention: Article 5(d)) 4. Research/educational and information programs: promotion of scientific and technical research; establishment of national or regional centers for training (1972 Convention: Article 5(c/e); implementation of measures to strengthen appreciation of and respect for heritage (1972 Convention: Article 27) 5. International assistance and cooperation: to respect, co-operate with and provide assistance to heritage organisations in other countries (1972 Convention: Article 6) 6. Fulfillment of responsibilities to the World Heritage Committee: submit an inventory of property (1972 Convention: Article 11), pay regular sums to the World Heritage Fund (1972 Convention: Article 16), invite donations to the heritage-protection cause (1972 Convention: Article 18) and submit reports on heritage-related activities (1972 Convention: Article 29)

续表见 P292 页 to be continued on page 292

treaties (conventions); non-binding policy documents (e.g. recommendations, declarations, charters); and other guidelines (manuals).

Note: Technically speaking, the Charter for the Conservation of Places of Cultural Significance cannot be counted as an international heritage conservation document as it was issued by Australia ICOMOS, a national heritage organisation. Nonetheless, given its wide international influence, it was included in the analysis.

To identify what kind of cultural heritage responsibilities the documents define, the content analysis was led by three main questions: (1) Which parties have these responsibilities? (2) What are the types and scope of the responsibilities? (3) How have the parties involved, and the types and scope of the responsibilities evolved over time? When it comes to content analysis, approaches can range from the purely quantitative, where frequencies are counted within categories, to qualitative techniques that focus on inductive reasoning and interpretation[24] [25]. Given the aim of the research (exploratory in nature) as well as the small sample of data, this study adopted a purely qualitative approach. First, all the documents were carefully read in order to grasp their general content. At the same time, texts regarding responsibility issues, notably those containing terms and phrases like "responsibility/responsibilities", "responsible for," "duty/special roles" and "function", were highlighted. Second, the highlighted texts were carefully read to identify to which bodies they ascribe specific responsibilities. This helped to answer the first two questions mentioned above. Third, in order to describe the evolution of heritage responsibility (question three), a diachronic perspective was added to the analysis. Specifically, the parties involved, and the types and scope of responsibilities were scrutinised in chronological order. In parallel, the general content of each document was also scrutinised in chronological order to gain an holistic understanding of changes in heritage responsibility over time.

FINDINGS

The parties involved and types of heritage responsibility

Six categories of parties with heritage responsibility emerged from the analysis (Table 2) and their respective responsibilities were summarised (Table 3). The 'parties of heritage responsibility are defined in this study as the groups, organisations or individuals responsible for the use and conservation of cultural heritage assets.

The first category comprises State Parties and their institutions, which hold primary responsibility for heritage conservation[1]. State Parties and their institutions are regarded as important agents during periods of armed conflict and in peacetime in almost all of the key documents published since the Venice Charter.

---

1 There are several reasons for the identification of State Parties as the agents who hold the chief responsibility for heritage conservation. As State Parties are responsible for identifying heritage sites and supervising and managing heritage conservation, the state-based heritage cognitive system is the most important paradigm in modern concepts of heritage responsibility.

续表 3 Continued

主体 Subjects	遗产责任类型 Types of Heritage Responsibility
国际组织 International Organisations	联合国教科文组织官方机构： 1. "大会在联合国教科文组织大会常会期间召开"（2013 操作指南 第 17 条） 2. "与缔约国合作"（2013 操作指南 第 24 条） 3. "为了促进《公约》的实施，委员会制定了战略目标，并对这些目标定期审查和修改，确保有效应对世界遗产面临的新威胁"（2013 操作指南 第 25 条） Official UNESCO institutions: 1. Organisation of regular meetings of State Parties to the 1972 Convention (2013 Guidelines: Article 17) 2. Co-operation with State Parties (2013 Guidelines: Article 24) 3. Stimulation of the implementation of the 1972 Convention; development of strategic objectives to ensure that new threats facing World Heritage Sites are addressed effectively (2013 Guidelines: Article 25) 世界遗产委员会咨询机构： 1. 为公约的实施提供咨询 (1972 世界遗产公约 第 13.7 条) 2. 协助制定和实施各项组织决定 (2013 操作指南 第 31 条 (b)(c)) 3. "对世界遗产的保护状况进行监测（包括应委员会要求派出的反应性监测及应缔约国邀请开展的咨询考察）并审核国际援助申请"(2013 操作指南 第 31 条 (d)) 4. "评估申请列入《世界遗产名录》的遗产……并向委员会呈递评估报告"(2013 操作指南 第 31 条 (e)) Advisory bodies of the World Heritage Committee: 1. Provision of advice on the implementation of the 1972 Convention (1972 Convention: Article 13.7) 2. Provision of assistance with the development and implementation of relevant organisational decisions (2013 Guidelines: Article 31(b)(c)) 3. "Monitor the state of conservation of World Heritage properties and review requests for International Assistance" (2013 Guidelines: Article 31(d)) 4. "Evaluate properties nominated for inscription on the World Heritage List and present evaluation reports to the Committee" (2013 Guidelines: Article 31(e))
旅游机构与国家旅游部门 Tourism Industry and NTOs	旅游业： 1. 提高当地居民的生活质量 (管理指南 第 10.1 条) 2. 加强对可持续发展的责任；承担一定程度的经济责任 (实践手册 第 2.6.6 条) Tourism industry: 1. Improvement of the quality of life of local residents (Management Guidelines: Article 10.1) 2. Increased responsibility for sustainable development; assumption of a degree of financial responsibility (Practical Manual: Article 2.6.6) 国家旅游部门： 1. 宣传一个国家的旅游景点；与旅游经营者和旅行社建立联系；举办宣传活动并提供研究数据 (实践手册 第 2.2.1 条) NTOs: 1. Promote a country's tourist attractions; establish relationships with tour operators and travel agencies; hold promotional events and produce research data (Practical Manual: Article 2.2.1)

续表见 P294 页 to be continued on page 294

State Parties are ascribed the primary responsibility for all aspects of heritage conservation (1972 Convention: Article 4).

The second category comprises international organisations. Indeed, the first heritage conservation documents were developed by international institutions, and their heritage responsibility can be traced back to the work of the League of Nations in the 1920s and 1930s, which initiated international cooperation for heritage conservation[26]. When the League of Nations was replaced by the UN at the end of the Second World War, UNESCO (part of the UN) began to call on and recommend State Parties to protect 'immovable heritage'. Later, the establishment of relevant UNESCO advisory bodies, including the International Union for Conservation of Nature (IUCN), ICCROM and ICOMOS, led to another shift in heritage conservation. The responsibility of international organisations for protecting the world's heritage was confirmed in the 1972 Convention and was emphasised in subsequent heritage conservation documents.

The third category comprises the tourism industry and national tourism organisations (NTOs). In response to the rapid development of heritage tourism since the 1990s, the tourism sector has been asked to contribute to heritage conservation through the 1993 Management Guidelines for World Cultural Heritage Sites (henceforth, Management Guidelines). The 2002 Managing Tourism at World Heritage Sites: A Practical Manual for World Heritage Site Managers (henceforth, Practical Manual) clearly states that the tourism industry should take more responsibility for sustainable development.

The fourth category comprises heritage monitoring organisations, such as indigenous custodians or owners, site managers and staff, groups of experts and NGOs (Management Guidelines: Chapter VII). The Management Guidelines recommend that heritage site committees of experienced professionals should be set up, and that their duties should be subject to international conventions and charters.

The fifth category comprises host communities, primarily consisting of local residents. The heritage management community did not itself become a subject of responsibility until the Nara Document. The Nara Document on Authenticity states: "Responsibility for cultural heritage and the management of it belongs, in the first place, to the cultural community that has generated it, and subsequently to that which cares for it" (article 8). With the development of community tourism, community participation has become a crucial element of tourism development, and communities have thus been given more responsibilities and obligations (International Cultural Tourism Charter, article 4).

The sixth category of agents comprises other individuals. "At the broadest level, the natural and cultural heritage belongs to all people, we each have the right and responsibility to understand, appreciate and conserve its universal values" (International Cultural Tourism Charter: The Charter Ethos). The responsibility of individuals was mentioned for the first time in the Nairobi Recommendation. Following a description of the importance of heritage conservation and threats to cultural property, the Nairobi Recommendation states, "This situation entails responsibilities for every citizen and lays on public authorities obligations which they alone are capable of

续表 3 Continued

主体 Subjects	遗产责任类型 Types of Heritage Responsibility
遗产监测机构 Heritage-Monitoring Organisations	本地经营者或业主："在旅游的语境中，对他们的资源、文化实践和当代文化表达进行识别、保护、管理、展示和阐释"（文旅宪章 第 4.1 条） 遗产地管理者：维护或恢复遗址的原有价值；为游客提供服务和管理；保护和修复遗产；促进遗产地和与利益相关者的沟通（实用手册 前言） 专家组：应充分利用他们的专业知识，加强对遗产地的监督（管理指南） 非政府组织：在私人部门与地方利益之间扮演中介的角色（实用手册 第 4.4.5 条）
遗产地社区 Host Communities	1. 保护和管理文化遗产；遵守国际宪章和公约（奈良文件 第 8 条） 2. 文化个性、生活方式和多样性的识别；与游客交流；传播和推广遗产（文旅宪章） 1. Conservation and management of cultural heritage; adherence to international charters and conventions (Nara Document: Article 8) 2. Identification of cultural personality, lifestyle, and diversity; communication with visitors; broadcasting and promotion of heritage (International Cultural Tourism Charter)
其他个人 Other Individuals	1. 对遗产普遍价值的理解、欣赏和保护（文旅宪章的精神） 2. 表达对遗产地阐释和展示的意见和观点（文旅宪章 第 6.3 条） 1. Understanding, appreciation, and conservation of universal heritage values (International Cultural Tourism Charter: the Charter Ethos) 2. Expression of opinions and perspectives on the interpretation and presentation of cultural-heritage sites (Cultural Heritage Site Charter: Article 6.3)

第一类是缔约国及其机构，它们对遗产保护负有核心责任[1]。在《威尼斯宪章》之后的几乎所有文件中，缔约国及其机构都被视为武装冲突和和平时期的重要责任主体，并应当承担遗产保护的各种首要责任（1972 世界遗产公约 第 4 条）。

第二类是国际组织。事实上，第一批遗产保护文件是由国际机构制定的，它们对遗产的责任可以追溯到 20 世纪 20 年代和 30 年代国际联盟的工作，正是国联最初发起了遗产保护的国际合作[26]。第二次世界大战结束后，当联合国取代国际联盟时，联合国教科文组织作为联合国的组成机构，开始呼吁并建议各国保护"不可移动遗产"。后来，联合国教科文组织成立了相关的咨询机构，包括世界自然保护联盟（IUCN）、国际文化财产保护与修复研究中心（ICCROM）和国际古迹遗址理事会（ICOMOS），这导致了遗产保护领域的另一个转变。1972 年《世界遗产公约》确认了国际组织保护世界遗产的责任，并在随后的遗产保护文件中予以强调。

第三类包括旅游业和国家旅游部门。为了应对自 20 世纪 90 年代以来遗产旅游业的快速发展，旅游部门因此被要求按照 1993 年《世界文化遗产管理指南》（后文简称《管理指南》）对遗产保护做出贡

1　将缔约国认定为遗产保护主要责任主体的原因有几个。由于缔约国负责认定遗产地，并对遗产保护进行监督和管理，基于国家的遗产认知体系是现代遗产责任概念中最重要的范式。

fulfilling". Therefore, this document puts individual citizens alongside governments with regard to responsibility for heritage conservation.

Evolution of the range of heritage covered by heritage responsibilities

Heritage responsibilities have evolved in two main contexts: in periods of armed conflict and in peacetime. The Hague Convention was the first document that focused exclusively on heritage conservation in the event of armed conflict. It outlined the obligation of states to protect cultural property in peacetime; but stated that this obligation "may be waived only in cases where military necessity imperatively requires such a waiver" (Article 4.2). To correct this apparent dispensation, a fourth chapter titled "Criminal Responsibility and Jurisdiction" was added to the Hague Convention in 1999, in which punitive measures against violations are legally mandated, and may be subject to international criminal responsibility. The later 2003 Declaration was a direct response to the "intentional destruction of cultural heritage", such as the destruction of the Buddhas of Bamiyan. This declaration extended the scope of responsibility from armed conflict to "intentional destruction" and made a clear distinction between state and individual criminal responsibility.

Responsibility for heritage expanded even more significantly in the documents that relate to peacetime. The Venice Charter advocated "the unity of human values" and "ancient monuments as a common heritage," warranting "common responsibility" for their conservation. The 1968 Recommendation then went a step further, suggesting nation states take full measures to protect and restore "cultural property". In the 1972 Convention, the concept of "cultural and natural heritage" was introduced for the first time, covering both natural assets and man-made monuments, groups of buildings and sites, and two special articles on "national policy" and "international co-operation" were added. The 1972 Convention put forward for the first time the concept of World Heritage with Outstanding Universal Value in the form of an internationally adopted convention. It not only specified the responsibilities of State Parties but also proposed the establishment of the World Heritage Committee and the World Heritage Fund to enhance the joint efforts of the international community for heritage protection, guaranteeing organisational and financial support.

To expand the sphere of protection for historic monuments, UNESCO added the responsibility for "historic and architectural (including vernacular) areas" in the Nairobi Recommendation, and stressed the important role that owners, local residents, users, and third sector organisations could play in heritage conservation. In a similar vein, ICOMOS extended the responsibility for conservation to cover historic gardens and historic towns in the Florence Charter and the Washington Charter, respectively. Moreover, the Council expanded the required protective measures from "conservation, restoration, excavation and publication" (Venice Charter) to "maintenance, conservation, restoration, reconstruction, legal and administrative protection" (Florence Charter), and the participation of community residents (Washington Charter). A similar trend could also be found in the Burra Charter which replaced both 'monument' and 'site' with the term 'place'[1], thus extending the sphere of historical

---

1 "Place means site, area, land, landscape, building or other work, group of building or other works, and may include components, contents, spaces and views" (Burra Charter: Article 1.1)

献。事实上，2002年《世界遗产地旅游管理：世界遗产地管理者实用手册》（后文简称《实用手册》）明确指出，旅游业应为可持续发展承担更多责任。

第四类为遗产监测组织，如本地经营者或业主、遗产地管理者和工作人员、专家组和非政府组织（《管理指南》：第七章）。《管理指南》建议成立由经验丰富的专业人士组成的遗产地委员会，其职责应服从于国际公约和宪章的规定。

第五类是由遗产地居民组成的社区。遗产社区直到《奈良真实性文件》（后文简称《奈良文件》）公布后，才成为一个责任主体。《奈良文件》指出："文化遗产及其管理的责任首先属于产生它的文化社区，然后属于关心它的人。"（第8条）随着社区旅游业的发展，社区参与已成为旅游业发展的一个重要组成部分，遗产社区因此被赋予了更多的责任和义务（《国际文化旅游宪章》（后文简称《文旅宪章》）第4条）。

第六类责任主体为其他个人。"在最广泛的层面上，自然和文化遗产属于所有人，我们每个人都有权利和责任理解、欣赏和保存其普遍价值。"（《文旅宪章：宪章精神》）《内罗毕建议》首次提到了个人的责任，并描述了遗产保护的重要性和对文化财产的威胁，指出："这种情况需要每个公民都承担责任，并依托于公共当局能够单独履行的义务"因此，在遗产保护责任方面，该文件将公民个人与政府并列陈述。

（二）遗产责任的演进

遗产责任的演变发生在两个主要背景下：武装冲突和和平时期。《海牙公约》是第一份专门关注武装冲突中的遗产保护的文件。它概述了各国在非和平时期保护文化财产的义务；然而，这种义务"只有在军事行动的必要性迫切要求被放弃的情况下，才可以放弃"（第4.2条）。为修正这一明显的豁免权，1999年《海牙公约》增加了标题为"刑事责任和管辖权"的第四章，其中对违反公约的惩罚性措施交由法定，并考虑了国际刑事责任。此后的《2003年宣言》是对"蓄意破坏文化遗产"的直接回应，如炸毁巴米扬佛像一事。本宣言将责任范围从武装冲突扩大到了"蓄意破坏"，并明确区分了国家和个人的刑事责任。

在那些和平时期制定的文件中，遗产责任的范畴得到了更为显著的拓展。《威尼斯宪章》主张"统一的人类价值观"和"作为共同遗产的古代遗迹"，将文化遗产保护上升为人类的"共同责任"。此后的《1968年建议》更进一步，倡议各国采取全面措施保护和修复"文化财产"。在《1972年的建议》中，"文化和自然遗产"的概念首次被提出，内容涵盖了自然资产（assets）和古迹、建筑群和遗址，并增加了两条关于"国家政策"和"国际合作"的特别条款。1972年《世界遗产公约》首次以国际条约的形式提出了"具有突出普遍价值的世界遗产"的概念。它不仅明确了缔约国的责任，还提出设立世界遗产委员会和世界遗产基金会，以促进国际遗产保护界的共同努力，确保组织和经费支持。

为了扩大历史遗迹的保护范围，联合国教科文组织在《内罗毕建议》中增加了"历史和建筑（包括乡土建筑）区"的责任，并强调了业主、当地居民、使用者和非政府组织在遗产保护中的重要作用。与之相呼应，国际古迹遗址理事会将保护责任分别扩展到《佛罗伦萨宪章》和《华盛顿宪章》中的历史园

monuments[26]. By 1990, archaeological heritage became a new focus of conservation policy-making, further extending the scope of heritage responsibility. The Archaeological Heritage Charter covers nine major components: integrated protection; the implementation of legislative and economic regulations; survey; investigation; maintenance and conservation; presentation; information; reconstruction; professional expertise; and international co-operation. These components clearly suggest the necessity of cooperation and common responsibility between multiple stakeholders regarding heritage conservation.

Given the increasingly close relationship between heritage and tourism development and the active call for community participation in tourism as essential for sustainable tourism development, heritage responsibility appears to have become a topic that is inseparable from the tourism sector and host communities, as reflected in the International Cultural Tourism Charter and Charter on the Built Vernacular Heritage. In the former, cultural tourism is no longer limited to visits to historical sites or World Heritage Sites, but tourist visits to all cultural heritage sites and their host communities. In the latter, the focus is on vernacular heritage, which is regarded as representing "traditional harmonies" that "constitute the core of man's own existence" and which are the "fundamental expression of the culture of a community". Furthermore, tourism, as an important channel of cultural communication, can play a critical role in communicating the importance and conservation of heritage. Yet the questions of "what to preserve, how to preserve it, and how it is to be presented to the public" (the Cultural Heritage Site Charter) can be confusing. In this respect, the Cultural Heritage Site Charter stresses the importance of public communication, stating that "it is the right and responsibility of all to make their opinions and perspectives known" (Article 6), and regards communication as central to various types of heritage conservation behaviours. To this end, whether heritage is understood and respected by the public, and whether the public is involved in heritage conservation and development, have become criteria for evaluating the fulfillment of heritage responsibilities.

Since the beginning of the 21st century, increasing emphasis has been placed on more diverse forms of heritage, such as underwater cultural heritage, digital heritage, and intangible cultural heritage. The 2001 Convention is an international law designed to protect underwater cultural heritage. It states, "all State Parties have a responsibility to protect underwater cultural heritage in the exclusive economic zone and on the continental shelf" (Article 9), and advocates strengthening cooperation through meetings of State Parties. The 2003 Charter was created in response to threats to digital heritage and required governments "to designate one or more agencies to take coordinating responsibility for the preservation of the digital heritage, and to make available necessary resources" (Article 10). Echoing the 1972 Convention, the 2003 Convention initiated the establishment of an Intergovernmental Committee for the Safeguarding of the Intangible Cultural Heritage and an Intangible Cultural Heritage Fund to facilitate the joint efforts of the international community for intangible cultural heritage protection. It also emphasised the importance of the protection of intangible cultural heritage by young people.

林和历史城镇。此外，委员会将必要的保护措施从"保护、修复、发掘和出版"（《威尼斯宪章》）扩大到"维护、保护、修复、重建、法律和行政保护"（《佛罗伦萨宪章》）以及"社区居民的参与"（华盛顿宪章）。类似的趋势也存在于《巴拉宪章》中，该宪章将"遗迹"和"遗址"都替换为"地点[1]"，从而扩大了历史遗迹的范围[26]。到 1990 年，考古遗产成为保护决策的新焦点，遗产责任的对象进一步扩大。《考古遗产宪章》涵盖了九个主要组成部分：综合保护、立法和经济条例的执行、调查、研究、维护和保护、展示、信息、重建、专业知识和国际合作，明确提出了关于遗产保护的多边合作和共同责任。

鉴于遗产与旅游业发展之间的关系日益密切，以及为了可持续旅游发展而对社区参与旅游的积极呼吁，遗产责任似乎已成为一个与旅游业和当地社区密不可分的话题，这在《文旅宪章》和《关于乡土建筑遗产的宪章》中得到了体现。在前者的概念中，文化旅游不再局限于参观历史遗址（historical sites）或世界遗产地，而是扩展到各种旅游相关的文化遗产地和当地社区。而在后者中，重点是通过建立乡土遗产，从而（将文化旅游）落实到社区层面。这被视为"构成人类自身存在的核心"的"传统的和谐"，是"社区文化的基本表现"。此外，旅游作为重要的文化交流渠道，在传递遗产的重要性和遗产保护方面发挥着至关重要的作用。然而，关于"要保存什么，如何保存，以及如何向公众展示"（《文化遗产地宪章》）的问题可能会令人困惑。在这方面，《文化遗产地宪章》强调了公共传播的重要性，指出"所有人都有权利和责任公开表达他们的意见和观点"（第 6 条），并将传播视为各种遗产保护行为的核心。为此，遗产是否被公众理解和尊重，以及公众是否参与遗产保护和发展，已成为评估遗产责任落实情况的标准。

自 21 世纪初以来，人们越来越重视水下文化遗产、数字遗产和非物质文化遗产等新型遗产。2001 年《水下遗产公约》是一部旨在保护水下文化遗产的国际法律。它指出"所有缔约国都有责任保护专属经济区和大陆架的水下文化遗产"（第 9 条），并主张应通过缔约国间会议来加强合作。2003 年《保存数字遗产宪章》是为了应对对数字遗产面临的威胁而制定的，它要求各国政府"指定一个或多个机构通过协作保护数字遗产，并提供必要的资源"（第 10 条）。与 1972 年《世界遗产公约》类似，《保存数字遗产宪章》发起成立了一个非物质文化遗产保护政府间委员会和一个非物质文化遗产基金，以促进国际非物质文化遗产保护界的共同努力。它还强调了青年人参与非物质文化遗产保护的重要性。

三、讨　论

本文的研究表明，自 1931 年以来，主要国际遗产保护文件中提到的遗产责任概念得到了极大的拓展。就主体而言，总的来说，所有遗产利益相关者通常都被囊括在最新的文件中，它们在这些文件中按以下时间顺序出现：各缔约国及其机构→国际组织→其他个人→旅游业及其相关组织，以及遗产监测机构→遗产（业主 host）社区。同样，遗产责任的对象也明显增多，从历史遗迹、建筑遗产和其他陆上物质遗

---

1 "地点 place"是指场地、区域、土地、景观、建筑或其他工程、建筑群或其他工程，可能包括构成 components、内容、空间和视野 views（贝拉宪章：第 1.1 条）。

DISCUSSION

This study suggests that heritage responsibilities, as defined in the most relevant international heritage conservation documents, have expanded significantly since 1931. All the heritage stakeholders are generally included in the more recent documents, appearing in the following chronological order: nations states and their institutions→international organisations→other individuals→the tourism industry and its relevant organisations, and heritage monitoring organisations→heritage host communities. Similarly, the scope of heritage covered by responsibility has expanded greatly, from historical monuments, architectural heritage and other tangible, onshore components of heritage, to intangible and underwater cultural property. The nature of these responsibilities has also increased greatly, expanding from criminal responsibility during wartime to general responsibility at peacetime, and from simple protective measures to a complex system of pro-active measures.

The heritage movement is contingent on and reflects the wider social environment[2]. Indeed, heritage is increasingly seen as a discourse with material consequences, as cultural practice or process, rather than just as a site or substantive object[27][28][29][30]. In the first half of the 20th century, the rise of the heritage conservation movement in Europe largely resulted from the damage caused to historic sites and buildings by war and industrial revolution[26]. Against this backdrop, international heritage conservation documents were developed, and the concept of responsibility for heritage conservation began to emerge. Subsequently, human practices like post-war urbanisation, new industrial revolution, and technological and informational development, have all presented new threats and challenges to heritage protection. Moreover, thanks to globalisation and modernisation, those with responsibility for heritage conservation are gradually becoming more interconnected. These increasingly complex relationships and emerging new conflicts /challenges over heritage require improvements to the mechanisms by which heritage conservation operates. As such, it is inevitable that the locus, scope and nature of heritage responsibility should each expand over time.

The different parties with whom heritage responsibility lies can have different perceptions of heritage as well as different interests regarding the development of each heritage site[31]. Overall, these stakeholders in the world heritage system can be grouped into three categories: international organisations ("a global stance"); State Parties and their institutions, the tourism industry and National Tourism Organisations (NTOs) ("a national stance"); and heritage management organisations, host communities and individuals ("a community stance") [32]. The nation-state is the fundamental unit of internal law and frames the prevailing social ideology and discourse, and hence is the fundamental unit in the world heritage system[32][33]. Furthermore, when nation-states engage in the development of international conservation documents, human beings are seen as a whole in a symbiotic relationship with the earth, thus the international community itself assumes responsibility for safeguarding the 'common heritage of mankind'. In this sense, it is not surprising that prior to the 1972 Convention, only State Parties

产组成部分，到非物质遗产和水下文化财产。具体责任也大大增加，从战时的刑事责任扩大到平时的一般责任，从简单的保护措施扩大到积极防护的复杂体系。

遗产运动取决于并反映了更广泛的社会环境 [2]。事实上，遗产作为一种文化实践或过程，越来越被视为一种能够产生实质结果的话语，而不仅仅是一个地点或"名词"或"事物" [27] [28] [29] [30]。20 世纪上半叶，欧洲遗产保护运动的兴起主要是由于战争和工业革命对历史遗迹和建筑造成的破坏 [26]。在这样的背景下，国际遗产保护文件应运而生，遗产保护责任的概念开始在这些文件中出现。随后，战后城市化、新工业革命、技术和信息发展等人类实践都对遗产保护造成了新的威胁和挑战。此外，由于全球化和现代化，遗产保护的主体逐渐相互联系起来。因此，日益复杂的关系和新出现的有关遗产的冲突／挑战需要改进遗产保护的工作机制。随着时间的推移，遗产责任的主体、对象和内容都会不可避免地相应扩大。

不同遗产责任主体对遗产的认知存在差异，对有关遗产地发展的利益诉求也不同 [31]。总体而言，世界遗产体系中的这些主体可分为三类：国际组织（"全球立场"）；缔约国及其机构、旅游业和国家旅游部门（"国家立场"）；遗产监测机构、遗产社区和个人（"社区立场"）[32]。民族 – 国家是国内法的基本单位、社会意识形态和话语的主导者，也是世界遗产体系的基本单位 [32] [33]。同时，当民族 – 国家参与制定国际保护文件时，人们被视为一个与地球共生的整体，因此国际社会应承担起维护"人类共同遗产"的责任。从这个意义上说，1972 年《世界遗产公约》发布之前，只有缔约国和国际组织在文件中被定义为责任主体，也并不奇怪。然而，自 20 世纪 70 年代以来，责任问题开始出现在"社区立场"上。可持续发展的概念是 1972 年在斯德哥尔摩举行的联合国人类环境会议上首次提出的，代际公平、社会正义和人文主义也得到了广泛认可 [34]。社区参与和遗产旅游开发在国际文件中被频繁提及。

到了 21 世纪，对"社区立场"主体的强调甚至变得更加明显。随经济形势的变化，遗产地人口格局也发生了变化。二者共同导致遗产社区个人和群体的增长，这些个体和群体成为作为遗产运动中的一支特殊力量。对"社区立场"主体的强调可能归因于这种变化所带来的威胁 [35]。例如，在《文化遗产地宪章》中，对文化财产的所有者和使用者，以及遗产社区的责任和利益给予了更多的尊重和关注。因此，遗产保护的焦点逐渐从政府导向向社会力量导向转变。

如今，人类现在已经进入了一个"后责任"时代，在这个时代中，主体的"责任感"将取代"道德秩序"，相应的，道德伦理将内化于每个人 [36]。然而，道德伦理的内化需要时间。虽然共同遗产的概念带来的共同责任已经在国际保护文件中得到了高度认可，但事实上，它未能解决谁有权拥有和阐释共同遗产的冲突。例如，1972 年《世界遗产公约》将世界遗产的所有权归属于两大互相较差的集团，即缔约国和全人类。同样，为纪念《世界遗产公约》发布 30 周年，（联合国教科文组织）举办了一次以"世界遗产 2002：共同遗产，共同责任"为主题的国际会议，联合国教科文组织副总干事 Barbosa [37]（在会上）强调"保护我们共同的人类遗产是我们的集体责任。这种责任，将过去、现在和未来的几代人联系在一个互惠互爱的链条上"。尽管如此，这种宏观的"叙述"对上述冲突的解决贡献甚微 [38]。因此，如何建立一个自下而上的遗产保护责任体系可能是值得我们探索的事情。

and international organisations were ascribed responsibility in heritage conservation documents. Since the 1970s, however, responsibility issues have begun to emerge in "a community stance". The concept of sustainable development was put forward for the first time in the United Nations Conference on the Human Environment held in Stockholm in 1972, which also acknowledged the concepts of intergenerational equity, social justice, and humanism[34]. Community participation and heritage tourism development were frequently noted in international documents.

The emphasis on stakeholders representing "a community stance" has become even more obvious in the 21st century. This change may be attributed to the challenges of changing population patterns that come with economic change, and result in the growing influence of individuals and interest groups within heritage[35]. In the Cultural Heritage Site Charter, for example, greater respect and recognition were given to the owners and users of cultural property, and the responsibilities and interests of host communities. Therefore, the focus of heritage conservation has gradually shifted from government-oriented to social-force-oriented approaches.

Humans have now entered an era of "post-responsibility", in which subjects' "sense of responsibility" will replace "moral order", and accordingly moral ethics will be internalised by individuals[36]. Nevertheless, such internalisation of moral ethics takes time. While the notion of a common heritage warranting common responsibility has been well-recognised in the international conservation documents, on the ground it fails to solve conflicts over who has the power to own and interpret our common heritage. For instance, the 1972 Convention attributes the ownership of World Heritage to two intersecting mega-constituencies: State Parties, and all mankind. Likewise, to mark the 30th anniversary of the 1972 Convention, an international congress on the theme of "World Heritage 2002: Shared Legacy, Common Responsibility" was held, and Barbosa[37], then the Deputy Director-General of UNESCO, stressed that "We have a collective responsibility to safeguard our common human heritage. It is a responsibility, furthermore, that links past, present and future generations in a chain of reciprocity and care". Such macro narratives, nonetheless, contribute little to the resolution of conflicts mentioned above[38]. As such, a bottom-up system of responsibility for heritage conservation may be worth exploring.

CONCLUSIONS

This study examines what kind of cultural heritage responsibilities are defined by the most relevant heritage conservation documents, based on a content analysis of 24 international heritage conservation documents since 1931. The findings suggest that the parties involved, and the types and scope of heritage responsibility have expanded significantly over time. The evolution of heritage responsibility in heritage conservation documents is a process of social construction, which results from the interplay of socio-economic, political, and cultural factors. The study calls for attention to be given to responsibility issues in heritage conservation, and particularly, for a bottom-up system of responsibility for heritage conservation.

结　论

本研究基于对自 1931 年以来 24 份主要国际遗产保护文件的内容分析，探讨了其所定义的文化遗产责任。研究结果表明，随着时间的推移，"遗产责任"的主体、对象和内容都有了明显的扩展。遗产保护文件中"遗产责任"的演变是一个社会建构的过程，是社会经济、政治、文化因素相互作用的结果。我们呼吁关注遗产保护中的责任问题，特别是一个自下而上的遗产保护责任体系的建立问题。

我们的研究对今后的研究有一定的启示。首先，本文的研究对象是最主要的国际遗产组织所发布的文件，未来的研究可能会将本研究作为出发点，以不同方法（如对文件编写者进行采访探讨其他组织（如不同级别的遗产组织或旅游组织））提出的责任问题。其次，遗产是在权力关系中产生和使用的 [28] [29] [39]，因此有必要探讨在保护和利用遗产方面权力和责任问题的相互作用。最后但并非最次要的是，虽然当前对"遗产责任"的探讨是基于二手数据进行的探讨，但需要对第一手材料进行实证研究，对责任问题进行扎实地探讨（例如，遗产利益相关者对责任的认知和承担），从而为遗产保护提供更实用的指导。特别需要指出的是，虽然从一般意义上讲，本研究专注于国际遗产文件中的遗产责任，但它指出了旅游业发展与遗产保护责任之间的联系。在一些最新的文件中，遗产社区、旅游业和国家旅游部门被认定为遗产责任主体。这一点证明了二者的联系。因此，随着遗产旅游业的蓬勃发展，探讨旅游利益相关者如何构建和理解遗产责任，以及这将如何影响遗产的保护和可持续利用，就显得尤为必要。

Some implications for future research can be obtained from this study. First, it focused on the documents produced by the most relevant international heritage organisations; future studies might take this research as a point of departure to explore responsibility issues as defined by other organisations (e.g. different levels of heritage and tourism organisations) and through different research methods (e.g. an interview with the document developers). Second, heritage is produced and used within power relations[28][29][39], and it is thus worth exploring the interplay of power and responsibility issues in the preservation and use of heritage. Last but not least, while the current research explores heritage responsibility based on secondary sources of data, empirical studies with first-hand data probing into responsibility issues on the ground (e.g. heritage stakeholders' perceptions of responsibilities, responsibility practices, etc.) are needed to offer more practical guidance for heritage conservation. While this study concentrates on heritage responsibility in international heritage documents in a general sense, it does show the relevance of tourism development to heritage conservation responsibility as demonstrated by the identification of host communities, the tourism industry and NTOs as bearers of heritage responsibility in some of these more recent documents. With a booming heritage tourism sector, it would be worth exploring how heritage responsibility is constructed and understood by tourism stakeholders, and how this can affect the conservation and sustainable use of heritage.

参考文献
Bibliography

[1] Bendix, R.F., Eggert, A., and Peselmann, A. "Introduction: Heritage Regimes and the State." In Heritage Regimes and the State, edited by R.F. Bendix, A. Eggert, and A. Peselmann. Gottingen: Universitätsverlag Göttingen, 2012:11-20.

R.F. 本迪克斯，A. 埃格特，A. 佩索尔曼. 简介：遗产制度与政府 [M]. R.F. 本迪克斯、A. 埃格特、A. 佩索尔曼编，遗产制度与政府. 哥廷根：哥廷根大学出版社，2012:11-20.

[2] 彭兆荣. 遗产：反思与诠释 [M]. 昆明：云南教育出版,2008.

Peng, Z.R. Heritage: Reflection and Interpretation. Kunming: Yunnan Education Press, 2008.

[3] Mckercher B., and Cros.H.d. Cultural Tourism: The Partnership Between Tourism and Cultural Heritage Management. Binghamton: The Haworth Press, 2002.

B. 迈克尔西,H.d. 克罗斯. 文化观光：观光与文化遗产管理 [M]. 宾汉姆顿：哈沃斯出版社,2002.

[4] Zhang, C.Z. "Heritage responsibility: Conception, characteristics and research issues." Tourism Tribune, Vol.29, 2014(11): 45-51.

张朝枝. 遗产责任：概念，特征与研究问题 [J]. 旅游学刊，卷 29,2014（11）:45-51.

[5] 国际古迹遗址理事会. 保护文物建筑及历史地段的国际宪章（威尼斯宪章）[EB/OL].1964-05-25.

ICOMOS. International Charter for the Conservation and Restoration of Monuments and Sites("The Venice Charter"). Second International Congress of Architects and Technicians of Historic Monument. Venice, May 25, 1964. http://www.international.icomos.org/charters/venice_e.pdf.

[6] 联合国教科文组织. 保护世界文化和自然遗产公约 [Z]. 第 17 届世界遗产大会通过.[EB/OL]. 1972-11-16.

UNESCO. "Convention Concerning the Protection of the World Cultural and Natural Heritage." adopted by the General Conference at its 17th session. Paris, 1972. http://unesdoc.unesco.org/images/0011/001140/114044e.pdf#page=134.

[7] GaliEspelt, N. "Identifying cultural tourism: A theoretical methodological proposal." Journal of Heritage Tourism, Vol.7, 2012(1): 45-58.

N. 加利埃斯佩尔特. 识别文化旅游：一份理论方法论提议 [J]. 遗产旅游杂志，卷 7,2012（1）：45-58.

[8] Macbeth, J. "Towards an ethics platform for tourism." Annals of Tourism Research, Vol.32, 2005(4): 962-984.

J. 麦克白. 走向旅游伦理平台 [J]. 旅游研究年刊，卷 32,2005（4）：962-984.

[9] Hultsman, J. "Just tourism: An ethical framework." Annals of Tourism Research, Vol.22, 1995(3): 553-567.

J. 豪斯曼. 公正的旅游：一个道德框架 [J]. 旅游研究年刊, 卷 22,1995（3）：553-567.

[10] Bianchi, R. "The critical turn in tourism studies: A radical citique." Tourism Geographies, Vol.11,

2009(4): 484-504.

R. 比安奇 . 旅游研究的关键转折：一份激进的批判 [J]. 旅游地理，卷 11,2009（4）：484-504.

[11] Pritchard, A., Morgan, N., and Ateljevic, I. "Hopeful tourism: A new transformative perspective." Annals of Tourism Research, Vol.38, 2011(3): 941-963.

A. 普理查德，N. 摩根，I. 阿泰列维奇 . 希望旅游：一种新的变革视角 [J]. 旅游研究年刊 , 卷 38,2011（3）：941-963.

[12] Caton, K. "Taking the moral turn in tourism studies." Annals of Tourism Research, Vol.39, 2012(4): 1906-1928.

K. 卡顿 . 旅游研究中的道德转向 [J]. 旅游研究年刊，卷 39,2012（4）：1906-1928.

[13] Farmaki, A., Constanti, P., and Yiasemi, I. "Responsible tourism in Cyprus: The rhetoric and the reality." Worldwide Hospitality and Tourism Themes, Vol.6, 2014(1): 10-26.

A. 法尔马季，P. 康斯坦蒂，I. 雅斯米 . 塞浦路斯的负责任旅游：言辞与现实 [J]. 世界餐旅及旅游主题，卷 6,2014（1）：10-26.

[14] Gao, J., Huang, Z., and Zhang, C. "Tourists' perceptions of responsibility: An application of norm-activation theory." Journal of Sustainable Tourism, Vol.25, 2017(2): 276-291.

高俊，黄琢玮，张朝枝 . 游客对责任的感知：规范激活理论的应用 [J]. 可持续旅游杂志，卷 25,2017（2）：276-291.

[15] Wells, V.K., Gregory Smith, D., Taheri, B., Manika, D., and McCowlen, C. "An exploration of CSR development in heritage tourism." Annals of Tourism Research, Vol.58, 2016:1-17.

V.K. 威尔斯，D.G. 史密斯，B. 塔赫里，D. 玛尼卡，C. 麦克科伦 . 遗产旅游中企业社会责任发展的探索 [J]. 旅游研究年刊，卷 58,2016:1-17.

[16] Wells, V.K., Manika, D., Gregory-Smith, D., Taheri, B., and McCowlen, C. "Heritage tourism, CSR and the role of employee environmental behaviour." Tourism Management, Vol.48, 2015: 399-413.

V.K. 威尔斯，D.G. 史密斯，B. 塔赫里，D. 玛尼卡，C. 麦克科伦 . 遗产旅游、企业社会责任和员工环境行为的角色 [J]. 旅游研究年刊，卷 48,2015:399-413.

[17] Zhang, C., Chen, P., and Wang, X. "Conceptualizing heritage responsibility in World Heritage Sites: Insights from Levinas' ethics of responsibility." Asian Journal of Tourism Research, Vol.2, 2017(3): 80-101.

张朝枝，陈朋，王雄志 . 概念化世界遗产地的遗产责任：来自列维纳斯的责任伦理的见解 [J]. 亚太旅游研究杂志，卷 2,2017（3）：80-101.

[18] Aas, C., Ladkin, A., and Fletcher, J. "Stakeholder collaboration and heritage management." Annals of Tourism Research, Vol.32, 2005(1): 28-48.

C. 雅斯，A. 拉德金，J. 弗莱彻 . 利益相关者评估和协作旅游规划：利益相关者的合作和遗产管理 [J]. 旅游研究年刊，卷 32,2005（1）：28-48.

[19] Araujo, L.M.d., and Bramwell, B. "Stakeholder assessment and collaborative tourism planning: The case of Brazil's Costa Dourada Project." Journal of Sustainable Tourism, Vol.7, 1999(3-4): 356-378.

L.M.d. 阿劳霍，B. 布拉姆韦尔 . 利益相关者评估和协作旅游规划：巴西科斯塔多拉大项目 (Costa

Dourada) 项目案例 [J]. 可持续旅游杂志，卷 7,1999（3-4）：356-378.

[20] Li, Y., and Caroline, H. "Community involvement for sustainable heritage tourism: A conceptual model." Journal of Cultural Heritage Management and Sustainable Development, Vol.5, 2015(3): 248-262.

李毓龙，H. 卡罗琳 . 社区参与的可持续遗产旅游：概念模型 [J]. 文化遗产管理与可持续发展杂志，卷 5,2015（3）：248-262.

[21] Van der Auwera, S. "UNESCO and the protection of cultural property during armed conflict." International journal of cultural policy, Vol.19, 2013(1): 1-19.

S. 范德欧威拉 . 联合国教科文组织和武装冲突期间的文化财产保护 [J]. 国际文化政策期刊，卷 19,2013（1）；1-19.

[22] Timothy, D.J. "Cultural Heritage and Tourism: An Introduction." Bristol: Channel View Publications, 2011.

D.J. 提姆西 . 文化遗产与旅游：简介 [M]. 布里斯托：海峡风景出版社，2011.

[23] Zhang, C.Z., Fyall, A., and Zheng, Y.F. "Heritage and tourism conflict within world heritage sites in China: A longitudinal study." Current Issues in Tourism, Vol.18, 2015(2): 110-116.

张朝枝，A. 法伊奥，郑艳芬 . 中国世界遗产地的遗产与旅游冲突：纵向研究 [J]. 旅游热点问题，卷 18,2015（2）：110-116.

[24] Fennell, D.A. "A content analysis of ecotourism definitions." Current Issues in Tourism, Vol.4, 2001(5): 403-421.

D.A. 芬奈尔 . 生态旅游定义的内容分析 [J]. 旅游热点问题，卷 4,2001（5）：403-421.

[25] Mehmetoglu, M. "Quantitative or qualitative? A content analysis of Nordic research in tourism and hospitality." Scandinavian Journal of Hospitality and Tourism, Vol.4, 2004(3):176-190.

M. 穆罕默德奥卢 . 定量还是定性？北欧旅游与酒店研究的内容分析 [J]. 斯堪的纳维亚餐旅与旅游期刊，卷 4,2004（3）：176-190.

[26] 张松 . 城市文化遗产保护国际宪章与国内法规选编 [M]. 上海：同济大学出版社 ,2007.

Zhang, S. City International Charter and Domestic Regulations for the Protection of Cultural Collection. Shanghai: Tongji University Press, 2007.

[27] Bendix, R. "Heritage between economy and politics: An assessment from the perspective of cultural anthropology." In Intangible Heritage, edited by L. Smith and N. Akagawa. New York: Routledge, 2009:253-269.

R. 本迪克斯 . 经济与政治之间的遗产：从文化人类学视角的评估 [J]. L. 史密斯， 赤川夏子编，非物质遗产 . 纽约：罗德里奇，2009:253-269.

[28]Mármol, C., Siniscalchi, V., and Estrada, F. "Reflecting on heritage and power: dynamics, strategies and appropriations in the Catalan Pyrenees and the French Alps." International Journal of Heritage Studies, Vol.269, 2016(5): 884-847.

C. 马尔默勒，V. 西尼斯卡尔奇，F. 埃斯特拉达 . 反思遗产和权力：加泰罗尼亚比利牛斯山脉和法国阿尔卑斯山脉的动态、战略和挪用 [J]. 国际遗产研究杂志，卷 269,2016（5）：847-884.

[29] Silva, L., and Santos, P.M. "Ethnographies of heritage and power." International Journal of Heritage Studies, Vol.22, 2012(3): 228-241.

L. 席尔瓦，P.M. 桑托斯 . 遗产和权力的民族志 [J]. 国际遗产研究杂志，卷 22,2012（3）：228-241.

[30] Smith L. Uses of Heritage. London: Routledge, 2006.

L. 史密斯 . 遗产的使用 [M]. 伦敦：罗德里奇，2006.

[31] Kaltenborn B. P., Thomassen J, Wold L. C, Linnell J.D.C. and Skar B. "World heritage status as a foundation for building local futures? A case study from Vega in Central Noaway." Journal of Sustainable Tourism, Vol.21, 2013(1): 99-116.

B.P. 卡尔滕博恩、J. 托马森、L.C. 沃尔德、J.D.C. 林内尔、B. 斯卡尔 . 世界遗产地位作为建立当地未来的基础？来自挪威中部韦加的案例研究 [J]. 可持续旅游杂志，卷 21,2013（1）：99-116.

[32] 彭兆荣，李春霞 . 遗产认知的共时向度与维度 [J]. 贵州社会科学 2012(1):5-11.

Peng, Z.R., and Li, C.X. "Heritage cognitive synchronic orientation and dimension." Guizhou Social Sciences, 2012(1): 5-11.

[33] Graham, B. "Heritage as knowledge: capital or culture?" Urban Studies, Vol.39, 2002 (5-6): 1003-1017.

B. 格雷厄姆 . 遗产作为知识：资本还是文化？[J]. 城市研究，卷 39,2002（5-6）：1003-1017.

[34] 邹统钎 . 遗产旅游发展与管理 [M]. 北京：中国旅游出版社 ,2010.

Zou, T.Q. Development and Management of Heritage Tourism. Beijing: China Travel and Tourism Press, 2010.

[35] Bohland, J.D., and Hague, E. "Heritage and identity." In International Encyclopedia of Human Geography, edited by N. Castree, M. Crang, and M. Domosh. London: Elsevier, 2009: 109-114.

J.D. 伯兰德、E. 哈格 . 遗产与身份 [J]. N. 卡斯崔、M. 克朗、M. 多莫什编，国际人文地理百科全书 . 伦敦：爱思唯尔，2009：109-114.

[36] Lipovetsky, G. Paradoxical happiness: Essay on hyperconsumption society[M]. Paris: Gallimard, 2007.

G. 利波维茨基 . 矛盾的幸福：关于超消费社会的论文 [M]. 巴黎：伽利玛，2007.

[37] Barbosa, M. "World Heritage 2002: Shared legacy, common responsibility." Adopted by an international congress. Venice (Italy), November 2003.

M. 巴博萨 . 世界遗产 2002：共同遗产，共同责任 [EB/OL]. 被国际大会采用 . 威尼斯（意大利），2003 年 11 月 .

http://whc.unesco.org/document/101842.

[38] 李春霞 . 世界遗产：人类共同继承的遗产 [J]. 重庆文理学院学报 .2008(2):5-11.

Li, C.X. "World Heritage: Common Heritage of Mankind." Journal of Chongqing University of Arts and Sciences, 2008(2): 5-11.

[39] Baird, M. F. " 'The breath of the mountain is my heart' : indigenous cultural landscapes and the politics of heritage." International Journal of Heritage Studies, Vol.19, 2013(4): 327-340.

M.F. 贝尔德 . "山之呼吸乃我心"：土著文化景观和遗产政治 [J]. 国际遗产研究杂志 . 卷 19,2013（4）：5-11.

INTERPRETING HADRIAN'S WALL FOR VISITORS

W.B. GRIFFITHS

Tyne & Wear Archives and Museums - Newcastle upon Tyne - UK

Abstract

The interpretation of Hadrian's Wall is constantly shifting due to new discoveries, better awareness of audiences and communities and their needs, and new technologies. Increasingly partnership working between the various organisations responsible for interpreting different parts of the monument is allowing more detailed and nuanced interpretation of the monument as a whole.

Keywords: Museums, interpretation, audiences, reconstruction, re-enactment

Hadrian's Wall receives an estimated 775,000 visitors each year[1]. They visit for the landscape and/or the heritage. Many visit its monuments and museums, while others simply walk the Hadrian's Wall Trail. This paper focuses on the interpretation of the archaeological heritage of the Wall, but it should not be forgotten that the interpretation of the natural environment of the World Heritage Site is also a significant factor in many visitors' enjoyment.

The interpretation of the Wall has been evolving since the 6th century AD when the monk Gildas claimed it was built in the 5th century AD around the time of the Roman abandonment of Britain. It was not until the early 19th century that it was first interpreted as having been constructed under the Emperor Hadrian[2].

As our detailed understanding of the frontier has increased, with excavations revealing more of the structures and the artefacts of daily life, and different academic interpretations to be shared with audiences, so too has our understanding of the visitors, actual and potential, to the Wall. This is driven in part by a need for institutions to demonstrate public interest and support for the monument, working to ensure the interpretation they provide is relevant and engaging for the audiences they are seeking to reach.

WHAT AUDIENCES WANT

Over the years a variety of audience segmentation techniques have been developed based on, for example, analysis of social class, interests, age and/or family status. The latest iterations are the 'culture segments' a psychographic model of segmentation based on people's deeply held values and their beliefs about arts and culture.(developed by MHM https://mhminsight.com/culture-segments)

Of course there are key audiences outside the segments too, such as schools and community groups, who

哈德良长城的观众阐释

比尔·格里菲斯
（泰恩·威尔郡档案博物馆，英国纽卡斯尔）

摘　要

随着考古的新发现，对不同观众和社区需求的更深了解和涌现的新科技，对哈德良长城的阐释也在不断变化。各机构不断加强合作，负责阐释遗迹不同部分，使得哈德良长城整体遗产得以进行更细致入微的阐释。

关键词：博物馆　阐释　观众　重建　情景再现

哈德良长城预计每年接待 775000 名游客[1]。他们大多是为景观和 / 或遗迹而来。很多人会参观遗迹和博物馆，而有些人只徒步于哈德良长城步道上。本文着重探讨对长城考古遗迹的阐释，同时，我们也不应忽视对世界遗产地自然环境的阐释，因为它也是吸引游客的重要因素。

对长城的阐释始于公元六世纪，此后不断演变。当时，吉尔达斯（Gildas）僧人主张长城建于公元五世纪，大约是罗马帝国放弃占领布列颠的时期。一直到 19 世纪初期，长城才首次被证实是在哈德良皇帝统治下建造的[2]。

随着考古发掘中建筑结构和日常用品的不断出土，以及大量学术成果呈现给公众的不同的阐释分析，使我们对哈德哈长城的理解愈加详尽，与此同时，我们对长城实际和潜在游客的认识也越来越深入。背后的部分动机是机构需要展示其公共责任和对古迹保护的支持，希望他们的展示阐释内容真实科学，并对目标观众有吸引力。

一、观众想要什么

多年来开发了多种观众细分方法，如基于社会阶层，兴趣，年龄和 / 或家庭差误的分析。最新的细分技术是基于"文化群体"，此模式按心理因素细分，基于人们内心深处的价值观及他们对艺术和文化的认知来区分观众（由 MHM 开发 https://mhminsight.com/culture-segments）。

当然，在这些观众群体之外还存在其他重要观众群体，例如学校和社区团体等。他们对长城阐释有特殊需求，比如希望能辅助教学，通过宣传当地历史促进社会参与，或是树立社区意识。

2011 年，哈德良长城发布了一份阐释框架文件。这份实用的文件将研究工作与观众和非游客结合起来，为哈德良长城罗马边疆遗址的展示阐释提出一系列的建议。此框架向所有负责阐释哈德良长城的机构公开，但需要指出的是它并不强行要求各机构严格遵循此框架。以下为其中的一些要点和提议：

have specific requirements from the Wall's interpretation whether it is to support study, inform engagement with their local place, or to create meaning for them as a community.

In 2011 an interpretation framework was published for the Wall. It is a useful document combining research into audiences and non-visitors and making a series of recommendations for interpreting the frontier. The framework is available to all the bodies who have a responsibility for interpreting Hadrian's Wall, although it should be noted that no one is required to follow it. It makes a number of key points and calls for:

'interpretation that is dynamic and people orientated, relevant (though potentially challenging) to their views, understanding and interest in the world around them - providing interpretation that is exciting, challenging, engaging, fascinating, participative, enjoyable and fun'[1][3].

Certainly today audiences are not looking simply to be educated, but to be engaged. An important aspect in interpretation is to consider relevance to their lives. This can seemingly represent a challenge to interpretation of a Roman frontier. However, stories can be brought out. A key example of this is the living frontiers gallery at Tullie House which sets Hadrian's Wall in the context of frontiers generally[4]. This responds to another of the principles of the interpretation framework that the Wall 'can act as a metaphor through which to explore contemporary issues, contributing relevance, meaning and value to the visitor experience.'[1]

Another aspect of interpretation for the Wall is the involvement of audiences and communities. Not least due to popular TV programmes about archaeology, the public are well informed about archaeological techniques such as geophysical prospection (Fig. 1), and have a real appetite for hearing about the latest discoveries. This is central to the displays at Vindolanda for example, where the museum has been designed to ensure that the latest discoveries from the excavations each summer can be incorporated into the galleries.

Increasingly audiences are also interested in areas of uncertainty in our understanding of the Wall, leaving them room to make their own minds up. For example, a reconstructed section of Wall at Segedunum displays a number of the ways in which the Wall might have been plastered over and decorated.

Hadrian's Wall is seeing programmes developed that involve communities in research and interpretation of the Wall. There is an active audience that wishes to participate. This has traditionally been through learned archaeological societies, but recent years have seen the rise of community participation projects. Examples include Wallquest (www.hadrianswallquest.co.uk) which saw members of the public join a programme to reveal more of the Wall on urban Tyneside. This included research into, and subsequent excavation and interpretation of, the bath-house at Segedunum. There is also an established group of volunteer Wall guides.

TECHNIQUES

To engage as wide a range of people as possible, with different interests, personality types and learning styles, means utilising a full array of interpretation tools and techniques including, on site interpretation panels, films, digital content, hands-on activities, reconstruction drawings and models[5]. Space does not permit a discus-

"阐释是动态的，以人为本的，切入人们观察周围世界的视角、理解和兴趣（虽然有时会挑战他们的观念）。呈现的阐释应该激动人心，富有挑战，引人入胜，激发参与，令人愉悦且有趣。" [1][3]

毫无疑问的，如今的观众并不想只是被动地学习，而是希望参与其中。阐释的一个重要方面就是要考虑内容与观众生活的相关性。对于罗马边疆遗产的阐释，实现这一方面似乎挑战很大。但是，我们可以呈现其中的故事。一个重要例子是在图利别墅（Tullie House）的边境生活展览馆，展示了哈德良长城边疆周围的普通生活 [4]。这也体现了阐释框架的另一个原则：长城"可以作为隐喻来探索当代议题，为游客体验添加相关性，意义和价值" [1]。

长城阐释的另一个方面是观众参与和社区参与。值得一提的是，由于考古电视节目的流行，公众对地理勘探等考古技术了解颇多（图1），并热衷于了解最新考古发现。这成为文多兰达的展览的核心内容，博物馆展陈的设计就是不断更新，确保每年夏天的最新发掘成果都能纳入展馆。

观众也越来越对长城的未解之谜产生兴趣，这赋予他们发挥自己想象力的空间。例如，在塞格杜努

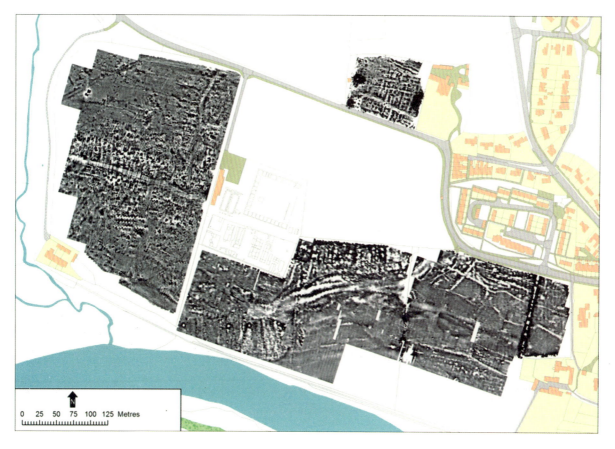

Fig. 1

Audiences engage with the latest research and are fascinated by archaeological techniques such as the geophysical survey of the Roman town at Corbridge (© Newcastle University)

图1

观众参与科布里奇罗马城镇的最新研究，并被地球物理调查等考古技术深深吸引（版权：纽卡斯尔大学）

sion of all the techniques, but a few are discussed here.

Publications: There are a bewildering array of publications about Hadrian's Wall, from authors presenting their overarching account of the frontier in a book, or focussing on points of detail in academic papers in a wide variety of journals. There are popular guides and travelogues aimed at the general reader, and of course books for children. Each has their place.

Exhibitions: The museum displays utilise a variety of interpretive techniques from traditional labels to 3D films reconstructing the frontier. These displays are most effective when the museum has considered what themes it can best focus on, rather than attempting to cover the full scope of the frontier. This is often linked to the Unique Selling Point of the site. For example, Segedunum concentrates on interpreting the functions of the various buildings in the fort as it has recovered almost the entire ground plan of the site. At Vindolanda parts of the display focus on the unparalleled collection of organic finds that survive in the almost unique environmental conditions at the site. In 2018 a new gallery 'Wooden Underworld' was opened, dedicated to displaying and interpreting the wooden artefacts from the site.

Fig. 2
Reconstructed buildings provide a sense of scale not possible in other interpretative techniques. The reconstructed West Gateway of the Roman fort at Arbeia, South Shields (© Tyne & Wear Archives and Museums)
图 2
重建建筑提供了其他阐释技术无法实现的规模感。图示为在南希尔兹镇阿尔比亚重建的罗马要塞西侧城门（版权：泰恩·威尔郡档案博物馆）

姆重建的一段长城展示了几种长城过去粉刷和装饰的可能方式。

哈德良长城也逐渐发展出社区参与长城研究和阐释的项目。也有一批观众积极性很高，愿意参与其中。项目原先是由学术性的考古团体执行，近年来则有越来越多的社区参与项目。案例包括"长城探秘"（Wallquest）（www.hadrainswallquest.co.uk），这是一个公众可以参与的项目，主要是在泰恩赛德城市地区深入探寻长城。项目包括对塞格杜努姆罗马浴室的研究，以及随后的发掘和阐释。还有一支由志愿者组成的固定长城导览队伍。

二、技　术

若要尽可能吸引拥有不同兴趣、个性特征和学习风格的广泛观众，我们就需利用各种不同的阐释工具和技术，包括在原址上的阐释讲解牌、电影、数码内容、实际操作活动、重建绘图和模型[5]。因篇幅所限无法讨论所有的技术，在此仅论及若干。

出版物：有关哈德良长城的著作令人眼花缭乱，有些作者将边境的总体描述著作成书，也有作者在大量期刊上发表学术文章，着重讨论部分细节。此外，也有针对大众读者的旅游指南和游记，以及儿童书籍。所有种类都不可或缺。

展览：博物馆在展览中使用一系列的阐释技术，从传统的标签方式到 3D 电影技术来重现哈德良。若博物馆策划好重点展出某个主题，而非试图呈现长城全貌时，这些展览技术的效果更佳。这通常需要确定各个遗址的独特卖点。例如，塞格杜努姆阐释的重点是要塞各建筑的功能，因为这里对大部分要塞建筑格局进行了发掘。在文多兰达，部分展出的重点为该遗址独特的环境中发现的绝无仅有的有机遗存物。2018 年一个新的展厅"木质地下世界"正式开幕，专门用来展示并阐释遗址中出土的木质文物。

情景再现：在英国的遗产阐释中，情景再现占据重要地位；演员大多都是由志愿者不计报酬地奉献自己的时间来完成。哈德良长城沿线的很多遗址都会举办多样的情景再现表演活动，可以很好地激发人们的想象力。优秀的情景再现演员通常会与学者合作，花很多时间研究装备。阐释哈德良长城时，其中一个挑战是罗马军队在此驻扎了将近三百年。在此期间，制服和装备都有所改变。越来越多的情景再现团体去表现罗马占领时期的不同时代，十分受欢迎，增加观众的参与感，丰富公众的认知，了解罗马士兵装备的演变。

重建：文多兰达、阿尔比亚和塞格杜努姆都重建了几处罗马设施（图 2）。因篇幅所限无法在此复述对这种重建的功过争论 [5]。但毫无疑问，对于偶尔到访的游客，这种展示方式为考古遗址提供了成效显著又能身历其境的阐释，带领他们进入一个数字模拟无法企及的三维世界。早期的担忧之一是重建会僵化公众对建筑的印象，但就笔者个人经验而言，实际状况完全相反。若阐释是以图画来呈现，则公众会漫不经心，但对于重建建筑，公众却会批判它的方方面面。若要成功地阐释遗迹，则重建需要有严格的学术研究基础。这应包括确保公众明白重建建筑中有多少是猜测的，这样至少反倒会加深公众的参与度。

反常规阐释方式有时也可以考虑——以出人意料或不同寻常方式让公众从不同角度了解遗迹。

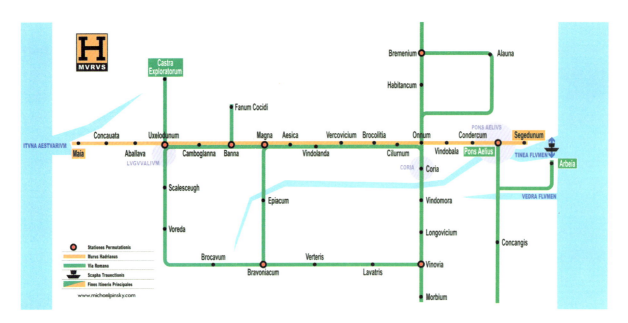

Fig. 3

Alternative methods of interpretation can capture audiences' imagination such as in this map of Hadrian's Wall and the road systems linking the Roman forts of the frontier presented in the style of a modern metro map. (© Tyne & Wear Archives and Museums)

图 3

不同的阐释方法可以激发观众的想象力，例如此幅地图，将哈德良长城及连接各罗马要塞的道路系统以现代地铁路线图的风格展现（版权：泰恩·威尔郡档案博物馆）

Re-enactment: Re-enactment is a key element in heritage interpretation across Britain, with the vast majority of re-enactors being volunteers, giving their time for free. On Hadrian's Wall many sites will put on re-enactment events of different kinds. They can be an excellent way of capturing imagination. The best re-enactors have spent many hours researching their kit, often in association with academics. One of the challenges in interpreting Hadrian's Wall is that it was garrisoned by Rome for almost 300 years. In that time uniforms and equipment changed. Increasingly re-enactment groups are covering different periods of the Roman occupation, which has proven to be a popular and engaging way of broadening the public's understanding of what a Roman solider may have looked like over time.

Reconstruction: At Vindolanda, Arbeia and Segedunum several Roman buildings have been reconstructed (Fig. 2). Space does not permit a rehearsal of the debates about the merits or otherwise of such reconstructions[5]. There is no doubt that for the casual visitor they provide effective and engaging interpretation of the archaeological remains they are based on - truly taking them into the third dimension in a way not achieved even with digital reconstructions. One of the early fears was that reconstructions would fossilise a view of a building in the public mind, however, in this author's experience, the opposite is true - with the public critically challenging aspects of the reconstructed building in a way they simply do not for an interpretation drawing. To be a truly

2003 年，画家麦克·平斯基（Michael Pinsky）受到委托，以艺术形式建立塞格杜努姆罗马要塞与沃森德（Wallsend）地铁站之间的联系。画家将地铁站指示牌用拉丁和英文双语重新印制，并制作了一幅地图（图 3）。

三、案例研究：哈德良骑兵——一个分散的展览

2017 年哈德良长城沿线的博物馆开展合作，在长城沿线共同举办了一个"分散展览"（展览的不同部分在不同博物馆展出，游客要看完所有展览内容需要参观所有相关的博物馆）。哈德良长城世界遗产地沿线有 11 座博物馆内有罗马遗迹，分别由五个不同的机构管理：泰恩·威尔地区档案及博物馆（管理阿尔比亚、塞格杜努姆罗马要塞遗址和汉科克大北方博物馆），英格兰遗产信托（管理考布里奇罗马城镇和切斯特罗马要塞、豪塞斯特兹和博得瓦德）、文多兰达信托（管理文多兰达罗马要塞博物馆和罗马军队博物馆）、图利别墅博物馆，以及森豪斯罗马博物馆。各博物馆合作展出的"哈德良骑兵展"由诺桑伯兰国家公园管理处支持，主要的资金来源则是英格兰艺术委员会的博物馆适应能力建设基金。博得瓦德罗马博物馆因在 2017 年重新装修而未能加入哈德良骑兵展项目。哈德良骑兵展在筹划阶段有三项目标：

·证明伙伴机构能够互相合作；

·探讨以往展览中受到忽略的骑兵的作用，包括其在整个罗马军队中的作用，尤其是在哈德良长城中的作用。

·举办一场出色的展览，以吸引更多游客参观长城。

在一般游客的想象中，通常是孤零零的步兵站在长城上把守，面朝北方观察入侵的迹象。实际情况则复杂得多，大约三分之一驻扎在长城的军队是骑兵，他们负责在大范围内进行巡逻。罗马骑兵往往配有最好的装备，其"盛装"包括装饰繁复的头盔、盔甲和骑具。展览筹备团队列了一个"愿望清单"，希望能从欧洲博物馆借得的精彩展品，其中包括大英博物馆。本以为大部分潜在的捐赠方会拒绝出借，因为这与一般博物馆间的文物出借相当不同。但是，我们联系的机构和个人都无一例外地非常乐意借出展品，并且其中一位私人捐赠者在我们原本要求的展品外还额外提供更多展品——这样我们就能够展出一套非常精美的文物。

除展览外，还组织了全方位的学校参与项目，以及一系列的情景再现表演。但是，该项目仍然还需要一个点睛之笔，以真正激发公众的想象力。

最终我们决定情景再现一支完整的罗马骑兵支队，这一场景自罗马时期结束后就没有在英国出现过。场面试图再现罗马骑兵操练表演（Hippika Gymnasia），这不仅是简单的文艺表演，而是作为考古学试验。在活动宣传中特别强调了这一性质，以此来增强该活动对公众的吸引力。为此集合了 30 名骑手（图 4），部分为角色演员，部分为专业特技演员，根据近 2000 年以前古罗马作家阿里安（Arrian）以及哈德良皇帝本人所描述的军事演习训练情况对他们进行训练。该活动最终也形成一个关于罗马时期骑兵的一小时记录片，在英国电视频道上播放（如需更多有关哈德良骑兵和其后世影响的信息，访问 www.hadrianswallcountry.co.uk/learning/ideas-and-inspiration/hadrians-cavalry）。

---

1 拉丁语，为一古罗马骑兵作战单位——译者注。

successful piece of interpretation a reconstruction needs to be based on rigorous academic research. This should include ensuring the public understand how much of the reconstruction is conjectural, not least as this creates greater engagement.

There is also room for quirky interpretation - doing things that are unexpected or at least unusual in order get the public to see the monument in a different way. In 2003 artist Michael Pinsky was commissioned to develop artist interventions that created a link between Segedunum Roman Fort and Wallsend metro station. Thus included reprinting the stations signs in Latin as well as English, and creating a map (Fig. 3).

CASE STUDY: HADRIAN'S CAVALRY - A DISPERSED EXHIBITION

2017 saw the Museums of Hadrian's Wall come together in a partnership, to mount a 'dispersed exhibition' (an exhibition in which several museums each display a different section of the exhibition so that to see it all visitors will need to visit all the participating museums) along the frontier. There are 11 museums with Roman remains on Hadrian's Wall World Heritage Site - managed by five different organisations - Tyne & Wear Archives and Museums (running Arbiea and Segedunum Roman forts and the Great North Museum: Hancock), English Heritage (Corbridge Roman Town and the forts at Chesters, Housesteads and Birdoswald), The Vindolanda Trust (Vindolanda Roman Fort Museum and the Roman Army Museum), Tullie House Museum and Gallery, Senhouse Roman Museum. Their partnership to deliver Hadrian's Cavalry was supported by the Northumberland National Park Authority and the project's main funder was Arts Council England's Museum Resilience Fund. Birdoswald Roman fort was being refurbished in 2017 and was not able to join the Hadrian's Cavalry project. Hadrian's Cavalry was developed with three purposes in mind:

- · To demonstrate that the partner organisations could work in partnership;
- · To explore the often under-represented role of the cavalry, in the Roman army in general, and on Hadrian's Wall in particular;
- · To deliver a stand out exhibition that would attract new visitors to the Wall.

The average visitor tends to imagine the Wall with lonely infantrymen standing on top of it looking North for signs of trouble. The reality was much more complex with approximately one third of the Wall garrison being cavalry who would carry out wide-ranging patrol work. Roman cavalrymen tend to have the best equipment, with their 'parade' armour including highly decorated helmets, armour and horse fittings. The project team drew up a 'wish list' of the finest examples to borrow from museums, including the British Museum, across Europe. It was thought that most potential donors would say no as this was a very different proposition to a regular inter-museum loan. However, without exception, the organisations and individuals we approached were more than happy in principle to lend items, indeed one private donor offered us more objects that we had originally asked for - meaning we were able to exhibit an exceptional group of artefacts.

Fig. 4
Re-enactment is a popular and effective way of engaging audiences - Turma![1] event in Carlisle both presented research and created a spectacle (© Graham Sumner)
图 4
情景再现是引起观众互动的一种广受欢迎且有效的方式—在卡莱尔举办的 Turma！活动不仅展示了研究成果，场面也蔚为壮观
（摄影：Graham Sumner）

那么总体而言，哈德良骑兵项目是否成功？可以肯定的是，它为哈德良长城带来了更多关注。在项目期间，有关项目的报道常常见诸旅游文章和网站。打头炮的是《每日邮报》（英国一家主要报纸）的周日版将它列为 2017 年世界上不可错过的 30 项活动之一，也是清单中唯一一个在英国举办的活动。2017 年哈德良长城的游客数量与 2016 年相比总体增长了 12%。长城和沿线的博物馆也见证了利益相关方更多的参与，这在英国公共部门资助减少的情况下至关重要。与此同时，合作伙伴也继续沟通并计划开展更多项目。

结　论

随着对学科本身和目标群体理解的加深，哈德良长城的阐释也一直在演变，发展出更多与当代人切实相关的细致入微的解读。继续发展和使用多种技术至关重要，从而可以尽可能地覆盖更广泛的观众群体。长城合作伙伴的合作也愈加频繁，前景看好，因为他们可以互相支持，确保哈德良长城和其蕴涵的无数故事能持续不断地吸引世界遗产地的观众。

Alongside the exhibition a comprehensive schools' engagement programme was developed, and a series of re-enactment events were delivered. However, the project needed a stand-out event to truly capture the public's imagination.

It was decided to recreate a full Roman cavalry turma, not seen in the UK since the Roman period, and try to recreate elements of the Hippika Gymnasia (the Roman cavalry drill display), not simply as a show, but also as an archaeological experiment, something made very clear in descriptions of the event, and which served to enhance its appeal to the public. This meant bringing together 30 riders (Fig. 4), some re-enactors, some professional stuntmen, and training them in drill described almost 2,000 years ago by the Roman author Arrian, and indeed by the Emperor Hadrian himself. The event was also the catalyst for a one hour documentary about Roman cavalry on British television (For more information about Hadrian's Cavalry and its legacy visit www.hadrianswallcountry.co.uk/learning/ideas-and-inspiration/hadrians-cavalry).

So was the overall Hadrian's Cavalry project a success? It certainly drew attention to Hadrian's Wall. It was regularly listed in tourism articles and websites over the year, starting with one of the UK's major Sunday papers, the Daily Telegraph, listing it as one of the top 30 things to do in the world in 2017, the only UK based item on the list. Hadrian's Wall in 2017 saw an overall 12% increase in visitors compared to 2016. The Wall and its museums have also seen an increased engagement of stakeholders, vital at a time of declining public funding in the UK, and the partners are still talking to each other and planning other projects.

CONCLUSION

The interpretation of Hadrian's Wall is constantly evolving as understanding of subject matter and audiences is developed, developing more nuanced understandings of what is relevant to people today. It is vital that diverse techniques continue to be used and developed in order to reach as wide a section of people as possible. The Wall partners are now starting to work in collaboration more regularly, which feels a very positive step as they can support each other to ensure Hadrian's Wall and the myriad of stories it represents can continue to engage audiences with the World Heritage Site for generations to come.

参考文献
Bibliography

[1] Adkins, G. and Mills, N. Frontiers of the Roman Empire World Heritage Site - Hadrian's Wall Interpretation Framework. Hexham: 2011.

G. 阿德金斯，N. 米尔斯 . 罗马帝国边境世界遗产地——哈德良长城阐释框架 [M]. 赫克瑟姆 : 2011.

[2] Breeze, D.J. Collingwood Bruce's Handbook to the Roman Wall (14th Edn). Newcastle upon Tyne：2006.

D.J. 布里兹 . 科林伍德·布鲁斯的古罗马长城手册（第 14 版）[M]. 纽卡斯尔 :2006.

[3] Adkins, G. et al. "The Hadrian's Wall Interpretation Framework: Audience Research." In Presenting the Romans, edited by N. Mills. Woodbridge： 2013: 157-169.

G. 阿德金斯等 . 哈德良长城阐释框架：观众研究 [J].N. 米尔斯编，展现罗马帝国 . 伍德布里奇 :2013：157-169.

[4] Mills, N., et al. "Applying the Hadrian's Wall Interpretation Framework." In Presenting the Romans, edited by N. Mills. Woodbridge： 2013: 180-192.

N. 米尔斯等 . 哈德良长城阐释框架的应用 [J].N. 米尔斯编，展现罗马帝国 . 伍德布里奇 : 2013:180-192.

[5] Griffiths, W.B. "Interpretation of Roman Archaeological Sites for Visitors." In Unidad y diversidad en el Arco Atlantico en epoca romana, edited by C.F.Ochoa and P.G.Diaz. Oxford: 2005:337-342.

W.B. 格里菲斯 . 为游客阐释罗马考古遗址 [J].C.F. 欧察和 P.G. 迪亚兹编，Unidad y diversidad en el Arco Atlantico en epoca romana. 牛津 :2005:337-342.

互联网如何为长城保护赋能——腾讯长城保护项目的经验分享

马　尧

（腾讯基金会，中国北京）

摘　要

腾讯基金会与中国文物保护基金会自 2016 年联合发起长城保护项目以来，在多个角度展开长城的传播与公众参与工作，本文旨在介绍中国长城传播的一些现实困境以及腾讯通过互联网手段面向年轻用户传播长城保护的手段和案例。

关键词：长城传播　IP 打造　长城内容　公益传播

一、长城保护的现状

长城是中国体量最大的文化遗产，自新中国成立以来就一直被认作是中华民族的象征，在许多场合被作为非常重要的图腾来进行展示和传播，包括中国的国歌和普通公民身份证的背面，都有长城形象的出现。因此，在中国，长城毫无疑问是最具有知名度的文化遗产。

然而提及作为文化遗产的长城，绝大多数的公众对其认知却非常局限，甚至是狭隘的。首先，在中国的长城宣传材料中，展示的长城形象往往是位于北京附近，按照最高标准修筑的八达岭明长城，而这种砖石搭建雄伟精致的长城段落，在国家文物局发布的中国长城资源调查数据中只占不到 2%，绝大多数由夯土搭建、形制多样的长城形象几乎不为国人所知。更不用说，绝大多数分布在胡焕庸线以西的长城段落，远离中国人口稠密的区域，人们既难以走近长城，在传播材料又看不到更丰富的长城形象，这直接造成大多数人对于这座最为知名的中国建筑的认知偏差巨大。

除去这种对长城形象的认知偏差，在许多宣传资料中，将长城的意象与中华民族的脊梁、钢铁军队等国家主旋律形象进行结合，也会影响到中国公众对于长城的认知。比如长城的修缮保护类的信息往往会被双重解读，不仅仅是因为长城是伟大而重要的文化遗产受人关注，而且有时会通过网上社交媒体将长城的民族意义、政治形象无限上升，也给从事长城保护工作的机构和个人带来许多意想不到的压力。

除去上面提到的公众对于长城形象的认知偏差，长城传播的话语体系也造成的受众的圈层化。我们曾经通过腾讯网的渠道面向公众开放过一场线下的长城专题讲座，邀请知名长城研究学者来从文化遗产的角度展示和介绍长城，报名到场的 200 名观众中，超过 90% 的参与者年龄都大于 50 岁。在互联网时代，传统的长城传播话题和材料，在让长城深入人心的同时，实际上也让长城（作为文化遗产的）爱好者越来越少，尤其是对于大多数年轻人来说，现在的长城是沉重、年迈的形象，加上不易走近（许多年轻人喜欢调侃嘲笑在假期去八达岭长城旅游排队的游客），事实上长城作为中国最为重要和知名的文化遗产，

HOW INTERNET EMPOWERS GREAT WALL PROTECTION - SHARING EXPERIENCE OF TENCENT'S GREAT WALL CONSERVATION PROGRAMME

Ma Yao

Tencent Foundation - Beijing - China

Abstract

Tencent Foundation initiated a communication and public participation campaign concerning the Great Wall when it launched the Great Wall Conservation Programme in concert with the China Foundation for Cultural Heritage Conservation in 2016. This paper aims to share some dilemmas facing the promotion of understanding of the Great Wall in China, as well as the means adopted and some cases in which Tencent promotes protection of the Great Wall among young users through the internet.

Keywords: dissemination of the Great Wall; IP branding; Great Wall content; promoting voluntary public activities

CURRENT STATUS OF THE CONSERVATION OF THE GREAT WALL

The Great Wall, China's most extensive cultural heritage site, has been recognised as a symbol of the Chinese nation since the founding of the People's Republic of China, and has been displayed and promoted as an icon on many occasions, including its presence in the national anthem of China and on the back of citizenship ID cards. Therefore, in China, the Great Wall is without a doubt the cultural heritage site with the highest profile.

Although the Great Wall is recognised as a cultural heritage site the vast majority of the public have limited, and even narrow, knowledge of it. For example, most of the publicity materials on the Great Wall reference only the Badaling section in close proximity to Beijing, which was built in the Ming Dynasty to the highest architectural specifications. Such majestic and exquisite brick sections of the Great Wall account for less than 2% the Great Wall as identified by the National Administration of Cultural Heritage. Images of earthen sections of the Great Wall are barely known to the Chinese. Of course, the vast majority of the Great Wall situated to the west of Heihe–Tengchong Line is far away from densely populated areas. It is difficult for people to access the Great Wall, and it is impossible for them to get a complete picture of the Great Wall from traditional promotional materials. As a result, most people have a grossly mistaken idea of this most famous Chinese monument.

In addition to this limited perception of the Great Wall, many publicity materials associate it with the ideas of the Great Wall as the backbone of the Chinese nation, the steel army and other national images, which influ-

图1

假期人山人海的长城景区 [1]

Fig. 1

Great Wall Scenic Area with throngs of visitors during holidays

在面对越来越广大的年轻人群体时，已经不再是香饽饽了（图1）。

二、腾讯对长城保护的思考

腾讯是从 2014 年开始关注到长城这一主题的，当时我们单纯是考虑从技术层面如何能助力长城的保护与传播。于是腾讯地图的技术测绘团队在中国西部省份采集制作了近 900 公里的 360° 高精度全景长城影像，并在地图平台面对用户线上展示。这些数据全部由高清晰高精度的采集设备和专业采集工程师沿长城步行采集，按照 150—200 米的间距，连续采集了甘肃、宁夏、陕西、河北和北京境内的多段长城，这些高精度的数据资料可以让用户非常清楚地看到不同形制的长城形象，以及它们所分布的地理环境，对于长城本体可以有一个较为全面和立体的观感，尤其是对于大多数没办法走近到长城的公众来说，这种全新有趣的体验方式可以丰富他们对于长城的认知，吸引更多人关注到作为文化遗产的长城。

ence the Chinese public's perception of the Great Wall. For example, the information on the conservation and protection of the Great Wall is often open to dual interpretation. The Great Wall attracts attention for its great and important cultural heritage significance. Also, its national and political symbolism are sometimes over-exaggerated through online social media, which often creates many unexpected pressures to institutions and individuals engaged in the conservation of the Great Wall.

In addition to the distorted public perception of the Great Wall, the framing of discussion and promotion of the Great Wall has previously been directed to limited audiences. We held a public lecture on the Great Wall (which was also broadcast online through the channel of QQ.com) during which leading research scholars were invited to present and introduce the Great Wall from the perspective of cultural heritage. Over 90% of the 200 participants present at the lecture were over 50 years old. In the age of the internet, traditional topics and materials are still used for the promotion of the understanding of the Great Wall and for raising the profile of the Great Wall. At the same time, the number of people who value the Great Wall as cultural heritage has been dwindling, especially among young people. The Great Wall has been seen as something which is old-fashioned and dull, and something which is difficult to engage with (many young people like to tease the tourists who queue to visit the Badaling Great Wall during the holidays). In fact, the Great Wall, although the most important and well-known cultural heritage site in China, is no longer sought-after among the vast majority of young people. (Fig. 1)

TENCENT'S THOUGHTS ON THE CONSERVATION OF THE GREAT WALL

Tencent began to pay attention to the Great Wall in 2014. At that time, we only considered how to harness technology to assist the protection and promotion of the Great Wall. Tencent Map's technical surveying and mapping team collected and produced 360° high-definition panoramic images of nearly 900 km of the Great Wall in the western provinces of China and displayed these on the map platform for users. This data was collected by professional engineers using high-definition equipment while walking along the Great Wall. At intervals of 150 to 200 m, they collected images of the sections in Gansu, Ningxia, Shaanxi, Hebei and Beijing. These high-definition images enable users to see clearly the different forms of the Great Wall and their geographical environments. It presents a comprehensive and three-dimensional view of the Great Wall, especially for the majority of the public who can't visit the Great Wall in person. This novel, interesting experience can enrich their knowledge of the Great Wall and can attract more people to be interested in the Great Wall as a cultural heritage site.

In mid-2016, the China Foundation for Cultural Heritage Conservation (CFCHC) began to make contacts with Tencent, in the hope of developing cooperation in the protection and promotion of the Great Wall. Given Tencent's concern for the protection of the Great Wall, this cooperation quickly matured. Tencent Foundation made a large donation (25 million RMB) to support the restoration of two sections of the Great Wall, and also set up a special grant fund (of 10 million RMB) under the CFCHC to protect and promote the Great Wall. Many

2016 年年中开始，中国文物保护基金会开始与腾讯侧接触，希望能够在长城保护与公众传播方面开展合作，基于以往腾讯对于长城保护工作的关注，这项合作很快达成。腾讯基金会则不仅捐赠大额资金（2500 万元人民币）用于支持两段长城段落的修缮工程，还在文保基金会下设立专项基金（捐赠 1000 万元人民币）专司长城保护与传播，同时推动腾讯旗下的多款业务团队深度参与项目。

在腾讯的长城保护项目团队成立之后，我们首先思考的问题就是如何吸引更多人，尤其是年轻人关心和喜爱长城。近些年在中国国内，以故宫为代表的一批国家级博物馆通过文创、特展以及与新媒体传播等的方式引发了大规模的文博热。以故宫为例，近年来组织的不少特展吸引公众熬夜排队参观，在电商上推出的部分文化创意产品受到用户追捧以至于千金难求。这些案例实际上说明，中国的公众并不是不喜欢文化遗产，合理地进行文创结合会收到远超传统推广模式的效果。

在中国，比故宫还要古老的长城面临着无人不知却少有人问津的现象，除去最著名的那一两个长城景区能吸引较多游客外，99% 的长城段落缺少公众的关注，更不要说走近它们。再加上年轻人对于长城这种高尚严肃的形象天然不感兴趣，如何吸引年轻人关注长城保护，对于腾讯来说是需要认真思考的问题，毕竟腾讯数以十亿计的用户中，大部分都是 35 岁以下的年轻人。

作为一家互联网公司，通过技术手段可以以相对容易的手段进行用户调研，经过对于 85 后、90 后、95 后甚至 00 后的全面用户画像调查，当代年轻人最喜欢的视觉语言基本都是电子游戏、二次元动漫、漫威电影等等，如果把这些流行介质提炼一下，我们可以认为——IP（Intellectual Property），即"知识产权"，是能够吸引年轻人关注、参与甚至衍生创造周边内容的核心要素。

在中国文化遗产领域，最知名的大 IP 一定是故宫，无论是台北还是北京的故宫博物院，近些年围绕皇室文化主题开发了各种 IP 内容，比如台北故宫博物院在文创商店销售的雍正手批"朕知道了"系列胶带文创产品在海峡两岸都受到年轻人热烈追捧（图 2），而北京故宫博物馆发布的线上 IPAD 游戏"皇帝的一天""韩熙载夜宴图"均获得苹果官方推荐，基于古老文化遗产的二次开发，不管是以文创商品还是新媒体的方式均大受欢迎。古老的文化遗产是可以通过 IP 开发焕发生命受到年轻人追捧的。

在前文里我们也提到长城在中国被赋予了过于严肃神圣意象，通常情况下，当代的年轻人会相对不容易受到这类内容的吸引。但是在前两年，中国网络上疯狂流传着一部动漫作品，叫《那年那兔那些事儿》，这部动漫把世界各个大国形象成各种动物，然后以"兔子"的形象代表中国，讲述了近百年的中国近代史上各个知名时期的知名事件，尤其着重描述的是中国共产党建立中华人民共和国所走过的各种艰难道路，像这样一种核心向的主旋律题材竟然受到大量年轻人追捧，许多人趋之若鹜像追美剧一样等待作者更新，并形象地自称"我兔"（图 3）。

图 2
台北故宫文创 – 朕知道了贴纸 [2]
Fig. 2
"I know it" sticker product by Taipei National Palace Museum

图 3
主旋律动画片《那年那兔那些事儿》[3]
Fig. 3
Cartoon movie "Those years those hares did those things"

of Tencent's service teams are deeply involved in the programme.

Since the establishment of the Tencent Team for Great Wall Protection Programme, our top priority has been to think about how to attract more people, especially young people, to care about and love the Great Wall. In recent years, a slew of national museums, led by the Palace Museum, have sparked a great boom for culture and museums by promoting culture and creativity, for example through special exhibitions and publicity through new media. Taking the Palace Museum as an example, many special exhibitions organised in recent years have attracted the public who queue overnight to visit. Some of the cultural and creative products launched via e-commerce have been so popular that stocks were sold out. These examples show that the Chinese public are enamoured of cultural heritage. An appropriate mix of culture and creativity will produce effects far beyond the traditional promotional model.

In China, visitors to the Great Wall, which is of greater antiquity than the Palace Museum, are few and far between. Except for the most famous one or two scenic spots of the Great Wall, 99% of the Great Wall receives scant attention, and even fewer visitors. Moreover, young people are not naturally interested in the traditional representation of the Great Wall which is too serious and dull. How to attract young people to become involved in the protection of the Great Wall is a serious consideration for Tencent. After all, a majority of Tencent's bil-

可见，具有严肃主旋律向的内容也是可以打造成大 IP 并吸引年轻人关注和喜爱的。

这样看来，无论是古老的文化遗产还是充满政治属性的形象都可以通过合理的 IP 开发来吸引年轻人关注，长城这样一个复合、复杂的身份形象应该是有机会打造 IP 传播的。腾讯作为中国最大的文化产业公司（腾讯有着中国最大的视频、动漫、游戏、文学、新闻等互联网文化内容平台，甚至还是世界上最大的游戏公司），如何利用旗下拥有十亿受众的互联网平台，向公众传达具有新意和吸引力的长城知识和长城保护号召，是我们需要思考和规划来做的事情。

三、腾讯对长城保护方面做出的尝试

经过公司内部多轮脑暴和创意策划，我们计划从几个层面来打造这个长城 IP：

（一）卡通形象

首先，我们设计推出了"长城小兵"（图4），三个可爱又各自带有明确属性的卡通人物分别代表了三座长城知名关卡。关小山，代表了山海关，一身的腱子肉，主业是修长城；手捧美颜相机自拍的关小小，代表了山西娘子关，特长是美颜长城，清扫掉破坏长城景观的留言和垃圾；而偏着头的小胖墩关小偏，则代表了知名关隘偏头关，他头盔上大大的问号说明他是个好奇宝宝，对于长城知识和考证非常在行。三个长城小兵分别代表了长城保护工作中的修缮保护与展示传播（知识与美）。

围绕三个长城小兵形象打造的微信公众号，通过小兵的形象组织各种长城相关的内容，包括长城保护理念、长城冷知识、长城历史故事等等方面的内容，以漫画、杂文、趣味段子等年轻人喜闻乐见的形式，在腾讯系的各种手机 app 上联合运营传播，公众号在没有任何作假的真实运营下，短短三个月（2017.07–2017.09）就突破了十万真实关注量，说明合适的 IP 打造结合具有创意的内容，是能够焕发原本古旧不吸引人的文化遗产重获关注的。

（二）长城专栏

伴随着微信公众号的创意运营，我们同时在中国最大的互联网新闻平台腾讯网上开设了"长城专栏"。其实写长城的文章非常多，但是许多文章都聚焦在长城久远的历史和各种纷繁的故事传说上，有些老生常谈的感觉。所以我们设立长城专栏的时候，对于内容的取舍是有考究的。

我们专栏首先关注的一个方面是"人的故事"，任何文化遗产，脱离了人的语境，总会被神化到不接地气，长

图4

长城小兵（左起：关小偏、关小小、关小山）（版权：腾讯基金会）

Fig. 4

Great Wall soldiers (from left: Guan Xiaopian, Guan Xiaoxiao, Guan Xiaoshan) (© Tencent Foundation)

互联网如何为长城保护赋能——腾讯长城保护项目的经验分享
HOW INTERNET EMPOWERS GREAT WALL PROTECTION - SHARING EXPERIENCE OF TENCENT'S GREAT WALL CONSERVATION PROGRAMME

327

lions of users are young people aged below 35.

As an internet company, Tencent can easily analyse users through technical means. After a comprehensive profiling exercise of users born after 1985, 1990, 1995, or even after 2000, we demonstrated that the most popular visual media among contemporary young people are video games, cartoons and animation, and Marvel movies. We therefore believe that developing new 'IP branding'[1] is the core to attracting young people to pay attention to, to participate in, and even create the spin-off content.

In the field of Chinese cultural heritage, the most well-known new 'IP branding' has been done by the Palace Museum. In recent years, the Palace Museum - both in Taipei and the mainland sites - has developed a series of 'IP brands' around the theme of royal culture. For example, various creative products such as adhesive tape bearing the words "I know it" hand-written by the Yongzheng Emperor, launched by the Palace Museum in Taipei are highly sought after by young people across the straits (Fig. 2). The online iPad games including "Daily Life of the Emperor" and "Night Revels of Han Xizai," launched by the mainland Palace Museum have all been officially recommended by App Store. After secondary development of new interpretive cultural heritage material, both cultural and commercial products and new media become smash hits. Ancient cultural heritage can become popular among young people through the development of these new 'IP brands'.

As mentioned above, the Great Wall has previously been presented as a very serious and dull subject in China. Contemporary young people are not usually receptive to such content. However, a few years ago, an animation work called "those years those hares did those things"[2], which went viral on the internet in China, describes each country as a different animal, and then tells the story of China through the character of The Hare. It narrates the famous events in China's modern history, especially the arduous road toward the establishment of the Communist Party of China and the founding of the People's Republic of China. The hare character is popular with legions of young people. Many people wait for the author to update the work, much like an American TV series, and fans call themselves "Us Hares" (Fig. 3). This shows that serious content with a strong theme or character can also create powerful new interpretive material and attract the attention of young people.

In this way, both ancient cultural heritage and serious themes can attract young people's attention through development of new interpretive material. The Great Wall, with its rich and multiple values, presents the opportunity to create new 'IP branding' for promotion. Tencent is China's largest cultural industry corporation (with the largest internet cultural content platform in China for video, animation, games, literature, news, and even the world's largest game company). Our focus is on how to harness its internet platform, with an audience of one billion, to convey to the public new and interesting information about the Great Wall and to encourage its protection.

---

1 IP stands for Intellectual Property. 'IP', 'IP brands' and 'IP branding are increasingly popular concepts in China. They refer to the development of brands which can be commercialised, particularly through internet platforms including apps, games, cartoons and movies but also then through associated branded merchandise. (Editors' note)

2 Meaning 'Those things by those hares in those years'. Please also note the Chinese word 'tuzi' can mean both 'hare' and 'rabbit' (Editors' note).

城就有这样的毛病，被主旋律拔得太高，脱离了人的叙事。关于人和社群的故事，我们关注的不是过去，而是此时，长城专栏中设定的《长城人》专栏，专门关注当今与长城有关联的人的故事，比如专注长城保护三十年的英国人威廉林赛，家住长城边兼职巡护长城的长城巡护员等等，通过"过去长城保护我们，今天我们保护长城"这样一个主题，引发了许多读者的共鸣（图5）。

专栏关注的第二个层面是与长城的互动，我们设立了《长城百问》专栏，通过设置问题，邀请意见领袖和公众参与回答和互动。比如"在今天修筑万里长城需要花多少钱？"等趣味问题吸引了企鹅号一百多位大V参加回答讨论，一百多万用户阅读和点赞留言。从一种更轻松和现实主义的角度来解构长城，让这个形象的话题讨论更具有趣味性。

我们设置的长城专栏第三部分是图片专栏《长城星空》（图5），事实上关于长城的审美虽然在国内出版物或摄影圈已经比较常见，但是主题还是比较保守和单一，多是突出墙体的巍峨、沧桑或者与春花秋叶的色彩比对，看多了难免审美疲劳。我们的图片专栏另辟蹊径，和专业的星空摄影师合作，邀请他们拍摄各地长城在夜色中的照片，浩渺的银河星空与古老的长城遥相呼应，充满神秘色彩与想象空间，专栏一经开辟便受到众多好评，许多人下载了图片用来做PC或者说手机的屏保桌面。这些优质的影像图片在受到作者的公益授权后，还用来做长城保护公共募款项目的宣传图片，为长城保护事业的资金募集贡献力量。

（三）植入游戏

通过长城小兵的IP形象、公众号以及长城专栏，我们是以长城作为核心内容去打造传播。与此同时，我们把长城也作为一种软性植入，加载在其他的一些载体里，通过巨大的访问流量来影响更多的人，比如电子游戏。提到游戏，在中国的许多语境里往往存在一些负面的印象，但是不可否认的是，游戏不仅仅是年轻人喜爱的内容形式，同时也是能够最生动展示内容演绎的介质。

图 5

长城人专栏与长城星空专栏（版权：腾讯基金会）

Fig. 5

Great Wall People and Great Wall Starry Sky Special Column (© Tencent Foundation)

互联网如何为长城保护赋能——腾讯长城保护项目的经验分享
HOW INTERNET EMPOWERS GREAT WALL PROTECTION - SHARING EXPERIENCE OF TENCENT'S GREAT WALL CONSERVATION PROGRAMME

329

TENCENT'S ATTEMPTS TO PROTECT THE GREAT WALL

After many rounds of brainstorming and creative planning, we have developed new 'IP branding' for the Great Wall at several levels:

Cartoon figures

Firstly, we have designed and launched the "Great Wall Soldiers" (Fig. 4). Three cute cartoon characters with particular attributes represent three well-known fortified passes of the Great Wall, respectively. Guan Xiaoshan, representing Shanhai Pass, is a muscular guy who is devoted in the construction of the Great Wall; Guan Xiaoxiao, a girl always holding her mobile for a selfie, represents Niangzi (or Princess) Pass in Shanxi, and specialises in beautifying the Great Wall, and cleaning the graffiti and rubbish that disfigure the Great Wall landscape. Guan Xiaopian, a chubby boy with his head always tilting to one side, represents the well-known Piantou (tilting) Pass. The big question mark on his helmet indicates that he is a curious boy, who is well-versed in knowledge of, and historical research on, the Great Wall. The three Great Wall soldiers represent the themes of restoration, protection, and promotion in the conservation of the Great Wall. (Fig. 4)

A WeChat public account set up for the characters of the Great Wall soldiers organises Great Wall-related knowledge through the characters of the soldiers. This includes ideas to protect the Great Wall, little-known information about the Great Wall, the Great Wall's history, etc. It is set out in the forms favoured by the young, including cartoons, short articles and funny stories, via mobile apps provided by Tencent. The account attracted 100,000 followers in only three months (Jul. 2017 to Sept. 2017). It shows that appropriate new 'IP branding', coupled with creative content, can inject vitality into the otherwise old-fashioned, unattractive perception of cultural heritage.

Special online column

With the creative promotion of the WeChat public account, we also set up the "Great Wall Column" on QQ.com, the largest Internet news platform in China. In fact, there were already innumerable published articles on the Great Wall, but most of these focused on the long history of the Wall and the numerous legends associated with it, which were uninspiring. We therefore developed some criteria to choose appropriate content when we set up the Great Wall Column.

Our column's top objective is to present human stories. In the absence of human context, any cultural heritage will be rarefied and only accessible to the experts. This has been the case for the Great Wall, which has been elevated so that it has become divorced from the human experience of ordinary people. Regarding the stories of people and communities, we focus on the present. The Great Wall People section in the Great Wall column focuses on the stories of contemporary figures related to the Great Wall, such as the Briton, William Lindesay, who

在这里我首先岔开一下长城，我们对比一下即使是中国人也非常熟悉的埃及金字塔和古希腊神庙，包括我本人在内的许多中国年轻人对于这两个伟大的世界文化遗产的印象首先都是来自于各种演绎的游戏或者电影。复活的木乃伊怪物、诸神的战争等等情节通过各种经典的电影和游戏走到我们面前，许多人在观看和游玩过有关这些文化遗产的娱乐作品后，通过阅读和博物馆参观去学习和了解它们背后真正的历史知识，通过文化遗产的 IP 开发和内容演绎，可以极大地扩展文化遗产相关内容的受众，而基数的扩大也一定会带来核心受众数量的扩大，因此，对于文化遗产的"硬核粉丝"也会随之增多。

我们也因此尝试把长城同 IP 打造和内容演绎等方式结合起来进行专项的传播。腾讯旗下两个非常重量级的游戏 IP 都加入到长城文化 IP 的打造和传播中来。比如月活跃度超过两亿，日活跃度超过 5000 万（意味着每月有两亿用户会打开这个游戏游玩，而每天会有超过 5000 万人打开王者荣耀游玩）的现象级游戏王者荣耀，从 2017 年中开始陆续推出"长城守卫军"系列的游戏英雄，通过设定英雄与长城的关联故事，并通过设置游戏周边讲堂，比如邀请知名作家马伯庸来制作"王者历史课"，连续五期都专门关注真实的长城历史与相关趣味知识，基于王者荣耀庞大的用户数量，有非常亮眼的传播数据。而且通过守卫长城的正派英雄形象，也将"保护长城"的概念与用户共情，让他们接受长城需要保护的理念（图 6）。

图 6
王者荣耀 长城保护计划（版权：腾讯基金会）
Fig. 6
The Honor of Kings - Great Wall Conservation Program (© Tencent Foundation)

互联网如何为长城保护赋能——腾讯长城保护项目的经验分享
HOW INTERNET EMPOWERS GREAT WALL PROTECTION - SHARING EXPERIENCE OF TENCENT'S GREAT WALL CONSERVATION PROGRAMME

331

has been protecting the Great Wall for 30 years, and the Great Wall Patrollers who live near the Great Wall and patrol it as a part-time job, and so on. The theme of "The Great Wall Protected Us in the Past, Today We Protect the Great Wall" has struck a chord in the minds of many readers. (Fig. 5)

The second objective is concerned with interaction with the Great Wall, and so we set up the "100 Questions on the Great Wall" section. We invited opinion-leaders and the public to participate in this Q&A session. Interesting questions such as "How much would it cost to build the Great Wall today?" involved over 100 key opinion-leaders on the Tencent platform in the discussion, and more than one million users read and 'liked' these questions. Interpreting the Great Wall from a more informal and natural perspective makes the discussion of ideas more fun.

The third part of the Great Wall column is the picture column "Great Wall Starry Sky" (Fig. 5). In fact, although Great Wall imagery is already commonly used in domestic publications or photography circles, the choice of images is conservative and simple, mostly highlighting the towering, ancient walls, or the contrasting colours of spring flowers and autumn leaves. Too many of these images will inevitably cause aesthetic fatigue. Our photo column adopts a novel approach by cooperating with professional photographers who take photos of the different sections of the Great Wall at night. The vast Milky Way echoes the ancient Great Wall, presenting a picture of mystery and imagination. These columns have been well received since their launch. Many people even download images as screensavers for PCs or mobile phones. These high-quality video images are also used as publicity pictures for fundraising for protection of the Great Wall. By authorizing the use of their pictures, photographers contribute to fundraising for the protection of the Great Wall.

Embedding the Great Wall into games

Through the new interpretive material of the Great Wall soldiers, the WeChat public account and Great Wall column, we use the Great Wall as the core subject for communication. At the same time, we embed the image of the Great Wall into other media and influence more people through high-traffic visits to items such as video games. When it comes to games, negative impressions exist in many contexts in China, but there is no denying that games are both the form of content preferred by young people and the medium that can most vividly showcase content.

Let's put aside the Great Wall for a moment and make a comparison with the Egyptian pyramids and ancient Greek temples, which Chinese people are very familiar with. Many Chinese young people, including myself, have developed our perceptions of these great cultural World Heritage Sites from games or films. The resurgent mummy monsters, the wars of the gods, and so on, are brought to life for us through a variety of classic films and games. After having watched and played games relating to these cultural heritage sites, many people then gain true historical knowledge about them through reading and museum visits. The development of new interpretive material can greatly expand the audience for cultural heritage-related content, and the expansion of the audience will surely bring about an increase in the core audience. Therefore, the number of 'hardcore fans' for

　　而另一款值得特别讲述的游戏合作就是"QQ飞车手游"，这样一款同样日活跃度超过两千万的"现象级游戏"与中国文化遗产研究院专司长城研究的年轻专家们一起合作，耗时六个月专门制作了一款"长城赛道"，用户在游戏里可以驾驶着赛车穿越多种形态的长城场景，游览众多非常重要但却并不知名的长城景观。不同于以往游戏里加入长城元素，仅仅是把一些同质化的八达岭砖墙放进游戏里，QQ飞车手游在赛道的设计上全面展示了夯土、石质和砖石长城的不同形制，对于特殊地理环境里的长城，比如黄河边的老牛湾长城，戈壁滩上的甘肃夯土长城以及海边的山海关等长城都进行了游戏场景中的展示（图7），同时在游戏中预埋了长城保护的彩蛋，包括长城小兵在内的IP形象会引导用户关注长城保护的口号。用户通过游玩游戏首先可以见识到长城的不同形态，还可以关注这个赛道的设计意义——即引起更多公众关注和参与长城保护事业，通过娱乐性很强的方式来进行公益理念的传播。

　　除去王者荣耀和QQ飞车手游这样的现象级游戏，腾讯旗下还有云裳羽衣等游戏用特有的形式植入长城的各种内容，来进行用户信息传达。我们认为这种基于庞大基数的软性公益传达是能影响到很多人对于长城保护这件事的看法的，而且是用大多数用户喜闻乐见的形式。

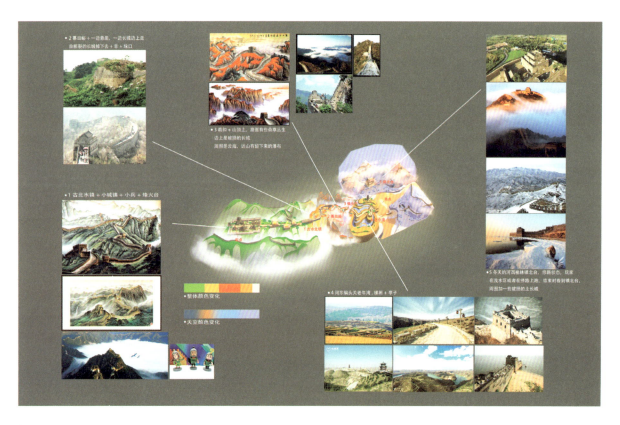

图 7
QQ飞车手游中的长城赛道（版权：腾讯基金会）
Fig. 7
Great Wall racing track in the QQ Speedo (© Tencent Foundation)

互联网如何为长城保护赋能——腾讯长城保护项目的经验分享
HOW INTERNET EMPOWERS GREAT WALL PROTECTION - SHARING EXPERIENCE OF TENCENT'S GREAT WALL CONSERVATION PROGRAMME

333

cultural heritage will also increase.

We try to combine the Great Wall with the creation of new interpretive material and content interpretation for special publicity. Tencent's two top games are involved in the creation and promotion of new interpretive materials on the cultural heritage of the Great Wall. For example, the Honour of Kings, with over 200 million monthly users and over 50 million daily users, launched the "Great Wall Guards" in mid-2017. We developed the stories linking the heroes with the Great Wall. For example, we hosted a lecture inviting the well-known writer Ma Boyong to produce the "History Lesson on the Honour of Kings" for five consecutive periods on the real history of the Great Wall relating detailed historical information. Thanks to the huge number of users of the game, the level of engagement is remarkable. Moreover, through the image of the upright hero who guards the Great Wall, the concept of protecting the Great Wall also resonates with the users, who accept the idea that the Great Wall needs protection. (Fig. 6)

Another cooperative game that deserves special mention is "QQ Speedo", a phenomenal game with over 20 million users daily. Together with the young experts of the Chinese Academy of Cultural Heritage in charge of research on the Great Wall, we took six months to create the "Great Wall Racing Track". Users can drive a car through various sections of the Great Wall, and they visit many important but little-known Great Wall scenic areas. Unlike previous games, which presented only the well-known Badaling brick walls, the QQ Speedo racing tracks showcase the different forms of the Great Wall made of rammed earth, stone and brick. The Great Wall in different geographical environments, such as the Laoniuwan section near the Yellow River, the rammed-earth section in Gansu in the Gobi Desert, and Shanhai Pass near the sea, are all displayed in the game scenes (Fig. 7). Interesting details on the protection of the Great Wall are embedded in the games, including images and slogans such as Great Wall soldiers that guide the users to think about the protection of the Great Wall. Users can see the different forms of the Great Wall through the games, and they can also learn about the purpose of designing this track - namely, interesting the public in the protection of the Great Wall, and promoting the public value of conservation in an entertaining way.

In addition to the games such as the Honour of Kings and the QQ Speedo, other Tencent games, such as "Muses", contain content about the Great Wall in a unique form for dissemination. We believe that this soft promotion of participation in charitable activities to a huge audience can influence many people's views on the protection of the Great Wall, and in the forms favoured by most users.

Public charitable fundraising

In addition to the creation of new 'IP branding' on the Great Wall, Great Wall content and Great Wall games, the core business of the Tencent Foundation is public participation. Tencent's public charitable donations platform is the largest online platform for fundraising through charitable donations in China and in the world as a whole. Tens of housands of projects use this platform for fundraising. Users can make donations to the projects that they follow through WeChat and QQ. They can also convert their user data into money for donations to the

（四）互联网公益捐赠

在长城 IP 打造、长城内容传播以及长城游戏等的形式之外，腾讯基金会的核心业务是公众的公益参与。腾讯公益平台不仅是中国也是世界上规模最大的互联网公益募款平台，数以万计的公益项目通过这个平台进行款项筹集，用户不仅可以通过微信、QQ 来给他关注的公益项目捐款，还可以通过腾讯公益平台捐赠移动设备所记录的运动步数、阅读时间等用户数据，我们称之为"行为公益"，兑换成资金捐入项目中。长城公益项目"保护长城，加我一个"（Protecting the Great Wall, count me in）在腾讯公益平台上线后（图 8），吸引了三十多万普通用户捐出了近 170 万元的善款，这笔善款已经被用于河北喜峰口长城的一段一百多米的工程修缮上，并且在 2018 年底工程完成。公益项目线上筹款实际上是提供给许多距离长城很远的用户一个参与长城保护的路径，他们可以通过捐赠资金或者行为给到公益项目，并且可以通过互联网持续收到项目的进展通知，建立用户和长城保护直接更多亲密的关联，能吸引他们持续关注和参与项目捐赠以及线下活动。借助互联网公益，更多的公众可以更方便地参与长城保护项目。

我们同时推动打造了围绕长城小兵的公益文创产品，由设计师和生产厂家协作生产出来的趣味文化创意产品（图 9），通过腾讯的平台对公众进行售卖，售卖后的费用在扣除生产运输成本后全部捐入中

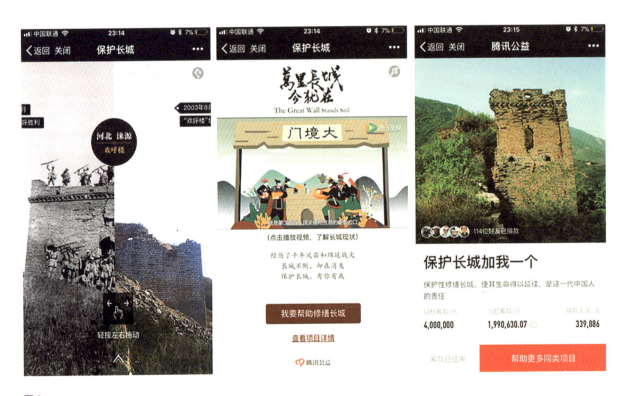

图 8
腾讯公益平台的公众筹款项目（版权：腾讯基金会）
Fig. 8
Public fundraising project on Tencent Public Platform (© Tencent Foundation)

图 9
长城公益文创产品（版权：腾讯基金会）
Fig. 9
Cultural and creative products for the Great Wall (© Tencent Foundation)

programmes, such as the number of exercise steps and reading time recorded by mobile devices, donated via Tencent's Charitable Donations Platform. We call this 'charitable donation through activity'. After its launch on Tencent's charitable donation platform (Fig. 8), the Great Wall project "Protecting the Great Wall, count me in" attracted over 300,000 ordinary users who donated nearly 1.7 million RMB. This fund was used for the restoration of over 100m of the Great Wall in Xifengkou, Hebei Province, which was completed at the end of 2018. Online fundraising for charitable projects is actually a way for many users far away from the Great Wall to participate in the protection of the Great Wall. They can contribute to projects through donation or activities, and they receive notifications on the progress of the project through the internet. This causes a direct, more intimate relationship between users and the protection of the Great Wall, and can attract them to think about and participate in project donation and offline activities. More people can participate in the protection of the Great Wall by virtue of the online charitable fundraising programmes.

At the same time, we promote the creation of cultural and creative products based on the Great Wall soldiers, which are produced in a collaboration between designers and manufacturers (Fig. 9). Products are sold to the public through Tencent's platform. The sales revenue, after deduction of production and transportation fees, is donated to the Great Wall Conservation Fund under CFCHC. It is also an embodiment of internet-based approaches that provide the public with many ways of participating in the Great Wall.

As mentioned above, Tencent Foundation donated 25 million RMB for the restoration of two sections of the Great Wall. This is the first time that a charitable institution has made a donation to the Great Wall conservation programme. Unlike traditional state-funded initiatives, new ways can be explored through the use of social funding. Regarding these two projects for the Great Wall, Tencent Foundation also encouraged innovations in terms of technology and use of funds, and in design and construction. With the support of these funds, archaeological work was incorporated in Great Wall restoration projects. Surveying and mapping technology applied to the online maps, such as tilt photography and 3D modelling, panoramic image data acquisition, and so on, were also used for the Great Wall maintenance project for the first time. The data collected during the restoration of the

国文物保护基金会的长城保护公益专项基金中，用于支持长城保护的公益项目。通过文创产品提供给公众参与长城公益的多种途径，也是互联网公益的一种体现。

在前文也介绍过，腾讯基金会针对两段长城修缮工程捐赠了 2500 万元用于支持工程，这也是首次有社会力量参与到长城保护的项目认领捐赠中来。由于是社会资金，不同于以往的国家财政支持长城修缮，可以在资金使用方式上作出一些新的探索。腾讯基金会也推动两个修缮项目在科技参与及资金使用、设计施工一体化等方面作出创新实施。在这些资金的支持下，长城修缮工程中有考古清理的项目介入，同时倾斜摄影三维建模、全景影像数据采集等最早在互联网地图上应用的测绘技术也首次应用在长城保护的项目中来，采集到的各修缮阶段的长城建筑数据也反推纠正施工中的小错误和瑕疵，帮助修缮项目能按照设计稿实现工程推进等等。这些都是在腾讯基金会与中国文物保护基金会的这次合作中跨界实现的。

四、小　结

以上这些就是这几年腾讯作为一家互联网公司参与长城保护作出的一些努力，希望我们的工作能够带给更多项目一些借鉴意义，帮助长城在内的众多优秀和重要的文化遗产能够在保护和传播中作出更多创新，吸引更多的公众和社区关注和加入到文化遗产保护的工作中来，让互联网赋予这种工作更多能力和效果，让科技赋予文化更多元的生命力和形式，能够更好地实现保护与传承，这也是我们最关注的方面。

互联网如何为长城保护赋能——腾讯长城保护项目的经验分享
HOW INTERNET EMPOWERS GREAT WALL PROTECTION - SHARING EXPERIENCE OF TENCENT'S GREAT WALL CONSERVATION PROGRAMME

337

Great Wall in turn helped in the stabilisation of structural weaknesses in the monument, facilitating implementation of the restoration. These benefits were achieved through cooperation between Tencent Foundation and the CFCHC.

CONCLUSION

These are some of the efforts made by Tencent - as an internet company - to participate in the protection of the Great Wall in recent years. It is hoped that our work is of value for other projects and that it can help many other outstanding and important cultural heritage sites in addition to the Great Wall to innovate as part of their conservation and promotional efforts. We aim to attract more people and communities to join in with heritage protection, to fully exploit the potential of the internet in this work, to endow cultural heritage with more vitality and variety through technology, and to achieve better protection of the legacy of our cultural heritage.

参考文献
Bibliography

[1] 图片来源：搜狐网 . 长城接待量再攀游客峰值 只见人不见景 [EB/OL].2017-10-04.

Image Source: Sohu.com. "Number of Visitors to the Great Wall Peaked, the Landscaped Overshadowed." [EB/OL].Oct 4, 2017.

http://www.sohu.com/a/196280037_100027668.

[2] 图片来源：

Image Source: http://www.npmshops.com/main/uploads/npmshops/PrdImg/3416649900033_x.jpg.

[3] 图片来源：故宫精品网路商城 [EB/OL].

Image Source: Online National Palace Museum Shop[EB/OL].

https://timgsa.baidu.com/timg?image&quality=80&size=b9999_10000&sec=1497938308262&di=b68e678
899b5a33e3136c0ca3456e21c&imgtype=0&src=http%3A%2F%2Fimg4.duitang.com%2Fuploads%2Fitem%2F
201608%2F03%2F20160803103433_M4iV3.jpeg

Chapter Five
Concluding Remarks

黑龙江金界壕（摄影：于 冰）
Jin Great Wall in Heilongjiang (© Yu Bing)

第五章
结　语

39 号里堡（版权：英格兰遗产委员会）
Milecastle 39 (© Historic England)

结　语

汉佛瑞·维尔法
（哈德良长城世界遗产合作委员会，英国卡莱尔）
于　冰
（中国文化遗产研究院，中国北京）

中国长城和哈德良长城有许多共同之处，这一点人尽皆知，无需额外解释。然而，两座长城的"品牌知名度"固然高，大众对此以外的了解却往往少之又少。追问下去，会发现许多人知道两座长城都是由帝国的掌权者建造，保护各自帝国不受外界侵害，但是真相却远为复杂，两座长城差异也很大。

我们所称的中国长城（英文由单数表示）其实是由许多不同防御系统构成；这些防御体系各自的规模都十分庞大——几乎足以构成一个世界遗产地系列——它们相互联系，建筑方式各不相同，所用材料形形色色，时间横跨逾两千年，用"墙"（the Wall）来通称这个庞大的防御综合体，实在是难以反映其全貌。相反，哈德良长城路线相对较短，总体设计和建造相对统一，实际使用时间只有大约 300 年。但两者区别不仅于此。对于晚期长城（明代），存有大量详尽且精美的历史图像和文献记载，而哈德良长城同时期的文献只局限于石头上寥寥数语的铭文及著名的文多兰达书简。这种一手资料缺失的状况，一定程度上被近三个世纪详尽的哈德良长城考古研究形成的丰富学术著作所弥补。

对于中国长城的特点，有一个方面英国同事在过去的认识并不充分，这就是中国长城各段的修筑时间跨度很大。现有的出版资料几乎都集中在明代长城上。明长城固然令人惊叹，但早期长城遗迹的研究、发掘和展示将对英国读者产生极大兴趣。另一方面，中国同事对英国哈德良中考古学和考古学家的主导地位印象深刻，他们不仅长期开展深入的哈德良研究，还广泛而积极地从事长城的管理、访客推广和公众参与等各个方面。中方要更好地研究和认识早期长城的价值，在这个领域还有很大追赶空间，同时这也将是中英双墙对话和合作的重要领域。

对于哈德良长城的特点，大多数中国人过去认识并不充分的是，哈德良长城只是庞大罗马帝国边疆防御体系的小小一部分。罗马边疆防御体系遍布三大洲的近 30 个现代国家。因此，就规模而言，两个军事系统在任何特定历史时期都可以媲美（例如，罗马边疆长城 5000 公里，明长城 8000 公里），而现存中国长城规模远远超过罗马边疆防御体系是由于超过其 2000 年的不断扩建和重建。认识到这一点对于双墙对话非常重要。首先双墙对话可以在更广泛的平台上开展，而现有和潜在的罗马帝国边疆世界路地和长城地段都可以作为案例。而且，考虑到它们在世界上无与伦比的重要性和复杂性，两个巨型系统的研究、保护和管理也具有十分宝贵的互相借鉴意义。

尽管有种种不同，两处长城依旧有足够多相似之处以作对话和对比。而在对话和对比之前，首先需要了解，即便专业人士也不例外。因此，在英国纽卡斯尔举办的这次研讨会，其首要目的就是使两国与会者开始介绍各自既有知识，并探索如何加强对各方遗产的保护和管理，以及遗产在当今社会的利用。

CONCLUDING REMARKS

Humphrey Welfare

Hadrian's Wall World Heritage Site Partnership Board - Carlisle - UK

Yu Bing

China Academy of Cultural Heritage - Beijing - China

Most people will accept at once that the Great Wall of China and Hadrian's Wall have much in common. This does not have to be explained. However, although the level of 'brand recognition' of the two Walls is very high, beyond that there is often little knowledge. More questioning will probably reveal that many people know that the Walls were built by imperial authorities to protect their empire from external threats, but the truth is rather more complex, and the two Walls are very different.

Many separate barriers make up what we call the Great Wall; they are of vast extent - almost a serial World Heritage Site in themselves - and their inter-relationships, their varied methods of construction, and the wide range of materials that were used, over two millennia, combine to make the whole defensive complex of 'the Wall' difficult to understand in its entirety. In contrast, Hadrian's Wall is relatively short, comparatively uniform in its general design and construction, and was only effectively occupied for about 300 years. The differences do not end there. Whilst there is a great deal of detailed and beautiful graphical documentation of the later (Ming) phases of the Great Wall, for Hadrian's Wall the contemporary written material is limited to short inscriptions on stone and the famous Vindolanda writing tablets. This lack of direct knowledge has been partly compensated for by three centuries of detailed archaeological research on Hadrian's Wall that has produced a huge academic bibliography.

One factor that is certainly not sufficiently appreciated in the UK is the span of time during which the different stretches of the Great Wall were constructed. Much of the readily available published material relates almost exclusively to the Ming Wall. Wonderful though this is, the analysis, excavation, and presentation of the remains from earlier dynasties would be of immense interest to many audiences. On the other side, Chinese colleagues are deeply impressed by the dominance of archaeology and archaeologists, not only in the research, but also in administration, visitor promotion, and public engagement in the Hadrian's Wall in the UK. There is a good opportunity for Chinese colleagues to create a better understanding of the Great Wall in earlier periods, and for UK-Sino cooperation. What most Chinese did not expect about Hadrian's Wall is that it constituted just a very small part of the extensive Frontiers of the Roman Empire, spreading over nearly 30 modern countries, across 3 continents. In terms of the scale, therefore, the two military systems can rival with each other at any given historic period (for example, 5000km of the Roman frontiers versus 8000km of the Ming Great Wall). The Great Wall grew far more substantially just because it was extended and reconstructed continuously over 2000 years. This is significant for the Wall-to-Wall dialogue. It could be developed on a wider platform, with existing and potential FRE WH sites and stretches of the Great Wall as cases. The research, conservation, and management of

这本文集记录了研讨会阐述及讨论的内容。与会者都意识到，囿于时间限制，他们只能介绍各自长城的基本情况和少数几个重点。即便如此，这些内容也足以激发我们获取更多知识、增强认知的欲望，并指出未来两国可进一步共同探索的若干主题。

研讨会最后一场要求每位与会者提出他们最感兴趣的主题及问题，同时为未来可以继续探讨和积极合作的机会建言献策。与会者涉及的一系列话题覆盖范围非常广泛，也充分展现了大家并不满足于仅仅简单的分享和交流知识分享，而渴望更深入的合作。讨论的结果形成一个非常清晰的愿望，就是举行第二次研讨会，更深入地探讨一些话题，同时进一步探寻实际的和潜在的合作领域。

不少与会者也表示需要更深入地理解历史上边界和防御体系的功能与运作。这种了解可以通过有选择地对具体点段长城本体和周边景观开展发掘、勘察以及理论研究得到增强。与会者也认为，重要的是应该让非专业人士也能更深入地了解历史上的边疆防御体系，将之与当今世界的其它边界联系起来。展览及相关出版物，尤其是那些可以比较两处长城（及其它的物质屏障）异同的展览和出版物，可以有效增强公众对中英长城遗产地的认识和欣赏。欣赏度的提高也被视为增强公众参与有效性的重要手段。在与考古遗迹联系最紧密的社区中，已经能看到这一手段卓有成效。通过价值传播，可以壮大志愿者队伍，从而为两处世界遗产地的保护与展示提供更多强有力的资源保障。因此如果有个人或机构希望开展遗产地志愿者合作，可以筹集资金策划项目。文化遗产保护意识的培养要从在校的孩子们抓起；已经有不少与会者表示愿意探索和扩大这方面的合作。

公众主动体验遗产，而不是被动接受知识的愿望已经愈来愈强。这也要求我们必须尽可能全面拓展公众接近考古遗址和古迹的渠道。研讨会展示了英国哈德良长城沿线国家步道的成功经验和发展前景，与会者也思考如何在中国推行相似的服务。与修建直接的、物理性的道路同样重要的是发掘、利用所有新兴技术吸引、陶冶和教育更广泛的观众群体。虚拟展览只需一瞬即可纵览世界，我们也可以做到收集、分析和监测若干年的游客数据。令英国代表印象尤为深刻的就是中国为吸引年轻群体而推出的游戏产品。

研讨会举行期间，组织参观了数个博物馆及阐释性展览，其中包括：位于纽卡斯尔市的汉考克大北方博物馆（旨在现场参观哈德良长城之前对长城有全面了解）、位于沃森德的塞格杜努姆遗址博物馆，还有豪塞斯特兹、文多兰达及切斯特要塞。讨论中，同样谈到中国长城沿线的博物馆，以及各个博物馆应如何不断发展以适应观众不断变化的需求。在沃森德和文多兰达，与会代表考察了一小段哈德良长城墙体复建工程。英中两国不同的处理方式也引发了更多热烈的讨论。很显然，这就是一个我们可以相互学习的领域。另一个类似的话题也与此相关，那就是对考古遗迹本体进行保护时，在材料的选用和干预的程度方面，可考虑采用哪些技术手段和方法。未来，这也将是一个引人探索的话题。

此番讨论的一个积极直接的成果就是在研讨会行将结束时，中国文化遗产研究院与英格兰遗产委员会分别表示愿意成为促进各自国家相关文化交流的桥梁，为更多的机构交流牵线搭桥。同时，这也为双墙以外的遗产合作打开大门，例如对工业建筑的研究和再利用。

尽管有着语言障碍，但感谢纽卡斯尔大学优秀的翻译团队，这一障碍得以化解，研讨会的专业探讨得以顺畅进行。这本基于研讨会上的演讲而正式出版的文集，无法充分反映和还原研讨会短短数日间两

the two giant systems will also be mutually inspiring considering their exceptional significance and complexity which is unparalleled in the world.

Despite the contrasts, the similarities remain and are powerful enough to justify comparisons. Before that can happen there is much to learn, even at the professional level, so the principal aims of the seminar held in Newcastle were for the participants from both countries to begin to explain what we have, and to start to explore how the conservation and management of this heritage might be improved, and how it can be used in contemporary society. This volume is a record of what was described and discussed. Participants were very conscious that only a general overview and a few highlights of each Wall could be presented in the time available. Even so, this was enough to stimulate an appetite for more knowledge and understanding, and to highlight topics that should be further explored together.

In the final session of the seminar, each participant was asked to identify those subjects and questions that had interested them most, and to suggest opportunities for further discussion and active collaboration. The range of subjects that were mentioned reflected the full breadth of the introductory presentations and amply demonstrated the desire to go beyond the simple sharing of knowledge. As a result, there was a clear wish that a second seminar should be held in which some topics could be examined in more detail, and when the practicalities and potential benefits of collaboration could be further explored.

Many of the participants expressed the need to reach a deeper understanding of the function and operation of boundaries and frontiers in the past. This understanding can be advanced through selective excavation and through the detailed analysis of sections of the landscape as well as by theoretical studies. It was thought important that non-specialists should also be able to learn more about the frontiers of the past, relating this to other boundaries in the modern world. Exhibitions and their associated publications, especially those that compare and contrast the Walls (and other hard barriers), could be a very effective means to increase public awareness and the appreciation of the heritage of each country. A heightened level of appreciation was seen to be essential to improving the effectiveness of public engagement and participation, something is already particularly productive among the communities most closely connected to the archaeological remains. The volunteering that can result from this engagement potentially offers a strong resource with which to enhance the conservation and presentation of both of these World Heritage Sites. Fundraising for additional projects can also be facilitated if individuals and organisations find that they can identify with this aspect of their heritage. Awareness should start with children while they are still at school; significant support was expressed for joint programmes to explore and expand this activity.

Increasingly, people wish to experience the heritage, rather than simply be told about it. This inevitably involves providing access to the archaeological remains and structures as widely as possible. The success and further potential of the National Trail along Hadrian's Wall was noted, and participants wondered how this sort of provision might be adapted and applied in China. Just as important as direct physical access is the need to explore and exploit all emerging technologies to engage, entertain and inform wider audiences. Virtual exhibitions can cross the world in seconds, and tourism data can be collected, analysed and monitored over many years.

国代表们之间分享的专业目标、友谊、热情和幽默。尤其是前往哈德良长城实地考察时，这种氛围尤为热烈，代表们对考古研究的求知欲及专业上的好奇心，引发了源源不断的提问和比较，极具感染力。代表们显然都已做好准备，分享真知灼见，互相取长补短，这也为未来成果更丰硕的合作奠定了良好基础。这种携手合作，以及跨越国界的理解认同，正是世界遗产的核心所在。

Delegates from the UK were particularly impressed by some of the gaming products that had been used in China to catch the attention of younger audiences.

During the seminar there had been visits to several museums and interpretative displays: The Great North Museum Hancock, in Newcastle (which is designed to provide an introduction to a visit to Hadrian's Wall itself), and to site museums at Segedunum (Wallsend), Housesteads, Vindolanda, and Chesters. There was some discussion about the comparable museums along the Great Wall, and about how every museum must continually develop to meet the changing needs of its audiences. At Wallsend and at Vindolanda the short reconstructions of portions of Hadrian's Wall were examined; these sparked more discussion as this is a topic in which the general practice of the UK and of China does differ. This is clearly an area in which we can learn from each other. Another such topic, closely related to this, is the consideration of the variety of technical approaches and methods that are available for the physical conservation of the archaeological remains, both in terms of the materials that are used and the extent of any intervention. It will be fascinating to explore this further in the future.

A very positive immediate result of the discussion at the end of the seminar was that CACH and Historic England each offered to act as a bridge for relevant cultural exchanges in their country, facilitating connections with a wider range of organisations. This has also opened the door to cooperation on heritage subjects that are not connected to the two Walls, such as the study and re-use of industrial buildings.

Despite the language barrier - greatly reduced by the excellent team of interpreters from Newcastle University - the professional conversations at the seminar were easy and flowed freely. This formal publication of the papers, based on those presented at the seminar, cannot adequately reflect the shared professional purpose, friendship, enthusiasm, and good humour that pervaded the few days together. This was especially evident during the field-trip along Hadrian's Wall when there was an infectious sense of archaeological enquiry and professional curiosity that stimulated a constant stream of questions and comparisons. The readiness to share ideas and to learn from each other was clearly apparent, and this provides a good basis for fruitful collaboration in the future. Such joint working, and the international understanding that comes with it, is at the very heart of World Heritage.